Shropshire

since 1900

A YEAR BY YEAR NEWS HISTORY

Toby Neal

LANGRISH
CAIGER
PUBLICATIONS

First published 2007 by Langrish Caiger Publications, PO Box 1916, Telford, TF7 5XZ

Cover design by Michelle Dalton

Printed by WPG, Welshpool

ISBN: 0-9548530-3-2

Introduction

To outsiders, Shropshire has a reputation of being a quiet rural county where nothing much happens. But it just ain't so.

Recent events bear this out. In early 2007, when a group of British service personnel were seized by Iranian forces, creating an international crisis, there was a certain inevitability that the young woman sailor who became the focus of media attention, Faye Turney, turned out to be a Salopian, the daughter of former Shrewsbury Town goalkeeper Alan Boswell.

And when car bomb attacks failed in London and Glasgow in the summer, one of those arrested was a doctor who had worked in Shrewsbury and Telford.

In journalistic circles in the county it is almost an article of faith that in any big event, either national or international, there is a Shropshire dimension.

This has held true for events as diverse as the Titanic disaster, in which there was a Shropshire victim, and the September 11 terror attacks on America, in which the only Briton to die on one of the hijacked planes came from Shrewsbury.

In World War Two, the first Army combat casualty was from the King's Shropshire Light Infantry, and the first operational RAF Fighter Command casualty was a young Shropshire pilot, who died in tragic circumstances.

Then there are events within the county itself. Two fires which hit the COD Donnington military complex in the 1980s were among the biggest peacetime fires, in terms of expense, in British history. A domestic siege at Weston-under-Redcastle in the 1960s remains the longest peacetime siege in modern British history.

Some high profile crimes which attracted both national and international attention were in Shropshire. A member of the royal family was killed in a plane crash on the county border and Shropshire didn't even escape being bombed during the Blitz.

This is a book of events and decisions which shaped the history of the county. Of course, history is more than just events and dates. For instance, at some point in the 20th century people stopped wearing caps and hats. Children started to smile for school photographs. And when answering the phone people stopped giving their phone number ("Shrewsbury 651, who is it please?").

I have used edited and adapted versions of the news stories of the day to tell of things which happened, and decisions which were made. They were the backdrop to the story of Shropshire and Salopians throughout the 20th century and beyond. Most of these news reports have come from the *Wellington Journal and Shrewsbury News* and, from 1964, the *Shropshire Star*.

It has not been practical to use the original headlines in most cases, but I have attempted to be true to their spirit and tone.

In a small number of cases there was no suitable contemporary news story – often because the significance of an event was not appreciated until long afterwards. In these cases I have synthesised a report from available sources.

By and large I have used the punctuation, style, and spellings of the original news reports, as this was part of their flavour (for example, for much of the first part of the 20th century the town of Ironbridge was generally spelt as Iron-Bridge). In other words, I haven't imposed a standardised "modern" style.

And in one or two instances I have taken the liberty of stepping slightly beyond the borders of Shropshire, for events which had reverberations within the county.

For instance, there was a terrible pool disaster in Bettisfield in 1905. It sent shockwaves throughout the surrounding area.

For those who want a more complete picture of what happened and when, I have included a detailed chronology, together with exact dates where I know them, in the appendices, together with other information of interest and use to local historians such as detailed lists of the county's MPs over the last 100 or so years.

There are many things I have left out, either because of lack of space, or because of lack of knowledge. But I have operated on the basis that an incomplete record is better than none.

A word of warning. There is some good news, and there is some bad news. Bad news which is beyond living memory is not normally a great problem. But inevitably any history book which reawakens memories of more recent tragedies can be painful for those involved.

We tend to think of history as the long-gone past. But the events in this book were once the living present for those who experienced them, just as our present will be viewed as history by future generations.

Shropshire's story continues to unfold, with a constantly changing cast.

Toby Neal

August 2007

Acknowledgements

This book is primarily based on information in old Shropshire newspapers, and I am therefore indebted to my editor, the Shropshire Star's Sarah-Jane Smith, for allowing me to use material and pictures in the Shropshire Newspapers archive.

I should also like to thank those who have given their blessing to my using various old photographs from their collections. They include renowned postcard collector Ray Farlow, Shrewsbury historian David Trumper, Shropshire Regimental Museum, and Shropshire Archives.

1900

DISASTER FOR REGIMENT

The War Office on Wednesday evening issued the following despatch from Lord Roberts:

"Pretoria, August 1. An unfortunate accident occurred yesterday near Frederickstad, on the Krugersdorp to Potchefstroom railway. The enemy had taken up some of the rails and a supply train, escorted by a detachment of the Shropshire Light Infantry, went off the line.

"Thirteen men, including the engine driver, were killed and 39 injured."

Hitherto throughout the whole campaign the regiment has been specially exempt from a long list of casualties. Most of the injured men hail from the neighbourhood of Wellington.

Cinematograph at Dawley

A crowded and enthusiastic audience filled the Town Hall when a cinematograph entertainment arranged by the Debating Society was given. The lecture was entitled "One Hundred Years of South Africa" and was well illustrated by many limelight views, and no less than 2,000ft of cinematograph film.

"It is unnecessary" says a correspondent "to go to London for the 'Hooligan' or Birmingham for the 'Peaky-Blinder'. They may be found in large numbers any evening in Shrewsbury streets, where juvenile rowdyism reigns.
This, to some extent, is probably due to the fact that the police, instead of looking to the good order of the town, are principally engaged in distributing all kinds of notices relating to laws which are never put into effect, or in matters of a civil character which might well take care of themselves."

KSLI soldiers advancing on Boer positions at Paardeberg.

Shropshires at Paardeberg

Angus, the special correspondent of the Journal with the Shropshire Regiment in the Orange Free State, contributes a highly interesting narrative of the regiment's conduct at Paardeberg:

"On the afternoon of 11th February we received sudden orders that we had been brigaded into the 19th Brigade, 9th Division, and that we were to move the same evening from Orange River – the destination being unknown. We were all pleased at the move towards the front, having been over two months in one place.

"We arrived at Paardeberg Drift at about 3 a.m. on Sunday, February 18, and then learned that Cronje's force was entirely surrounded.

"After a short rest of one and a half hours we were ordered into action, our battery of 15 pounders first firing a few rounds of shrapnel. The Shropshire battalion was ordered to ford the Modder River, the enemy being in strong force along the bed thereof. The water was deep at the drift, and reached up to the men's breasts. F and H Companies crossed the river later, at a higher point, under fire.

"Arriving on the further side of the river the remaining Companies of the Shropshires, under the command of Lieut.-Col. Spens, were extended for attack, and ultimately took up a position on a small kopje overlooking the Boer position and at once came in for a shower of bullets. No. 5,800 Private R. Chinnery was the first man wounded, the bullet passing through the right shoulder and out of the left breast.

"F and H Companies, under command of Capt. Gubbins and Lieut. Sowray, met with a rather warm reception and had four men killed.

"A hot fire was kept up until dark, the enemy being gradually driven back towards a large laager, and our men posted on outposts. The battle lasted about 14 hours.

"On Tuesday, 27th February, great was the surprise and pleasure when news was received by signal at 8-30 a.m. that Cronje had surrendered. Our officers and men cheered heartily when the tidings were read to them by Lieut.-Col J. Spens. In the evening Cronje, accompanied by his wife and 4,060 prisoners, were despatched under a strong escort."

1901

DEATH OF THE QUEEN

It would probably be safe to say that not 28 individuals in each of the 28,000 inhabitants of Shrewsbury had ever seen Queen Victoria, yet there was no name and no personality more beloved than hers.

It was impossible by Monday to escape the conviction that the Angel of Death was hovering over the Sovereign's chamber and when on Tuesday evening it was authoratively announced that the illustrious patient had peacefully passed away, sadness and not surprise was the pronounced characteristic of the inhabitants.

Strong men could not restrain their tears. The darkness and dreariness of the evening added to the mental gloom and the aspect was one of the deepest mourning.

The old bell in the Mayor's Court was the first to give tongue to the sorrowful information; but it was soon much more widely disseminated by the doleful pealing of muffled bells at St Chad's, St Alkmond's and St Mary's.

The first intimation of the sad news was received at Wellington shortly after 7 o'clock on Tuesday evening when a telegram was posted in front of the "Journal" office and eagerly scanned by a large number of people.

The news rapidly spread throughout the town and was received with deep regret. The Parish Church bell was tolled and later a muffled peal was rung.

Shocking Westbury tragedy

About ten o'clock on Saturday morning a terrible crime was committed at Westbury. A young woman named Mary Eliza Bowen, a barmaid at the Lion Inn, which is situated in the village, adjoining the main road leading from Westbury to Worthen, was murdered, it is alleged, by a Shrewsbury butcher named Richard Wigley, by cutting Miss Bowen's throat with a pocket-knife.

The deceased was a farmer's daughter, her home being at Penybryn, Llanfair, near Welshpool.

No-one actually saw Wigley commit the crime, but from a subsequent statement made by him there can be little doubt that he has brutally murdered the young woman, with whom he had fallen in love.

The news of the murder rapidly spread, and in Shrewsbury and other localities extraordinary reports were circulated. Even rumour, however, could not supply anything more revolting and abhorrent than the actual circumstances.

He had known the deceased for some time and, though married himself, and a man of about 50 years of age while the deceased was only 28, he was living apart from his own wife, having conceived a more than ordinary regard for Miss Bowen, whose acquaintance he made while both lived at Berrington, near Shrewsbury, in the service of different employers.

Wigley made no attempt to escape and was heard to remark: "I've done it, my girl, this time; she's dead enough. I did it for love, and I'll die like an Englishman."

Excavation work taking place at Shrewsbury railway station to create a lower level under the existing, inadequate, accommodation.

Furious driving case

Carl Lawton, gentleman, Mossley, near Manchester, was summoned at Shrewsbury for furiously driving a motor-car so as to endanger the life or limb of any street passenger in Mardol. He was fined £2.

Use of the telephone

The Finance Committee of Wellington Urban Council recommended that a telephone be placed in the surveyor's office. Moving the idea, Mr G.W. Harvey said the telephone would be very useful.

1902

Unfortunate incident hits "The Musical Snowmen"

The fifth annual cycle and floral carnival was held at Shrewsbury. The Shrewsbury Handbell Ringers, who played on their bells and designated themselves "The Musical Snowmen," being dressed all in white, were second in the procession.

An untoward accident, and one of a somewhat serious character, occurred during preparations for the night assemblage. "The Musical Snowmen" were at the house of one of their number in Smithfield Road. As the party rose, a spark from the fire fled out and ignited the cotton wool in which Alfred Teckoe was dressed and, as the others rushed instinctively to put out the flame that suddenly darted up, their own costumes caught fire.

They were burned more or less seriously on the hands and necks. As soon as possible they went to the Infirmary and had their injuries attended to. They were also detained. Five were burned including Alfred Teckoe, painter, Roushill Bank (very badly).

Wigley executed

Richard Wigley, found guilty of the murder of Eliza Mary Bowen, barmaid at the Lion Inn at Westbury, suffered the extreme penalty of the law within the precincts of Shrewsbury prison on Tuesday morning at 8 o'clock, in the presence of the chaplain and officials of the gaol. Hundreds gathered outside to witness the hoisting of the black flag.

Hinstock fire

A serious fire took place in Hinstock National Schools, doing considerable damage.

The whole of the contents of the infants' and girls' schools were totally destroyed, only the bare walls being left standing; most of the contents of the boys' school, including the piano &c., were saved.

Ludlow mishap

Considerable excitement was caused in Ludlow and in Ludford by the bursting of one of the large water mains which is to convey the water from Wales to Birmingham. A great volume of water rushed down the roadway like a river – down Ludford Bank, over Ludford Bridge, and into the houses in Lower Broad Street.

Crowds gather outside the Shirehall in Shrewsbury to welcome home the 2nd Volunteer Service Company of the 2nd Battalion of the King's Shropshire Light Infantry on its return from the Boer War.

Iron Bridge in collapse

Great was the consternation in Iron-Bridge on Sunday night, when the news rapidly spread throughout the town that the famous old iron bridge had fallen in, and in less than half-an-hour nearly the whole town was out to see what really was the matter.

The report of the collapse was like that of a gun, and on inspection it was found that about 30 feet of the palisading had fallen into the Severn below, taking with it the end of the footplate.

The place is being visited daily by hundreds of people. The Trust are having the bridge examined by experts. It is conjectured that the foundations have been shaken through the recent pipe laying.

The bridge is private property, and a small charge is made to pass over it, a bugbear which the inhabitants would like to see removed at once. Shortly before the accident people were observed lounging against the palisading, and it is nothing short of a miracle no-one was injured.

1903

PROTECTION AGAINST RECKLESS DRIVING

A largely-attended public meeting was held in the Corn Exchange, Shrewsbury, to protest against the high rate of speed at which motor-cars were now driven, and to form an association to institute legal proceedings against offending motor-car drivers.

The chair was occupied by Mr R. Blakeway (chairman of the Roads and Bridges Committee).

The Chairman said that the meeting was not called to wage war against motor-cars generally, but against what was considered to be the reckless manner in which they were driven. (Applause).

He considered that a great many cars were put into the charge of incompetent people, and it would be well perhaps if a law were introduced to compel drivers to serve some sort of apprenticeship and gain a certificate of qualification.

A motion "That this meeting protests against the reckless manner in which motor-cars are being driven to the danger of the public and resolves to form an association called the Shropshire Association for Protection Against Reckless Motor-Driving" was passed.

A temporary wooden cross was erected at the corner of Castle Street and High Street in Shrewsbury to commemorate the 500th anniversary of the Battle of Shrewsbury.

'Buffalo Bill' visit

Buffalo Bill's "Wild West" performed at Shrewsbury in a field adjacent to the Barracks in Copthorne.

Thousands of people were seated round the arena, and gazed admiringly and with amazement on a succession of life representations of scenes upon the Western American Plain, a unique assemblage of cowboys, Cossacks, Mexicans, Arabs, Gauchos, Indians &c. upon whom to look was an education in itself.

After the performance, the Mayor of Shrewsbury (Mr H.R.H. Southam), with his little daughter, paid a visit to the Indians' tents and presented the children in them with dolls, &c. In the evening, Colonel Cody ('Buffalo Bill') dined with the Mayor at the Crown Hotel.

'Bribery for years'

The Shirehall, Shrewsbury, was crowded when Mr Commissioner Morton William Smith sat in connection with the Shrewsbury municipal election petition. It was lodged by Liberal candidate Mr John Barker against the return of Conservative Mr F G Morris as a member of the Shrewsbury Town Council for the Castle Fields Ward in the November 1902 election. Morris received 367 votes, Barker 294.

Giving evidence, John Henry Cookson, a labourer, of Stanley Terrace, Castle Fields, was asked by counsel: "Were you surprised to hear that you could get 2s 6d for voting?" "No; you can always get that," he replied.

Asked if she had received half a crown at previous elections, Isabella Knox testified: "We have had it for years before, and we have not had all this bother."

Morris' agent John Edward Wyke admitted bribing voters: "It is absolutely necessary. If you want them to give votes, you must pay them, on both sides."

In his subsequent report Mr Morton William Smith said: "From the hold which corrupt practices have on the Shrewsbury voters, and the indifference with which the leaders of the political parties in the town seem to treat the subject, I firmly believe that the corrupt practices, which (on the admission of everyone) exist and flourish in this town, and at almost every kind of election, will never be checked or eradicated until an example has been made of some of those who bribed, or authorised bribing."

He estimated that of the 661 votes cast, over two-thirds were as a result of bribes. He declared the seat vacant. Nine people were jailed.

1904

Shropshire war memorial unveiled at Shrewsbury

To commemorate the heroism and devotion of the officers and men of the Shropshire Regiment who died either from wounds received in action or from disease contracted during the South African War, a handsome memorial was unveiled at Shrewsbury with all the pomp and circumstance associated with such functions.

The position selected is a prominent one in close proximity to St. Chad's Church, where all the other memorials of the Shropshire Regiment are placed, and where also repose the revered old colours of the 53rd Regiment.

The memorial consists of a figure in white Sicilian marble representing a soldier of the Shropshire Light Infantry in full marching order, in mournful attitude, both hands resting on the butt of a reversed rifle.

SAD COLLIERY FATALITIES

There was much consternation at St George's, near Wellington, when the news was circulated that a serious accident, in which three men lost their lives, had occurred at the Lilleshall Company's Granville Pit.

Residents of the district flocked to the pit, and it was ascertained that the unfortunate men who were killed were William Latham (61), New Buildings, St George's; William Dawes (27), St George's; and Ernest Stanworth (33), Wrockwardine Wood.

A large timber rod connected with the pumping machinery had broken in the water shaft of the pit, and this put a stop to work in the mine. The task of putting in the new rod began. The timber rod was 45 feet long, 13 inches square, and weighed about two tons.

When everything was in readiness for the timber to be lowered the three men entered one of the cages. Suddenly, without the slightest warning, when the lowering had commenced, the rod slipped from the "hitch" and fell on to the cage containing the men, carrying the cage and men and a large quantity of debris with it to the bottom of the shaft. The report caused by the accident resembled the roar of artillery.

On Thursday Lord Barnard laid the foundation stone of the New Market Hall and offices which are being erected at Wem. A large crowd assembled.

The Lady Forester Hospital in Much Wenlock was opened in March.

Child killed by motor car

An inquest was held at the Pant, near Oswestry, concerning the death of a boy named Alfred Ditcher, aged four and a half years, son of Thos. Ditcher, a labourer, residing at the Pant.

Mr Gerald Dugdale, of Llwyn, Llanfyllin, said he was driving a motor car from Llanfyllin to Oswestry. As he and his party neared the Pant he saw a ginger beer cart draw up alongside the road, and some children almost in the centre of the road. He blew his horn several times, shut off the engine, and applied the brake, and the children moved away.

Just as the car was passing the cart, however, a child ran out from behind the cart. Witness immediately attempted to draw up, but the distance between them was so slight it was impossible to do so in time to avert an accident.

He wished to express publicly, on behalf of himself and his parents, his deep regret for this unavoidable accident, and to tender the bereaved family their sympathy and condolences.

The Coroner, in summing up, said that one point was quite clear, and that was that the car was not proceeding at a greater pace than 10 m.p.h., the limit allowed by the Act of Parliament being 20 per hour. The jury returned a verdict of "Accidental death."

(*This tragedy appears to have been the first motoring fatality in Shropshire*)

1905

Kangaroo shot

A kangaroo made its appearance on Lawrence's Hill, in proximity to the Wrekin, and its career was cut short by a shot from a keeper, who appeared to have been in ignorance of the actual nature of his "game" and was greatly astonished when he found it out.

It appears that three kangaroos of this kind known as wallabies, a small species, were introduced into Attingham Park, near Shrewsbury, by Major Atterley. A kangaroo had been missing from the park for about a week.

The historic main building of Shrewsbury School at Kingsland has been partially destroyed by fire, the second conflagration in the county town in a short period.

The bellringers assembled at Norbury Church. The clergyman, bride and bridesmaids, and friends were also there to celebrate the marriage of "a loving couple" from Churchstoke, but at the appointed hour the bridegroom was not in waiting, nor could he be found; and the party, after waiting for some time, had to abandon the proposed "happy event".

Later in the afternoon the bridegroom turned up. Whilst walking from Wentnor, where he had stayed overnight, he had felt tired and sat down by the roadside, and fell asleep. When he awoke he found himself too late for the wedding.

Bad fire in Shrewsbury

A fire, the most disastrous that has occurred in Shrewsbury for many years, broke out at the Perseverance Ironworks, Castle Foregate, Shrewsbury, the property of Mr. Thomas Corbett, J.P., in the early hours of Monday morning; and before the majority of the inhabitants of the town had risen from their slumbers, damage to the extent of some thousands of pounds had been done.

The buildings, which it is considered were the most handsome and compact of their kind in the Midlands, comprised, when intact, spacious storage rooms, whose front elevation skirted the thoroughfare – and high above rose an imposing clock tower – a foundry, saw mill, timber store, pattern shops, and many other departments.

It was between three and four o'clock when Edward Hughes, who is employed in the new yard of the London and North Western Railway Company at Castle Foregate, discerned flames rising from the building.

Volumes of choking smoke ascended upward to the sky and were illuminated by the long, lurid tongues of flame, which rose with a wave-like motion, and then darted this side and that, searching into every cranny, devouring and destroying as they swept along. The destructive element embraced the clock tower.

Shocking ice accident at Bettisfield pool

The quiet district of Bettisfield, near Ellesmere, was startled by the news of a terrible ice accident, by which the lives of five children were lost.

The disaster happened in the school children's interval for the midday meal. A number of the youngsters, directly after being released, made their way to what is known as Kynaston's Pool, a pit which is little more than a quarter of a mile away from the school house. The pool had a covering of thin ice, and on this the children ventured, with the intention of sliding.

They had scarcely been on more than a minute when the ice, rendered weak and treacherous by the thaw, gave way.

With startled screams five children, two girls and three boys, whose names were Evelyn Hughes, Lucy Morris, Percy Moore, William Spekeman, and Jack Beckett, disappeared from sight through the large hole to the intense horror of those who stood on the bank.

1906

On August 22 a balloon called "Wulfruna" giving captive ascents at Shrewsbury Flower Show broke free, to the surprise and consternation of both the crowd and the passengers on board. The balloon eventually came down safely at Knightley Eaves, north of Gnosall. The passengers were charged for a captive ascent – five shillings – instead of the 50 shillings which would normally have been charged for a cross-country flight.

Fancy dress ball

At the invitation of the Mayor and Mayoress of Shrewsbury (Mr. and Mrs. T. Corbett), several hundred children attended a fancy dress ball held in the Music Hall on New Year's Eve.

The spectacle will long live in the memory of the hundreds of people who were able to witness it.

The pride of the parents of the children was reflected in the elegant and costly costumes they wore, the great diversity of characters being an interesting study in themselves, while the variety and richness of the colours produced a splendour that little could surpass.

Our picture shows Dorothy and Vincent Evans as "Pierrette" and "Pierrott".

Prime Minister interrupted

As a crowning point to the multitude of public meetings held in Shrewsbury during the present campaign in support of the candidature of Mr. E.G. Hemmerde, the Liberal candidate for the borough, a great demonstration took place in the General Market Hall.

Interest in the event was, as might easily be supposed, intensified by the fact that Sir Henry Campbell-Bannerman, the Prime Minister, was announced as the principal speaker.

When one looked in at the Market Hall shortly before the meeting was timed to commence, the transformation was strikingly pleasing. Rows of flags in their hundreds ran from pillar to pillar. They were all shapes and sizes, while the names of the Prime Minister and members of the cabinet and the Shropshire candidates were exhibited in white on a red ground.

The audience cheered long and loud when the Premier arrived in the hall, accompanied by Mr. Allan Bright and Mr. and Mrs. Hemmerde and although he looked tired after delivering two speeches at Chester and Wrexham, his countenance betrayed his gratification at the magnificence of his welcome to Shropshire's county town.

When the cheering had subsided it was soon evident that there was to be a good deal of opposition from a section in the audience at the back of the hall.

Sir Henry Campbell-Bannerman tried to make himself heard above the din that soon prevailed. Mr. Hemmerde repeatedly appealed to the men of Shrewsbury to give the Prime Minister a hearing.

After speaking for about half an hour, and being subject to almost continual interruption, the Premier announced that he could not proceed further.

He said – "I am perfectly unable, after what I have been going through for the last day or two, to continue to struggle against this noise."

He resumed his seat, and the vast audience cheered him to the echo.

1907

TERRIBLE SHROPSHIRE RAILWAY ACCIDENT

A catastrophe, one of most exceptional character in the annals of the railway services of England, occurred on the London and North-Western line, within 50 or 60 yards of Shrewsbury Station, on the Castle Foregate side of the town, to a train in the "North and West Express" service from Crewe to Bristol.

It was the mail train timed to arrive at Shrewsbury shortly after 2 o'clock a.m. and, in addition to the heavy mails, conveyed a large number of passengers, of whom many were either killed or sustained injuries of a more or less serious character in the shocking crash ensuing.

The accident appears to have occurred in the fact of the train having been driven at full speed ("sixty miles an hour" being surmised by some railway witnesses) right up to the approaches of Shrewsbury General Station, and consequently "jumping" from the rails of the sharp curves of the railway over the viaduct which spans Castle Foregate close against the station.

That which happened in the twinkling of an eye to what on leaving Crewe a short time previously was described as "a magnificent train" is nearly impossible of description. It was of course absolutely wrecked, and the wonder is that it did not crash over the viaduct into the street below.

Why the train was driven at this great speed right up to the station is of course a problem of which experts are endeavouring to suggest some solution, "sleep", "intoxication", "collapse" and other conditions of driver and fireman being only suggested to be scouted as impossible.

Whatever the cause, and it does seem wonderful beyond reason to comprehend, the engine plunged over the rails, crashed on for some little distance with its train following, and became a practically shapeless wreck, the carriages being piled up almost over the engine, which had turned right over on to its side.

Then began the dreaded discoveries of dead and injured. Buried beneath a mountain of debris were scores of passengers who found themselves in sudden darkness owing to the lights going out. In a few moments the rescue work began, and this continued throughout the night and the following day. Eighteen passengers and crew were killed.

1908

Lively reception of Suffragettes

Shrewsbury was disturbed by its first attack of election fever on Wednesday evening.

Up to that period the Newport by election contest had occasioned no excitement in the borough, but the advent of members of the National Union of Women's Suffrage Societies was attended with demonstrations of the liveliest character.

The announcement that the Suffragettes would hold an open-air meeting in the Square on Wednesday evening caused some thousands of people to assemble there, and when three members of the union put in an appearance they had a mixed reception.

Mrs Stanbury, the leader, stood on a chair under the shadow of Clive's monument and endeavoured to explain the objects of the union. She was greeted with shouts of "Go to the washing" and "Where's your bell?" but, after appealing to the interrupters to be Englishmen, she succeeded in getting a fair hearing.

Occasionally unsympathetic members of the crowd endeavoured to poke fun at the speaker, but Mrs Stanbury's repartee was unusually clever, and she invariably turned the laugh against the interrupters.

At the close of Mrs Stanbury's speech she called upon Miss Rowlette, but before that lady could climb on the chair a policeman intimated that as the crowd now extended all across High Street, the Suffragettes must move into the Square. They endeavoured to do so, but the rowdy element became so demonstrative that it was found absolutely impossible to resume the meeting. Mrs Stanbury and her friends were hustled all over the place, and the crushing was so severe that women and children cried out in terror, but happily no one was injured.

Mrs Stanbury took temporary shelter at the Police Station, and was none the worse for her experience.

The Suffragettes took the opportunity to hold meetings at various towns during the Newport by election campaign to spread their message. Below is Miss Howey, far right, addressing a crowd in Park Avenue, Whitchurch.

BADEN-POWELL IN SHREWSBURY

General Baden-Powell visited Shrewsbury to explain his "Boy Scouts" scheme, as he had already done in various parts of the country.

Lively memories of some of the most exciting experiences of the war in South Africa ensured for the "Hero of Mafeking" a rousing reception, and as much for the purpose of according the great soldier a welcome to Shrewsbury as for listening to his lecture, hundreds of people flocked to the Music Hall (to which scores were unable to gain admission).

Oswestry murder

A sensation was caused in Oswestry on Good Friday when it became known that a murder had been committed at Ffynnondeg, Sychtyn, a neighbouring hamlet, the previous evening.
The victim was Annie Lloyd, aged 75, who was found strangled.

Vicar dies in Alps

The Rev Frederick Wale, vicar of Holy Trinity, Shrewsbury, who had been staying at Blonay, near Vevey, left on an excursion to the Pleiades, where a fine view is obtained of Lake Geneva and Mont Blanc, and later his mutilated body was discovered in a crevasse.

The statue of Hercules at Shrewsbury is at present a somewhat sorry sight. Daubed in dull red, the strong man looks much like an old British warrior in his war "paint". Over his head and body are stuck downy feathers, and the general appearance is extremely ludicrous. Some people suggest that the joke has been played by some Old Salopians.

1909

Webb memorial

Recent attempts to swim the English Channel led to the suggestion that a permanent national tribute to the memory of the late Captain Webb should be erected in Dawley, the birthplace of the gallant swimmer.

The opening ceremony took place on Saturday evening. It was intended that the ceremony should not last more than half-an-hour, but even this had to be slightly curtailed, as at the time announced for it rain was descending heavily, and did not abate for some time afterwards.

The fountain is a very handsome one. The inscriptions on it are, "Nothing great is easy. Erected by public subscription to the memory of Captain Matthew Webb who, in addition to feats of life-saving, swam the English Channel.

"Captain Webb was born at Dawley on January 19th, 1842, and lost his life in an attempt to swim Niagara Rapids on July 24, 1893.

"He was born in a house which formerly occupied a site a few yards from this memorial."

Thousands turned out to see the opening of the bridge on June 26.

Opening of new bridge

Saturday was quite a red letter day in the history of the borough of Wenlock, when the new traffic bridge at Jackfield was declared open by Mr Thomas Parker. The town of Iron-Bridge was gaily decorated, and near the approaches of the bridge (The Blockhouse) were garlands, with the words "Success to the New Bridge and Prosperity to All".

The Alexandra Theatre was also prettily decorated for the occasion, whilst the bridge itself was decked with flags. Notwithstanding the inclemency of the weather, something like 5,000 people were present, and took a lively interest in the proceedings. The conveyance contained the Mayor (Councillor B. Maddox), Mr T. Parker, JP, Councillor Davies (Cardiff), member of the Severn Commissioners, Councillor W. Roberts, and Mr J. W. White (treasurer).

The Mayor, in introducing Mr Parker to open the bridge, said that indeed it was an auspicious day in the history of that part of the Severn Valley. For the first time they were able to see erected across the river a free bridge (Applause). The party drove over the new bridge, which was also crossed by the thousands present.

At night the Wellington mail cart from Broseley came over the Severn for the first time free of toll, and the driver was cheered as he drove through the crowded streets.

Lloyd George motor promise kept

A few years ago two gentlemen were dining at a Shrewsbury hotel, when a lumbering car was driven into the yard.

Like many of the earlier motors, this one was neither silent nor odourless, and one of the diners, pointing to the snorting machinery, observed to his friend, "If I should ever become Chancellor of the Exchequer, those are the things I should make contribute pretty generously to the finances of the country."

The speaker was Mr David Lloyd George, now the Chancellor.

Hill's column hit

The colossal figure that surmounts Lord Hill's Column has been struck by lightning. Pieces have been chipped off the figure in three places, but fortunately the monument is in no danger of collapsing, and the necessary repairs can be carried out without the statue being removed.

1910

PIT CAGE DISASTER

A gloom was cast over the town of Madeley when it became known that a shocking disaster had occurred at the Kemberton Colliery, the property of the Madeley Wood Colliery Company, whereby seven lives were lost.

Eleven men, under the charge of Fireman George Gough, were to have gone down to do some repairs in preparation for the 200 or 300 miners who should have begun work in the early hours. At the time for descending the shaft, however, only nine men and youths had put in an appearance, and the fireman directed that two of the men should await the arrival of the absentees, and go down into the pit by the next cage.

The signal was given for the descent, and when the cage had gone down about forty yards the rope suddenly snapped and the cage containing the men was precipitated to the bottom of the shaft, some 800 feet below, with terrible consequences, the seven miners being dashed to pieces.

They were brought to the surface and placed in the engine room for identification, and here some heart-rending scenes were subsequently witnessed, when the widows and families of the men and other relatives and friends were summoned to the spot.

The victims were George Gough, Prince Street, Madeley (who leaves a wife and four children); Arthur Wilton, Park Lane, Madeley (wife and two children); Richard Rogers, Victoria Road, Madeley (wife and two children); Thomas Glenister, Dawley (wife and eight children); Alphonso Stanley, Shifnal, 19, single; Randolph Cecil Miles, Prince Street, boy, 14; and Albert Jones, Church Road, Dawley, boy, 14.

Up to the present the reason of the rope breaking is a mystery. It had been tested on the day of the accident and appeared to be in perfect condition.

New football ground

Shrewsbury Town played their first match on their new ground, the Gay Meadow, Abbey Foregate, on Saturday last, when they were defeated by the odd goal in three by the Wolves' Reserves.

The Gay Meadow is nicely situated, and the Town Football Committee are making every effort to put it into first class order.

It is hoped that the grandstand will be completed in time for the Halesowen match, on the 24th inst.

The grandstand of the previous ground at Copthorne was destroyed in a gale in February.

Park opened

The opening ceremony in connection with Caeglas, the new park in Oswestry which the Corporation have acquired for the use of the public, has taken place. The function was favoured with ideally fine weather, and a large number of townspeople assembled to witness the ceremony.

The proclamation of the new king, King George V, in Oswestry on May 10.

Disastrous fire at Pontesbury

A fire broke out in the Deanery Hall, Pontesbury, and so strong was its hold that it completely gutted the premises.

Regrettable as the occurrence would be in any circumstances, it will be considered doubly so from the fact that the hall, a new one, has only just been completed, and had not even been formally opened.

This function was to have been undertaken by the Bishop of Hereford on the 26th inst.

1911

HOTEL FIRE AT SHIFNAL

A serious fire broke out at the Star Hotel, Shifnal. The licensee, Mr Henry Hews, retired to bed about an hour after closing time, when everything was quite safe.

When the outbreak was discovered it was found that the flames had got a firm hold of the building, and it was not long before the roof of the hotel fell in.

Then the bedroom floor collapsed, the debris falling into the billiard room, and a billiard table was completely destroyed.

The licensee managed to escape from the doomed building just in time through one of the windows. It was not until nearly six o'clock that the conflagration was got under control by the Shifnal Fire Brigade, who got their supply of water from the adjacent hydrants.

They worked exceedingly hard, and had many narrow escapes from the falling building, several large chimney pots falling into the roadway. The premises next door were also slightly damaged.

The hotel was completely gutted, only the outside walls of the building being left standing.

How the fire originated is unknown, but the damage, which is estimated at something like £3,000, is covered by insurance.

The Star Hotel is close to the railway station.

After lying derelict for over a quarter of a century, the Shrewsbury and Llanymynech and the Kinnerley and Melverley sections of "The Potteries, Shrewsbury, and North Wales Railway" have been quickened into life, and were formally reopened for traffic as the Shropshire and Montgomeryshire Light Railway.

Plane lands near Madeley

Valentine's aeroplane drew huge crowds when it landed on July 31.

In connection with the £10,000 prize aerial race, Mr James Valentine, the English airman, alighted about 7.15 on Monday morning on his journey from Manchester to Bristol in a field occupied by Mr Smith of Brockton, a distance of one mile from Madeley and 100 yards outside the Wenlock Borough.

The report of his descent spread like "wild fire". People from all over Shropshire quickly assembled on the scene in motor cars, motor cycles, cycles, waggonettes, brakes, and others on foot.

Mr Valentine, who appeared in capital condition, was generously entertained at breakfast by Mr J Cock, manager for the Madeley Wood Company. The airman was very affable and chatted with anyone, and he must have been tired of signing his autograph.

There must have been nearly 8,000 people present when he resumed his journey in the evening amid the vociferous cheers of a delighted crowd. He had about 12 hours' stay.

During Mr Valentine's rest his machine was strictly watched, and the people kept in good order by Supt Tait, Sergeants Morris, Durnall, Harries and Police-constables Wakeley, Plant, Reeves, Edwards, Griffiths and Lowe.

(This was the first well documented appearance of an aeroplane in Shropshire).

Shropshire Sanatorium opened

Long and devoted efforts in an attempt to stamp out tuberculous disease in Shropshire had a gratifying consummation when the new County Sanatorium, which has been erected at Shirlett, was formally opened by Her Royal Highness Princess Alexander of Teck.

It stands on the summit of a fir-studded acclivity approached by pastoral slopes, and is situate about three miles from Much Wenlock, on Lord Forester's Willey estate, 700 feet above the level of the sea.

1912

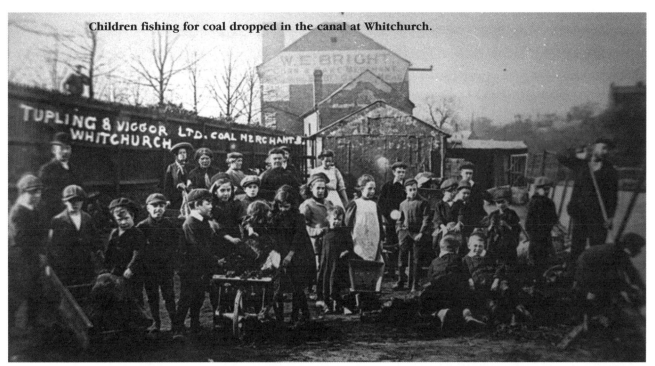

Children fishing for coal dropped in the canal at Whitchurch.

Coal strike – suffering among the poor

A week has now passed since the coal strike became general, and there is no indication of any appreciable progress towards peace.

Reports from various parts of the country indicate that distress among the poor is increasing, and there is a further large addition to the number of workers thrown out of employment in other trades than the coal industry.

The conduct of the Shropshire miners during this workless week has been exemplary in every respect.

So far it has been a peaceful strike, and the men as a whole have shown no inclination to act in any but an orderly and law-abiding manner.

Passing through the whole area affected by the strike between Madeley Wood and Wellington, a JOURNAL representative was impressed with the transformation in the out-look across the country and on the horizon.

Vulcan had quenched his fires, and the Cyclops slumbered. Nowhere could be heard the throbbing of the winding engines of the collieries, nor the rattle of the ropes bringing their black burdens from the dismal depths of the coal seams.

No sombre columns of smoke ascended from the towering tops of furnace chimneys, but the sun shed effulgent rays over a landscape as pure and picturesque as could be found in the country.

The scene was Elysian; but hidden away from its glitter and glory were the possibilities of a tragedy which may become appalling.

(The miners strike, over a minimum wage, lasted from March 1 to April 6 and caused great hardship)

Shropshire Titanic victim

It has now been definitely ascertained that the ill-fated Titanic claimed a Shropshire victim. The second steward of the luckless vessel was Mr Leopold Turner of Church Stretton.

His friends and relatives have hitherto been labouring under the mistaken belief that he was on the Olympic, but have now discovered that he transferred to the Titanic just prior to its sailing, and went down with that vessel on the anniversary of his 28th birthday.

Composer in home town

A memorable performance took place at the Whitchurch Town Hall when the Whitchurch Choral Society presented Edward German's concert version of "Merrie England" before one of the largest audiences ever seen in the hall.

Mr German conducted the performance in his home town personally, and this, of course, was the great attraction. It is some 25 years since his last public appearance in the Hall, although of course he visits the town frequently.

1913

Lovers drown at Colemere

Dr Alymer Lewis, district coroner, Oswestry, and a jury, inquired into the circumstances attending the death of a youth named Henry Wilkinson (17) and of Ethel Mary Owen (26), who for some time past had been in service as head housemaid at Frankton Grange, near Cockshutt.

Wilkinson had been employed at the same place as footman for about two years. He was a native of Knowbury, and Ethel Owen belonged to Clungunford.

The day after Owen had visited a medical man, she and Wilkinson were missing from Frankton Grange. Their bodies were found in Colemere, Ellesmere.

The Coroner elicited the statement that Dr Bathurst found that the woman was an expectant mother. Owen told him that it was impossible for her and Wilkinson to marry.

The Coroner, in addressing the jury, said the case was one of the saddest he had had to inquire into for some years.

One could not help regretting that the couple could not face the music and that they should have taken their fate in their own hands. He was of opinion that the jury might safely return a verdict to the effect that the two committed suicide while of unsound mind. A verdict to this effect was returned.

A combined project which probably will come to be regarded as one of the most important recorded in the annals of Wellington had a delighted consummation when, under auspices of the most favourable description, the "John Crump Bowring Memorial Cottage Hospital" and the "John Crump Bowring Recreation Ground" were opened to the public.

It was Empire Day, and brilliant sunshine lent lustre to the function (see picture above).

It will be recalled that under the will of the late Mrs J C Bowring a piece of land about three acres in extent, prettily situated on the south side of Haygate Road, Wellington, was left on trust for the purpose of erecting thereon a Cottage Hospital.

The opening ceremony was performed by the Earl of Powis (Lord Lieutenant of the County) in the presence of a vast assembly.

THE BOLAS ROMANCE

Thousands of persons were attracted to the Parish Church of Whitchurch, near Cardiff, to witness the wedding of the Rev Joseph Miller, Rector of Bolas Magna, Salop, whose age was given as 74, and Miss Dilys Wynne Roberts, school teacher, aged 20, of Llandaff North, near Cardiff.

It was only comparatively a few weeks ago that Miss Roberts came to Bolas as assistant teacher at the village school, and naturally the announcement of the engagement between her and the Rector, which was made shortly after her advent into the parish, caused some surprise and much interest in the locality.

The wedding was fixed for 2-30, but the vicar of the parish explained to the bridegroom that the bride had not arrived. "Good gracious, that's strange," replied Mr Miller.

Minute after minute passed until five minutes to three arrived. More than once the bridegroom looked as if he would burst into tears and as he stood with bent shoulders he presented a pathetic figure. He looked all his 74 years.

It was within two minutes of the fatal hour of three – after which no marriage could be solemnised – that the cry went up from the outside, "Here she comes!"

The bridal party came in a taxi. By the hiding of faces attempts were made to baffle the battalion of cameras in front. As they hurried into church the girl's father, a distinguished-looking man, shook his fist at the photographers, and said "I shall sue you for this if you put the photographs in."

EUROPE ABLAZE

All efforts to secure peace between the great European Powers have failed, and war is raging throughout Europe.

Never has there been a war of such monstrous size, as the number of combatants so far involved totals more than twenty millions. Great Britain has at last herself been drawn into the struggle.

Immediately on it becoming known that there was a likelihood of this country being engaged in the war with Germany, in all local and military circles great activity commenced to be shown, and consequently all arrangements were quickly complete and in readiness to carry out the orders of mobilisation.

Shrewsbury has been greatly excited the whole week with the comings and goings of soldiers of all branches of the Service, and the enthusiastic scenes witnessed in the streets have clearly shown how earnest everyone is in this war that has been thrust upon the country.

In Oakengates and St George's district a good number of Germans have been employed in the various local works as officials and workmen, and these have obeyed the call to their "Fatherland" and on Monday and Tuesday left the district en route for Germany.

Great excitement is prevailing in Oswestry, as elsewhere over the war, and on Wednesday evening a large crowd assembled at the Great Western Railway Station to give Oswestry Territorials a send off. The Mayor (Alderman Chas. E Williams) was present, wearing his chain of office, and addressed the Territorials prior to their departure, wishing them god speed. They were heartily cheered by the assembled crowd as the train steamed out of the station.

The Shropshire Yeomanry departs from Ludlow on August 8.

Royal Show visits Shrewsbury

For the third time in its history of 80 years the Royal Agricultural Society of England held its annual exhibition in Shrewsbury.

In the main streets and avenues converging on the Racecourse, glitter and gorgeousness were the dominant features. In many towns a general holiday had been declared so as to afford traders and their assistants an opportunity of seeing his Majesty. Many additional trains had to be requisitioned to Shrewsbury.

Long before the scheduled moment for the King to be present people filled the Square (see picture) and every available vantage ground for sightseeing was occupied.

1915

GERMAN POWS ESCAPE

Alarm was caused in Shrewsbury by the escape of two German soldiers from the Prisoners' of War Barracks at Abbey Foregate, but we were unable to publish anything as the military authorities refused to give any information, and said there was nothing for publication.

Next day, however, the authorities changed their attitude, and issued a full description of the runaways, with the result that they were captured the same evening.

Meanwhile, it is stated, the Germans had been seen by a number of people, but, in the absence of official information of the escape, they were not aware that this little excursion was not according to programme and part of our humane and considerate method of dealing with the prisoners of war.

The escape was made in broad daylight. They were arrested on the highway at the Garreg, about five miles out of Welshpool.

When accosted they offered no resistance.

Chief constable dies

We announce with deep regret the death in a French hospital from wounds received in action of the Chief Constable of Shropshire, Captain Gerald Lysley Derriman, of the 2nd Grenadier Guards.

Sir Arthur Conan Doyle, before a great audience assembled in the Speech Hall, Shrewsbury, gave a graphic story of the four great battles of the war.

The lecture was arranged by the Abbey Foregate Literary Society. Sir Arthur vividly described the incredible gallantry of our men at the front.

Big camp at Prees Heath

Work in progress on the wooden huts at the Prees Heath camp.

One of the most interesting spots in Shropshire just now is Prees Heath, where a wooden town is rapidly being erected for the accommodation and training of some 18,000 soldiers.

Those who knew and loved the heath in its wild state will regret the change, but pleasure must give way to utility, and few more suitable or healthier spots for a big encampment could be found.

The golf links have entirely disappeared. East and west and north and south workmen are engaged erecting endless rows of huts, stabling for horses, laying tramways and making roads, and the place is a hive of industry, to the great benefit of Whitchurch and neighbourhood.

A siding has been made connecting the heath with the London and North Western Railway.

Altogether it is intended to build 900 huts, besides officers' quarters, riding schools, and a drill yard with cement floor.

Ultimately it is anticipated the camp will extend to Prees Village.

Another camp is to be formed in the Deer Park at Bettisfield.

In all probability a rifle range will be prepared on Whixall Moss, but nothing has yet been definitely settled.

The arrangements for the Park Hall Camp at Oswestry are as follows: Cheshire Regiment, Lancashire Fusiliers, and the East Lancashire Regiment, with Territorial Force units, a total of about 20,000.

Defence of the Realm Act case

At Shrewsbury Borough Police Court Alice France (24), servant girl of 17 Hill's Lane, Shrewsbury, who is employed at Mr Hayes's, builder, Abbey Foregate, and her mistress Mrs Mary Teresa Hayes, were charged with acting in a manner likely to be prejudicial to the defence of the realm, in writing and signalling to a prisoner at the Coleham prison camp.

France said she wrote merely out of friendship. Mrs Hayes drafted the letters. Mrs Hayes was fined £10, and France £2.

1916

TALLY HO! VC

Colonel John Vaughan Campbell, DSO, of Broomhall, Oswestry, has been awarded the Victoria Cross for conspicuous bravery on the Western front.

Following are the official particulars published yesterday that earned the high distinction: "For most conspicuous bravery and able leading in an attack. Seeing that the first two waves of his battalion had been decimated by machine-gun and rifle fire he took personal command of the third line, rallied his men with the utmost gallantry, and led them against the enemy machine-guns, capturing the guns and killing the personnel.

"Later in the day, after consultation with other unit commanders, he again rallied the survivors of his battalion, and at a critical moment led them through a very hostile fire barrage against the objective. He was one of the first to enter the enemy trench.

"His personal gallantry and initiative at a very critical moment turned the fortunes of the day, and enabled the division to press on and capture objectives of the highest tactical importance."

Colonel Campbell is a Master of the Tanat Side Harriers and it is stated that in the desperate assault on the German trenches he rallied his men to the sound of a huntsman's horn.

Colonel Campbell entered the Army in 1896, was promoted lieutenant 1898, Regimental Adjutant 1900, Captain 1903, and Brevet-Colonel last January.

He took part in the South African War, and was engaged in the advance on Kimberley, in the operations in the Transvaal, Orange River Colony, and Cape Colony, for which he was awarded the DSO and Queen's and King's medals.

Col. Campbell's father, the Hon Ronald G E Campbell, was second son of the second Earl Cawdor, and married Catherine Susannah, daughter of Bishop Claughton of Rochester.

Prees discovery

An exceedingly interesting discovery of human remains of a prehistoric age has been made in the course of excavations which have been carried out at Prees Heath recently. The remains are authoratively stated to belong to the Neolithic age.

In the early hours of Wednesday morning a fire was found to have broken out at the tannery of Messrs Cock and Sons, Barker Street, Shrewsbury, where, in less than an hour and a half later, damage to the extent of about £50,000 was caused.

The lurid light of the angry flames lit up the whole town, and the strange illumination in itself, at a time when the borough should have been in total darkness, alarmed many a wakeful inhabitant, but not so much perhaps as a number of successive explosions, probably from the bursting of barrels of liquids, which suggested to not a few that Zeppelins were at work over the town.

Soldiers of the 1st Battalion of the King's Shropshire Light Infantry emerge from trenches near Ginchy.

1917

Mrs Harley killed in town bombardment

Feelings of deepest sympathy and great regret were elicited in all parts of Shropshire, and indeed throughout the Kingdom, when it became known that Mrs Harley of Condover, whose name has been so prominently associated with hospital work both in France and Salonika, had succumbed as the result of a wound in the head caused by an enemy shell fired on the open town of Monastir.

Mrs Harley was a sister of Viscount French and widow of Col G E Harley, C B, of Condover House.

Mrs Harley went to France early in the war with the Scottish Women's Hospital, which was raised by the National Women's Suffrage Societies. In July 1916 she took charge of a flying column of motor ambulances in Macedonia to be attached to the Serbian Army there.

Last December she left the Scottish Women's Hospital in order to work an independent motor ambulance unit for the civilian Serbian population of Monastir, and she was engaged in this work when she met her death.

One of the most touching features of her death is the fact that she had just been engaged in distributing food to some half-starving Serbians assembled in her house at Monastir. Her daily distribution of food was over, and she was sitting alone by the window when the usual evening bombardment of the town began. A shrapnel burst close to the window and a fragment struck Mrs Harley in the head.

For some years previous to the war Mrs Harley, together with her sister Mrs Despard, took a prominent part in the movement for securing the Parliamentary vote for women.

The River Severn froze over at Buildwas in February. Enjoying a spin on the ice is Charlie Bagley with passengers Billy Brown and Beattie Brown.

NO LEAVE FOR SHROPSHIRES

Considerable excitement was shewn throughout the county on Saturday last when it became known that the 1/4th King's Shropshire had arrived in England from the Far East.

Telegrams were received by many of the wives and relatives of the men and preparations were made to give them a hearty reception after their absence for nearly three years. Two or three towns displayed flags, and bands were hastily got together to meet the trains on which the Shropshires were expected.

Several of the railway stations were besieged with anxious crowds.

In the meantime the Battalion had been embarked for "somewhere in France", whither they were sent in their Colonial kit, which attracted much attention wherever they went, as the men were suffering from cold.

To those at home, it appears to be the refinement of cruelty to take these men without allowing them short leave to see their friends after so long an absence, and there is very much discontent and dissatisfaction throughout the county.

The men were sent to France in "shorts" with nothing but their packs.

Cox executed

Thomas Cox (59), hawker, Ludlow, who was sentenced to death at the last Salop Assizes by Mr Justice Atkins, for the murder of his wife, was executed at Shrewsbury.

Cox one night in August attacked his wife while she lay in bed and cut her throat with a razor. His appeal on the grounds of insanity was rejected.

Shot at dawn

Private Denis Jetson Blakemore, aged 28, son of George and Sophia Blakemore, of St George's Street, Mountfields, Shrewsbury, was executed near Scherpenberg at 4.30am on July 9 for desertion. He was in the 8th Battalion North Staffordshire Regiment and was arrested in Boulogne after he disappeared from the trenches.

1918

THE ARMISTICE

News leaked out in Shrewsbury between 8 and 9 on Monday morning that the Armistice had been signed. The putting out of a Union Jack from the Post Office and the singing of the National Anthem by the operatives gave credence to the report, and the glad news was taken up with fervour by the populace.

Immediately all the places of business in the principal thoroughfares were beflagged and before noon the smaller and side-streets followed, being transformed into a many-coloured canopy of flags and streamers.

The town was visited by many American troops, who joined in the general rejoicings. Throngs of people assembled at various centres, more especially in the Square. Each hour witnessed crowds of increased dimensions, and the streets for the remainder of the day and well into the night were packed with joyous people, most prominent among them being a large sprinkling of wounded heroes, who were loudly cheered wherever they appeared. Then the bells of St Chad's rang out the glad news, and the sky was soon crowded with intrepid airmen, who gave a remarkable exhibition of "stunt" flying and other evolutions.

In Wellington large numbers of people assembled in the streets eager to know the results of the Allied demands, and when telegraphic communications announced the signing of the armistice and the fact that firing would cease at 11 o'clock there was jubilation.

Mr J W Clift (chairman of the Urban Council), from a balcony in the Square congratulated the throng upon the memorable event, and the National Anthem was sung.

On the whole the people appeared to be dominated by a spirit of subdued exultation and restrained joyfulness, probably because in so many among them were awakened sorrowful memories of what victory had cost.

Battle of Bligny

The 4th Battalion of the King's Shropshire Light Infantry has been awarded the Croix de Guerre by the French for its heroism in taking Bligny Hill, near Rheims, under heavy fire. The attack was led by Lieutenant Geoffrey Bright, who was, because of heavy casualties, the senior officer in the front trenches.

Park Hall, near Oswestry

Park Hall, near Oswestry, one of the best preserved houses of its type in the country, has been destroyed in a fire. The requisitioned 16th century mansion near Oswestry was the headquarters of the West Lancashire Brigade. As flames consumed the hall, the Inniskilling Fusiliers toiled, moving furniture, papers, and paintings from the house.

First Victoria Cross for KSLI

Sergeant Harold Whitfield, KSLI, has won the Victoria Cross for bravery in action in Palestine.

During the first and heaviest of three counter-attacks made by the enemy on a position which had just been captured by the battalion, this gallant soldier, single handed, charged and captured a Lewis gun which was harassing his company at short range. He bayonetted or shot the whole gun team and, turning the gun on the enemy, drove them back with heavy casualties.

Sergeant Whitfield, son of the late Mr John Whitfield of Oswestry, is the first member of the KSLI to receive the much-coveted distinction of the VC during this war.

And of six Victoria Crosses conferred by the King in recognition of most conspicuous bravery in the Zeebrugge and Ostend naval operations, one has been bestowed upon Lieutenant Richard Douglas Sandford, R N, a scion of one of Shropshire's oldest county families (the Sandfords of Sandford, near Whitchurch).

1919

Shropshire's tribute to her fighting sons

Favoured with glorious sunshine, the welcome and the reception at Shrewsbury on Tuesday to Shropshire officers and men who served overseas in the Great War was a magnificent success.

The day was recognised as a general holiday, all places of business in the town, with the exception of the refreshment houses, being closed.

The townspeople turned out en masse to greet our heroes, while from all parts of the county came heavily laden trains and the streets during the day and well into the evening were packed with large crowds, the town having the appearance of a pre-war Floral Fete day.

Shrewsbury excelled itself in the matter of decorations, which were profuse, patriotic, and in the best taste.

It is estimated that quite 50,000 men and women of Shropshire have been engaged in the Army and Navy either overseas or in home service.

St Chad's bells rang out merrily. The words of greeting which stretched across the streets were well chosen, "Salopia salutes her sons", "Victory; Peace with Honour", "We never forget", "Welcome Home, Shropshires", "We thank you all", "Honoured sons, in honoured footsteps tread", "Your town and county thank you", "Well done, Shropshires", "Welcome

to hearth and home".

The day was given over chiefly to joyous festivities, but all were deeply moved who witnessed something of the touching scenes in front of the Free Library Buildings during the morning, pictured above.

Here on the greensward between the beds of glowing flowers was raised a cenotaph in the form of a cross ten feet high, mounted on a base so constructed as to add greatly to the beauty of what it held, and to afford space for hundreds of wreaths and other floral tokens that parents bereaved by the war placed on them.

Lilleshall Hall sold

The Duke of Sutherland's former Shropshire residence, Lilleshall Hall, has been bought by Sir John Leigh, the philanthropist. Included in the estate is the historic Abbey of Lilleshall.

It is pleasing to record that the new owner has announced his intention of putting no restrictions upon the liberty of the public to visit the ancient shrine. It will be recalled that Lilleshall House and 606 acres were sold by the Duke in 1917 for £45,000.

Admiral von Reuter at Oswestry

Admiral von Reuter and his comrades on Tuesday detrained at Gobowen. There were two trains, each carrying 30 officers and 400 men, closely guarded by a strong escort of Gordon Highlanders.

Admiral von Reuter was motored to Park Hall Camp, Oswestry, where he is under close arrest. The men were marched through the village to Henlle Camp, adjoining Park Hall Camp, still led by their officers and under strong local guard of the Royal Defence

Corps, which reinforced the Highlanders.

Their attitude was proud, defiant and arrogant. They marched like haughty victors, singing and whistling, till brought to their senses by women of Gobowen who hooted, booed, and shook their fists at them.

(Admiral von Reuter and his sailors had just scuttled the German fleet at Scapa Flow, where it was lying at anchor under the terms of the peace treaty).

1920

DAWLEY VICTIM

St George's Hall, Garrick Street, Wolverhampton, a building used as a billiard hall, collapsed.

It is estimated that there were between thirty and forty men and youths in the hall at the time.

Two men were killed, and five are detained in Wolverhampton General Hospital with serious injuries. The killed were Harry Plimmer, Bank Road, Dawley; Alfred Breakwell, 6 Herbert Street, Wolverhampton, railway porter. Harry Plimmer (36 years of age) was killed while passing the building at the time of the collapse. He was employed at the Sunbeam Works and was on his way to the factory when he was knocked down by falling masonry.

Mosley wedding

With almost regal splendour, the wedding of Mr Oswald Mosley, MP, and Lady Cynthia Curzon was solemnised at the Chapel Royal, St James's Palace, London.

The King and Queen were there. The bridegroom is the eldest son of Sir Oswald and Lady Mosley. Lady Mosley resided for a number of years at Beech Hill, Newport, and was very popular in the district, being keenly interested in social work. She now has her residence at Betton House, Market Drayton, and in this neighbourhood too she is doing splendid work.

Townshend wins

Polling took place in the Wrekin Division to fill the vacancy caused by the death of Mr Charles Palmer, late member for the constituency. The Independent candidate General Townshend, the hero of the siege of Kut, won with a majority over Mr Charles Duncan of the Labour Party of 3,965.

First women jurors

For the first time women jurors took part in the business at the Shrewsbury Borough Quarter Sessions held before the Recorder (Mr J W St Lawrance Leslie).

Before the ordinary business of the Court began, the Recorder said that that was the first time they had had the pleasure of seeing ladies serving on the jury panel. He could only say that he hoped – and he believed they would – that ladies, when serving on juries, would emulate the virtues that men had so long displayed.

For centuries men had made trial by jury in England the admiration of the civilised world, and he was sure that women, in the course of their duties, would emulate them.

In a case that followed the jury of 12 included Mary Elizabeth Hayward, Clara Parry, and Mary Constance Halford.

A large crowd watches the unveiling of Wem war memorial on December 19.

Ascent of Wrekin by motor-car

On Sunday visitors to the Wrekin witnessed the unusual spectacle of a motor-car making a clean ascent of this formidable hill.

The car was an 11 h.p. Riley of Coventry make, being an absolutely standard chassis, fitted with rough test body. It had received no special tuning whatever, and was driven by Capt. Riley (late of the RAF) who, when flying over the Wrekin on several occasions during the war, had often thought that it would be amusing to attempt to climb the hill in a motor-car.

Last Sunday an opportunity was presented to gratify this wish, while on a week-end visit to Wellington. Miss "Pat" Riley, of "Westcote", Wellington, volunteered to come with him as passenger.

The route taken was the usual one, viz: from the gate near the Forest Glen.

Although many motor-cyclists have successfully negotiated the hill, it is understood that this is the first time that a car has completed the climb.

1921

New hospital opens

The founders of the Shropshire Surgical Home at Baschurch in 1900 can have had little idea that their scheme would assume the character of a national institution with a world-wide reputation as a hospital for alleviating the suffering of crippled children.

With the closing of the Park Hall Military Hospital, that hospital was purchased after prolonged negotiations "for conversion into an open-air orthopaedic hospital". The transfer was completed on February 1, and the new Shropshire Orthopaedic Hospital, near Oswestry, was formally opened by the Marchioness of Cambridge before a representative gathering.

Unfortunately the proceedings were marred by heavy rain, and the ceremony had to be held in one of the open-air wards.

Lady Harlech (to sit at Oswestry) is the first lady magistrate to be appointed in the county, and one of the first to be appointed in the kingdom.

Royal shopping trip

Shropshire has been honoured by a visit from the Queen and Princess Mary, who have spent a long week-end with the Marquess and Marchioness of Cambridge at Shotton Hall. The Marquess is the Queen's brother and the gathering at Shotton Hall was in the nature of a family reunion on the occasion of his birthday. He was 53 on Saturday.

The visit was marked by an entire absence of ceremony, a great deal of their time was occupied in visits to places of interest in Shrewsbury and district, and they were recognised and loyally welcomed by the inhabitants.

On Saturday afternoon the Queen, accompanied by Princess Mary and the Marquess and Marchioness of Cambridge, motored into Shrewsbury and indulged in a little shopping tour.

They walked down to the shop of Mr G.L. Reynolds, antique dealer, in Dogpole. The proprietor was absent, and his assistant, Mr Bromfield, was taken somewhat at a disadvantage.

"I was cleaning a piece of furniture and was up to my elbows in soda water," he told our reporter, "when I heard somebody enter the shop. To my astonishment I saw it was the Queen and Princess Mary."

The news of her visit soon spread, and a large crowd assembled outside the establishment. The Queen was evidently not aware that she had been recognised, for as she turned to leave the showroom, after making a purchase of china, she caught sight of the crowd and gave an exclamation of surprise.

Afterwards they visited several other establishments, showing a preference for those in which antique goods were displayed.

While in one shop it was pointed out to her that the crowd had assumed considerable dimensions, and a suggestion was made that the car should be sent for.

"Oh, don't do that," said the Queen, "We'll walk."

And they did.

An observant friend of mine tells me that the short skirt fashion has enabled him to make an interesting discovery, namely, that among the girls of Shrewsbury shapely calves and ankles are more plentiful than beautiful faces.

He says that where you see a girl with a fine figure and the trimmest of ankles her face is generally as plain as ----. I have not noticed this myself. Perhaps some reader of this column may like to give his opinion.

"GOSSIP OF THE WEEK"

Billingsley pit closes

Billingsley Colliery, near Highley Colliery, which was taken over by the latter company during the war, has closed down, and this will have the effect of adding about 200 persons to the list of unemployed.

The pit is to be boarded up and the machinery and pit ponies are being brought up. A number of enginemen and others are engaged clearing up.

This is a disaster to the district, following the long spell of unemployment caused by the coal strike, the effect of which has been felt by practically every household in Highley.

1922

NEW WAR MEMORIAL

With due reverence the ceremony of unveiling the fitting memorial which Shropshire has raised to her honoured dead who fell in the Great War and to all who went out from the shire to fight for their country, took place on Saturday.

The memorial, a magnificent example of the sculptor's skill, occupies a site in the main avenue of the Quarry at Shrewsbury, near the principal entrance. In form it follows a classic temple, circular in plan and surrounded by six Ionic columns supporting a hollow dome. On

the floor are carved the Arms of the county, the Croix de Guerre, the badge of the King's Shropshire Light Infantry, a cross and an inscription which reads as follows: "Remember the gallant men of Shropshire who fought for God, King and Country, 1914-1919."

Princess Mary Fund total

The fund, which we have been glad to raise for the dual purpose of relieving distress in Shropshire and of presenting a wedding gift to her Royal Highness Princess Mary, is now closed, and the total subscribed by our readers is close upon £500. Grants in relief of distress have already been made by the Committee amounting to £244, and there remains about £130 still available for distribution.

French honour for Territorials

S aturday was a red letter day, not only in the stirring history of Shrewsbury, but also in the military annals of the whole county, which are considerably enriched by the public recognition of the distinguished services of one of its Territorial units in which all Salopians have cause to feel proud.

Many thousands assembled in the Quarry grounds at Shrewsbury to witness the bestowal by a famous general on behalf of the French nation of its highest mark of honour and appreciation – the Croix de Guerre (with palm) – awarded for highly distinguished service by the 4th Shropshire L.I. (T.A.) who contributed so important a part in the great struggle of 1914-18 for freedom and humanity.

General Berthelot made a special visit in person to affix to the battalion's regimental colour the emblem of gratitude and esteem for their meritorious stand at Bligny and for their part in the subsequent defeat of the common enemy.

It is now four years (June 6, 1918) since the officers and men of the 4th Shropshire Light Infantry covered themselves with glory in action at Bligny on the Western front while in co-operation with the 5th French Army.

General Berthelot addressed the Battalion in French (the English translation being afterwards read out by a staff officer).

"There are pages in history which can never be disowned, and you have just cause to be proud of yours," he said.

Cinema opening

The opening of the new "Empire" Cinema, Mardol, provides the town with one of the best designed and most completely equipped picture houses in the provinces.

The building, which has seating accommodation for 1,000 people, is the product of experts. Every seat in the building was occupied for the opening ceremony, the audience assembling in response to personal invitation of the directors, who occupied seats on the stage.

A new secondary school at Bishop's Castle was opened by Lord Powis on October 25.

1923

Exciting incident on River Severn

Considerable interest was aroused in Highley and district by the appearance on the river of a hydro-glider.

The designer of this ingenious craft is Mr Walter F W Davies of Dudley. As its name implies, it is designed to glide across the top of the water at great speed and does not take more than a few inches of water. Saturday's experiment was the third of its kind.

The trip was intended to extend as far as Shrewsbury, but within five miles of the goal they were defeated by flood waters.

All went well on the return journey until Iron-Bridge was reached, when the currents went awry, with the result that the craft crashed into the bridge.

Matters were adjusted in a short time, away went the boat and a successful trip was made as far as Bridgnorth, and here a stay was made for the night.

On Monday morning the boat left Bridgnorth but unhappily the ferry crossing at Potter's Loade, near Highley, proved to be its undoing. At this point there is a rope across the river, and although the designer and pilot Mr Davies was aware of the fact, the conditions of the river rendered a collision unavoidable. The three occupants had an unexpected immersion.

Flooding hit several areas, such as Ironbridge, seen here on March 1.

Shrewsbury Town success

The Shrewsbury Town Football Club will be able to look back upon the season of 1922-23 as the most successful in its history from the point of view of honours gained.

Altogether 88 matches were played by the first and reserve teams, of which 59 were won, 19 lost, and 10 drawn. The first team won the Birmingham League Championship Shield for the first time in its history, and the Shropshire Senior Cup, and were runners up for the Shropshire Senior Charity Cup.

Of the 47 games played by the first team, 33 were won, 10 lost, and four drawn. Between November 20 and January 13 there was a sequence of 11 victories. Altogether 118 goals were scored, against 60.

Jack Williams heads the list of goal scorers with 35 to his credit.

With commendable enterprise the club has carried out considerable ground improvements, including the erection of a commodious new stand and dressing rooms, which would not disgrace any first league club.

All hunting stopped

The Ministry of Agriculture issued a new order on Wednesday night prohibiting hunting in any foot and mouth disease infected area.

As far as Shropshire is concerned the order will make little difference as practically all the local packs had previously suspended operations.

Up to the time of going to press the number of outbreaks on Shropshire farms since September was 90.

Girl killed by tree

During a gale, estimated to be blowing at 50 to 60 miles an hour, on August 2, one of the famous lime trees in the main avenue of the Shrewsbury Quarry was blown down.

A four-year-old child, Marjorie Adams, whose home is in Castle Foregate, who was caught by the tree, was killed instantaneously, while her two playmates had miraculous escapes.

Dr Downer of Shrewsbury has written to the "British Medical Journal" on the effect on two young Shrewsbury girls on sniffing tobacco powder containing hashish. The one girl was sick and the other acted as though she was intoxicated.

Dr Downer says it is very disturbing to find so large a proportion of hashish in a popular brand of cheap tobacco sold all over the country. The two girls, it is understood, sniffed at tobacco dust lying at the bottom of a pouch.

1924

Remarkable discovery

Many and wonderful "finds" were made at Uriconium in the course of excavating a large and remarkable building.

So extensive was the structure that even now, after four months' labour, it is still only partly opened up, and how much more has yet to be dealt with cannot confidently be said.

Though the ruined foundation works now exposed have been very extensively plundered for their stone, there is nevertheless much of the greatest interest yet remaining in original position.

No colonnade of equal extent has been excavated in England before. The wide spaced columns appear to indicate the main entrance or portico of the building.

The extent of the whole building may be speculated upon thus: Allowing that the Roman taste for symmetrical layout obtained in this structure and that therefore the portico was set in a central position in the facade, then the northern length of the colonnading would correspond with that of the southern and a total frontage length of some 300ft would be occupied.

If the cross colonnade of the courtyard lies on the transverse axis of the building, then its total width from east to west would be about 360ft. If further excavation goes to prove this, it will expose a monumental structure indeed, one well worthy of the efforts and success of the Emperor Hadrian in whose honour, as the inscription records, it was dedicated.

Mr Thomas Dutton passed away at Market Drayton at the age of 70 years. He was known as the Shropshire Giant, and when in his prime was 7ft 4in in height, and proportionally built. Some 40 years ago he was commissionaire at Lewis's of Manchester, and afterwards travelled in different parts of the globe.

Everest disaster

The Mount Everest Committee received on Friday the following cablegram: "Mallory and Irvine killed on last attempt. Rest of party arrived at base camp all well."

It is believed that the disaster was due to the most unfavourable conditions of weather and snow.

Mr A C Irvine was an old Shrewsbury schoolboy. He was well known as an oarsman, and was in the Shrewsbury Eight who won the Elsenham Cup.

Earthquake

On Saturday at 1am there was a distinct shock of earthquake felt at Ludlow.

There was first a rumbling noise as though a very heavy motor lorry was passing up the street; then the houses began to shake, and people who were in bed were awakened by the rattling of the windows and crockery. The shock lasted only a few seconds.

1925

TWO DROWNED

During the Shrewsbury floods two families suffered bereavements of the saddest kind.

Samuel Braddick had come into the town to procure provisions and, not being adept himself in manipulating a coracle, sought the assistance of a friend, Joe Davies, of Frankwell Quay, an expert in the management of these little boats.

The two men set out towards Braddick's home at the cottages near the Barge Gutter during the later afternoon, and they had gone some distance when their craft overturned. Both drowned.

A gloom has been cast over this district by the fact that the Bog Mines (below) closed down last week, thereby throwing a large number of men out of employment. A number of the men at Snailbeach Mine also ceased work on Friday.

English Bridge – collapse of an arch

While the work of demolishing the old English Bridge at Shrewsbury was in progress the third arch from the town side suddenly collapsed.

Reconstruction under way of the old English Bridge.

Part of the side of the structure fell on to the adjacent arch with a loud crash, but most of the masonry fell into the river. A number of men were on the bridge at the time, but fortunately no-one was working on the arch or on the nearest side of the adjacent one, so that the damage was confined to the structure itself, and no-one was injured.

The fall of the heavy masonry into the water caused a tremendous splash and drenched a number of men who were working near the pile driver. Work was immediately put in hand to shore up the remaining arches to avoid any further collapse.

It is stated that the incident is not likely to throw the bridge work back at all.

A pile trestle bridge has been built to take traffic from the English Bridge while the latter is being reconstructed.

Queen of Rumania misses crowds at Shrewsbury

The news that Queen Marie of Rumania was to visit Shrewsbury on her way from Broadway, Worcestershire, to Portmadoc, attracted a large number of people to Castle Street.

The Rumanian flag was flown outside the Raven Hotel where the Queen and her party of five had ordered luncheon for 1pm, but some disappointment was experienced when the royal party did not arrive.

Many people waited over two hours, but as it was apparent that the party had made other arrangements the crowd gradually began to disperse and the flag was hauled down.

At 3.20pm, however, the party arrived by motor car. The cause of the delay was a late start from Broadway and some mechanical trouble some distance out of Shrewsbury.

A special luncheon was served, and at 4.10pm Queen Marie left for Portmadoc, gracefully acknowledging the crowd's farewell.

1926

Lords reject Shrewsbury Bishopric

The Shrewsbury Bishopric Measure received the approval of the House of Commons by a majority of 24. The resolution in favour of the measure was moved by Lt Col Windsor-Clive (Ludlow). He said: "I rise to move this resolution by which the House is asked to agree to a measure, which was passed by a large majority of the Church Assembly, for the creation of a new diocese of Shrewsbury as soon as sufficient funds have been collected."

The resolution was carried by 57 votes to 33.

Later the measure came before the House of Lords where the Bishop of Manchester moved that the House direct that the measure be presented for the Royal Assent.

He said everybody was agreed that the county of Salop would make an admirable diocese, with its chief town in the centre and accessible from all parts.

Lord Forester opposed the motion. He was proud to be a Salopian, but he was every bit as proud to belong to the ancient and historic diocese of Hereford.

The only reason given for ruthlessly breaking up this ancient and historic diocese was, so far as he had been able to discover, the relief of the diocese of Lichfield. It was not for the general good of the Church that relief should be given by doing injury to another portion of the Church.

The Bishop of Durham said the measure was unique in that it was the first of its kind to propose the breaking up of an ancient see against its will, and without any compensating advantages.

The motion directing the measure to be presented for the Royal Assent was rejected by 61 votes to 60.

Shrewsbury's police-run fire brigade testing hydrants in 1926 at Welsh Bridge.

GENERAL STRIKE

It is estimated that there are 4,000 men on strike in Shrewsbury area. The rumour that a striker has been killed at Oakengates in a police scrimmage is false.

News of the progress of the strike from the strikers' point of view is being posted daily outside the Co-operative Stores in Beatrice Street, Oswestry.

Several wireless firms in the town have erected loudspeakers outside their premises, and large crowds assemble at the hours when news is being broadcast. Wireless apparatus has also been installed at the police station, and the public are invited to attend there at 10am, and 1, 4, and 7pm.

The best of humour prevails in the town, despite the general discomfort.

End of Coalport works

A stranger to Coalport would never imagine that the small red brick buildings like cottages on each side of the road housed one of England's great china works. Such a state of affairs is not conducive to economical management and this is one of the main reasons why the whole works is being transferred to Stoke on Trent.

Gobowen bypass

On Tuesday Col Heywood Lonsdale, chairman of Salop County Council, opened at Gobowen the first bypass road in Shropshire.

The new road, half a mile long, obviates Gobowen village crossroads, the most dangerous place in Shropshire.

There are in the county more than 40 dangerous corners to be dealt with.

At the invitation of the authorities, the Mayor of Shrewsbury (Mr R D Bromley) made the first call by ringing up the Deputy Mayor (Mr Bates Maddison) over the new automatic telephone system which has been introduced to serve the Shrewsbury district.

Installed at the cost of many thousands of pounds, the new apparatus is the last word in telephone equipment; there is, it is claimed, nothing better in the world of its class.

The official royal opening of the English Bridge on October 26 was cancelled.

DEATH OF MARQUESS

The death of the Marquess of Cambridge, brother of the Queen, took place in the Shropshire Nursing Institution, Shrewsbury, on Monday, following upon an operation for internal trouble earlier in the day.

The Marquess became critically ill at his home, Shotton Hall, near Harmer Hill, on Sunday, and early on Monday morning was conveyed to the nursing home, where an operation was performed shortly afterwards by Mr Arthur D. Haydon, a member of the honorary staff of the Royal Salop Infirmary, and who has a private practice in the town.

For a short time the Marquess felt a little easier, but soon his condition grew worse and he died in the presence of the Marchioness of Cambridge and the Earl of Eltham, his eldest son. The cause of death was a perforated intestinal ulcer.

Shortly after the serious illness of the Marquess became known, a notice was issued that all the ceremonies arranged at Shrewsbury for Wednesday, on which day the Prince of Wales was to have visited the town, were cancelled.

On Thursday the body of the Marquess was conveyed by road from Shrewsbury to Windsor to await the funeral.

The coffin, covered by a Union "Jack", was placed on a motor hearse. As the hearse moved from Quarry Place the police led the procession. The procession took the route along Murivance and Town Walls, passing over the English Bridge, where, on the right hand side, was drawn up a guard of honour.

(The Prince of Wales had been due to officially open the English Bridge on October 26. A twist of fate meant instead that it was used the following day to carry the coffin of the Queen's brother. As it happened, Queen Mary had passed over the bridge earlier, on August 13, during a visit to Shrewsbury in which she went to the flower show and did some shopping. Hers was the first car to pass over and, in the light of the subsequent events, this date was adopted as the "royal opening" of the bridge.)

Cartland wedding

The Bishop of Dover officiated at St Margaret's Church, Westminster, at the marriage of Mr Alexander George McCorquodale, of Cound Hall, Shrewsbury, with Miss Mary Barbara Hamilton Cartland, of Chelsea.

The church was thronged with fashionable guests, for Miss Cartland is very popular and extremely clever, having had published at the age of 22 her first novel. The bride intends to go on with her writing after marriage.

They will settle down in a beautiful house in Culross Street, just off Park Lane.

Through the generosity of the bridegroom's father, a party of 35 employees of Cound Hall and Cound estate made the journey to London to see the wedding.

Castle Hill landslide

Considerable excitement was aroused in Bridgnorth when it was discovered there was a slip of rock on the south side of the famous Castle Walk, nearly opposite the railway station, and adjacent to the war memorial.

It has been estimated that 200 or 300 tons of earth and sandstone fell into New Road which is, of course, the main vehicular route, connecting as it does High Town and Low Town.

It was a matter of good fortune that no one was injured when the debris fell, although a few passengers and two motor-cars were close by at the time.

It is to be hoped there will be no continuance of the slide, for if such was the case, then the famous Bridgnorth Castle would possibly be endangered.

The manufacture of beet sugar at the sugar beet factory at Allscott commenced when the machinery was put in motion by Mr E.W. James (managing director), and it is expected that the finished article will be placed on the market this weekend.

1928

Statue breaks youth's leg

Tired, perhaps, after so many years' vigil, the 6ft effigy in stone of Earl Roger de Montgomery, a prominent figure in the main room of Shrewsbury Castle, fell and was shattered and in its fall struck a youth named Ernest Evans, of 46 Severn Street, Shrewsbury, breaking his leg.

The accident happened when the castle was thronged with visitors. The figure stood on a wide stone plinth on the ground floor, and was in all over 8ft above the floor. It appeared to have broken off at the feet, but there is no explanation as to the cause of the fall.

Easthope church burnt down

Easthope suffered an irreparable loss in the entire destruction of her old church by fire on Thursday.

The rood screen of ancient oak, a peal of six bells with keyboard, the organ, the beautifully carved oak pews, and an hour glass, which projected from the pulpit, one of the very few of its kind in the country – are all destroyed.

The church was built in the 13th century, contained a pulpit dated June 28, 1623, and the hour glass is in the year 1662. As the roof and the greater part of the fittings of the church were of old oak, the fire gained an immediate hold, and before anything could be done was blazing throughout.

A wedding had been held earlier in the day.

At present the origin of the fire cannot be definitely determined.

Posthumous praise for Salop writer

During his speech at the dinner of the Royal Literary Fund, Mr Stanley Baldwin, the Prime Minister, referred in terms of high praise to the literary work of Mrs Mary Webb, a comparatively unknown authoress from Shropshire, who, "The Times" states, "was probably at her death on the verge of making a great reputation." She died last October..

By our own representative.
Glasgow. Thursday.

With the picturesque ceremonial befitting the occasion, HMS Shropshire, the latest addition to the Royal Navy, was launched this afternoon at the Dalmuir shipyards of Messrs. Beardmore by the Countess of Powis, wife of the Lord Lieutenant of the county.

The event was of particular importance to Shropshire people, for this is the first of His Majesty's ships to bear the name of the county, although the name Shrewsbury has been identified with the Royal Navy at intervals since 1694.

The conferring of the county name upon the new cruiser is mainly down to the good offices of the Rt Hon W C Bridgeman, First Lord of the Admiralty, who has represented the Oswestry Division of Shropshire in Parliament for 22 years.

The morning was dull and cloudy, but at the moment of launching the sun burst through the clouds, and the "Shropshire" slowly slipped into the Clyde bathed in glorious sunshine. The ceremony was witnessed by a large and representative assembly.

After a short religious service, Lady Powis pressed a key, releasing a bottle of champagne, which crashed against the bows, at the same moment turning a miniature steering wheel, which set in motion the launching machinery.

The new ship belongs to the "London" class and is one of the Washington Treaty type of cruisers, standard displacement of which is limited to 10,000 tons.

1929

Police court sequel to caning

At Newport Police Court Walter Samuel Brooks, headmaster of Newport Grammar School, and William Harmon and L.S. Lowe, two assistants, were charged with assaulting Frank Douglas Wright, the 16-year-old son of the chairman of the Urban Council.

After prayers the headmaster had dismissed all the school below 5B, leaving the senior school there, and then called Wright and a school friend named Williams forward.

He told him he had been seen smoking in the street, and Wright admitted this. Brooks then said: "It is against the school rule, and I am going to make an example of you and flog you."

Wright made a rush for the library stairs, but Harmon and Lowe caught him and he was badly knocked about. He was put across the desk and held in that position by Harmon and Lowe, and was then and there flogged in no gentle manner.

Williams was then flogged, while Wright was still held down by Harmon and Lowe. Wright was released and then further flogged, and had to apologise before the boys for his behaviour.

The chairman of the court, the Hon Gerald Clegg-Hill, said the Bench was quite clear that the headmaster was quite within his rights to administer corporal punishment. It would have been far better had the boy taken his punishment like a man.

The case was dismissed and the Bench considered it ought never to have been brought.

(The boy's father, who had given his son permission to smoke, later took the case to the King's Bench Division of the High Court of Justice. It turned on the extent of the school's power to punish a boy smoking in the street with the permission of his parent. The court upheld the magistrates' ruling).

'Talkies' at the Empire

The proprietors of the Shrewsbury "Empire" made local history when they commenced, for the first time in Shropshire, the exhibition of sound films, popularly known as the "Talkies".

The Mayor and Mayoress, and a representative company of townspeople, attended the evening show, and must have been impressed by the excellence of the entertainment provided.

Following on the completion of a "silent" film, it came as something of a shock when a pleasantly modulated voice, apparently emanating from the screen, announced that the "Movietone News" would be displayed. Then followed a collection of news pictures, in each case accompanied by the appropriate sounds – the singing of choirs at a Roman Catholic celebration; the roar of engines in a speed-boat race, and the halting speech of the recipient of the cup; the bleating of sheep and barking of dogs in a pastoral scene were faithfully reproduced.

The main item in the programme, the "Movietone Follies," provided an admirable test for the apparatus. Depicting the production of a new revue, it introduced song and dance, "close-up" dialogue, the playing of the orchestra, with solos by individual instruments and incidents "behind the scenes".

Synchronisation of sound and movement was perfect, and the effect was altogether satisfactory.

On June 23 a loaded Chevrolet truck became the first lorry to drive to the top of The Wrekin in a feat watched by thousands of spectators. It was a stunt to promote Vincent Greenhous' fourth annual motor show in Shrewsbury.

At the monthly meeting of the Much Wenlock WI the members expressed very decided opinions against the suggested revival of long skirts.

The following resolution was unanimously passed: "That this meeting, representing 130 women, view with alarm the threat of long skirts, and think the time has come for concerted action, and call upon the 4,376 WIs to speak with no uncertain voice and to ask the co-operation of the Press to help to stop this menace to health, cleanliness, and comfort."

1930

End of church spire at Wenlock

The demolition of Much Wenlock church spire has aroused great interest in the town during the last week.

The decayed condition of practically the whole of the woodwork is very noticeable. The charred state of part of the spire is apparently proof of its being at one time struck by lightning. An old resident states that this happened in 1887.

Messrs. Thompsons' of Peterborough are making satisfactory progress with the foundations of the tower, the grouting machine doing excellent work in the strengthening process, large amounts of cement being used.

The parochial church council have this week circulated an appeal for financial help.

It is interesting to note that a series of photographs have been taken of a crack in the tower wall, and the various stages of demolition of the spire, and of the ravages of the death watch beetle in the timber of the spire, which will be of great interest in years to come.

Shrewsbury man in R101 tragedy

Shropshire and the neighbouring counties, in common with the rest of the country, were profoundly shocked when the news was received that the airship R101 had been wrecked near Beauvais, about 40 miles north west of Paris, while on the first stage of her flight to India.

To Salopians the shock was all the greater in that one of the 48 victims was Squadron Leader F M Rope, a native of Shrewsbury.

Squadron Leader Fredk. Michael Rope was assistant to the Assistant Director (Technical). He was the son of the late Dr Rope, of Shrewsbury, and of Mrs Rope, who at present resides at The Priory, Shrewsbury. He had two brothers, Dr A D Rope, of Quarry Place, Shrewsbury, and the Rev H E G Rope, Cleobury Mortimer, and seven sisters.

Squadron Leader Rope was educated at Shrewsbury School. From 1921 to 1924 he was Technical Staff Officer, RAF, Iraq, and was then appointed to the Royal Airship Works, Cardington.

He played a considerable part in the designing of the R101. In July 1929 he was married to Miss Jolly, of Kesgrave, near Ipswich.

A Requiem Mass was said at the Shrewsbury Catholic Cathedral by the Rev Monsignor A J Moriarty.

It was specially appropriate in view of the fact that the town was so deeply concerned in the tragedy through the death of Squadron Leader Rope.

Near the altar rails stood a bier covered by an RAF standard with Squadron Leader Rope's uniform cap and three medals placed on top.

Criftins School destroyed by fire

Criftins village school has been gutted by fire.

The outbreak was discovered by a girl, and the headmaster marched all the 135 scholars out in two minutes. Less than two hours later the school was a heap of ruins. The building was a wooden structure, roofed with corrugated iron.

Mr Poynton, the headmaster, was taking a class when a little girl pointed behind him and shouted "Look Sir! The wall is on fire." He turned round and saw that the wooden wall near the stove was alight. The fire alarm was sounded, and the children jumped to attention and filed out of the school in perfect order.

Although the general opinion is that the erection of electrical standards has a tendency to disfigure the countryside, Mr J Nelson of the Central Electricity Board told Wenlock Town Council: "The towers have been designed to be as pleasing as possible to the eye.

"I am sufficiently optimistic to say that they will be hardly noticed in a few years."

1931

By the felling of the chimney stack of the old paper mill at Tibberton the countryside has been robbed of a familiar landmark which has been visible for miles around for nearly 60 years.
The erection of the chimney, which was 154ft high, was commenced in 1873, and completed in 1874.
Previously there had been another chimney on or near the same spot which fell upon an adjoining cottage, killing a man, woman, and little girl.
The chimney, which was last used in 1913, was generally in a very sound condition and perfectly safe, but the factory inspector had pointed out to the present owner that repairs were required at the top.

'Castle' falls down

The quaint round building which has stood on the summit of Haughmond Hill for some generations, a conspicuous object for many miles around, has been so badly damaged that one side of it collapsed on Wednesday.

At one time, not many years ago, the place was habitable, but for some time past it has been closed. It is know locally as "The Castle".

Mr Anthony Hall, of Hereford, who was formerly an inspector in the Shropshire Constabulary and was stationed at headquarters in Shrewsbury, has lately secured much publicity for his claim to the Throne of England.

He visited Ludlow on Saturday and delivered a speech in Castle Square, during which he alleged that he was descended from Henry VIII and was the rightful heir to the Throne, now occupied by King George V.

His remarks were received with amused tolerance.

3,000 Salopians in London

Over 3,000 people from all parts of the Wrekin Division participated in a "birthday party" to celebrate the first anniversary of the adoption of Col J Baldwin Webb as prospective Conservative candidate for the Wrekin.

The event took the form of a trip to London, and notwithstanding the huge size of the party, the day's proceedings were carried through with clock-like precision. The only drawback was that rain fell uninterruptedly, but everybody spent a thoroughly enjoyable day.

The party was conveyed in five special trains, each of which was coloured and named, and badges were issued to each person corresponding with the colour of the train.

Over 6,000 meals were served en route, comprising hot luncheon and cold supper.

On arrival at Euston 50 guides from the Royal Army Service Corps Regimental Association and the British Legion (Upper Norwood branch) met the party and conveyed them to a fleet of motor-coaches (120 strong) in which the sightseers were conveyed to the Houses of Parliament.

A trip through various parts of London followed, wreaths being laid on the Cenotaph by Col Baldwin Webb, Miss Webb and others, after which the party were entertained to tea and a cabaret at Lyons' corner restaurant, Coventry Street.

First electricity showroom opens

The first showroom in Shropshire in connection with the electrical scheme of the West Midland Joint Electricity Authority has been opened at the YMCA buildings in Wellington.

Alderman Bell, chairman of the authority, said that in Wellington 200 consumers were connected to the mains, and in Newport there were 150 consumers.

Mr H W Pearce (chairman of the Wellington Urban Council) said that the supply of electricity would prove a boon to the district.

1932

RUINED ABBEY MYSTERY

Unaccountable subterranean noises near the Abbey ruins at Lilleshall Hall – once the estate of the Dukes of Sutherland and now owned by the Lilleshall Estates Co Ltd and used as a pleasure resort – have led to Mr H Ford (managing director of the company) to send out an "SOS" in which a reward of £50 is offered to a diviner or archaeolo- gist who can locate the entrance to an underground passage believed to run from the Abbey.

Weird sounds stated to resemble the rumble of thunder, tinkling of bells, groans, and rustling of paper, and the banging of doors, have be heard for some time, and they have generally occurred after midnight.

Recently the noises have become worse and have repeatedly awakened the warden of the Abbey and his wife (Mr and Mrs R Bellingham) and other members of his family.

One theory is that running water may be in the passage, another is that it may be possibly "haunted" by a murdered monk, or the uneasy spirits of monks who are returning to the scene of their former ministrations.

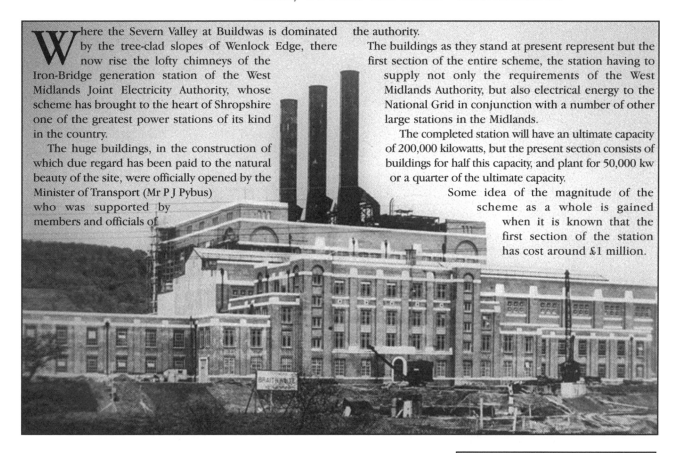

Where the Severn Valley at Buildwas is dominated by the tree-clad slopes of Wenlock Edge, there now rise the lofty chimneys of the Iron-Bridge generation station of the West Midlands Joint Electricity Authority, whose scheme has brought to the heart of Shropshire one of the greatest power stations of its kind in the country.

The huge buildings, in the construction of which due regard has been paid to the natural beauty of the site, were officially opened by the Minister of Transport (Mr P J Pybus) who was supported by members and officials of the authority.

The buildings as they stand at present represent but the first section of the entire scheme, the station having to supply not only the requirements of the West Midlands Authority, but also electrical energy to the National Grid in conjunction with a number of other large stations in the Midlands.

The completed station will have an ultimate capacity of 200,000 kilowatts, but the present section consists of buildings for half this capacity, and plant for 50,000 kw or a quarter of the ultimate capacity.

Some idea of the magnitude of the scheme as a whole is gained when it is known that the first section of the station has cost around £1 million.

Forbra wins the Grand National

Mr William Parsonage, the popular Ludlow racehorse owner and former com- mission agent, achieved the height of his ambition when his horse, Forbra, jumping perfectly, showing clear superiority over the selections of the racing "experts", won the Grand National in convincing style.

Mr Parsonage was overwhelmed with congratulations when he returned to Ludlow on Saturday night.

Ludlow has provided two previous winners of the Grand National, Mr More's Liberator, which was trained at The Vinnals, and Mr Weyman's The Colonel, trained at Richards Castle.

Miss Shropshire

Mrs J C Beckett, Miss Pontesbury, was chosen as Shropshire's beauty queen at Shrewsbury Music Hall on Tuesday night.

The series of dances leading up to the selection of Miss Shropshire was the brilliant idea of Mr J W Noble, chairman of the carnival dance committee.

1933

OPENING OF SHREWSBURY BYPASS

The Princess Royal received a true Shropshire welcome when she visited the county for a series of engagements, which included the opening of the new bypass road at Shrewsbury and an inspection of the Shropshire Orthopaedic Hospital at Gobowen near Oswestry.

Large and enthusiastic crowds greeted Her Royal Highness during her visit, buildings and streets were gaily decorated with flags and bunting and, as though to add the finishing touch to a festive occasion, the sun shone forth in all the splendour of a glorious spring day.

The visit to Shrewsbury was the second which Her Royal Highness has made to the borough within the past four or five years. On the occasion of her previous coming she opened a new wing at the Shropshire and North Wales Eye and Ear Hospital, and on Tuesday the princess, who travelled from London during the morning, opened the new Shrewsbury bypass road, constructed with a view to relieving the congestion of vehicular traffic in the county town, at an approximate cost of £130,000.

The new bypass road, which has been under construction for the past two years, connects up with the London to Holyhead road at Emstrey on the one side of the town and at Shelton on the other.

The opening ceremony took place at the Shelton end of the new road, which is near the junction of the Welshpool and Holyhead roads.

Shropshire honours Gordon Richards

Shropshire has never before, perhaps, had the opportunity of welcoming such a distinguished gathering of sporting people as was the case when there took place several functions organised to celebrate the pre-eminent position to which the famous Shropshire-born jockey, Gordon Richards, has attained by beating the record of 246 winners in one season set up by Fred Archer nearly half a century ago.

It was appropriate that the first function should take place within a couple of miles of Wrockwardine Wood, where Gordon was born, the ceremony here taking the form of a presentation of an address, contained in a casket.

The Market Square at Oakengates where the first function took place was quite inadequate to accommodate the large number of people desirous of paying tribute to the Shropshire hero, and the roars of cheering which greeted Gordon at the reception could not possibly have been given with greater lustiness or sincerity.

The Rev Gordon Cartlidge, left, watches the cutting of the first sod on the Charlton Mound, Oakengates, at the beginning of a project involving international student volunteers to remove the massive spoil heap dominating the western approach to the town.

Hospital name

The Shropshire Orthopaedic Hospital is to be known in future as "The Robert Jones and Agnes Hunt Orthopaedic Hospital."

The name commemorates the connection with the hospital of the late Sir Robert Jones and founder Dame Agnes Hunt.

Messrs Furrows, Ford agents for Shropshire, conducted a test of one of the new 8 h.p. models with a non-stop 72-hour run from Shrewsbury via Newport and Market Drayton. The total distance of 2,032 miles was covered without any trouble of any kind.

For 72 hours the engine ran without ceasing, and the car covered the course 32 times.

1934

BLACKSHIRTS MEETING HELD IN SHREWSBURY

Sir Oswald Mosley visited Shrewsbury and addressed a large gathering at the Music Hall.

He explained the policy of the British Fascists, especially with regard to agriculture, and also made a spirited reply to attacks made against his movement following certain incidents at a recent meeting at Olympia.

There were a large number of members of the movement in the hall, clad in their black shirts. Sir Oswald (pictured right, before the meeting), who was also wearing a black shirt, was given a good reception.

For nearly an hour after his address he was kept busy answering questions that were put to him from all parts of the hall.

Although before the meeting there were rumours that a party of Communists was to be present from Birmingham, there was no unruly incident.

Referring to the charges that methods of violence had been used by members of his movement at Olympia, he said there was no single case on record of meetings being attacked or broken up by Fascism. What they did was to defend their own meetings against organised Red violence.

"It was time some movement stood up to the Red Terror in this country," he added, amid cheers.

Answering questions, Sir Oswald said one of his first Acts would be to suppress the Communist movement.

Asked what he would do if the blackshirt movement was outlawed, he replied: "That has not yet been suggested, but in any case I do not tell my enemies in advance of what action I propose to take."

Football flare up

Deplorable incidents were witnessed on the Buck's Head ground when Wellington and Oakengates met in the extra-preliminary round of the FA Cup.

Scenes, regrettable in the extreme and unprecedented in the history of the Wellington club, occurred, which necessitated the game being abandoned 20 minutes from time.

The culminating point was reached when a section of the crowd encroached on the field.

A commission of the FA later sat and ordered that Wellington Town ground be closed for 14 days and the match be replayed at Shrewsbury.

Historical pageant

The Shropshire Historical Pageant and tercentenary celebration of Milton's Masque of "Comus" in the grounds of Ludlow Castle was a great success. The unbroken spell of glorious weather helped towards the realisation of the originators' ambitions, and thousands of people visited Ludlow every day. Nearly 8,000 people – a record attendance for the week – saw the final performance.

The iron toll bridge at Iron Bridge has been closed to vehicular traffic and scheduled an ancient monument. Salop County Council has resolved to build another bridge, subject to funding.

When Mrs Marion Cock is elected first lady Mayor of Shrewsbury today she will put on a robe which will be practically identical with those worn by her male predecessors.

There will, however, be differences in the headdress and adjustment of the cravat. It is customary for Mayors to wear a collapsible court hat, but in the case of a lady Mayor, a tricorn is worn.

The town clerk has issued a letter for the guidance of all concerned as to the correct way in which Mrs Cock should be addressed.

1935

This season's annual Good Friday "Derby" between Wellington and Shrewsbury will go down in history as the most brilliant spectacle ever staged in a Birmingham League match.

Not only was there the excitement provided for a record crowd by the match itself, which was made doubly keen in view of the high positions occupied by the two teams, but there were other attractions which have never been witnessed on the Buck's Head ground before.

Attendance was 11,836, the largest in the history of the Birmingham League.

Long before the kick-off the ground was a seething mass of people, in possession of a "News Chronicle" community song paper.

In the playing arena stood the band of the 2nd Battalion of the King's Shropshire Light Infantry, together with Mr T P Ratcliffe, of Wembley fame, and for an hour before the kick-off there was community singing to the accompaniment of the band.

But the spectacular event of the afternoon was the display of the combined military and drum and bugle bands of the Shropshire's famous regiment at the interval. This was a sight which will long be remembered.

Wellington lost the match 2-1.

Return of the Shropshires

Another milestone in Shrewsbury's long and stirring history was reached when a crowd estimated to number nearly 60,000 saw the Duke of York present new Colours to the 2nd Battalion King's Shropshire Light Infantry.

The ceremony in the Quarry was an impressive and colourful one, and the vast crowd of onlookers was thrilled with the brilliance and precision of the military evolutions.

It was the culminating point of the visit to Shropshire of the 2nd Battalion after an absence from the county of more than a century.

During the battalion's march from Lichfield to Shrewsbury the old Colours were carried by officers and guarded by men with fixed bayonets.

It is 117 years since the 2nd KSLI last visited Shropshire, and at each place they reached during their march by easy stages from their Lichfield barracks they received a great welcome.

That of Shrewsbury (right), the birthplace of the regiment, was perhaps outstanding.

1936

Miss Pargeter at work at Bemrose's chemist in Dawley.

A SHROPSHIRE GIRL NOVELIST

Dawley has not even got a railway station, and there is nothing there that visitors go specially to see, but probably in a few more years it will have an inrush of people interested in places of literary connections, who will pause before a certain little chemist's shop and an equally small house in King Street to admire the workplace and home of Miss Edith Pargeter, the rising novelist.

Perhaps I am wrong, and it will be Horsehay, the place of her birth, which will attract the visitors.

Already Miss Pargeter has breasted the first slopes of the difficult hill of success, for she has had two novels published, "Hortensius" and "Iron Bound", and a third is in the press, while she is only 23. She has been writing ever since she can remember, mostly poems when she was a child. Her pet subjects at school were composition, Latin, and art.

She wrote a novel when she was 15 and sent it to Heinemann's. She thinks now that, though it is meant for quite a serious story, she finds it laughable.

She works for Mr Bemrose in Dawley as a chemist's assistant and dispenser.

As to her opinion on marriage, it can better be summed up in her own words: "Wait for Mr Right or have nobody. Better to be single than to have a second best."

Pupil dies in storm

One of the worst thunderstorms experienced in Wellington for several years broke over the town and caused the death of an 11-year-old Wellington schoolboy.

Dennis Crane was a scholar at the Wellington Constitution Hill Senior Boys School.

A tall chimney of the caretaker's house, which adjoins the school, appears to have been first struck. A large amount of debris crashed through the skylights of two class-rooms, where a number of scholars were assembled.

Ancient coins find

More than 200 pennies coined a thousand years ago when Edward the Elder, son of Alfred the Great, reigned as king of the West Saxons, have been unearthed in Castle Foregate, Shrewsbury.

The coins were found by workmen while engaged on excavations for a new garage on the premises of the Shrewsbury Industrial Co-operative Society.

The coins were only of paper thick-ness and all but seven, which have been placed in the public museum, have practically resolved into dust.

First nursery school

Unknown to the majority of Salopians, a nursery school – the first in Shropshire, and one of the first, if not the first, of such institutions in rural England – is in operation in the village of Hodnet.

Splendidly situated, the new school has only been opened for the admit-tance of "scholars" –- the age is two to five years – a short time and at present the number on the register is about a dozen.

It has, however, accommodation for about 30. The curriculum is similar in many respects to kindergarten.

1937

Shrewsbury tribute

History was in the making at Shrewsbury, Mr Clement Davies MP (Montgomeryshire) said in a speech he delivered from the stairway outside the Shrewsbury Castle, after he had raised the national flag of Wales to fly for the first time over the historic pile on St David's Day.

Outrage at Wem

Intruders who made an unwelcome call at the Wem Methodist Church evidently included a gifted artist who left behind on the Sunday school blackboard, drawn in chalk, a wonderful likeness of Herr Hitler, the German dictator, complete with Swastika.

The last trip was made on the old Bishop's Castle Railway when the B.C. Co's old engine Carlisle worked the trip into Craven Arms goods yard, where she will be cut up.

Fell to death from airliner

Mr Max Wenner, of Batchcott Hall, Leebotwood, fell to his death from a Belgian air liner when it was thousands of feet above unbroken clouds over the Meuse district between Cologne and Brussels.

Mr Wenner (left) was one of 10 passengers in the machine, which was flying from Cologne to London, via Brussels.

The fall was not seen by any of the passengers or crew, but the fact that Mr Wenner had vanished was realised before the plane landed at Brussels.

Shortly before he was missed he was seen writing letters. It was later found that a floor door had been damaged, and it is assumed that Mr Wenner disappeared through that door.

Two of the passengers, who were sitting opposite Mr Wenner in the plane, on arrival at Croydon said: "We saw a man writing a letter. He hurriedly put it into his pocket, carefully placed his suitcase and hat on one side, and left the compartment. Some time afterwards – it may have been 10 minutes – we felt a bump, and later we heard that the passenger who had been opposite to us had vanished from the plane."

His body was found later. He had travelled to Germany on a family visit.

(The manner of Wenner's death and his links with Germany prompted lurid rumours which persist to this day. He had taken measures which made him unpopular. As owner of the shooting rights on the Long Mynd, his staff had tried to make sure walkers at the beauty spot kept to the paths, and he had won an injunction against the Midland Gliding Club, forcing it to move from its initially chosen site. He had also abruptly sacked his staff at Batchcott Hall. However, an investigation concluded his death was an accident).

POLICEMAN DIES SWIMMING RIVER AFTER RUNAWAY

The funeral procession for Shrewsbury police officer Harry Speake.

Whilst swimming across the River Severn at Emstrey in pursuit of one of three boys who had absconded from Saltersford Training School, Holmes Chapel, Cheshire, Police-constable Henry Geo. Andrew Speake, aged 21, of the Shrewsbury Borough Police Force, suddenly disappeared beneath the water, and repeated efforts to locate him were unsuccessful.

The boys had run off after being seen in Heathgates.

Two were caught, but the third boy swam to the other side of the River Severn and ran off, and it was while swimming after him that PC Speake lost his life.

His body was recovered later.

A postmortem found no signs of drowning and it was concluded PC Speake had died of heart failure.

Emperor of Abyssinia in Shropshire

On Tuesday midday the news was made known that the Emperor of Abyssinia, Haile Selassie, was breaking his journey from London at Craven Arms to spend a few days as the guest of Messrs. Ronald and Noel Stevens, of Walcot Park, Lydbury North, the well known Midland hardware manufacturers who have spent thousands of pounds in converting the park into a bird sanctuary.

The Emperor arrived at Craven Arms at 3.10 on the express train from Bristol, which was stopped for a few moments to enable him and his retinue to alight.

A large crowd which gathered outside the station gave the Emperor a rousing welcome.

He was accompanied by his daughter, the Princess Tenange, and several of his attendants.

SHREWSBURY 'BOMBED'

A "high explosive bomb" dropping near Shrewsbury's famous Column and sending it "crashing to the ground and damaging several buildings in its fall" was one of the incidents designed to bring into action the borough's ARP services during a two hours "blackout" on Thursday evening.

Some 400 square miles of country in and around Shrewsbury were enveloped in total darkness for two hours and the whole of the ARP services for this huge area underwent a realistic test of what might be expected of them in an emergency.

The "blackouts" extended over an area comprising the borough of Shrewsbury, Atcham rural district and Church Stretton urban district. In these areas the co-operation of the public had been sought to ensure that as far as possible no light should be visible between the hours of 6pm and 8pm to the RAF planes which flew overhead.

Throughout the borough the public responded excellently and the "black-out" was very effective. The small crowds who assembled near the scenes of the various incidents behaved extremely well and took a keen interest in them.

In Shrewsbury the 'blackout' was ushered in at 6pm by a continuous warbling up and down note on the two official sirens for two minutes and shortly afterwards could be heard "explosions" as "bombs" fell in different parts of the borough and the clanging of fire bells.

Huge Wem fire

One of the most disastrous fires ever seen in Wem occurred when business premises in the town were totally destroyed.

The premises, which are among the oldest in the town, consisted of half-timbered property.

In Market Street firefighters fought valiantly to prevent the flames spreading in a block which forms the centre part of the town in High Street, Market Street and Noble Street, and which includes many prominent structures.

Legend says that the one building which was destroyed was formerly a meeting place where such eminent divines as Coleridge and Haylett delivered discourses.

On November 15 Shrewsbury's new technical college buildings were opened by Kenneth Lindsay, parliamentary secretary to the Board of Education.

1939

CROWDS PELT BLACKSHIRTS

Scenes perhaps unprecedented in the history of Wellington took place in the Square when members of the British Union of Blackshirts arranged another public meeting and several ugly incidents were staged by the crowd before the Blackshirts were eventually escorted out of the town guarded by police.

At their previous meeting the Blackshirts announced their intention of holding another meeting. A huge crowd assembled and the numbers were increased after the Blackshirts, composed of males and females, marched from Park Street into the Square, carrying with them the Union Jack and their own banner.

After their arrival a large contingent of police formed a human ring round the Blackshirts.

Every bit of space was occupied in the Square by the crowd, from which came many catcalls; there was considerable shouting, hand bells were rung, and whistles blown, while in another section of the crowd an attempt was made to sing "Rule Britannia".

Later one section of the crowd surged forward and the real trouble commenced when one or two eggs were thrown at the Blackshirts.

This started the pandemonium and in the next minute dozens of eggs, tomatoes, oranges, cabbages etc went hurtling through the air from various parts of the crowd and blows were freely exchanged.

Eventually Major Golden (chief constable of the county) went to speak to one of the Blackshirts and they afterwards made an attempt to sing the national anthem, but the din continued and the crowd were still demonstrative.

Ultimately the police succeeded in forming an outlet for the Blackshirts to leave by way of Duke Street at the entrance of which a final rush was made by a certain section of the crowd.

Sandbagging under way at Wellington police station.

Shropshire was prepared

News of war found Shropshire ready, so much so, in fact, that there was little apparent alteration of the normal routine of life. The county ARP organisation was immediately placed in readiness for whatever demands might be made upon it, and is remaining so.

There are indications, of course, such as the sudden increase in the number of uniformed figures, the increase of the population in many areas owing to the influx of evacuees, and the digging of trenches for protection against air raids, and the sandbagging of important buildings and centres, the closing of the cinemas, the shaded traffic signals, and the whitened pavement edges.

School children and others evacuated from congested areas began to arrive in Shropshire on September 1, mainly from Liverpool, Manchester and Birmingham areas. The children, who were smiling and cheerful, were given a cordial welcome at the various stations (such as at Wellington railway station, below) before they were taken to the houses where accommodation for them had been arranged.

A Shropshire fighter pilot has become Fighter Command's first operational casualty after his aircraft was shot down by mistake.

Pilot Officer John Hulton-Harrop, aged 26, of Betton Strange, near Shrewsbury, was in one of two Hurricanes shot down by Spitfires on September 6. The incident has become known as "The Battle of Barking Creek".

And acting Corporal Thomas William Priday of the King's Shropshire Light Infantry became the first British soldier killed in action in the war. He was killed by a mine on December 9.

1940

BLITZ ON SHROPSHIRE

Five people have been killed in bombing raids on Shropshire towns within the space of two days. Two women died when a German raider dropped a string of 12 high explosive and incendiary bombs across Bridgnorth early on August 29. Three explosive bombs landed close to St Leonard's Church.

One struck Cliff Cottages occupied by two sisters, the Misses Maynard, and one of them (62-year-old Miss Josephine) was fatally injured. Another hit a house in Church Street, killing Mrs Hand and severely injuring her husband.

Another bomb landed at the junction of Pound Street, Listley Street, and St Mary's Street, severely damaging the Squirrel Hotel and nearby properties.

In Shrewsbury, a woman and her two grandchildren, who were staying over from their Llangollen home, were killed when a bomb fell on a cottage on the outskirts of the town just

before midnight on August 31.

The German raider first dropped some incendiary bombs, which fell harmlessly on pasture land and then, it is believed, two high explosive bombs were dropped, one of which hit the cottage and the other buried itself in the roadway nearby.

The victims were Mrs Jessie Mary Broxton, aged 43, of Armstrong Cottages, Ellesmere Road, and her grandchildren John Terrence Meredith, aged four, and Margaret Eileen Meredith, aged six.

The three had gone to bed, but her husband Bill was downstairs having a final smoke before retiring.

He was rescued from beneath five or six feet of debris, suffering from shock and cuts. A dog was also rescued alive from the wreckage, and emerged from his "nest" wagging his tail.

In other bombing raids a number of airfields in Shropshire were attacked.

The aftermath of the deadly Shrewsbury attack.

Wrekin MP killed

The torpedoeing of the children's evacuee ship City of Benares in the Atlantic brought a severe bereavement to the Wrekin Division, which has lost its MP, Col James Baldwin-Webb.

He had been on his way to Canada and America to raise funds for the provision of additional ambulances and when last seen was helping women and children to safety.

Heroism of air ace

Shot down 21 "Jerries" in 19 days (three of them in one afternoon) – baled out three times in as many weeks – wounded in the left leg.

Such is the story of Pilot Officer Eric Lock, 21, son of Mr and Mrs Charles Lock, Eastington, Lyth Hill Road, Bayston Hill, who has just been awarded the DFC.

At the moment he is spending a period of leave with his wife, formerly Miss Peggy Meyers, of Percy Street, Shrewsbury, whom he married in July.

COs get the sack

Salop County Council decided at its quarterly meeting at Shrewsbury to dispense with the services of employees who were conscientious objectors, members of subversive organisations, or of organisations which encouraged conscientious objection.

Dr J.A. Ireland said: "We have got our backs to the wall solidly and definitely and we are here today in the position of being for the country or against it. There is no such thing as neutrality in England today."

1941

Fighter ace Lock is missing

Reported missing... the report that Flt Lt Eric Stanley Lock, DSO, DFC and bar, was missing following recent flying operations was sad news for all and sincere sympathy is extended to his wife and parents in their anxiety.

The news came 10 days after a public presentation by inhabitants of his native village, Bayston Hill, attended by his wife. Flt Lt Lock was unable to attend.

He is one of the most famous fighter pilots the Battle of Britain produced. He gained the Distinguished Flying Cross last September and a higher honour, the Distinguished Service Order, before Christmas.

It was awarded as the result of an extraordinary feat of courage and endurance. Having shot down two of the enemy, he was then himself severely wounded, but managed to bring his damaged machine down safely.

The official announcement of the decoration stated he had shown exceptional keenness and courage in his attacks. This same courage he displayed during the long recovery from his wounds and, once well again, he rejoined his unit with the rank of Flight Lieutenant.

He was recently presented with the Eagle's Feather (being one of 11 recipients in the RAF) from a Red Indian organisation in Chicago.

Eric Lock, nicknamed "Sawn-off" Lockie because of his height – about 5ft 7ins – is one of the leading aces in the

RAF, with a tally of 25 enemy aircraft destroyed.

He was on a low-level attack mission in a Spitfire and was last seen near Boulogne.

(For years the disappearance of Lock, whose death was presumed, was a mystery. However modern research cross checking his flight with Luftwaffe combat claims suggests he was shot down off Calais by a German fighter ace).

Town hall destroyed

Whitchurch Town Hall, erected 65 years ago, has been totally destroyed as the result of a fire.

Nothing could be done to save the upper part of the premises which when daylight broke were nothing but a mass of twisted girders and smoking ruins.

The Town Hall, which is known as the Regent Cinema, seats many hundreds of people and the whole of the furnishings and the seating, together with the operating box, were lost.

Worst for 60 years

Details of Shrewsbury's great flood – almost to the day the highest for 60 years – which blocked main roads, marooned whole rows of houses, cut off the electricity supply in the centre of the town, and drowned sheep and pigs in the abattoir, may now be revealed.

It was the aftermath of the worst snowfall within living memory. The river was 18ft above ordinary low water level – highest since February 13, 1881.

Dr Benes visits

Dr Benes, President of the Czechoslovak Republic, accompanied by Mrs Benes, paid a visit on July 11 to the Czechoslovak State School at Hinton Hall, Whitchurch, the only Czechoslovak Secondary School not under German domination and the centre of education for the many Czechoslovak refugee children in this country.

Dr Juraz Slavik, Czech Minister for the Interior and Education, was also present.

1942

Enemy "invasion" of Shropshire

The military and civilian defence exercises which took place all over Shropshire during the weekend provided the authorities with some valuable experience.

The defending troops were members of the Home Guard and some regular troops, and the "enemy" were regular troops, some of whom during the night operations had blackened faces in the accepted Commando style and they included small detachments of parachute troops with a specified list of objectives in all parts of the county.

The aim of the defenders was to search out and exterminate the invaders. Fully 90 per cent of the Home Guard took part in the operations. In many cases the "enemy" captured their first objectives but in most instances the positions were retaken, there being sufficient reserves in the neighbourhood to mount counterattacks.

Exceptional keenness was shown by the Home Guard, who used to the full their special knowledge of the lie of the country and showed considerable ingenuity in covering and defending vulnerable points. One country company put out a patrol mounted on horseback during the night operations, making it a mobile and comparatively noiseless force.

The hostility of the inhabitants to the "invaders" was an important factor in favour of the defenders, who in many cases were given information of the disposition and movements of the "enemy".

The liaison between the military and civil authorities appeared to work well.

At Shrewsbury a number of positions were captured by the "enemy" but were all regained before the end of the operations. The Castle was one of the places taken, but was quickly recaptured, the walls being scaled by means of ladders, while a plentiful supply of smoke bombs were used in ejecting the "enemy".

In an attack in the Ironbridge district, a platoon of the Home Guard mounted on cycles recaptured an important position.

GAY MEADOW BASEBALL

A large crowd visited the Gay Meadow, Shrewsbury, when two teams from an American Army Air Base met in a baseball match in aid of the Red Cross Fund.

The teams were the Yankee All Stars and the Flying Eagles.

In his welcome, the Mayor of Shrewsbury, Captain Harry Steward, expressed the belief that this was the first baseball game ever played in Shrewsbury. During the game, however, a programme was handed up by one of those present of a game played at Shrewsbury on September 21, 1918, between the Canadian and American forces.

King George VI and Queen Elizabeth made a hush-hush visit to COD Donnington on July 16. The Queen is with Brigadier de Wolff, the first commandant of the base, with the King following behind.

Scouts' VC for Broseley boy

Broseley Parish Church was crowded when Major-General H D O Ward, of Linley Hall, Broseley, presented the Bronze Cross (the Scouts' Victoria Cross) to the mother of Patrol Second L H E Humphries, the 13-year-old Broseley Scout who was posthumously awarded the Cross for his bravery in attempting to save a fellow Scout from drowning in the River Severn at Sheinton last summer. Both, however, were drowned.

The official mascot of a King's Shropshire Light Infantry battalion – a nearly full-grown bear – has had to be shot. It broke loose and mauled its keeper, Private Percy Pritchard, of Wellington, who is now in hospital. The bear was owned by Captain Wycherley, who had it as a cub and presented it to the battalion.

1943

FIRST DEATH IN 51 YEARS

About 4.45pm on Wednesday an accident occurred at Bridgnorth Castle Hill Railway – the shortest and steepest in England – involving the death of the engineer attendant, Harold Augustus Howes, 36, of 26 West Castle Street, Bridgnorth.

This is the first fatality on the Lift Railway since it was opened over 50 years ago.

The railway has been closed since before Easter to permit of repairs, including the fixing of new cables, and at the time of the accident the carriages were disconnected from the cable.

It is understood that Howes, who had been employed by the railway proprietors for the past 14 years, was engaged on some work on the top carriage, which broke away and crashed into the bottom station, wrecking the carriage and causing considerable damage to the premises. Howes was apparently trapped in the water tank underneath the carriage and was carried from top to bottom, his legs protruding from the end of the carriage. He was extricated by Police Sergeant Jones and others who were quickly on the spot and was attended by Dr J L Lloyd Jones, who immediately gave him morphia. Mr Howes had multiple injuries and died within a short time.

Homeland defenders – officers of G Company, 2nd Battalion, Shropshire Home Guard, comprising men from villages in the Oswestry area.

Double tragedy at Sleap

The control tower of a Shropshire airfield has been hit by a double tragedy with bombers crashing into it twice within the space of a few days, leaving many dead and injured.

In the first incident at Sleap airfield, near Wem, a Whitley bomber swung on landing on August 26 and ran into the tower. The pilot and bomb aimer were killed and the rest of the aircraft crew, together with three people on the ground, were seriously hurt. Others had miraculous escapes.

The hole in the control tower was quickly bricked up and it was able to resume operations.

Then, soon after midnight on September 7, another Whitley bomber hit the tower while taking off and burst into flames. Seven died – four in the plane – and, on the ground, Norman Peate and WAAFs Vera Hughes and Kitty Ffoulkes. The tail gunner was badly injured and two WAAF Met staff were badly burned.

The tower is being repaired but some have claimed it is now haunted by the ghosts of the two WAAFs.

US man cleared of Forest Glen murder

"The Court acquits you of all the specifications in the charge."

When these words were spoken by the President of the US Court Martial in the West Midlands on Tuesday, Sergeant Michael Pihosh, 22-year-old military policeman, walked from the Court a free man.

He had been charged with the murder of an ATS Private, Louisa Edith Jenny Price, aged 18, of 15 Greenway Road, Higher Tranmere, Birkenhead, by striking her on the head with a stone.

Price's body, mutilated and partly stripped, was found by quarrymen in the woods of the Wrekin on the morning of September 9 after she had attended a dance given by American soldiers at the Forest Glen Pavilion, near Wellington, the night before.

The trial had lasted seven days.

KSLI LAND ON D-DAY

The King's Shropshire Light Infantry were among the troops who landed in Normandy on D-Day. They did not have an easy landing for, when they left their landing craft at La Breche d'Hermanville, they plunged into between four and five feet of water. There was a heavy sea running and the beach to which they made their way was under shellfire.

The regiment was swiftly engaged in stiff action. They rode on the tanks of a yeomanry regiment towards Caen but their advance was hindered by minefields.

One company met its first group of the enemy on a ridge overlooking the sea. The company cut its way forward through cornfields towards the enemy positions. Here and there, hidden among the tall corn, were machine gun nests and the company advanced spread out in a loosely linked line, looking as an observer put it like so many beaters walking up game.

(The 2nd Battalion of the KSLI fought their way to Lebisey on the out-skirts of Caen and claim to have made the deepest inland penetration of any of the Allied troops on D-Day).

Troops of 2 KSLI capture a Polish soldier serving in the German Army in Caen on July 10. This sequence was re-enacted for the benefit of newsreel cameras and shown in cinemas all over Britain.

"Great Escape" Salopian shot

Friends over a wide area were profoundly shocked when it became known that Flight Lieutenant Cyril Douglas Swain had been shot by the Germans in the mass escape attempt from a prison camp.

One of the gallant officers to whose courage and high sense of duty Mr Anthony Eden paid tribute in the House of Commons last week, Flight Lt "Sid" Swain was the second son of Mr and Mrs Percy Swain, Belle View, Wem. He was 31.

After many operational flights, his machine was shot down over enemy territory and on November 28, 1940, he was made a prisoner of war.

(Swain was one of those shot for taking part in the "Great Escape" of March 1944)

Mrs Peggy MacNeece, eldest daughter of Mrs G. Hincks, Fourways, Copthorne Road, Shrewsbury, has married Lt Col. Brian Frederick Montgomery, brother of General Sir Bernard Montgomery, at Caxton Hall, London.

Mrs MacNeece has been a voluntary worker at the American Red Cross Club, Shrewsbury.

General Montgomery was unable to attend.

Meanwhile, "a proud Salopian" has the coveted position of head chauffeur to the famous general.

Born in Shrewsbury, the man is Sergeant W E Edwards, and he is a son of Mr E Edwards, formerly of Wenlock Road, and Monkmoor Road, and of the late Mrs Edwards.

V1 ROCKS NEWPORT

A V1 flying bomb which landed near Newport in the morning of Christmas Eve has caused extensive blast damage in the town.

Windows were shattered but there were no casualties and no structural damage.

The "doodlebug" had been launched from the air by a German bomber and came down in a field a mile to the east of the town, near the railway line close to the "Griffy Bridge". The scene was quickly sealed off, but some schoolboys who were first on the scene reported that the bomb was still largely, or partly, intact.

The bomb, it is said, contained what purport to be letters from prisoners of war. The letters are in both photostatic and printed form and are marked "V. P.O.W. Post."

It is believed that the letters may be a propaganda ploy or a ruse to discover where the bomb landed.

The letters have been confiscated by the authorities.

1945

Towns celebrate VE Day

Heavy rain on Tuesday morning which ceased about midday, only to give way to dull skies, rather damped the pleasure of the first day's victory celebrations in Shrewsbury.

There were, however, plenty of people in the streets and public and private buildings were decorated with the flags of the Allies.

The town presented a more festive appearance as dusk approached, when the Castle and the Public Library buildings, some of the schools and the war memorial were floodlit. The number of people in the streets had by this time largely increased and many were drawn to the Square by the music of an I.T.C. band.

As far as possible, full street lighting was given in as big an area as possible after darkness fell.

On Monday night in Meadow Place a piano was brought into the street together with a drum and singing and dancing were enjoyed. About 120 children from Albert Road and Sentinel Gardens attended a party on Wednesday in the Sentinel Waggon Works canteen. Later a bonfire was lit in which an effigy of Hitler was burned.

In Wellington, a jolly and at the same time thankful spirit prevailed. There was dancing in the Square and in other parts of the town until the early hours of Wednesday.

A VE Day street party in Rope Walk, off Beatrice Street, Oswestry.

Labour election win

The General Election has resulted in a sweeping Labour victory. By capturing well over 200 seats the Labour Party has secured a clear majority over all other parties in the House of Commons.

The Liberal Party fared badly and has been practically extinguished.

Shropshire held out better than most Conservative strongholds, three of the four seats being held. In the only Shropshire seat gained by Labour, the Wrekin, Mr Ivor Thomas had a 5,000 majority.

Cinema hit by fire

The famous old Shrewsbury County Theatre (late Theatre Royal) has been seriously damaged by fire.

Huge crowds gathered to watch. All the balcony was severely burned and the circle badly damaged. One fireman was injured when a beam fell on him.

German POWs shot

Two German prisoners of war, Grenadier Mullenhordd and Lance Corporal Frederick Wolter, have been shot dead while reportedly trying to escape on May 1 from a military site near Wem. The funeral took place at Wem Parish Church, with eight German POWs forming the bearer party under armed escort.

Shrewsbury to 'adopt' blitzed Dutch town of Zutphen

Shrewsbury is going to show practical sympathy with the unfortunate people of Holland by "adopting" the town of Zutphen, with which it shares the memory of that great hero and pupil of Shrewsbury School, Sir Philip Sydney.

During the next few weeks a concentrated effort will be made to collect in Shrewsbury and district clothing, furniture,

cooking utensils, crockery and other articles of which the people of Zutphen are greatly in need.

They have practically nothing to call their own. Zutphen, only 17 miles from Arnhem, was right in the battle area. It has been bombed, shelled, flooded, and looted. Sir Philip Sydney was mortally wounded at the siege of Zutphen in 1586.

1946

First town with 999

Shrewsbury is the first town in the county to be equipped with the "999" scheme for emergency telephone calls.

The new scheme enables users, by dialling "999" instead of "0", to secure the immediate attention of operators for calls to the police, fire or ambulance services on occasions of emergency.

The system was inspected by the Chief Constable of Shrewsbury, Mr G H Macdivitt, who, in the telephone exchange at Pride Hill, heard the buzzer sound as a call came in from the borough police station.

Mr Thrower arrives

Mr Percy John Thrower, Shrewsbury's energetic new 33-year-old parks superintendent, who was chosen from no fewer than 72 applicants for the position, after the resignation of Mr G S Ingle last November, took up his new duties on New Year's Day.

He says he looks forward greatly to working towards Shrewsbury's first post-war flower show, and is anxious also to get on with the task of reconstruction in the Quarry, to make it even better than before the war.

Bananas at last

Good news on the fruit front! More than 700,000 bananas have arrived in the county, the first for over six years.

The bananas, fine Jamaican ones, have been delivered to the ripening stores of wholesale fruit merchants. Sufficient bananas will be available to provide 1lb per ration book.

Mr Harry Rogers, the well-known coracle man of Ironbridge, will be seen over the air by holders of television sets when he takes part in a television programme on October 5. He is believed to be the first Shropshire man to be televised.

THE GREAT FLOOD

Vehicles negotiate the floods near Shrewsbury Abbey.

The worst flood in living memory in Shropshire and the Welsh border counties left behind it a tale of widespread damage and loss.

Agricultural livestock and poultry suffered heavily and there was great damage to property, while during the flood gas and electricity services were interrupted to many parts, householders suffered great inconvenience, and in many places road and rail traffic was dislocated.

Consternation was caused amongst people living near the Rivers Severn and Vyrnwy and isolated farms between Shrewsbury and the Welsh border, where miles and miles of countryside were swept by flood waters. Both the Shropshire and Montgomeryshire police were out on rescue work with boats and their job was a most hazardous one because of strong currents and concealed hedgerows, gate posts and underwater obstructions.

So great was the task that the military were called upon to assist and several Army "ducks" manned by military crews were in service, carrying passengers, rescuing people and animals, conveying milk churns and food.

The current reply to the question – of academic interest only to Shrewsbury's 600 householders who were the chief sufferers – "Was it a record flood?" is difficult to give. It was certainly higher than the 1941 flood, itself a record for 60 years, and probably higher by a few inches than the 19ft 4ins on December 20, 1869. But whether it beat the known all time best – or worst – of 20ft 3.5 ins in 1795, is not known.

Certainly in one respect it must have established a record, and that was in the rapidity of its approach. In the 12 hours from 9.30pm on February 8 the Severn rose 4ft and it was this which contributed more than anything else to the conditions which followed, suitably described by the Mayor of Shrewsbury as "widespread misery".

At Ironbridge the police organised a soup kitchen and the distribution of sandwiches, the materials for which were contributed by local butchers and other tradesmen.

One of the busiest workers over the weekend was Mr Harry Rogers, who manipulated his little coracle across the flooded roads to take water, milk and provisions to families who were marooned.

1947

Crowds watch the floods from the Welsh Bridge, Shrewsbury, on March 20.

Second great flood equals that of 1946

After the frosts, the snow and the gales of this most severe of all winters comes the flood, which on Thursday reached the same level as the great flood of last year, when a record which has stood for 150 years was broken.

On Thursday afternoon the level at Montford Bridge was 18 feet 9 inches, exactly the same as last year's peak level. Since noon the river at Montford Bridge had remained at that height, and as a drop of three feet was reported at Welshpool it was expected that the peak had been reached.

At 4pm on Thursday at Montford Bridge the level had dropped two inches and the gauge read 18 feet 7 inches. The river dropped 1 foot 3 inches at Montford Bridge and 1 foot at Shrewsbury during Thursday night.

The flood brought the usual sombre story of impassable roads, of acres of farm land under water, farms and cottages isolated, dwellings and shops by the riverside flooded to a depth of several feet.

There is the usual tale of loss and damage to be faced by householders and farmers, this year more severe than ever because of the great losses already caused by the weeks of snow and frost. Farm work, already delayed by the arctic weather, has had another setback.

Movement by boat became the only means of transport in many areas of the countryside, and much help was given in this by the Army, who supplied DUKWs and folding boats to take food to marooned families and in many cases to rescue stock from the flood waters.

Police force farewell

Shrewsbury no longer has a police force of its own.

The Shrewsbury Borough Police Force amalgamated with Shropshire Constabulary on April 1.

Weds PM's girl

Scientist Harold Shipton of Shrewsbury married Janet Attlee, daughter of serving Prime Minister Clement Attlee, at Ellesborough Church, Buckinghamshire. The reception was at Chequers.

A runaway lorry careered down Tontine Hill, Ironbridge, hitting and overturning another lorry before crashing through a wall into the River Severn, taking a parked van with it. A number of people had amazing escapes. The driver struggled from the partly submerged cab.

1948

Disastrous hospital fire

The 500 patients of the Shropshire Orthopaedic Hospital at Park Hall, Oswestry, were moved to safety on Tuesday night when the most disastrous Shropshire fire of the century – in its effects – destroyed four of the 15 wards of the hospital and gutted the laboratory, stores, kitchen, dispensary, massage and gymnasium departments.

Nurses, doctors and staff, villagers, and over 300 soldiers and ATS from the nearby Park Hall Camp rushed to the rescue and pushed the wheeled beds out into the driving rain, where they were protected as much as possible by mackintoshes and water-proof bedding.

No-one was hurt.

About 250 patients were wheeled down the road half a mile to the Derwen Training College for Cripples, and others were pushed the two miles to Park Hall Camp and to the hospital's

annexe at Aston Hall.

By 10.30 all were safely indoors and were supping the hot drinks provided by willing helpers.

A small number were sent to the Royal Salop Infirmary and the C.C. Hospital, Berrington, on Wednesday evening.

Within 48 hours, said Mr J C Menzies (secretary/superintendent), he hoped they would all be back at the hospital, though there may be a little overcrowding. Some would be brought back immediately.

"You can do us a good turn by assuring your readers that everyone is quite all right, and that the only things which have gone up in smoke are bricks and mortar," said Mr Menzies, who, though his face was grey with fatigue, courteously replied to the press bombardment of questions.

Typhoid deaths

Seven people died and over 100 were infected in a typhoid epidemic at the Shropshire Orthopaedic Hospital, which began in September and ended on October 23.

Despite a top level investigation, the cause has not been positively discovered, although contaminated milk is suspected. Another suspect is Argentinian corned beef.

Billy Wright to captain England

A great honour has been bestowed on "Billy" Wright in being selected to captain England in the international match against Ireland.

Shropshire is justly proud of Wright who has had all the honours of the game showered upon him and who is probably the finest footballer the county has produced.

The "skipper" of the Wolves is only 24 and should be good for many years of international football.

He is a native of Iron-Bridge and, a player of the best type, is a fitting personality to lead the English side both on and off the field.

Dame Agnes dies

Founder of an institution known all over the world, a pioneer in the work for cripples, and regarded by thousands of patients who had passed through the institution she loved so much as a "Florence Nightingale" of the wards, Dame Gwendoline Agnes Hunt, of Boreatton, Baschurch, has died at her home, after a long illness, aged 81. She founded what was to become Shropshire Orthopaedic Hospital in 1900.

The post-war housing crisis has led to squatters seizing former military camps. Squatters took over the old ATS camp at Harlescott in a night time operation staged on May 14 and were joined by their wives coming over the fence next morning.

1949

Good television in Salop

The opening of the BBC television station at Sutton Coldfield on December 17, despite the early "hitch" due to a faulty valve, has given great satisfaction throughout Shropshire, where television has been eagerly awaited, along with other Midland areas.

Shrewsbury's first televisions arrive at Mitchell's.

Shrewsbury, it was thought, would lie upon the fringe of the area covered by the transmitter, but there is now ample evidence that reception is being obtained much further west, and there have been reports of reception from as far away as Rhyl.

About 300 sets have been installed by Shrewsbury radio engineers in the town and district during the past few months and smaller numbers in Wem, Whitchurch, and Oswestry and surrounding districts.

Towards the south of the county tests are still being made in various areas, there being possibilities of interference from the Clee Hill, Wenlock Edge, and, further to the west, from the Longmynds.

When the Sutton Coldfield station opened up there were scores of "TV parties" in Shropshire, and the radio dealers who served the sets have in practically every instance received reports of perfect vision and excellent sound.

Many have thought succeeding programmes have been even better, and firms are inundated with inquiries from people eager to take up sets.

Shrewsbury's Royal week

Cheering crowds massed in streets which had been transformed by a wonderful show of flowers, flags and bunting presented unforgettable scenes as Princess Elizabeth and the Duke of Edinburgh drove through Shrewsbury on their official visit to the Royal Show.

Cool, dull weather contrasted sharply with the warmth of the affection and loyalty shown by the thousands upon thousands of "Proud Salopians" to whom the sight of the Royal car was the signal to let themselves go in a great and sincere welcome.

Although they had passed through the town a few weeks before, this was their first official visit to Shrewsbury, to which fell the great honour of receiving its fourth Royal Show since 1845 – the biggest ever in the long history of the Royal Agricultural Society of England.

The 115 acre site at Sundorne changed from green fields to a small agricultural town.

Gone to Earth shooting starts

Much Wenlock has had an experience which has never hitherto fallen to its lot – assisting in making a film in which famous actors and actresses are appearing.

The film starring Jennifer Jones, Dame Sybil Thorndike and David Farrar has been written and is being produced under the direction of Mr Michael Powell and is based on episodes in "Gone To Earth", one of the Shropshire novels of Mary Webb.

The appearance of some of the shops in High Street and the Square has been changed to give the impression of an earlier epoch.

Field Marshal Viscount Montgomery made a short halt in the centre of Newport on his journey from Hodnet to Lichfield and a huge crowd gave him an enthusiastic reception. Alighting from his car by the parish church, Lord Montgomery strolled 100 yards or so up the main street.

1950

HUGE FACTORY BLAST

ire which broke out on the afternoon of May 12 at the Madeley Wood factory of the Ironbridge Metal Company, a two-storey building stacked with some hundreds of tons of aluminium foil, was followed by a terrific explosion in the furnace room at the far end of the building, resulting in the managing director of the company, Mr Ferdinand Frankel (57), of Westwood, Holyhead Road, Wellington, and a woman employee, Mrs Kate Healey (47), of 24 Paradise, Coalbrookdale, being trapped in the wreckage.

The body of Mr Frankel was recovered from the debris on Saturday morning and Mrs Healey was found by firemen in the early hours of Monday morning.

Seven of the firemen who were fighting the outbreak where it had originated in the furnace room were burned and injured in the explosion, and were conveyed to hospital by ambulances, two of them being in a critical condition.

Three employees of the firm were also taken to hospital. At least three of the firemen had to be dug out of the fallen masonry.

The explosion shook houses in Ironbridge over half a mile away, and the blast shattered some windows of nearby houses.

The side of the kitchen of the Madeley Wood Methodist Manse, the nearest building to the end of the factory, was blown in, and Mrs Bower, wife of the minister, the Rev James Bower, had a very narrow escape.

Emergency services sift through the wreckage of the factory.

Third Division football at Meadow

In 1886 Shrewsbury Town Football Club came into existence, and played its matches before a few hundred spectators on the old Shrewsbury Racecourse, devoid of stand, terracing or even an enclosure.

And now, 64 years later, after 15 years of battling against the "closed shop" principle in the English Football league, Shrewsbury have gained admission to the Northern Section of the Third Division.

A picture used in Shrewsbury's brochure sent to all League clubs as part of their "election campaign" was taken during the big benefit match at the end of last season when a crowd of about 9,000 attended. The club confidently expects an average "gate" of similar size for every home match next season.

There was great excitement in Shrewsbury when the good news came through.

Much has already been written about Shrewsbury's successful bid for League status, and perhaps, it is best summed up by the club's chairman, Mr Bernard Hayes, when he said to me on his return: "It was a great day for Salop".

Yes, it certainly was a great day; not only for the sportsmen of the town and the county, but also for every Salopian, for there is no doubt that the club's admission to the Football League will do much to help to put Shrewsbury on the map.

Worst year for polio

The number of deaths in Shropshire from polio has hit 11, making it the worst year on record. There have also been 62 notifications of the disease.

Film premiere

About £800 will go to various charities as a result of the provincial premiere of the film "Gone To Earth" at the Granada Cinema, Shrewsbury.

Every seat was taken, although some Salopians did not attend because they could not approve of the performance being held on a Sunday.

1951

COUNTY CRIME WORST EVER

"An appalling increase in crime" is referred to in the report for 1951 of the chief constable of Shropshire, Mr D. Osmond.

Mr Osmond states: "It is difficult to say to what this can be attributed, but it is fair to comment that there is a feeling amongst service police officers that we are beginning to see the reaction to years of increasingly lenient treatment of offenders. The general lack of discipline in all walks of life and the absence of deterrents to wrongdoing seems to be breeding an indifference to the rights of property which is reflected in these rising crime figures.

"The year has been the worst on record for crime in Shropshire. This county is not alone in this respect and there is reason to believe that throughout the country 1951 will be one of the blackest years in respect of crime in our history."

The report shows 3,295 offences, the previous highest number being 2,746 in 1948.

KSLI escape

When part of a Company of the 1st Battalion King's Shropshire Light Infantry was captured by Chinese in Korea, disarmed and told to file down a hillside towards enemy lines, the men obeyed the order, but took a sharp left turn and ran straight to the lines of a neighbouring Commonwealth unit.

They were rearmed and returned to the fighting. This incident is related in a despatch from the Korean battle-front, which describes great and bitter defensive actions fought by the KSLI and the 1st Battalion Royal Leicestershire Regiment against heavy attacking forces.

Licensee killer hanged

Frank Griffin (40), sentenced to death by Mr Justice Cassels at Shropshire Assizes for the murder of Mrs Janet Edge (74), licensee of the Queen's Head Inn, Ketley, near Wellington, was executed by the public executioner, Albert Pierrepoint, in the permanent stone execution shed at the rear of Shrewsbury prison.

Present outside the prison to see Chief Prison Officer H A Ling post at 8.14am the two notices of the execution were Mrs Edge's two sons, John and Bert Edge, who had travelled by train from Wellington to arrive outside the prison just after 8am.

Also outside the prison gates were about 50 people, including three women. One of these women had been the first to arrive and was seen to go on her knees and pray.

The one notice was a certificate by the prison doctor, Dr A V Mackenzie, of the death of Griffin.

The second was a declaration that judgment of death had been duly executed, and this was signed by Mr M de C Peele, the Under-Sheriff, Major James S Haywood, the prison governor, and the Rev A H Bird, prison chaplain.

The last execution at Shrewsbury prison was on July 23, 1923, when William Griffiths, aged 57, a joiner of Eccleshall, was hanged for the murder of his mother at Eccleshall.

Easy does it... The central span is put in place for the new Castle foot-bridge in Shrewsbury, which was opened in November.

Many people who were unable to be present at Shrewsbury when she came to the Royal Show two years ago had a further opportunity of seeing Her Royal Highness, Princess Elizabeth, when she visited Newport and district.

The main purpose of her visit was to perform a double opening ceremony – a new hall of residence at Harper Adams Agricultural College, Edgmond, and the National Recreation Centre which has now been established at Lilleshall Hall – but she had graciously consented to make a short stay in the Church Square, Newport, en route to Lilleshall, in order to receive a Loyal Address of Welcome.

1952

Jackfield *on* the *move*

For some weeks now the surface of Salthouse Road, Jackfield, which has suffered through the recent subsidence, has gradually been cracking up and taking on the appearance of a switchback, making it extremely dangerous for traffic.

The GPO has refused to allow their

mail vans along the road which leads to Jackfield Post Office.

The "top" road is still being used by traffic with difficulty, and like the lower road is getting worse. Five houses affecting 14 people have so far been evacuated and a number of other houses are now becoming affected by the continued movement of the ground.

Gangs of workmen are still engaged on the stretch of railway line by the Jackfield Halt where hundreds of tons of ash are being used as ballast for the rails which are continually altering position through the underground movement.

Pear Tree Cottage, the first house to be evacuated in Salthouse Road, is split in two where the extension was added and the part of the house nearest the river leans at an angle of about 70 degrees, appearing as if it might topple over at any minute.

Steeplechaser
**John Disley
from Gobowen
won a bronze
medal at the
Olympic Games in
Helsinki.**

The Queen and Duke at Shrewsbury School.

THOUSANDS WELCOME QUEEN AND DUKE

It was an unforgettable scene at Shrewsbury as thousands of cheering "Proud Salopians" and people from the surrounding counties lined the narrow winding streets of the ancient borough to greet Queen Elizabeth II and the Duke of Edinburgh.

A great concourse of people, including thousands of children, watched from their vantage spots the royal procession move slowly through streets gay with stately banners, flags and bunting and their minds must have flashed back to a similar visit just over three years ago when the Queen, then Princess Elizabeth, and the Duke of Edinburgh visited the Royal Agricultural Show at Shrewsbury in July 1949.

To many, it was the first occasion on which they had seen a reigning monarch, for the last official visit to Shrewsbury by a reigning monarch was 1914, when the late King George V visited the Royal Agricultural Show at Shrewsbury and, appropriately enough – for yesterday's royal visit was primarily concerned with Shrewsbury Schools – laid the foundation stone of the new library at Shrewsbury Schools.

1953

SIR GORDON IS FETED

Over 40 years ago a small boy named Gordon Richards had his first ride on a pony. Later he became a warehouse clerk at the Lilleshall Company's New Yard but in his spare time he still practised his riding and all the time cherished dreams that one day he might become one of the great figures of the Turf.

This week that same boy, still small, but now Sir Gordon, returned to the district of Donnington Wood, where he was born, and the parish of Wrockwardine Wood, where he was raised, with his dreams amply fulfilled.

He came back to receive the hearty congratulations of everybody in the district in a three-day programme of celebrations arranged by Oakengates Urban Council and Oakengates Chamber of Commerce to demonstrate the people's pride at the knighthood conferred upon their favourite son and the fact that at last he had succeeded in winning the Derby riding Pinza (below) – the only major honour which had constantly eluded him in the 28 years he has remained at the top of his calling.

Mrs Muriel Taylor gives a lesson at Marton "Rebel" School.

Marton's 'Rebel' School

Ever since their village school was closed by Shropshire Education Authority in 1949, villagers of Marton, nestling in the hills near Chirbury, have been campaigning to get it reopened.

When the County Education Committee closed the school, and all the children were told to go to Chirbury, four miles away, things did not go to plan. The older children went "on strike" and, with the approval of their parents, refused to go to Chirbury, until pressure from the education authorities made them reluctantly move to Chirbury.

But parents of some infants too did not like the idea of five-year-olds travelling to Chirbury. Rather than send the infants there, local people banded together and, at their own cost, formed their own private school in the village hall, situated only a stone's throw from the closed, and now cobwebbed Church of England School.

Not only does the new school cater for the infants, but also for many children whose parents prefer them to be taught nearer home than at Chirbury. Today the little Marton private school has some 20-odd children, ages ranging from five to 11.

Although the private school is running successfully, it is the big aim of all the villagers that the school should be reopened by the authority.

(The parents won their battle when, in October 1953, Salop County Council agreed to reopen Marton School. In an apparent move to save face, it reopened as an annexe to Chirbury School in 1954).

Cheers from nearly 400 villagers echoed among the hills bordering the picturesque valley of the River Teme at Llanfair Waterdine. Colonel John Hunt, leader of the successful Everest expedition, and his wife, Joy, had come home.

Arriving from London, they found the villagers waiting to meet them, with some strong ropes and a blue governess cart, at the border between England and Wales. Colonel Hunt and his wife were asked to step out of their car and into the cart, to be hauled on the last leg of their journey by 40 villagers.

1954

Tong Castle goes up in smoke

Tong said goodbye to its castle on Sunday. One minute, there it was – the gaunt, ruinous shell which has been a local landmark for years. A puff of smoke, and there it wasn't. All that remained was a heap of rubble to mark where it had been.

The castle had been empty since 1908, so its demolition presents no housing problem. And it was built as late as 1760, and was never considered to be of any great shakes as an architectural showpiece, so nobody fought for its preservation.

It was not really a castle at all – just a country mansion with a pretentious title. The original castle disappeared centuries ago. The Durant family occupied the house from 1760 to 1885. It was finally abandoned in 1908, and was partially demolished after the First World War.

Recently it was decided that it must go because it had become unsafe. So on Sunday a company of T.A. sappers from Cannock came along to perform the last rites. They laid 120lb of standard Army explosives at appropriate points. Lord Newport, on whose estate the ruins stood, pressed the button which fired the charges, and the ruins disappeared in a cloud of smoke.

The rubble which remains will be put to various uses on the estate. Hundreds of people watched the demolition.

Myxomatosis here

Myxomatosis, the disease which has been reducing the rabbit population in other parts of the county, has now spread to Shropshire, although at present it is confined to between 100 and 200 acres at Marshbrook, near Church Stretton. Mr J S Watts, county pests officer to the agriculture committee, believes it was not introduced into the district deliberately.

Oil blaze danger

A fire at the oil refinery of Morris & Co Ltd, Castle Foregate, Shrewsbury, in the late evening of April 30 threatened to involve a quarter of a million gallons of oil and so great was the potential danger that occupants of houses opposite to the refinery were evacuated and many more in the area were warned that it might be necessary to evacuate them. It was probably one of the town's biggest ever fires.

Apart from police officers, reporters and photographers, only one man stood outside Shrewsbury prison at 8am on Tuesday, January 26, the time when Desmond Donald Hooper, 28, a gardener, of Atcham Camp, near Shrewsbury, was being executed for the murder of 12-year-old Betty Selina Smith, also of Atcham Camp.

1955

The news that the Minister of Housing and Local Government contemplates building a new town to house 100,000 of Birmingham's "overspill" has aroused interest in the industrial area of East Shropshire.

It has been known for some time that discussions between the planning officers of the City of Birmingham, the planning department of the Salop County Council and officers of the Dawley Urban District Council have been taking place.

Suggestions have been put forward that with Dawley as a centre, a town of 100,000 could be developed in the surrounding areas, using mostly semi-derelict land. The area has direct rail and road links with Birmingham.

When asked for his comment on the Ministry of Housing and Local Government's proposals for a new satellite town for Birmingham, Mr. Charles Savage (surveyor to Dawley Urban District Council) said: "As far as Dawley Urban District is concerned provisional plans have been produced to allow for an overspill population from Birmingham of 10,000. Dawley in itself is not large enough to accommodate 100,000, and any decision on such a matter must involve other adjoining authorities."

KSLI AMBUSH TRAGEDY

Lieutenant Colonel Cuthbert Brooke-Smith, Commanding Officer of the First Battalion of the King's Shropshire Light Infantry, was accidentally killed in an ambush set by his own men in Mau Mau country, 35 miles from Nairobi in Kenya. His home was at Mynd House, Little Stretton, where his widow, two sons and one daughter are living. He was 39.

Appointed to command the battalion only two months ago, Lt.-Col. Brooke-Smith was on patrol when he walked into an ambush set by men of his battalion in a Kikuyu forest during anti-Mau-Mau operations. He and his party were not recognised.

He was a son of Captain L A Brooke-Smith of the Royal Naval Reserve and he was educated at Birmingham preparatory school and at Shrewsbury School. He was appointed Officer Commanding on May 6 this year and sailed for Kenya on May 17.

(Brooke-Smith's name was added to Church Stretton war memorial in 1998 following a campaign by his brother, Captain Louis Brooke-Smith).

KSLI troops embark on the Empire Halladale at Liverpool bound for Kenya.

All Black weds

The wedding took place at Dawley Parish Church of Miss Dorothy Prudence Browne, eldest daughter of Dr and Mrs S.N. Browne, The Terrace, Dawley, and Dr Ronald Rutherford Elvidge.

The bridegroom is a former captain of the New Zealand "All Blacks" rugby team, and is at present a member of the staff of a Shrewsbury hospital. They will live in Shrewsbury.

Floodlight history

To an amateur club has fallen the honour of being the first in Shropshire to introduce full-scale floodlighting to football.

History was made when Wrockwardine United, the Wellington and District League club, turned on their new floodlighting system for the first time and played a full-scale practice game.

A new secondary modern school for boys was opened at Trench when the boys from Wrockwardine Wood Modern School moved there and handed the Wrockwardine Wood school over entirely to the girls.

The headmaster, Mr Harold Fletcher, moved with the boys and immediately brought into operation a new idea. As a result of this idea, Brigadier Sir John Hunt, leader of the successful Everest expedition, is now "godfather" to the 260 boys at the school.

1956

Shrewsbury's new cattle market

Over a thousand people visited the new attested cattle market at Shrewsbury on the opening day, and hundreds crowded into the sale ring for the opening ceremony itself, performed by the Earl St. Aldwyn, Parliamentary Secretary to the Minister of Agriculture, to the whirr of television cameras.

Thus was completed the first stage of a project which will give Shrewsbury one of the finest cattle markets in Europe. The site of the new Harlescott market is one of 25 acres, compared with the four-and-a-half acres of the older one at Smithfield Road, Shrewsbury, which was built in 1850.

In future sales of attested dairy and store cattle will take place at Harlescott. Sales of other classes of animals will continue at Smithfield Road until the remainder of the new smithfield is completed.

Many doubts have been expressed about the wisdom of moving the market from the town centre.

A general view of the first sale at Shrewsbury's new attested market. Earl St Aldwyn assisted by Alderman H.O. Ashton (managing director of a local firm of auctioneers) sells the first animal. The champion cow belonged to Mr B.J. Whittingham senior, of Bomere Heath, who is standing in the corner behind the cow, which sold for £115.

Tommy Nicholls is home

Shropshire's silver medallist from the Melbourne Olympics, southpaw featherweight boxer Tommy Nicholls, of Wellington, arrived back in his home town on Thursday afternoon – but it was no noisy hero's welcome which greeted him. When he got off the London train accompanied by his wife and his father, this unassuming little man manhandled the bulk of his suitcases along the platform.

It was only when the flash bulbs started to explode that the other travellers realised that they had had a celebrity in their midst. He captained Britain's most successful Olympic boxing team ever.

Refugees welcomed

Shropshire extended a warm welcome to 35 Hungarian refugees who arrived in the county and who are taking up residence at Ash Grange, near Whitchurch.

Ash Grange has been handed over by the Salop County Council, free of rent to the Red Cross for accommodation for Hungarian refugees.

Rock and roll fear

At Ludlow Magistrates Court, Supt. J. Taylor opposed an application for a bar at a dance advertised as "Dixieland with a difference. Rock and roll..." He said in view of what was read in the papers, this "might give vent to an outburst of some kind of hysterical business."

Children from Much Wenlock School examine a mosaic pavement they helped to unearth during excavations at the site of a Roman villa at "Yarchester", near Harley. The excavations were later covered over again.

DANGERS OF SMOKING

While children are awaiting vaccination against poliomyelitis, a health official will talk to them of the dangers of smoking and the attached risk of developing lung cancer in later life.

A campaign on these lines is to be carried out in the schools throughout Shropshire during the next few months, Dr Tom Hall (county medical officer of health) said.

At a Press conference to give details of the latest arrangements for the registering of children for vaccination against polio in the New Year, Dr Hall said that we had, hitherto, done little or nothing in preventive work in the lung cancer direction.

It seemed clear that we should encourage our children not to learn to smoke and now it seemed likely that school medical officers would seize the opportunity offered by the new polio protection campaign to talk to them.

Lightning scare

During an evening performance a cinema audience at the Majestic Theatre, Whitburn Street, Bridgnorth, had a frightening experience when the building was struck by lightning at the height of a particularly severe thunderstorm which broke over the Bridgnorth district.

Women screamed and some fainted, while others rushed for the exits. The lightning strike happened during the screening of a gun battle scene in a Western.

The Captain Webb Memorial at Dawley has been taken down and moved to a prepared site in front of the County Library to allow for road improvements at the busy road junction of High Street, New Street and King Street.

Runaway ferry escape

Mr William J Parkes, 66-year-old ferryman at Hampton Loade, near Bridgnorth, had an alarming experience which he is unlikely to forget and he considers himself most fortunate to be alive.

Shortly before 10pm he was preparing to make a normal late crossing of the River Severn at Hampton Loade when suddenly the guide hawser snapped and the squat, 18-foot flat-bottomed boat was swept away downstream into the darkness, out of control, by the fast flowing flood waters. All day the river had been rising and at the time it was some seven feet above normal with a strong current running.

Hearing Mr Parkes' shout, a local resident, Mr J P Dodd, dashed to the nearby public house, The Lion, to give the alarm, and the licensee, Mr Claud Duval, immediately phoned the police at Bridgnorth.

At Highley a rope was slung across the river but when the ferry struck it the boat, with the strong current forcing against it, started to capsize, and Mr Parkes had to cling for his life to the hawser guide pole of the ferry. Then the rope snapped and on his now partly submerged ferryboat Mr Parkes continued his nightmare trip.

When this rescue attempt failed, the police raced by car to the next ferry place on the river at Arley where ferrymen, by the lights of cars drawn up on the river banks, had got out their boat on its towline.

As the "runaway" ferry came alongside there was almost a head on crash but Mr Parkes, without a moment's hesitation, leapt aboard to safety.

1958

Salk polio vaccine used for first time

The Canadian anti-polio Salk vaccine was this week used for the first time in Shropshire. It is an initial supply of 900 doses, part of bulk supplies of the Salk vaccine from America and Canada which, it is expected, will be received now at regular intervals and in sufficient supplies to meet the needs of the county.

This initial 900 doses is being administered to those children on the second register of priority – children born in 1955 and 1956.

This week the county MOH department has completed and sent to the Ministry of Health the total of requirements of anti-polio vaccine for the county's third register of priority.

This was the result of a recent offer to children, expectant mothers and certain other classes in the county for anti-polio vaccination.

It was thought there might be anything up to 70,000 people coming within this category.

The final number of people and children agreeing to the vaccination was 40,933, and the majority of these agreed to either the British vaccine or the Salk vaccine.

This number, stated a county MOH department spokesman, was considered very satisfactory.

There will, of course, be greater supplies of the Salk vaccine than the British vaccine, and so those who have stipulated British vaccine only may have to wait longer than those who have agreed to either British or Salk vaccine.

Prime Minister Harold Macmillan was served cake by Mrs Maud Leighton at her home at 1 West Road, Wellington, during a "meet the people" tour. Wrekin MP Bill Yates served the tea.

Overspill arrivals

The first Birmingham families to move to Dawley under the overspill agreement have been handed their new homes.

The building of houses on the Langley Farm Estate in the Shropshire town is now in an advanced stage and the influx of Birmingham families in the new year will rapidly increase.

Cock island goes

Salop County Council workmen are tearing up the Cock Hotel road island at Wellington – one of the five busiest traffic spots in the county – as the first step in a Ministry of Transport scheme. The scheme includes the provision of traffic lights and alteration of the kerb lines.

Goal ace Rowley joins the Town

The formalities of signing were completed on Thursday afternoon when George Arthur Rowley, prolific scoring centre or inside forward (he has also played on the left wing), who did so much to take Leicester City to the First Division, became Shrewsbury Town's first player-manager since they entered League football.

He becomes Shrewsbury's fifth manager since entering League football in 1950.

Shrewsbury Town had to pay their highest fee ever for a player.

Many of the 500 men of the 522 Company, Royal Pioneer Corps, Donnington, have made a spontaneous demonstration against their food.

All but 30 or so boycotted the three meals in the cookhouse as a protest against the standard of their messing. But the C.O., Major T. Hanlon, said: "I tried the evening meal and although it had gone cold, I could not find anything to grumble about."

1959

Mothers and babies and expectant mothers from the maternity unit, and patients from a private ward at the Royal Salop Infirmary in Shrewsbury were evacuated when tons of earth fronting part of the river side of the hospital slid on to the gardens below.
Trees, shrubs and a heavy brick inspection chamber were carried away by the landslip, which tore a 30ft wide chasm in the steep banking leading up to the infirmary on its river side.
The gap came within a few feet of the foundations of the building and was 40ft deep.

Pagan rites tree ban

Worldwide newspaper publicity linking Princess Margaret's recent visit to Salop with long-forgotten pagan fertility rites associated with the famous Arbor Tree at Aston-on-Clun has resulted in the Parish Council deciding to ban the annual Sunday pageant and dedication ceremony of flags on the tree.

In the story, first published in an English national daily just before the Royal tour, a gossip writer mistakenly reported that even if the Princess did not stop to see the Arbor Tree, she would be given a cutting from it when she reached Craven Arms.

Since then several childless women in various parts of the world have written to the village asking for "magic fertility twigs" from the tree.

The rector of Hopesay, the Rev T S D Barrett, who is chairman of the parish council, received one from a woman in America and soon afterwards he called a special meeting of the council. And the decision was made to ban the Sunday ceremony which follows the "dressing" of the tree with Commonwealth flags on May 29 every year.

The rector said: "These poor women seemed almost to believe that even if they merely stood in the shade of the tree they would have babies. The Church scotched all this old superstitious nonsense centuries ago."

Parish councillor Mr W H B Naylor said: "When we received these requests for fertility twigs it was like getting back to the days of witchcraft. These women must be daft to think that the Arbor Tree can help them."

Mr Frank Jones, the parish council's clerk, says: "Our chairman considered that the church and the village should have nothing to do with anything that might cause a revival of superstitious pagan beliefs."

The decision has split the village. Some people are saying that the matter should have been decided at a parish meeting where everybody could have a say.

To mark the 250th anniversary of the founding of the Coalbrookdale Company in 1709, a set of commemorative gates leading to the newly excavated furnace site was officially opened by Lady Bridgeman. A museum has been established to mark the 250th anniversary of the first smelting of iron by coke by Abraham Darby in 1709.

End of furnaces

The Lilleshall Iron and Steel Company Limited has announced the closure of the blast furnaces at Priorslee, the last operating in the county, although in 1870 there were about 68 blast furnaces in operation in Shropshire.

Ace racing driver Stirling Moss and his wife Katie were injured when they were in a head-on-collision with another car at Chetwynd, near Newport. It was near the scene of an accident earlier this year involving former world motor-cycling champion, Geoff Duke.

1960

Stirling Moss loses licence

Famous car ace, Stirling Moss (30), star of the international motor racing world, was found guilty at Shropshire Quarter Sessions of driving a "Baby" Austin dangerously at Chetwynd, near Newport, on September 29 last.

He was fined £50 and his driving licence was suspended for 12 months.

The case was a sequel to a head-on collision. Moss was driving an Austin Seven, which he had had out on test, and was returning from the Oulton Park racing track.

After the jury had returned their verdict, Moss's counsel said that it would not prevent him driving on race tracks. He holds an international driving licence as well as an American licence. But he would not be able to race in this country in any event less than an international one.

Moss in Shrewsbury for the trial.

Shropshire saw its worst flooding for many years. At Shrewsbury the River Severn rose from its comparatively low winter level to well over 18 feet – the highest since 1946.

Demolition work nears completion on the historic Raven Hotel in Castle Street, Shrewsbury, which was making way for a new Woolworth's store.

Last National Servicemen

Thirty-seven soldiers, composing the last National Service intake to be trained at the Regimental Depot of the King's Shropshire Light Infantry at Shrewsbury, passed out on Thursday.

The inspecting officer was the Mayor of Leominster, Councillor C P Goodwin, and he was accompanied by Major General W R Cox, Colonel of the KSLI.

The Mayor spoke of the occasion as being rather a "sad" one.

Major Cox said that Thursday was "a bit of a landmark in the regimental history. It is the last Regimental parade which is to be held on this square and in one way it may be a sad occasion as the Mayor has said.

"But I would not like you to go away with the impression that it is sad at all, for the Regiment remains. The home of the Regiment will always be here."

He said that in one way the Regimental Depot could say that it had become the "centrepiece" of the Light Infantry Brigade, as it had been chosen to be the Brigade's Depot.

Although National Service call-up does not cease until the end of 1960, the Depot is unable to absorb any more National Servicemen because of the rebuilding programme at present taking place at the barracks.

KSLI goodwill march a triumph

The "Getting to know you" route march of the King's Shropshire Light Infantry through the towns and villages of Shropshire created an unprecedented amount of goodwill.

The battalion marched through Shropshire and Herefordshire for a fortnight to "Show the flag" to the people of the counties and wherever they went they received tumultuous welcomes.

1961

Riley executed

Despite dramatic last minute efforts to save his life or to obtain a stay of execution pending further inquiries, George Riley, 21-year-old Shrewsbury butcher's assistant, went to the gallows in the permanent stone execution shed at the rear of Shrewsbury prison at 8am on Thursday.

And so was written the last chapter of a murder drama which started just four months ago when on the morning of Saturday, October 8, frail and slightly built 62-year-old widow Mrs Adeline Mary Smith, of 47 Westlands Road, Shrewsbury, just opposite to where Riley lived at 38 Westlands Road, was found lying on the floor of her bedroom battered to death.

George Riley had been convicted at Stafford Assizes of the capital murder of Mrs Smith. On Thursday he paid the penalty.

It had been a dramatic week in this closing stage of a murder drama. The events of the past few days have received nationwide publicity on television, by radio and in Sunday and national newspapers.

There were probably up to 200 people including many press photographers and reporters outside Shrewsbury prison at 8 o'clock on Thursday morning. The crowd waited on, expecting notices to be posted on the prison doors. But that practice has ceased now for some years. It was felt that it merely incited demonstrations. So as the word spread around people began to drift away, but it was about 9am before everyone had gone.

(He was the last man executed in Shropshire)

Rowley joins soccer immortals

Down into the football records goes the name of Arthur Rowley, who, with the equalising goal in Shrewsbury's last but one League match of the season against Bradford City on Saturday, beat the aggregate goalscoring record of Dixie Dean of England and Everton fame.

It was a beautiful header, finishing off a movement Rowley had engineered himself shortly after the start of the second half, which did the trick.

He jumped for joy at having passed Dean's 379 League goals (scored in 437 matches) in this, his 507th League match.

The players joined with him in acclaiming this feat and the rather smallish crowd roared its approval.

At the end of the match the players formed an escort for Arthur and, in the dressing room, champagne, kept on ice for several matches, was at hand for players of both sides to toast Arthur and his record.

Five die in ambulance tragedy

Five people died in the worst tragedy of its kind within living memory in Shropshire.

An ambulance taking outpatients from the Donnington, Wrockwardine Wood and Wellington districts to Shrewsbury hospitals burst into flames and became a raging inferno when, it is believed, the petrol tank exploded after the rear nearside wheel of the vehicle had come off at Atcham. Within seconds the ambulance was a blazing furnace.

The people of Baschurch will never forget the horror of the "silent" train crash in which three men died.

Few people heard the collision. Scores of firemen and volunteers worked frantically on the twisted engine "Haberfield Hall" which lay on its side, tangled with a coach which had catapulted over it.

A nationwide police search for two prisoners – one a Shrewsbury man – who escaped from Shrewsbury Prison ended dramatically with the announcement of their recapture in Manchester after six days on the run. The escape has been described as one of the most daring from Shrewsbury Prison for many years.

1962

Phantom clock raider strikes again

The clock climber who has risked his life in insisting that time should stand still in the ancient borough of Shrewsbury has dramatically carried on his daring exploits this week.

The self-styled Pimpernel of the Clocks has struck four times and stopped just as many principal public timepieces.

A fifth, thought at first to have been damaged accidentally, might have received the same treatment.

In each case it looks as though the agile joker – considered by police to be an expert climber – has scaled almost unclimbable buildings.

Last clock to be stopped was at Morris's Oil Works in Castle Foregate. A few hours before this, an anonymous message was left in a local newspaper office saying that the time-takers had struck for the last time and advising clockmakers to carry out repairs.

Police think the hoaxer is doing it all for a bet.

First strike came just before Christmas when a daring character removed the hands from the old Shrewsbury Technical College clock.

Second strike came about a fortnight ago when Shrewsbury School's clock was stopped. Third strike came last week when the public library clock was a casualty. Fourth strike was at St Chad's Church where the hands were missing.

Police dog handler Constable Bob Roberts, stationed at Knockin, has been awarded the George Medal. Constable Roberts, pictured with police dog Taxel, is one of four police officers awarded the medal for the parts they played in capturing an armed man near Machynlleth.

New town at Dawley

After months of waiting and conjecture, the big news East Shropshire has so long awaited came on Tuesday – there WILL be a new town at Dawley.

In the House of Commons the Minister of Housing, Dr Charles Hill, announced that the new town will be built to relieve congestion in the Birmingham area. He was answering a question by Mr William Yates, Wrekin MP.

He said that having considered a report made to him, he believed that a satisfactory new town could be built at Dawley to include ultimately 80,000 to 90,000 people, of whom he hoped that over 50,000 would come from Birmingham.

Now, the next big question being asked in Dawley and elsewhere is – how long before the derelict pit mounds begin to disappear and new buildings take their place? Estimates as to how long it will be before the new town is built vary between five to 15 years and one estimate given is that it might take two years or more before building starts.

In the meantime the announcement has been enthusiastically welcomed both at Dawley and Birmingham.

Shropshire had its coldest Christmas Day since 1943.

Shawbury meteorological office recorded a minimum temperature on Christmas Day of minus 10 degrees centigrade.

All parts of Shropshire had snow over the Christmas period, but none had snow on Christmas Day.

1963

THE BIG FREEZE

The big freeze-up looks as though it will smash all records in Shropshire.

Cost of the cold spell to Salop has already just about reached £100,000 – the figure reached in the 1947 shiver. And Shawbury weathermen were claiming this week: "We can't be sure – but we think we have got 1947 beaten."

The situation worsens. Hundreds of outdoor workers have been laid off, buses, trains and cars froze up and were brought to a standstill. The local electricity authority say voltage reductions and even power cuts may follow if the freeze-up continues and coal supplies are getting low.

A county council spokesman revealed this week that no new supplies of salt were forthcoming at the moment. There was some reserve of salt, but a shortage is likely.

Snow ploughs were out again day and night over the weekend. Later this week only the minor hill roads throughout the county were still blocked.

Men used a pneumatic drill to break up the 20ins thick ice which formed on Shrewsbury's 4.5 million gallon reservoir. In Shrewsbury's 4,500 council houses alone there have been over 800 bursts.

New town go ahead

Sir Keith Joseph, Minister of Housing and Local Government, has confirmed an order designating 9,100 acres at Dawley for a New Town with a target population of about 90,000, with a possibility of further growth.

Its primary purpose will be to provide housing and employment for people in Birmingham and the Black Country, particularly Birmingham, and to relieve congestion in that area.

Dawley will be the 13th New Town in England and Wales.

The Beatles, whose latest waxing "From Me to You" is riding high, sign the "Book of Stars" which, when full, will be auctioned by the Shropshire "Freedom From Hunger" Campaign Committee for their funds. They entertained, for the second time since their meteoric rise to fame, at Shrewsbury Music Hall on April 26. With them is committee vice-chairman Tex Llewellyn.

Closure of RAF Bridgnorth

The Royal Air Force was grateful for the spirit of goodwill and co-operation that had been extended to RAF Station, Bridgnorth, by the Town Council, RDC, local organisations, and not least the people themselves, said Air Vice Marshal A A Case.

Air Officer Commanding on No 22 Group, Air Vice Marshal Case was speaking to civic dignitaries, service chiefs and guests, after he had reviewed the last passing out parade at RAF Bridgnorth.

He said: "The establishment of good relations between a Royal Air Force station and the local district is always important and at Bridgnorth we have been particularly fortunate."

The RAF was particularly grateful for the honour of the Freedom of Entry which the Borough of Bridgnorth conferred on the station in 1950.

He said the parade which they had seen that morning marked the cessation of training at Bridgnorth – "a sad occasion for us all."

The streamlining of the RAF had made available a number of permanent RAF stations with modern barrack blocks, messes and training accommodation. It was the Air Council's policy to deploy to such stations units which still occupied hutted accommodation, not only because of the improved living conditions that could be offered, but also because temporary accommodation was very expensive to maintain.

It was this policy which had led to the decision to move the School of Recruit Training from Bridgnorth and so close down RAF Bridgnorth.

THE WREKIN TO LOSE ITS BEACON

It is said that a Salopian will never settle down away from the red beacon on the Wrekin... a light which means home to the younger generation and which for older people holds a host of wartime memories.

Servicemen coming on leave looked for it – it signalled the end of their journey, maybe from France, India, Burma or Singapore.

Salop airmen on night patrol could see it from miles away – on a clear night from as far away as Merseyside. It brought warm and nostalgic thoughts.

But next week the beacon will blink its last. It is being dismantled.

The light has blinked over Shropshire – and Staffordshire – like a watchful guardian angel since the war years. From its 1,334 feet high position on what is believed to be Europe's oldest mountain, it has brought comfort to

many an airman during the war; it has brought contentment to Salopians during peace.

The light was installed after a number of aircraft crashes. Young trainee American pilots stationed at Atcham were, apparently, prone to hitting the sides of the Wrekin.

A spokesman for the RAF at High Ercall said that the light was outmoded – "It is like a beacon after the Armada.

"In these days of planes flying six miles high and at great speeds, the pilot who wants to land at High Ercall or Shawbury would have to start preparing to come down when he was over Much Wenlock. I realise, though, that the light is looked on with affection."

(Although due to be switched off on January 31, it was given a last minute stay of execution by the Air Minister following local protests. Later the beacon was handed to a trust committee which kept it flashing until the end of the year.)

A new evening newspaper, the first since the war, was launched in Shropshire on October 5. The *Shropshire Star* uses revolutionary photocomposition and web offset printing technology. It takes the place of the old Shropshire edition of the *Express & Star*, which had a nightly circulation of around 19,000.

Queen's joy for Brightwell

The Queen has wished Shropshire's Robbie Brightwell and his fiancee, Ann Packer, good luck for their wedding in December.

It happened at Buckingham Palace when Robbie, Great Britain's athletic team captain in the Olympic Games, and Ann, who won a gold medal in the women's 800 metres event, attended an Olympic luncheon after returning from Tokyo.

Being named as the athletic team captain was the climax to a wonderful career in sport by the tall, fair-haired sprinter from East Avenue, Donnington.

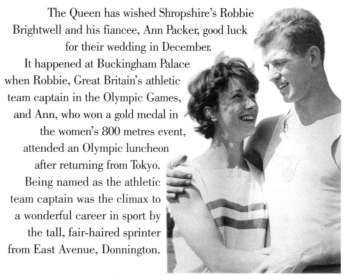

1965

Farewell to the great man – Arthur Rowley leads out Shrewsbury Town at the Gay Meadow for his last League game on April 10.

They're off – building new town

It has started! Development of Dawley New Town officially began on November 15. A bulldozer moved on to waste ground near Cuckoo Oak, Madeley, to begin preliminary site work on the new Tweedale industrial zone.

By the end of February, Dawley Development Corporation is expecting the first bricks of the new factories to be built there to be laid.

Site works for the first housing estate, at Sutton Hill, nearly half a mile away from Tweedale, are scheduled to begin in January.

Accent initially will be on building small factories on Tweedale. Later next year, work will start on building factories up to 18,000sq ft.

Welcome back to the beacon

At exactly ten minutes before midnight on April 20 the Wrekin beacon – switched off nearly four months ago because of lack of support to save it – began blinking once more.

It was turned on at a barbecue and hillbilly held on the Wrekin by the beacon's preservation trust and attended by about 500.

The switching-on ceremony was performed by 16-year-old Sally Pilkington, of Roseleigh, Bratton, near Wellington, who had the winning ticket in a draw to pick someone for the honour.

The beacon, declared "redundant" by the air authorities, was saved by donations from a number of people in the district, including a group of businessmen.

The trust now has funds to keep the beacon working for a year, and during the next few months will be appealing for more money.

(The money must have soon run out because the beacon had gone off forever by the beginning of 1966).

National Trust buys Long Mynd

The 4,500-acre Long Mynd range of hills has become the property of the National Trust.

At an informal ceremony near the summit of the 1,700ft hill area, Miss D G Outlaw, secretary of the Wolverhampton Centre of the National Trust, handed over the title deeds.

They were received by Mr John Cadbury, president of the appeal committee which has raised the money to buy the hills, and a member of the Trust national executive.

The £18,500 needed for the purchase and endowment of the property was raised in seven months by a public appeal.

The moorland extends for four miles on the west of the Church Stretton valley and provides views to the Black Mountains and to the Shropshire and Cheshire plains.

Stone me! but it was an earbusting night at the Granada when the Rolling Stones hit Shrewsbury on Wednesday.

Pandemonium broke loose when the Stones appeared on stage and a solid wall of screams accompanied their entire act. As Mick Jagger pranced and danced on stage girls fainted, ambulance men reached to help, attendants pleaded with girls, their arms raised to the heavens in ecstasy, to be quiet and boys sat with their fingers in their ears.

1966

Lilleshall 'ideal' for Ramsey's men

Twenty-seven of the cream of England footballers sweated under a sweltering Shropshire sun on the bone-hard pitches at Lilleshall Hall yesterday preparing for the World Cup games next month.

Watched by a crowd of pressmen and others who visited the training camp on their first "open day" the players looked in great spirit, and Wolves' Ron Flowers summed it up afterwards.

"The facilities here are first class. I can't name anything which they haven't got. This is an ideal place to spend 10 days. It's not too long to get bored. If you were here longer than that it might be a burden."

Ron said there was plenty to interest the players when the training was over.

"We have several films of matches and also some ordinary films, and also games like tennis, table tennis, badminton, golf and volleyball. And the food is very good. Everybody is very happy here."

Flowers added as he relaxed after a tough two hours in the sun: "If we are not fit after this we never shall be."

Two players missed yesterday's training – Bobby Tambling and Ray Wilson. Tambling, said Alf Ramsey, fell down a bank when chasing a ball and had a slight injury, but was doing light training. Wilson had a recurrence of a slight back injury.

How do the players spend their days at Lilleshall, where they stay until today week?

Ramsey said the bell goes at 8.30 and breakfast is at 9 o'clock. After breakfast they have a medical examination. Vaccinations are being carried out, also the players have polio vaccine and tetanus injections where necessary.

At 10.30 the training programme starts and there is a break at 12.30 with lunch at one o'clock. Then the players rest and go out on the field again at 3 and work until 4.30. Then comes a "cuppa" and a biscuit and more work before dinner at 7.

After this comes recreational games or films. In addition to football films the players can see others including Peter Sellers and a cowboy feature.

Ramsey doesn't insist on a lights out curfew – "They start moving away to bed about 10.30."

This week the training has been aimed at fitness, but from today the accent will be more on actual football.

(The players were at the National Sports Centre at Lilleshall as part of their final preparations for the 1966 World Cup. At the end of the stay in June Alf Ramsey named his 22-man squad).

End of the line

Oswestry's last remaining link with main-line trains was broken on Saturday evening when passengers travelled for the last time between the town and Gobowen.

The twin car diesel, packed with about 100 travellers, left Oswestry punctually at 10.24 and, after brief stops at Park Hall and Gobowen, where about 50 more people boarded the train, made the return journey twenty minutes later.

A £100,000 mystery blaze has gutted a complete wing of Ellesmere College. Smoke was first seen seeping from the gabled day-room in the centre of the north wing at about 7 o'clock last night. Within minutes the blaze spread and smoke from it could be seen from six miles away.

1967

FOOT & MOUTH STRIKES

A massive police hunt is going on today for animals sold at Oswestry Smithfield yesterday. The beasts were sold and had left market before an outbreak of foot and mouth disease four miles from the town was confirmed.

Two thousand other animals still at the Smithfield were locked in the stalls overnight and are likely to be slaughtered today. At Oswestry, Chief Inspector Colin Evans said today: "We now have the colossal task of tracing every beast which left the Smithfield before the outbreak was first suspected at 4.15pm yesterday.

"This means contacting buyers as far north as Glasgow and as far south as Devon.

"And I am afraid there is going to be slaughter on what in my experience is on an unprecedented scale."

The drama began when Mr Richard Ellis, of Bryn Farm, Nantmawr, called in his veterinary surgeon to examine a sow and her piglets. The vet suspected foot and mouth disease and an immediate standstill order was imposed over a five mile radius, including the Smithfield where earlier in the day Mr Ellis had sent cattle to be sold.

Samples from the suspected pigs were rushed to the Ministry of Agriculture laboratories in Shrewsbury for analysis. Meanwhile police cordoned off the Smithfield, sealed exits from the town and turned back some lorries which had already left. At 5pm the outbreak was confirmed and today 272 beasts at the farm were slaughtered.

The stench of disinfectant hung over Oswestry cattle market today. The whole of Shropshire, Cheshire, Montgomeryshire, Flintshire, Denbighshire, and Staffordshire have come under a control order forbidding

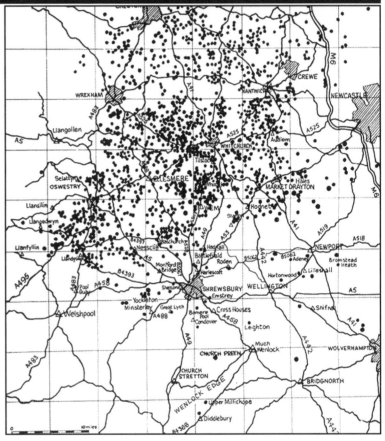

This map from February 1968 shows how foot and mouth disease spread across Shropshire and into neighbouring counties.

the movement of livestock within these counties without a special licence.

(This was the start of Britain's worst foot and mouth outbreak which was to cost over £100 million and see more than 421,000 animals slaughtered)

Huge crowds for Queen

Pandemonium threatened minutes after the Queen's arrival in Shrewsbury today.

Hundreds of schoolchildren, eager to get a closer look, surged through a police cordon. But order was soon restored.

She went on formally to open the new Shirehall and was then going on to visit the Dothill junior and infants schools in Wellington; Wrekin College; and the beginnings of Dawley New Town at Tweedale and Sutton Hill.

1968

24 KILLED IN SHELTON BLAZE

Twenty-four patients died and 12 were injured when fire swept through two floors of a women's wing at Shelton Hospital in Shrewsbury today.

The blaze was discovered at midnight and within an hour 50 firemen from all over Shropshire had it under control. But by that time the 24 patients had died – choked in their beds by dense smoke.

Several hours later the matron, Miss Rosamond Butters, said it could not have happened in a worse ward. Beech Ward, where most of the victims were, is the hospital's only locked ward, she said. She has no idea how the blaze started but said that patients in the ward are careless with their cigarettes. She was told about the blaze by the night porter.

"There's a fire and it's pretty grim," he told Miss Butters on the phone.

"When I got there," Miss Butters said, "everyone was busy – the firemen, ambulances and staff. Everyone seemed to be well organised.

"Firemen were going into the building and bringing out people. Ambulances were taking them down to the Royal Salop Infirmary as quickly as possible.

"I think the doctors and everyone did a grand job. I am sure it could have been far worse," she said.

Experts from the Forensic Science Laboratory visited Shelton Hospital this afternoon to probe the cause of the fire.

Mr Arthur Bloomfield, Chief Fire Officer for Shropshire, said that the means of escape at the hospital were "quite adequate."

Moments later, he opened fire

Seconds after this picture was taken, gunman John James opened fire, sending the photographer and police diving for cover.
James was holed up in a lonely farmhouse at The Slade, Weston-under-Redcastle, with his wife and children as hostages. At one point an Army Saracen armoured personnel carrier moved in, carrying six police officers armed with tear gas grenades. But a shot hit the radio antennae and, pinned down and unable to get out, the vehicle withdrew. *(The 17-day siege, the longest peacetime siege in modern British history, ended when a hostage grabbed the gun while James slept and threw it out of the window. James was later sent to Broadmoor).*

Now it's TELFORD new town

Dawley is OUT. It's Telford New Town. Housing Minister Mr Anthony Greenwood has decided to name the Dawley-Wellington-Oakengates triple town after the famous engineer, Thomas Telford.

And in doing so the minister rejected a suggestion by his inspector that the town should be called Wrekin. Mr Greenwood said that he wanted a distinctive name.

Dawley Development Corporation will be renamed Telford Development Corporation and will now be responsible for the planning and development of the enlarged new town.

The area will eventually house about 220,000.

Dawley, designated as a new town in 1963, was intended to take 50,000 people from Birmingham and the Black Country. Telford will take 100,000 from the area by the mid or late 1980s.

1969

Curtain drops on Highley

I t was the end of the road in the mining industry for over 400 men as they surfaced from the 1,040ft Highley pit to collect their cards.

It has taken the National Coal Board a year to decide ultimately that the mine had to close – for economic reasons. Many men, such as those on the last shift, above, will be unemployed after today, but hope to filter into other industries.

Mr James Coleman, 61, a mineworker for 16 years at Highley, said: "The men have done their best."

Coal has been mined at Highley since the 1870s and the closure marks the end of an era.

The final decision to "axe" the pit was made by the Coal Board after 12 months of reprieves and appeals.

The men were told that the pit was losing money.

It's a Knockout

Shrewsbury are joint winners of the 1969 "It's A Knockout" competition. And they have the magnificent gold and amethyst trophy plus £3,000 to prove it.

They share their victory with the German team from Wolfsburg, with whom they tied in the competition proper at Blackpool.

The estimated 100 million viewers who watched on the Eurovision link believed Shrewsbury had been pipped at the post when they lost the play-off to Wolfsburg. But the tie breaker was merely to decide which team would hold the trophy for the next 12 months.

And at a reception later it was announced that the German team had decided to hand the trophy over to Shrewsbury. Wolfsburg will now be presented with an exact replica of it.

Troops in Belfast

Armed British troops are moving onto the streets of Belfast, capital city of Ulster, now the focal point of gun-fights in the Irish troubles.

The order was given by British Prime Minister Harold Wilson following an urgent request from Ulster's leader Major James Chichester-Clark.

Many Shropshire men were among the 600 of the Third Battalion, Light Infantry, which flew in six aircraft from RAF Lyneham, Wiltshire, to Belfast today. The battalion was formerly the 1st Battalion King's Shropshire Light Infantry. The troops are being led by 39-year-old Lt Col John Ballenden, of Whitehall, Pontesbury.

Independent colour television comes to Shropshire in a few weeks' time, but only a few homes have sets that can pick up a colour signal because the cost of the sets is so high.

1970

A dripping floral disaster

Shropshire Horticultural Society is today counting the cost of the most disastrous flower show in its 96-year history. And, as the rain-wrecked event is expected to finish £15,000 in the red, an appeal for donations has been launched to offset the deficit.

Already gifts have started to reach the show offices.

Yesterday's pay-at-the-gate customers totalled only 9,553 – a drop of 17,090 on last year.

Takings were £7,097 down and, added to Wednesday's loss, totalled £9,231 for the two days.

That, however, does not account for the pre-show ticket sales or the number of members, both of which are expected to be on a par with last year.

Estimated attendance on the two days of the show was well below 40,000.

Society chairman, Mr Denis Salt, said that records showed there had never been two completely wet days in the show's history and the last time there was a continuous downfall on one day was in 1909. Takings that year were cut by a third.

The appeal for donations was made by Captain Richard Corbett, the president, and the vice-president, Councillor Vic Pierce, Mayor.

Captain Corbett said the two wet days had so severely affected the attendance that the society faced a deficit for the fifth successive year.

"I believe this was the best show we have staged," he said.

"Now we need help if we are to maintain our tremendously high standards and reputations."

Two lonely little boys waiting in vain in the pouring rain for the band to start playing at the sodden flower show.

The six week old GKN Sankey strike, which has cost the motor industry more than £40 million and made more than 25,000 workers idle, is over. The 5,000 strikers decided by more than a two thirds majority at a 30 minute mass meeting at Sankey's stadium at Hadley today to accept the firm's wage offer and return to work on Monday. The vote is pictured above.
(The strike cost the company £6 million in lost production)

First cinema shuts

The oldest cinema in all England and the first to open in Shropshire is to close next month.

The lease of Ludlow's Picture House to the Regal Cinemas Ltd has come to an end and the property is for sale.

The Picture House opened its doors before the 1914-18 war when a May Fair showman, a Mr Temple, decided to stop roaming with his "penny gaff" and settle down.

The long-awaited "green light" by the Minister of Transport giving the go-ahead to reopen the 5.5 mile stretch of disused railway line between Bridgnorth and Alveley means that the energetic Severn Valley Railway Company can now "steam" confidently in the 1970s.

Now, scheduled fare-paying passenger services between Bridgnorth and Hampton Loade are a reality.

1971

Miracle of Willows Road

Nine people, including four children, escaped from their wrecked homes in Oakengates in a Monday morning miracle.

One house was demolished and two others made uninhabitable by an explosion which shattered shop windows in the town centre and woke families throughout the area.

But everyone escaped and only one person is still detained in hospital. He is Mr Roy Nock, of 48 Willows Road, whose home was flattened by the first of two explosions. He is in hospital with burns.

The second explosion, seconds later, blasted the home next door of Mr Ivor John Lees, 32, his wife Hilda, 33, and their two children Paul, five, and Joanna, two. The outside wall and ceilings of 46 Willows Road were blown in.

Police constable Mark Wrycraft had just arrived to investigate a complaint about a smell of gas. He was standing less than 25 yards from the house as it was ripped apart.

"It was just a ball of fire and then the next door house went up a second later. I saw four people come out of one house and I put two of them in my van. Some people took the others into their homes.

"An old lady was hanging in the rafters of one of the houses. We left her there for a little while because she was alive. We had people shouting and so we dug them out first then went back to the old lady." Many residents on the estate were treated for shock.

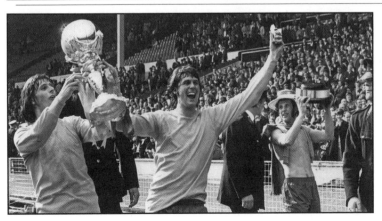

Telford win the cup

Telford won the highest accolade that non-league football has to offer on Saturday with an FA Challenge Trophy triumph that matched the magnificence of its Wembley setting.

Fighting back with tremendous courage and determination, they turned a 2-0 half time deficit against Hillingdon into a 3-2 victory that will forever be inscribed in Telford's history.

Only rarely in the illustrious history of Wembley Stadium can there have been such a dramatic reversal. Pictured on the lap of honour are Johnny Ray and Geoff Croft.

1972

POWER CRISIS WORSENS

Many Shropshire homes have received their last sacks of coal until the miners' strike ends.

Most of what little is left in Shropshire merchants' yards is being kept now for the old and needy.

With many Shropshire coal yards already bare, householders will not be able to obtain more until the strike is over.

With Britain reeling under 15 per cent rota blackouts and warnings of extra five per cent cuts tonight, the Central Electricity Generating Board today described the power prospects as grim.

"The situation is deteriorating all the time," said a spokesman.

The CEGB said that today's 15 per cent rota cuts began at 6.30am. Shortly after 7am voltage had to be reduced by three per cent for one and a half hours.

And more voltage reductions might be imposed later today, the board warned. The threatened extra five per cent stage of disconnection – producing a massive 20 per cent blackout – would affect medium risk customers.

Among the businesses affected are GKN Sankey in Hadley, and the wheel shop stood silent on February 16 as a result of the government emergency measures to preserve power. The Corbett Tank Works at Wellington was forced to lay men off for the first time in its history.

All evening sessions at libraries are being discontinued, and evening activities at Shropshire schools have been cancelled. The Shropshire Journal stopped publishing colour pictures in the national interest to use as little electric current as possible.

An end of Paradise

Police officers keeping watch at the Paradise Lost Club at Hadley saw "lewd and obscene striptease shows", it was alleged at Wellington.

Men in the audience were able to fondle the strippers and take part in other lewd and obscene acts, Mr Colin Evans said. He was making an application on behalf of the police to have the club's licence withdrawn.

Mr Ray Hutchinson, chairman of the Wrekin magistrates, said the club certificate would be cancelled. The premises were disqualified from use as a club for two years.

(A highly sensational court case was to follow at the end of which two men were jailed on disorderly house charges. The judge said what went on was "almost unimaginable filth").

Picket violence

Windows were smashed, walls damaged and workmen threatened when building trade pickets hit Telford to try to bring other workers out with them in support of a pay dispute.

They arrived at the Brookside development, where McAlpine's are building 800 houses. About 250 pickets poured out of the six coaches.

Roman discovery

Archaeologists working for the Department of the Environment at the site of the Roman City of Viroconium at Wroxeter have discovered the foundations of a baths basilica which could be unique in this country.

A team of over 70 volunteers is working on the dig.

Death of a royal

Prince William of Gloucester, piloting a Piper Cherokee, crashed at the start of the main air race at Halfpenny Green, near Wolverhampton, this afternoon.

It is believed his four seater aircraft exploded on impact. Emergency services immediately turned out.

No definite news was immediately known of the prince or his pilot, Mr Vynell Mitchell. Prince William is 30.

The crash occurred at the end of Runway 04 after the aircraft had disappeared over the horizon from people standing near the control tower.

In August last year Prince William became the first member of the royal family to pilot himself in an air race.

He was one of the 40 competitors who entered the King's Cup Air Race. *(Both on board were killed when the plane came down in a country road. In an effort to save time, the prince had started to turn while too low and clipped a tree.)*

1973

Telford shops open

Telford's new town centre got under way today with the opening of the first phase of the massive £22 million complex.

The controversial Carrefour hypermarket and a large Sainsbury supermarket were the only two shops open for business today. But most of the remaining 23 shops and businesses in this £2 million first phase are expected to be in operation by Christmas.

Several hundred people gathered outside the giant hypermarket before the opening at 9am.

An "action squad" of Wellington traders put up 25 fluorescent posters on the approach roads to the centre which they fear will have a serious effect on their business.

Posted in the night, they read "Stop – shop at Car Free, Carefree Wellington, Telford's leading market town."

Cricket delight

Over the moon was how county secretary Harold Botfield described the feeling in the Shropshire cricket camp after yesterday's magnificent victory over Staffordshire at Shrewsbury. It clinched the Minor Counties championship for Shropshire for the first time in its history.

Petrol coupons

The big petrol coupon rush began in Shropshire as motorists with surnames beginning A and B queued for their ration books.

Post offices reported a scramble for coupons first thing this morning. But there were signs later in the day that the rush was easing off. Most post offices have brought in extra counter staff to cope with the rush and some are planning to open in the evenings.

Ludlow gas blast havoc

West Midlands Gas engineers are probing the cause of an explosion in Ludlow which ripped through a row of houses at Temeside.

Two homes were demolished and two others and an office block were damaged.

Two people were seriously hurt and others had amazing escapes.

A family of seven escaped unhurt after dashing down a blazing staircase.

Fire engines, ambulances, police and gas men raced to the scene. The blast was heard several miles away.

Mr and Mrs John Williams, of 40 Temeside, were seriously injured and taken to the Royal Salop Infirmary. Mrs Williams was later transferred to Copthorne Hospital.

A gas board spokesman said: "We are working on the assumption that it was a gas explosion."

Mrs May Lewis, of 38 Temeside, said that people in the area had been complaining about the smell of gas for some time.

Demonstrators make their way through Shrewsbury as the trial starts.

Protest march halts town

About 1,500 demonstrators marched through Shrewsbury today calling for the release of the building strike pickets. As the trial judge left the Shirehall courtroom for the luncheon adjournment an empty soft drinks can and a newspaper were thrown in the direction of his car.

Both missed the police-escorted car carrying Mr Justice Mais and fellow judge Mr Justice Neild.

Shrewsbury traffic was halted by the procession of demonstrators which stretched over a mile.

As the judges left for lunch about 800 demonstrators again took up chants they shouted when the judges first arrived.

A cordon of police held back the demonstrators as they shouted "Free the 24".

Twenty four men were committed for trial but six are being dealt with separately.

Trade unionists from all over the country had congregated outside the court.

The men are charged with conspiring to intimidate workers on building sites to compel them to abstain from their lawful work.

(The prosecution said a frenzied mass of 300 flying pickets tore through building sites in Telford and Shrewsbury "like a horde of Apache Indians" during the 1972 building strike. Three of those on trial were jailed including Ricky Tomlinson – later a famous actor).

1974

Three day week bites

Nearly 8,000 workers in Shropshire are laid off today because of the three day week.

And the picture could become worse next week when more firms are expected to start back after an extended Christmas break and more employees claim benefits.

So far employment officials are coping well with the emergency and there have been few queues for benefit with most payments being made at factory wages offices.

Shropshire employment officials are unable to estimate how many have been laid off, but are not yet claiming.

Some Shropshire firms are keeping going with workers operating manual processes or doing maintenance work on non-power days.

Unemployment benefit paid per day will vary between £1.23 for a single person to £3.68 for a married man with seven children.

(Industry was put on a three day week on January 1 to save power due to industrial action – an overtime ban – by the miners.

Among the measures was a 10.30pm curfew on television programmes. The crisis culminated in Prime Minister Edward Heath calling a general election in February on the basis of the question: "Who runs the country – the Government or the miners?" He lost and a Labour Government came to power led by Harold Wilson.)

PODDY DOES A VICTORY HOP

Derek Podmore, dressed in full frogman's outfit, did a victory leapfrog today after magistrates dismissed a case involving him swallowing a frog.

Mr Podmore – known in Market Drayton as Poddy – of no fixed address, appeared at Market Drayton court dressed in a frogman's suit, large flippers, a wig and a large feather behind each ear.

He denied causing unnecessary suffering to a frog by swallowing it at the Railway Hotel, Market Drayton. Reporter Mr Frank Fuller told how he went to see Mr Podmore after hearing he was intent on beating the world record for frog swallowing.

Apparently dissatisfied after swallowing a small living frog, Mr Podmore produced a larger one. He took a drink, put the frog in his mouth, and swallowed it, and then took another drink.

Prosecutor Colin Evans said Podmore told police he could not understand why swallowing a frog was considered cruel but fishermen impaling hooks into fish was not.

'Terror attack' troops open fire

A top level investigation was ordered today after a 25-year-old farm worker was shot and seriously injured by soldiers near Oswestry's Park Hall Camp.

David Parry Jones, of Old Port Cottages, Oswestry, was out duck shooting when the shooting occurred.

One of his companions today accused the Army of giving absolutely no warning before the soldiers opened fire.

Mr Jones was taken to the nearby Shropshire Orthopaedic Hospital with lower abdomen and spinal wounds. Duck shooting with Mr Jones were his friends Mr Huw R Edwards, who runs a chemists shop in Church Street, Oswestry, and Mr George Kay, an Oswestry tobacconist.

The shooting happened between 8.15 and 8.30 last night. Mr Jones was in a duck shooting party in a cornfield next to the camp. Soldiers on guard duty heard shots and called the police.

But when the firing continued a senior officer in charge of the guard authorised the issue of ammunition. Soldiers then fired into the field and Mr Jones was hit in the lower part of the stomach.

(The soldiers said they thought they were under terrorist attack and were cleared of blame).

The last meeting of Wellington Rural District Council, on March 14. In April a local government reorganisation saw many of the old rural and urban councils across Shropshire swept away. In Telford area they merged to form a new council – Wrekin District Council.

1975

KIDNAP HUNT FOR LESLEY

Police hunting for 17-year-old Highley heiress Lesley Whittle, who has been kidnapped from her home, said today that the deadline for the £50,000 ransom demand has expired.

Instructions left at Lesley's Highley home on four lengths of coloured plastic tape revealed the deadline for the handover was at 1am this morning.

The Whittle family had the cash ready as demanded in used £5 and £1 notes but no contact was made, Detective Chief Superintendent Robert Booth, head of West Mercia Police, who is conducting the inquiry, said today.

Most villagers first heard of news of Lesley's disappearance on the radio and television last night.

In a statement West Mercia Police said

Lesley, a member of a coach business family, was a student at Wulfrun College at Wolverhampton, and lived with her mother at Highley.

"Inquiries show that from about 8.30 on Monday evening she was alone at home while her mother was out with friends. When her mother returned at about 1.30am she saw that Lesley was in her bed in her room. At about 7am Lesley's disappearance was discov-

ered from the house and it was established that the only article of clothing missing with her was a pale blue candlewick full length dressing gown.

"Lesley is 4ft 11ins to 5ft tall."

Before the first press conference last night there had been a clampdown on information. News of the kidnapping is understood to have been kept quiet for several hours while police investigated the possibility of the girl's disappearance being linked with a rag stunt.

(Her body was found on March 7, in a drain at Bathpool Park, Kidsgrove. On December 11 Donald Neilson – a serial killer dubbed the "Black Panther" – was caught in a struggle with two police constables near Mansfield and charged with Lesley's murder).

M54 opens to fog

Fog shrouded the opening of Shropshire's first 4.5 miles of motorway this afternoon – and police switched on hazard warning lights between Ketley and Hollinswood.

Workmen lifted the barriers at 12.10pm as police radioed to officers at each of the interchanges to ensure all side roads were opened simultaneously on the M54.

The opening of the "Wellington bypass" was delayed for 10 minutes as police made sure that the road was clear.

26 rescued from hospital blaze

Nurses and staff braved flames, smoke and falling debris to push and carry patients to safety from a burning ward in a £70,000 fire at Shrewsbury's Copthorne Hospital.

The ward was completely cleared of 26 women patients – some of them seriously ill – in six minutes and saved them from injury.

Teams of firemen battled to prevent the flames spreading but Ward 7 – where the fire began in the roof space – was com-

pletely gutted and the neighbouring intensive care unit damaged. As columns of smoke towered 100ft above the hospital, Salop Area Health Authority chairman Mr Frank Leath ordered it clear of all visitors, who were hindering evacuation operations.

Praising the efforts of staff and firemen, Mr Leath said the newly-introduced fire procedures had proved their worth in their first big test in Shropshire.

Poison drama

Six workmates fought for their lives after being overcome by deadly poison fumes at a Shropshire factory.

Teams of doctors and nurses battled throughout the night to save the men in what was described as the Royal Salop Infirmary's biggest-ever medical emergency.

The men are thought to be suffering from arsine poisoning. The men collapsed within minutes as they were handling zinc waste at a small steel fabricating factory at Tern Hill, near Market Drayton.

Immediately the firm, Wheeler and Pearsall, based at the Rose Hill Industrial Estate, was closed down. One of the men later had a relapse and died.

TV mast a winner

Telford people are getting "wonderful improvement" in television reception from the new mast on The Wrekin – but viewers in Shrewsbury are suffering.

This is because Shrewsbury aerials point at The Wrekin and are blasted by the powerful signal, while those in Telford face away from the new mast and pick up a weaker signal.

In Shropshire there was a 63 per cent turnout for the referendum on whether to stay in the Common Market, with 113,044 voting yes (72.3 per cent) and 43,329 voting no (27.7 per cent). Total nationwide yes was 67.2 per cent against 32.8 per cent no.

1976

Hot weather sparks water crisis

Workshop staff at Shrewsbury Fire Station prepare a Green Goddess fire engine for service for use during the drought.

As Britain faces its worst water crisis for nearly 20 years, a hosepipe ban is being introduced in Shropshire and Mid Wales.

This means that people in this area – the Severn Trent Water Authority's Upper Severn division – must not use hosepipes for watering private gardens or washing cars. News of the ban today – which could be Shropshire's hottest of the year – comes only hours after the government announced emergency powers to deal with the drought.

In a statement today, the authority says that the continuing abnormally dry hot weather has resulted in unprecedented demands on the water system throughout the Upper Severn division.

In the Shrewsbury area last week, demand was about 3.6 million gallons a day, and this had jumped by one million gallons a day at the beginning of this week.

Yesterday was one of the hottest July days on record. Temperatures reached a scorching 90F in north Shropshire.

GUILTY OF MURDER

Donald Neilson has been found guilty of the murder of Shropshire heiress Lesley Whittle.

The jury of 10 men and two women took just an hour and 55 minutes to reach their verdict at Oxford Crown Court. When the verdict of guilty was announced there was clapping and cheering from the public gallery. When Neilson heard the verdict his face twisted and he dropped his head slightly.

(Neilson was not sentenced for another three weeks following his trial and conviction for a series of other murders. He was unmasked as the notorious "Black Panther", Britain's most dangerous criminal. He was jailed for life with the judge saying "in your case life must mean life".)

Final service

Five hundred years of worship ended when the final service was held at St Leonard's Church, Bridgnorth.

Parishioners from every age group packed the church for the historic and moving occasion.They were reminded in the sermon by the Bishop of Hereford, the Rt Rev John Easthaugh, that the closing of the church should not affect their worship and their faith in God.

The rector, the Rev Donald Phillpot, stressed the need for the congregation to continue their worship, although he made no pretence that the closing of the church was not a great personal sadness to him.

1977

End of an era as patients leave RSI

The draughts whispering through deserted wards and echoing corridors played a last requiem yesterday for 200 years of hospital tradition in Shropshire.

After surviving innumerable crises, the Royal Salop Infirmary in Shrewsbury finally faded into history as a red lettered notice board went up on the doors which stayed open day and night throughout the centuries.

But two and a half miles away champagne corks were popping to usher in a new era as the £9.5 million Shrewsbury Hospital, Copthorne (North), took over its role. In the biggest operation seen in the West Midlands for ten years, a fleet of ambulances ferried patients – many of them seriously ill – from the infirmary to Copthorne.

At 8am a notice went up outside the RSI to say its casualty department was closed and had moved to the new hospital.

Just over an hour later the first patient limped into the new department to be met by dozens of pretty nurses and popping champagne bottles.

An incredulous Terry Barratt, 27, from Sutton Hill, Telford, who hurt his foot at work, said: "I was amazed. I thought they were expecting royalty."

The move was christened Operation Changeover and began with the transfer of 38 patients from the present Copthorne Hospital to the new north block. That left 74 patients to be moved yesterday, 22 between the hospitals at Copthorne and 52 from the RSI. Eight ambulances did the job in two and three quarter hours, virtually half what was expected.

Meanwhile the old RSI – the favourite of so many people – waits uneasily for a new future.

Jubilee tribute

Thousands of people braved the rain to see the lighting of the jubilee bonfire on top of The Wrekin.

But the 8,000 or so people who attended caused a few traffic problems. The bonfire was one of a network of 102 beacons throughout the British Isles which were lit after the Queen had ignited the first bonfire at Windsor.

The Wrekin beacon was lit at 10.24 pm after the sighting of the previous beacon in the chain at Walton Hill. After the sighting, the Lord Lieutenant of Shropshire, Mr John Dugdale, lit The Wrekin bonfire.

A flare was also sent up so that the next bonfire in the chain at Cader Bronwyn could be lit. Site organiser of the bonfire, Mr Tommy Eade, said that many more people turned up than had been expected.

Huge crowds gather on The Wrekin for the Queen's silver jubilee bonfire.

Sex Pistols cause little trouble

Police arrested four punk rock fans when the Sex Pistols appeared at The Village nightclub in Newport.

Extra police, including dog handlers, were brought in to keep the crowds of fans under control.

Four people were arrested for offences which Chief Inspector Doug Powell of Wellington described as "abusive or insult-ing words or conduct".

"While there were no excessive prob-lems, I think that this could possibly have got out of hand," he said.

Manager of The Village, Mr John Broome, said there had been no real problems, but this might have been down to the extra security brought in from Wolverhampton.

Telford squeeze

In an anxiously-awaited Commons state-ment on big cuts in new town development, Mr Peter Shore, Environment Secretary, said that Telford must accept a reduced population target.

He said "natural growth" should result in a population of about 150,000 in 1990, compared with the original long-term target of 220,000.

1978

THEATRE HIT BY BIG BLAZE

Shropshire's biggest permanent theatre has been badly hit by a fire just hours before the opening night of a week-long operatic production. But the show WILL go on.

The fire caused thousands of pounds worth of damage and destroyed much of the stage. It burned out electrical fittings at The Little Theatre at Donnington, Telford.

But undeterred by the setback – which comes only 12 months after an £8,000 facelift at the theatre – the Donnington Garrison Amateur Dramatic and Operatic Society said the show will be staged.

Now its production of Gilbert and Sullivan's The Pirates of Penzance will be performed at the Donnington Garrison Church.

Towers lit up

Mr Tom Honess, chairman of Ironbridge Gorge Museum Trust, has pressed a button to floodlight the four 375ft cooling towers of Ironbridge Power Station.

This is the first time that cooling towers have ever been floodlit in Britain.

The reception to mark the floodlighting was the first of a series of events to mark the bicentenary programme of the Iron Bridge which will be 200 years old next year.

Telford's Tessa strikes gold

Shropshire javelin star Tessa Sanderson has soared into the Commonwealth Games record books. The 22-year-old secretary from Telford set a Games record of 61.34 metres – 201ft 3in – to collect the gold medal and confirm her supremacy in Commonwealth javelin throwing. Tessa is a member of Wolverhampton and Bilston AC who moved to Randlay in Telford earlier this year.

Royal honour for new hospital

It was a right royal day for Shrewsbury today – for as Prince Charles arrived to open the new £12 million hospital at Copthorne, Mr Frank Leath, chairman of Salop Area Health Authority, announced to a packed reception that the Queen had given her consent for it to become the Royal Shrewsbury Hospital.

Thousands of cheering spectators met Prince Charles as he flew into Shrewsbury. Thirty this week, the birthday prince was carrying out the official opening of Shrewsbury Hospital, Copthorne, just three days before its own first birthday.

The prince landed in a helicopter of the Queen's Flight but for once was not at the controls himself.

He stepped out to meet thousands of people including many children, some of whom had waited for hours to greet the royal visitor.

Prince Charles was welcomed by the Lord Lieutenant of Shropshire Mr John Dugdale who introduced him to other leading dignitaries before the prince began his tour.

The 300-bed hospital centralises accident and emergency services for Shropshire and Mid Wales.

Prince Charles at the reception to open the new hospital.

1979

Turner's Tigers go up in style

Champions! Graham Turner and his players celebrate promotion to the Second Division for the first time in their history.

The whole of Shropshire was still buzzing today with the excitement of Shrewsbury Town's promotion to Division Two for the first time. Congratulations were pouring into the Gay Meadow and player manager Graham Turner paused from opening telegrams to declare: "It was a superb night." Less than 12 hours before, his players had beaten Exeter City 4-1 to clinch the Third Division title.

It was a success which sparked emotional scenes the like of which have never before been seen at the Gay Meadow. Thousands of fans swarmed over the walls on to the pitch, singing, chanting, and waving banners.

They refused to budge until Turner and his men had made several appearances in the director's box. Afterwards, the champagne corks popped in the dressing room and the board room as players and club officials celebrated the finest hour in the club's history.

Health fears as rubbish piles up

Experts were called in today to investigate large mounds of rubbish piling up around Shropshire hospitals for potential health risks.

With the worsening effects of the ancillary workers' dispute, hospitals are now seeing a "marked lowering of standards" in non-patient areas. Corridors are dirty, rubbish is piling up and some non-clinical supplies are running low, says a report.

Meanwhile members of Salop Area Health Authority are being deluged with offers of help from the public. But volunteers will still not be brought in for the moment for fear of exacerbating the situation and putting at risk the agreement with the unions allowing emergency services to be maintained.

At Shrewsbury alone, nearly 800 people lost their appointments during the first two weeks of the dispute.

(The dispute was just one part of the so-called "Winter of Discontent" which saw industrial action by a wide range of workers in early 1979, including water workers, ambulance drivers, sewerage staff, and dustmen. Schools, hospitals and transport were all affected).

Birthday bridge

The Iron Bridge celebrated its 200th birthday in style today. Thousands crammed the streets to join in the celebrations and the bridge itself seemed in danger of buckling under huge crowds.

Festivities got under way with a colourful and musical procession. Then it's all set for Prince Charles to visit later.

Granville gone

Shropshire's last remaining pit at Granville Colliery, Telford, has finally stopped production because of a geological fault on the remaining coal face. The National Coal Board is now putting into operation plans to close the pit down, which include interviewing the 391 men – 296 of whom work underground – and offering them alternative work.

IT'S GOODBYE TO SALOP!

From April 1 people in this county will live in Shropshire – not Salop. An overwhelming vote in favour of the name change was carried at a special county council meeting.

Those in favour of the change needed a two-thirds majority. In fact, there were 48 in favour, and only five against.

The proposal came from Colonel John Kenyon who said he had found 90 per cent of people supported the change.

Councillor David Lloyd supported Colonel Kenyon's "peaceful revolt" and said the name Shropshire was written in people's hearts.

The name change will mean altering headings on council stationery and forms, signs on buildings, signs on vehicles and at county boundaries. This can be done by deferring alterations until repainting and replacing is needed in the usual course of things.

Deputy county secretary Mr Hugh Blofield said all official bodies had been notified. Salop County Council now becomes Shropshire County Council.

Colonel John Kenyon celebrates the success of his Shropshire campaign.

Lady Diana Spencer, latest girlfriend of Prince Charles, watched him at Ludlow Races.

LADY DI ON THE RAILS

It was a day of delight for Lady Spencer at Ludlow Races. Lady Diana leapt up and down as Prince Charles galloped home in the three-mile Clun Amateur Riders' Handicap Chase.

The elegant blonde, said to be the latest in a long line of royal girlfriends, watched the heir to the throne take second place in only his second steeplechase.

A broad grin on her face, a blushing Lady Diana was first to the rails of the unsaddling enclosure as Prince Charles led his horse Allibar in.

Lady Diana, who is 19, could scarcely conceal her delight.

Dressed in green coat and tartan tights, Lady Diana had arrived with two female companions shortly before the prince.

She has watched the prince playing polo and fished with him at Balmoral in recent months.

1981

Big demo greets Prior

Employment Secretary James Prior faced the fury of Telford's jobless when he visited the new town last night. A noisy crowd of about 500 demonstrators erupted when he arrived at the Charlton Arms Hotel in Wellington around 8pm to speak at a Wrekin Conservative Association supper.

The crowd, chanting "Tories out", surged towards the entrance of the hotel, and police battled to hold them back as at one stage it looked as though the seething mass would crash against the locked doors.

There were some minor scuffles before the strong contingent of police with locked arms managed to force the crowd back and clear the entrance area.

An apparently unruffled Mr Prior had disappeared into the hotel before the full force of the surge.

"I know how strongly people feel. It's per-

fectly understandable," he said when asked about the reception.

Mr Prior's visit came the day after the shock news of almost 1,000 redundancies at GKN Sankey's Hadley Castle plant in Telford, underlining the new town's position as the West Midlands unemployment blackspot.

The latest toll has made the Telford unemployment rate one of the highest in the country, and Mr Prior had agreed to meet area union leaders for emergency talks about the jobs crisis in the town.

Mr Prior met a deputation in the Charlton before his speaking engagement.

Shop stewards from the Sankeys plant had called for a mass demonstration at the Charlton by all Sankey workers and jobless people.

He promised his support if there was an application for special government aid.

Torrent hits Oswestry

Millions of gallons of water exploded through the streets of Oswestry today when a massive 100-year-old water main burst at 2am – ripping up roads, washing away gardens, flooding shops and houses, scattering debris through the streets, and sweeping a fireman from his motorcycle.

Damage will run into thousands of pounds. One eyewitness said it was as if a dam had burst. The force of water rolled back tarmacadam on roads like a carpet.

The burst blew a crater several feet deep under a stone wall round Brogyntyn Park about 100 yards from Oswestry Fire Station.

The 39-inch cast iron main laid in 1880

carries 20 million gallons a day to Liverpool from Lake Vyrnwy. Between two and three million gallons of water cascaded down Mount Road and Willow Street, which hours later looked like the bed of a river.

The alarm was raised by Fireman Mike Wilkinson. He was on his way home with his wife, Jane, from a fire service cheese and wine party.

"We were walking up Mount Road when all of a sudden we heard this gush of water," said Mike, of Park Avenue, Oswestry.

"There was a loud roar, like a river in flood. It was unbelievable."

Friends Around The Wrekin

Around 17,000 strangers became Friends Around The Wrekin on Monday as people of all ages and walks of life joined hands to make a charity event one of the biggest and most successful in the history of Shropshire.

Organisers were overwhelmed by the response from the thousands who came by road, rail, or on foot to support Hands Around The Wrekin, an attempt to put Shropshire into the record books.

The Shropshire Weekly Newspapers team was only expecting half the number who actually turned up despite the grey skies and steady drizzle during the morning. And the huge success of the link up was a tribute to the comradeship and community spirit of the people who live in the shadow of Shropshire's world-famous landmark.

Hands Around The Wrekin had succeeded on a scale hardly imagined as the world's largest human chain – eligible for the Guinness Book of Records – crept around the path.

Eventually their hands met and, as if on cue, the overcast sky parted to let the sun shine through.

Prime Minister Margaret Thatcher aims a snowball at a Press photographer during a visit to Walford Farm Institute at Baschurch. She scored a direct hit.

The Shropshire and Mid Wales Cobalt Unit Fund – after a two year fundraising marathon – has reached the golden target of £1,250,000. And money is still coming in to the coffers.

The appeal was launched by Councillor Bernard Lingen in the middle of 1979 when he was mayor of Shrewsbury.

1982

LORRY DISASTER

The lorry lies embedded in the building, left.

Four people were killed and eight injured when a runaway lorry careered down a steep hill and crashed into a row of shops in Ironbridge.

The picturesque town was packed with tourists and shoppers when the 16 ton lorry began its journey of destruction.

Eye witnesses spoke of the lorry driver desperately trying to control his vehicle as it thundered down Madeley Hill into the centre.

It crashed into five cars, smashed the front of a former betting shop, and ploughed into a tea shop.

The town was brought to a standstill within seconds of the horror crash. But people in the town said it could have been worse as the streets were busy with shoppers and tourists and a group of about 40 children were near the Iron Bridge. The entire front of The Wharfage Tea Shop and the former betting shop next door were ripped away.

Two women and three children escaped death by seconds as they stood by their car which was buried in the rubble.

An estate agent inspecting the former betting shop which was the home of Mr Mark Stafford-Lovatt and his family leapt for his life and escaped through the back seconds before the house crumbled.

Rubble was strewn across the road alongside the River Severn in the shadow of the famous Iron Bridge.

Emergency crews clawed their way through the debris to reach the dead and injured. They were all in the vicinity of the tea shop and police said some of them were in cars.

The drama began when the lorry, carrying 16 tons of coal slack, went out of control on Madeley Hill.

The coldest winter in modern history has seen temperatures plunge to record lows, blizzard conditions, villages cut off, and dozens of school closures across Shropshire.

Ice floes were spotted on the River Severn in both Shrewsbury and Ironbridge. After 1981 saw the coldest December since 1890, and a combination of cold and snow not exceeded since 1878, the New Year got off to a similarly shivery start, and on

January 10 Shropshire had the honour of seeing the lowest temperature ever recorded in England – minus 26.1C (minus 15F).

It was recorded by Edgmond resident Bill Burrell at Harper Adams Agricultural College, Newport. Temperatures have plunged so low that breathing in the cold air is painful, and hairs in nostrils freeze.

The winter has been compared to that of 1947 or even of 1684.

Shropshire plans for completing the county's changeover to comprehensive education have been rejected by Education Secretary Sir Keith Joseph.

He has decreed that Newport, the only remaining area with a grammar and secondary modern system, is to stay that way and keep its division of children at 11-plus.

1983

Huge blaze grips depot

A massive blaze gripped Shropshire's giant army base at COD Donnington, Telford, today. A pall of smoke over 1,000ft high could be seen for miles around and flames were billowing hundreds of feet as explosions ripped through part of the complex.

Hundreds of army and civilian staff are employed at the depot but initially there were no reports of casualties.

Fire engines from all over the county raced to the scene to battle the inferno in one of the depot's main buildings. The depot's own firefighting force was also helping to bring the flames under control.

Pieces of blackened charred paper were being carried by the wind several miles into Wellington town centre and other villages in the area.

Eyewitnesses talked of the sky around the depot suddenly going dark as if a storm was brewing because of the huge pall of smoke from the fire.

An employee who saw the fire at close quarters said it was building B6 that was involved.

"The whole building has gone. The building has collapsed completely," he said.

"It went up quickly. By the time the depot fire brigade got there the flames were high," he added.

The sky turned black downwind of the huge blaze which is at Europe's biggest army stores depot. Fire crews from the neighbouring West Midlands and Staffordshire fire brigades were called in to help.

Nearby residents said they heard a series of loud bangs from the area of the fire. It is thought the bangs may have been caused by exploding batteries.

Building B6 is known to store textiles.

(The fire was Britain's most costly blaze to that date, with a final bill put at £165 million. Asbestos from the roof was scattered over 15 square miles of east Shropshire, causing a major clear-up operation. A top level Board of Inquiry failed to find the cause of the fire).

New motorway opens in the rain

Telford was plugged in to the national motorway network when Transport Secretary Nicholas Ridley officially opened the M54 link with the M6. Even pouring rain did not dampen the enthusiasm when the minister cut a ribbon to mark the opening of the £65 million, 17.5 mile long motorway.

"This road will provide much better communications to Telford, to the area beyond, and into Wales," he said.

Telford's long-awaited £27 million new hospital is finally going ahead – but only on the most perilous of margins.

After years of arguing, pleading, and now heartsearching, Shropshire's number one health project won approval last night – on the casting vote of Shropshire Health Authority chairman Mr Frank Jones.

1984

DI CHARMS THE CROWDS

A radiant Princess Diana provided an early Christmas treat for the huge crowds which turned out to celebrate her visit to Shropshire today.

Thousands of shoppers and well-wishers packed into Castle Street, Shrewsbury, to catch a glimpse of the princess on her first official function in the county.

And they were not disappointed as the smiling Diana caused anxious moments for police and security men, insisting on an impromptu walkabout which set back her schedule by some 12 minutes.

The crowds sang and waved, chanting her name and as cameras clicked incessantly, she moved from one side of the street to the other, chatting and shaking scores of hands.

Who killed Hilda?

An elderly woman who was one of the most devoted conservationists in Shropshire has been found murdered in the countryside she loved.

Sixty police officers are today hunting the killer of 79-year-old Miss Hilda Murrell, whose body was found at the weekend in a lonely wood near the Haughmond Hill beauty spot just outside Shrewsbury.

She had multiple stab wounds, although police said the cause of death was hypothermia.

Miss Murrell, of Sutton Road, Shrewsbury, was a botanist, ornithologist and rose expert of international repute, well known in conservation circles. Her body may have been there for several days and a full scale murder inquiry is now under way with officers combing the countryside.

Miss Murrell lived alone in Sutton Road and disappeared last Wednesday morning. The same afternoon her white Renault 5 car was spotted six miles away slewed into a hedge and ditch along a narrow country road at Hunkington, between Haughmond Hill and the village of Withington.

On Saturday a police officer out searching with the local gamekeeper's wife found her body nearly half a mile away across a wheat-field and in a small wood known locally as The Moat.

Detective Chief Superintendent David Cole said the car had initially been treated as an abandoned vehicle. On Friday evening, however, it was still there, and police visited her house, obtained no reply, and returned on Saturday.

Then, again getting no reply, they forced entry and found evidence of a disturbance. A detailed search of the area around the car was then ordered and her body found.

He said the police were keeping an open mind on exactly what happened.

(This was the beginning of one of Britain's most baffling and bizarre murder mysteries in the last quarter of the 20th century. It was the subject of various conspiracy theories. One theory was that she caught an intruder at her home searching for documents relating to the Falklands War, in which her nephew had served, and another theory had it that her killing was connected with the public inquiry into the Sizewell B nuclear power station. Her killer was finally caught almost 20 years later by DNA evidence. Police turned out to have been right all along in their own simple theory that it was a "burglary gone wrong".)

Movies in town

The clock was turned back in Shrewsbury's Square with amazing effect yesterday as the film makers came to town.

It was a winter scene straight out of Victorian times, and the onlookers loved it.

Thousands of Shrewsbury people went along for the first day's filming of Charles Dickens' A Christmas Carol, a £2 million-plus Christmas epic starring a line-up of famous names.

And although the big names were absent yesterday – George C Scott and the others will be appearing on and off during the next five weeks – the crowds enjoyed the occasion, witnessing the incredible transformation of The Square and old market hall, with artificial snow.

Soccer school

The seeds of England's soccer future were sown at Lilleshall with the opening of the Football Association–GM Soccer School at the National Recreation Centre.

Top 15-year-old footballers in the country will be groomed for success in England boss Bobby Robson's vision for the future.

The school is costing £2.5 million.

Armed raiders escaped with about £474,000 after hijacking an armoured security vehicle. The seven-man gang, armed with shotguns and a pistol, held up the vehicle on a country road leading from the A49 to the village of Weston-under-Redcastle using two lorries.

1985

Sandy wins the Open

Shropshire's Sandy Lyle has proved that nice guys don't always come last, by capturing Britain's top golfing prize, the Open.

For, instead of being locked away with advisors this morning planning how to capitalise on his achievement, Lyle was getting ready to fulfil a longstanding charity engagement.

He spent his first day as Britain's champion playing in a pro-am tournament at Sunningdale to raise money for the dependents of golfer Guy Wolstenhome, who died recently.

Sandy, the son of the Hawkstone Park professional Alex, snatched the title in style at Royal St George's, Sandwich, yesterday.

He is the first Briton to win the championship since Tony Jacklin in 1969 and it could not have come at a more opportune moment for 27-year-old Lyle as it was his first tournament victory of the year.

But what a way to win as he came from behind over the tough closing holes of this fearsome course to overhaul German Bernhard Langer, Australian David Graham, and his playing partner, Irishman Christie O'Connor Jnr.

However, after playing a real handicapper's chip shot to drop a stroke at the 72nd hole, Lyle had to suffer the agony of waiting nearly 30 minutes before he could raise his arms to salute his greatest triumph before thousands of adoring fans packed around the last green.

Lyle, charged with emotion as he savoured the glory, was driven in an electric buggy to receive the championship trophy – already engraved with his name.

Lyle told the vast crowd that, while he waited for Langer and Graham to finish, he had phoned his parents, Alex and Agnes Lyle, who were "too choked" to say much to him.

Radio station on air

Radio Shropshire went on the air today. The station was heard loud and clear on the county airwaves at 6.29am. The first voice heard live this morning was breakfast show presenter Diane Kemp, who admitted to being up in the air with excitement.

But the station's attempt to launch a hot air balloon from the grounds of Attingham Park, near Shrewsbury, was foiled by high winds.

That apart, Radio Shropshire got off to a flying start.

The 30th BBC local radio station arrived on St George's Day and this afternoon Radio Shropshire was inviting anyone, including domestic animals, with the name of George, Georgie, and Georgina to the studios in Shrewsbury and Telford.

"We know already that among those coming to the studios between 3pm and 6pm will be a goose and a rabbit," news editor Bob Calver said.

Stan hits back

Telford United manager Stan Storton has defended his team against allegations that they played it too rough in their FA Cup fifth round clash at Everton.

"I think it's a disgrace what some sports writers have written about us," said Storton as he reflected on his side's 3-0 defeat.

Much has been made of Everton's casualty list, but Storton pointed to the fact that his men had hardly come through unscathed either. He said he felt sorry for his team after they were booed off Goodison Park.

Stunt rider Kirk Owen came to grief trying to cross the River Teme near Ludlow in a record attempt. He landed short and spent weeks in hospital, but made a good recovery from serious injuries.

1986

World honour for Gorge

One of Shropshire's most famous landmarks has been named a World Heritage Site by a United Nations organisation.

The Ironbridge Gorge was chosen out of seven sites in Britain to receive the award from Unesco, the United Nations Educational, Scientific and Cultural Organisation.

"I'm absolutely delighted," said Mr Stuart Smith, director of the Ironbridge Gorge Museum.

"It's the ultimate accolade," he said.

Mr Smith said the award was made to places of world importance and would come into effect on January 1 next year.

People in the gorge area would be able to use the special World Heritage site logo which is a circle with a square inside it.

"It has enormous potential in marketing terms," he said.

Unesco officials and Government ministers would be present at a ceremony to erect a plaque in the area next spring, Mr Smith added.

There are 200 World Heritage sites throughout the world and the Gorge was chosen over sites such as Durham Cathedral, and three castles in Wales.

Stonehenge was rejected as a possible choice for the shortlist.

GREAT MAMMOTH DISCOVERY

The remains of a woolly mammoth have been found by workmen at a sand and gravel pit near Shrewsbury. Natural history experts, who have described it as a significant regional find, are now examining the bones at Ludlow Museum to establish exactly what they are.

The identity of the quarry is not being disclosed because its operators and the county museum service fear that amateur bone hunters could descend on the site, with a resulting risk of accidents, or theft of other specimens.

The mammoth remains were discovered by contractors using an excava-tor to strip off the top layer of soil at the pit to get at the sand and gravel below.

The county museum service was called in, the bones were taken to Ludlow and excavating is continuing under supervision in case other remains are uncovered.

Mr Tim Robson, senior technician with the sand and gravel company operating the site, who is also a geologist, said the bones were the vertebrae, part of a pelvis, leg and jaw bones of a mammoth.

The mammoth had probably wandered onto some vegetation, had sunk into a bog and died.

The whole area from Newport to Shrewsbury had been a gigantic glacial lake – Lake Lapworth – formed by the retreating ice damming the River Severn, which had eventually burst out south through Ironbridge Gorge.

(The Condover mammoth turned out to be 12,700 years old, a major find proving they had survived in Britain until far later than had previously been thought)

Hall demolished

The demolition of Ludlow Town Hall is well under way with the focus switching to whether anything of the 99-year-old building will be retained.

South Shropshire District Council says work will stop when the building is structurally sound – but permission has already been sought from the Department of the Environment to clear the whole site, if necessary.

No decision has been taken on whether the groundfloor market hall can be reopened with a temporary roof and councillors are awaiting a progress report before taking any further the issue of selling the land to private developers.

The Labour administration on Shropshire County Council is surveying the wreckage of the falling rolls secondary education package after being defeated on a whole series of major points.

A number of rural schools which were in line for closure were reprieved following massive protest campaigns.

1987

Health cuts demo

Five black coffins signalling the "death of the NHS in Shropshire" led a protest demonstration around Shrewsbury as hundreds of angry health workers took part in a last-ditch stand against health cuts.

In the second demo in a month, once again the banners flew and the placard boards were waved in the spring sunshine as nurses, ancillaries, and other health staff showed their strength of feeling over the row.

Despite the flurry of negotiations with the West Midlands Regional Health Authority no more cash has been forthcoming for Shropshire and the authority is still being asked to make savings worth £5 million over the next few years.

Train collision

A major inquiry was under way into how two passenger trains came to crash head on at Westbury.

The Sprinter trains collided near the level crossing on the B4387 Westbury to Halfway House road at about 9pm.

A fleet of ambulances ferried injured passengers to the Royal Shrewsbury Hospital, which mobilised its own major accident procedure.

Amazingly only five people were detained in hospital overnight. Most of the 47 people taken to hospital suffered only shock and minor injuries including whiplash injuries and cuts and were allowed home.

A montage photo capturing Concorde swooping over the Iron Bridge in a special diversion during her flight over Shropshire for the centenary Shrewsbury Flower Show.

Balloon pair in rescue drama

Adventurers Richard Branson and Per Lindstrand escaped with their lives when they ditched their hot air balloon in the Irish Sea.

The magnificent Virgin Atlantic challenge came within an ace of ending in tragedy when pop millionaire Branson and Oswestry's Per Lindstrand plunged into the water.

The two were within a whisker of completing an almost perfect crossing of the Atlantic when their heroic effort came to grief off the coast of Scotland.

For two frantic hours it was feared that Lindstrand may have perished in the chill waters before he was hauled aboard a rescue craft. He leapt 70 feet into the sea after explosive bolts – which should have blasted the capsule free from the massive hot air balloon – failed to operate leaving the Atlantic Flyer to drift helplessly out of control.

The pair were later credited with making the longest hot air balloon flight.

Mugged by a mutt

Shoppers stood in amazement as a dog snatched a tray of chops from a display outside a Telford butchers – and dropped his haul by a waiting getaway car.

The woman driver grabbed the pork chops and sped off down the road, hotly pursued by the butcher's young assistant. But the car and dog disappeared without trace after the daring snatch from butcher Bob Holmes, High Street, Dawley.

Mr Holmes said the alsatian had been casing the joint for several minutes before making his move.

The cunning canine had struck at the shop only the day before, making off with a 5lb pack of sausages from the same display.

Warrant for mace MP

Telford magistrates issued a warrant for the arrest of mace-dropping MP Ron Brown.

Left-winger Brown failed to appear in court to answer a private prosecution alleging that he damaged the ceremonial mace during a House of Commons debate in a case brought by Telford solicitor John McMillan.

Mr McMillan, outlining the case, said at the end of the debate on Supplementary Benefits Appeals, Brown, MP for Edinburgh Leith, threw some papers on to the floor, picked up the mace and threw or dropped it to the ground.

"The House of Commons mace is property of the Crown. It dates from the 1600s and is of silver gilt. It is probably the same mace which was described by Oliver Cromwell as 'that bauble' when he had it removed by armed force from the House of Commons on April 20, 1653.

"It is a national treasure, the symbol of Royal authority and of Parliament's authority."

It was damaged at both ends said Mr McMillan. The Crown jewellers' estimate for repairs was about £1,500.

(The DPP later stepped in to halt the prosecution)

T'Pau wow Telford

"We're proud to be home," said Carol Decker, and thousands of Shropshire rockers roared their approval.

The Shrewsbury songbird, who fronts Britain's best-selling new band, T'Pau, put her heart and soul into a blistering 90-minute performance at Telford Ice Rink.

In front of 3,500 devoted fans, the band blazed through the material from their number one album, Bridge of Spies.

Debut chart single Heart and Soul was greeted with roars of approval as Carol performed a raunchy duet with boyfriend Ronnie Rogers.

But the biggest cheer of the night came in the encore as keyboard player Michael Chetwood, who hails from Ketley, struck up the familiar opening bars of China in Your Hand.

Firemen from all over Shropshire raced to COD Donnington this afternoon when another massive fire broke out at the depot. A massive pall of smoke hundreds of feet high shrouded the new town and drifted away in the direction of Shrewsbury. It was a carbon copy of the multi-million pound inferno five years ago which engulfed a warehouse at the depot.

Big manhunt as search for Anna goes on

Police searching for missing teenage schoolgirl Anna Humphries today alerted ports and airports in their hunt for farm labourer David Evans.

Detectives, who now fear Anna is dead, put out a nationwide alert for the 31-year-old bachelor.

But they warned the public: "Do not approach him."

Evans vanished from his home in Bettisfield on the Shropshire-Wales border,

just hours after 15-year-old Anna went missing on her way home from school a couple of miles away.

Detectives have now revealed that Evans took his passport and spare clothing.

There has been no sign of Anna since she vanished on the way to her home in Hampton Wood near Ellesmere as her parents were held up in the traffic on the way to pick her up.

Hundreds of volunteers joined in a

search for the missing girl.

Police have pleaded with women and children in the area not to venture out alone.

(Evans, a convicted rapist, was eventually arrested in France after which Anna's body was recovered from the River Severn at Hampton Loade on November 27. Evans was subsequently jailed for life for her murder, with a recommendation he serve at least 30 years)

1989

IRA BLITZ ON TERN HILL

Devastated accommodation blocks after the IRA attack

The Shropshire base of the Parachute Regiment has been rocked by three bomb blasts, which ripped buildings apart. The explosions came minutes after sentries opened fire on two fleeing IRA terrorists.

Several shots were fired as the bombers – one armed with a handgun – were challenged.

Forty soldiers were woken and ordered from the barracks only minutes before their accommodation blocks in Clive Barracks at Tern Hill were ripped apart by the massive explosions.

One man was believed to have been injured by flying glass, but the rest were evacuated safely. A thick pall of smoke still

hung over the base six hours after the explosions, which blew away the roofs of the accommodation quarters.

The two bombers were being hunted across three counties by the police and the military. Road blocks were set up on all routes leading from the base and helicopters were being used to search the countryside.

The Parachute Regiment has been hated by the Provisional IRA since the Bloody Sunday shootings during the 1970s, and the elite 2nd Battalion of the regiment has completed many tours of duty in Northern Ireland.

Normally there are around 550 men at the barracks, but many were away on leave.

The 2nd Battalion was coming to the end of a three year term at Tern Hill and was due to leave in the summer.

The drama began at 3.20am when two sentries challenged two men seen acting suspiciously inside the camp. The men fled when challenged by the guards, who fired a number of shots at them.

The guards immediately raised the alarm, and the accommodation blocks were evacuated just minutes before the first explosion was heard. Mr William Edwards, who lives opposite the base on the A41, told how he was awoken by blasts which sounded like thunder.

"I looked out and saw flames leaping from the roofs in the barracks," he said.

Three hurt in building collapse

Three people were hurt – one seriously – when the front of a three storey building crashed into Newport High Street.

Shoppers, pedestrians and motorists rushed to help two men and a woman who were caught under the falling scaffolding and rubble in Newport High Street.

They desperately held the weight of the scaffolding off the seriously injured man, who was trapped beneath the scaffolding and rubble, as emergency services fought

to save him.

Witnesses described a scene of chaos and mayhem in the immediate aftermath of the collapse.

They feared using cutting equipment might set off a gas blast.

The empty building, the old Tuckers ironmongers, is undergoing renovation.

Disaster struck shortly after 11am. Police, fire and ambulancemen searched frantically through the wreckage.

First patients

Shropshire's biggest single hospital project in history, the £27 million Telford Hospital, has opened its doors to its first patients.

Miss Dorothy Collett, 77, of Priorslee, was the first through the doors.

But several hospitals have been closed in a package of spending cuts. Among those axed in the first wave are Oswestry and District Hospital, Monkmoor Hospital, Newport Cottage Hospital, and Broseley Cottage Hospital, with more to follow.

FRENCH COACH CRASH

Six Shropshire people were among 11 killed in a French coach crash. They are a 10-year-old schoolboy, an 18-year-old woman, a 30-year-old man, and three women.

The majority of the seriously injured are also from the county. Three people from Wolverhampton and one from Oldbury also died.

The double decker crashed south east of Paris, leaving 11 dead and 61 injured.

Twenty nine people from Telford were on board the coach which skidded several hundred yards along the motorway before rolling over and plunging into a ditch beside a wheatfield.

The holidaymakers were returning from a holiday in Spain's Costa Brava when the tragedy happened.

The luxury coach was carrying 69 passengers, six couriers and two drivers. It was operated by Montego European, of Leek, Staffordshire, and was on hire to Pineda Holidays, of Paddock Mount, Dawley.

It is believed the coach driver lost control after the vehicle suffered a tyre blow-out at 7am on the A6 motorway near Joigny about 80 miles south east of Paris.

Clun rocks

The epicentre of the earthquake which rocked Britain has finally been tracked down – to a south Shropshire farm.

Earthquake experts broke the news to the shocked Gwilliam family living just outside Clun.

The quake was caused by a fault in rock, hundreds of millions of years old, under Guilden Farm.

"We were in the sitting room when we heard this tremendous rumble and very loud noise,"' said Mrs Rosalind Gwilliam.

"The whole house shook like a leaf which was quite a shock as it is built on solid rock," she said.

In the ancient settlement of Clun just over a mile away the castle remains were seen to shake and stones fell off. A number of houses were also slightly damaged.

The quake measured 5.2 on the Richter scale.

Poll tax fury

Furious demonstrators tried to storm Wrekin Council's meeting as the district's poll tax was set amid scenes of mayhem.

Hundreds of chanting, placard-waving protesters laid siege to the council's Malinslee House headquarters in Telford town centre.

Inside the packed council chamber proceedings were repeatedly disrupted by the public gallery. One man was ejected.

Shocked councillors were barracked, jeered, sworn at and abused, stink bombs were let off, and an egg was thrown at the Tory opposition – which missed and hit a radio reporter.

Finally chairman Councillor Phil Heighway abandoned the meeting after a bomb threat – but not before councillors set a local poll tax of £383, although the exact amount will depend on which parish people live in.

A crowd of around 700 – some estimates have put it as high as 1,200 – were demonstrating outside. At one point, to a rallying chorus of "Here we go, here we go, here we go," a section suddenly surged towards the wood and glass entrance doors.

Police helmets were sent flying as about a dozen policemen were crushed against the doors, which seemed in danger of breaking.

Three policemen were injured and a girl protester was slightly hurt after being caught in the eye by a piece of broken placard.

Despite the trouble police, who seemed to be adopting low-key tactics, only made one arrest.

And angry and violent protests marked the historic setting of the poll tax in Oswestry last night. One man was arrested, several people were slightly hurt.

Borough councillors were stranded inside their council chamber as an angry crowd of more than 500 people chanted threateningly outside.

Councillors from all across the political spectrum were yelled at, jostled and pelted with makeshift missiles as they stood at the chamber door.

The night started quietly with most councillors arriving early for the 6.45pm meeting.

A few were taunted mildly as they went in to officially set the £325.30 tax.

Only 25 protesters were allowed into the small council chamber. Five police officers guarded the chamber steps, keeping the remaining crowd at bay.

Chants of "Maggie, Maggie, Maggie, Out, Out, Out" and "We won't pay the poll tax" were shouted throughout the debate – even during the prayer given by the Mayor's chaplain.

An hour later, with the tax set, members of the public, reporters and councillors spilled out on to the council steps to a reception of hostile jeers and a barrage of eggs.

More attempts by councillors to leave the building during the next half hour resulted in similar violent scenes.

Police battle to control the poll tax demonstrators outside Malinslee House

1991

POLICE SHOOT MAN DEAD

A gunman was shot dead by police today after being chased through the streets of Wellington by a SWAT-style police team.

He was Ian Garfield Gordon, the brother of Olympic judo medallist Elvis Gordon.

Gordon was shot at the top of steps behind The Duke pub in Wellington, after being challenged by crack marksmen.

Witnesses – who said it was like a scene from Starsky and Hutch – heard two shots.

West Mercia Police said the man had pointed a weapon at the officers and was challenged three times before they opened fire.

Armed police were still surrounding a house in Wellington this afternoon where they believe another man may be hiding.

Gordon has lived at several addresses in Telford. He had been lodging at a house in Walker Crescent, St Georges, and at one time lived in Oakengates.

Gordon was seriously injured in the shooting incident and was taken unconscious to Telford's Princess Royal Hospital, where he was pronounced dead, said police.

Later gangs of marauding youths went on the rampage in Telford after it was revealed that the 24-year-old was armed with an unloaded air pistol.

The youths, some of them wearing masks, ran amok as they vented their fury.

First they gathered outside Wellington Police Station to protest at the killing. Stones were thrown and some windows were smashed.

Then they moved on to Hadley, home for many in Telford's ethnic minorities, where disturbances flared up involving 100 people, and the police house there was among the targets.

At least two petrol bombs were thrown during the melee in Hadley, one aimed at a police van, and another thrown into the bar of the Kings Head pub. Neither exploded.

Some in the groups of people milling around shouted "Murderers" at police, who were pelted with stones and bottles.

Windows were smashed at a number of premises in Hadley centre.

Rubble and debris was strewn across the main road through Hadley. The main body of the crowd congregated chiefly in the Manor Heights flats area.

Today the controversy continued over the shooting, with police saying Mr Gordon pointed a gun at officers saying: "You're dead! You're dead!"

Ian Gordon, whose death at the hands of police sparked riots in Telford

TDC finally wound up

Goodbye Telford – that was the message from Telford Development Corporation staff today.

The corporation was being officially wound up, closing an era of massive redevelopment which was begun by the old Dawley Development Corporation set up in 1963 and continued when the new town was expanded to create Telford in 1968.

The Commission for New Towns will inherit all the corporation's remaining assets – and is taking on about 45 of the corporation's remaining 200 staff.

And the workload for Wrekin Council will be hugely increased. It is taking on about 4,300 former corporation homes and about 2,000 acres of open space in Telford.

A newly created Telford Development Agency will continue the job of promoting the town and attracting more investment.

A decade ago the dream was just beginning. Yesterday the Shropshire and Mid Wales Hospice received a truly royal blessing.

And at the end of a memorable day made perfect by the care and attention of a great lady, everyone within the hospice walls felt the richer.

The Duchess of Kent's commitment to the hospice movement is well known. Now Shropshire has seen it in action at the £1.25 million purpose-built haven on the outskirts of Shrewsbury which costs over £1,500 a day to run with next year's costs topping £750,000 to be raised from and by the public.

The official presentations, the opening ceremony plaque unveiling, and the royal signature were all right and proper parts of the occasion.

TOWN'S DAY OF TERROR

Terrorists today firebombed Shrewsbury's historic castle and a nearby shopping centre. The attacks are thought to be the work of the IRA.

Two incendiary devices were used to start fires in a military museum at the castle, causing £250,000 damage.

A third went off at the Charles Darwin shopping centre nearby, and a fourth was later found at Wades furniture store in Shoplatch. The fourth device went off during the night but caused little damage.

Most of the town was sealed off for seven hours during the huge security alert which followed.

Although there was no immediate admission of responsibility for the 1.30am attack, the incident bore all the hallmarks of the IRA tactic of using small devices to cause severe damage.

Mr David Thursfield, West Mercia Police Assistant Chief Constable, Operations, said he had spoken to Commander George Churchill-Coleman, head of New Scotland Yard's Anti-terrorist Squad, who had offered "full facilities".

Experts on terrorist attacks are travelling to Shropshire.

Mr Geoff Parfitt, curator of Shropshire Regimental Museum, said today: "We sus-pect that it probably is the work of the IRA. It is a total disaster.

"It is sick and sad. With all the historic military material inside it has caused at least £250,000 damage. We just hope it is not more."

Emergency services were called to the town centre after an explosion on the ground floor at the castle, which houses the regimental museum.

A second blaze then broke out at the Staks soft furnishing store in the Charles Darwin centre.

More than 50 firemen led by Shropshire's fire chief Ian Kerr were called in to deal with the outbreaks.

The majority of Shrewsbury's town centre was sealed off as police continued checking for firebombs.

Shrewsbury, with its military links, has long been feared as a prime target for the IRA, with the presence in the town of a regional Army headquarters and main barracks.

If the latest incident is the work of the Irish terror group, it will be its second attack in Shropshire in the past four years.

In February 1989 IRA bombers struck at Tern Hill barracks, causing 50 sleeping paratroopers to scramble from their beds minutes before explosions tore through their accommodation.

Shropshire Regimental Museum curator Geoff Parfitt surveys the damage

It was the death of a hero... the sad end of a campaign which touched the hearts of thousands of Shropshire rail lovers.

The champion of the county's commuters was given a glittering send-off. When the final InterCity service drew slowly into Shrewsbury railway station at 10.41pm last night, it was met by a fanfare of photography.

Rail buffs from up and down the country jostled for position on the platform to capture their own slice of InterCity's last encounter with Shropshire.

As the crowds paid their final respects, Telford Railway Society member Keith Perry summed up their feelings.

"This is a sad, sad day for everyone in Shropshire. It did not have to happen," he said.

Yet there had been signs of exactly why it had happened from the moment the 7.40pm service from London Euston prepared for its final voyage.

Even the razzmatazz surrounding the pilgrimage – and the train's unique naming as "The Salopian" – failed to fill half the seats.

Pictured: Assistant Driver Nigel Harkness of Wellington, and Driver Ray Lovatt of Wolverhampton, before the last journey.

1993

DISASTER NIGHT

Flames grip the Cox's Chemicals plant at Overley during Shropshire's night of disaster

Shropshire came desperately close to a major disaster with two separate incidents in one night.

They came within hours and a few miles of each other and stretched emergency services to the limit.

With true "Blitz spirit" firemen braved toxic debris and exploding barrels of chemicals to fight a massive chemical plant blaze near Wellington.

And at Shrewsbury hundreds of homes were successfully evacuated in an all-night operation involving all the emergency services.

Main roads linking the two towns were sealed off as toxic fumes spread from the devastated Cox's Chemical Works at Overley Hill.

More than 70 firefighters, some wearing gas and chemical suits, battled to contain the huge blaze. Some 20,000 litres of chemicals, including pesticides and fertilisers, and four tons of mercury were involved in the fire.

Nearby residents and councillors said the chemical plant was a "disaster waiting to happen".

Shrewsbury meanwhile was hit by its biggest emergency for years when a petrol tanker overturned, spilling thousands of gallons of fuel.

Fire chiefs warned that a single spark could have set off a catastrophic explosion, which would have devastated rows of houses in the immediate area.

Hundreds of people were evacuated in a World War Two-style relief operation as firefighters worked ankle-deep in a river of petrol.

The crisis arose at 6.45pm as a 38 tonne tanker made a delivery to Copthorne Service Station in Frankwell.

It tipped over on steep Copthorne Road, rupturing a tank and releasing 7,000 litres of fuel.

Half a million in just 90 seconds

Masked raiders wielding baseball bats took just 90 seconds to snatch nearly half a million pounds worth of gold and watches from a Shropshire jewellers.

It is possibly the county's biggest ever jewellery robbery. And the luckiest. For, by chance, the robbers stumbled upon a sales rep, who was visiting Robinsons Jewellers in Shrewsbury. The raiders grabbed his two cases, crammed with gold jewellery and by doing so, they increased the value of their haul more than seven times.

Brinks Mat heist

Armed raiders hijacked a security van and abducted two couriers at gunpoint outside a Shropshire bank today.

The raiders escaped with a Brinks Mat van containing £400,000 from outside Lloyds Bank, in High Street, Broseley.

Treasure sensation

Forgotten treasures worth up to £2.5 million which lay undisturbed for over 50 years have been discovered packed into attics and cellars at a Shropshire mansion.

Thousands of works of art were carefully stored at Stokesay Court, near Craven Arms, after the outbreak of the Second World War.

They were discovered by relatives after the death of the custodian of the mansion, Lady Jewell Magnus-Allcroft.

More than 5,000 objects, including furniture, paintings, glass and ceramics are packed into every available space in the house, built in 1892 by the millionaire glove manufacturer, John Derby Allcroft. The treasure trove is expected to raise around £2.5 million in a four day auction by Sotheby's in the grounds from September 28. It will be the biggest country house sale in Britain for a decade.

Lady Magnus-Allcroft, granddaughter of John Derby, died in 1992. Her mother, Cissy, had personally supervised the packing and storage of Stokesay's contents when the house was requisitioned in 1941 by the Army as the Western Command Junior Leaders School.

Jewell denied permission for anyone to go into the cellars and attics and the discovery of their contents came as a complete surprise to her executors.

The items have survived in pristine condition because they have remained out of use and protected from daylight.

The colours are, in many cases, as strong as the day the objects were made because they have been protected from sunlight for so long.

There are hundreds of exotic objects in the mansion which were brought back from several world tours by Jewell's father Herbert Allcroft.

The most valuable piece of furniture is a 1710 French Louis XIV boulle commode, estimated at £80,000 to £120,000.

(The items sold in the four-day "sale of the century" auction for a total of £4,217,644)

Screen heart throb Hugh Grant steamed into Shropshire to film part of his new movie "The Englishman Who Went Up A Hill But Came Down A Mountain." He and co-star Tara Fitzgerald had time for a smile during a break from filming on the Severn Valley Railway at Hampton Loade, near Bridgnorth. They are also filming in and around Llanrhaeadr-ym-Mochnant, near Oswestry.

Spill hits homes

Shropshire was at the centre of one of Britain's largest water pollution scares after a huge chemical spill was traced to an industrial estate in Wem.

Drinking supplies to nearly a quarter of a million people in Worcestershire and Gloucestershire were affected – but Shropshire homes were not hit as they receive underground supplies from a different source. The spill, believed to be as much as 10,000 litres, was said to be a solvent. It entered the River Roden near Wem, and eventually reached the River Severn.

Wrekin tragedy

Two men were killed when their light aircraft crashed and exploded on the summit of The Wrekin.

The accident happened in dense fog as dusk fell.

The aircraft smashed into the famous Needle's Eye landmark, just 30ft below the top of the 1,300ft hill.

VANDALS RIP UP "STONEHENGE"

The cost of repairing "Shropshire's stonehenge", which has been ruined by vandals, could be as high as £23,000, conservation experts say.

Two standing stones at Mitchell's Fold stone circle, an important Bronze Age ancient monument at Stapeley Hill, near White Grit, have been ripped out.

The stone circle, which dates back to 1500BC, is a county landmark and popular attraction for visitors.

English Heritage boss, Glyn Coppeck, said: "Basically they were pulled over by some sort of machine."

Plans are already in hand to right the stones. Below, Eddie Lyons of English Heritage inspects the damage.

1995

A Shropshire town hall was destroyed in a massive blaze which ripped through the building.

Over 60 firefighters battled to control the fire at Wem Town Hall and the town centre was cordoned off. Hundreds of people gathered to watch the drama and at its height flames could be seen three miles away.

The town hall, owned by North Shropshire District Council and built in 1904, is a focal point used by many groups including the town council and a regular market.

Apart from the destruction to the building, it is feared council papers and regalia have been lost in the flames.

Investigators say there are no immediate indications that the cause is suspicious.

A woman fears a curse has descended on her village after an ancient boulder was removed from its resting place.

Mrs Mary Davies, of Ellerdine Heath, said at least five neighbours had fallen ill after the Ice Age glacial debris was moved from a field yards from her home by a farmer unaware of its significance.

Yesterday the stone was put on public view after it was donated by the farmer to Ellerdine Village Hall.

Mrs Davies said she hoped the stone's return to public view would put the villagers of Ellerdine and Ellerdine Heath back on the road to good health.

'Scrapyard' artwork sparks row

A storm of protest has greeted a newly installed artwork on a Telford road island funded by National Lottery money.

The ambitious £30,000 Wrekin Council project aims to transform Forge Island in the town centre, but has come under attack for "looking like a scrapyard" and has been described as a monstrosity and a waste of money.

But a council spokesman defended the artwork saying: "The island will grow and develop and the trees will grow and blossom which will soften the effect greatly. We're asking people to give it a chance."

Arbor tree collapses

More than 200 years of history came tumbling to an end today after south Shropshire's most famous tree fell down.

Residents in Aston-on-Clun, near Craven Arms, were left stunned after the huge Arbor Tree in the centre of the village dramatically fell to the ground hitting a car just before 9.30am.

The old black poplar tree, which was the object of a centuries-old south Shropshire tradition, blocked Mill Street in the village and caused only minor damage to the parked car. The recent heatwave is thought to have contributed to the collapse of the ancient hollow tree.

Arbor Day celebrations were first held in the village in 1786 when the tree, dressed with flags, was the focus of festivities. Chairman of the Arbor Day organising committee Mrs Pam Booth said she was stunned.

"It really is a terrible mess," she said. "This tree is known throughout the world and now it's gone.

"The whole village is shocked but we are obviously thankful that no-one was hurt in the tragedy," she added.

"We all knew the tree had to go sooner or later, but we can't believe what's happened today. I'm sure the heatwave caused the tree to snap," she said.

Villagers surrounded the tree today and collected pieces of bark for souvenirs as the flags were taken off the branches and the area cleared up.

Former tree warden Mr Frank Pashley said the tree had been leaning over for some time.

"The tree was very old and last night's heavy rain obviously pulled the weight of the tree over," he said.

Only this year the Arbor Day tradition was threatened with extinction as too few volunteers had come forward to help.

But it was saved at the last minute as local people stepped in to ensure the celebrations continued.

Villagers examine the remains of the historic tree in Aston-on-Clun.

1996

BSE crisis bites

The leader of Shropshire's farmers has called for urgent action to save his industry from being destroyed by the BSE scare.

County NFU chairman Neale Dalton – who farms on the outskirts of Telford – said the Government had to act now to restore confidence in British beef before it was too late.

He was speaking to more than 200 angry farmers at a crisis meeting in Shrewsbury.

They claim they face financial ruin as the BSE scare continues to wreak havoc on British agriculture.

"Now is not the time for recriminations or apportioning blame," Mr Dalton, of Sutton Maddock, told them.

"We need to be moving the issue along in order to save this very valuable industry before it reverberates throughout the whole of the agricultural sector."

His comments came hot on the heels of the announcement that a major French supermarket chain has now slapped a ban on British lamb.

This latest threat was revealed this morning to Craven Arms abattoir Euro-Quality lamb. Its managing director, Mr Sattaar-Mohammed Khalid, said his French orders for lamb had plunged by half and he accused the French of "over-reacting and jumping on the bandwagon."

Meanwhile beef has been banned from menus in all 250 schools run by Shropshire's local education authority.

Shropshire County Council has joined several other councils in taking beef off menus at all of its schools across the county.

The decision comes into effect immediately following the latest medical fears over links between mad cow disease – BSE – and its human equivalent Creutzfeldt-Jakob Disease.

But it has brought despair from the county's beef farmers.

Ghost mystery

Wem has been gripped by ghost fever amid claims a sensational picture shows a spirit haunting the fire-gutted Wem Town Hall. Amateur photographer Tony O'Rahilly says it shows a young girl standing in a doorway as the fire rages behind her. Residents have officially labelled Wem a ghost town by changing entrance signs to the town.

COUNTY FAIR DEAL DEMO

The people of Shropshire have spelt out a message to the Government in a big way. Hundreds of people climbed Oswestry's ancient hill fort carrying pieces of a special mosaic.

Then, on a command, they all linked up spelling out the words, A Fair Deal for Shropshire.

The words summed up a countywide campaign in support of improved funding for county council services and were captured by TV crews flying over the scene in a light aircraft.

There were mums and dads, toddlers, teenagers and grandparents, all concerned about the funding in schools. And there were others, worried about other county council services, from the youth service to services for the elderly, road gritting and the libraries.

The mosaic was the idea of Simon Greaves, of Weston Rhyn, a leading member of the Oswestry Cares group which has been at the forefront of the campaign for more money for the county council.

Campaigners are celebrating a shock decision to axe Shrewsbury's hugely controversial flood defence scheme.

The National Rivers Authority says it has abandoned the £6 million project after failing to win the backing of Shrewsbury and Atcham borough councillors.

Bedstone School has been severely damaged by fire. The school had broken up for the summer holidays when the blaze was accidentally started by workmen.

1997

HERO OF THE NATIONAL

Shropshire's Grand National hero Lord Gyllene – the horse which the IRA couldn't beat – was the toast of both sides of the Irish Sea today.

The victorious nine year old arrived home at his stables at Preston on Severn, Uffington, near Shrewsbury, last night to a rapturous reception from nearly 100 friends and also wellwishers. Champagne corks popped and Tina Turner's Simply the Best belted out around the yard as the celebrations began.

A red carpet had been laid out for the champion's homecoming after victory in the race which had been postponed by an IRA bomb warning.

Shrewsbury and Atcham Borough Council is now planning a civic reception for its equine hero.

Chief executive Douglas Bradbury said they wanted to invite trainer Steve Brookshaw to bring Lord Gyllene into the town centre so that the people of Shrewsbury could see him.

A makeshift banner at the stables summed up reaction to the Shropshire triumph: "Gyllene First, IRA Nowhere."

Mr Brookshaw, 46, said if the Grand National had not been run,
no British sporting event would ever be safe.

"It's a great British tradition and I'm glad the decision was taken to re-run the race, otherwise who knows what would be targeted next?" he said.

Celebrations were also continuing in the Northern Ireland town of Downpatrick at the home of jubilant Ulster jockey Tony Dobbin, who romped to victory at Aintree by 25 lengths.

The 24 year old Roman Catholic was widely applauded for hitting out at the terrorists whose bomb scare forced the 49-hour postponement of the historic race.

"I'm embarrassed. It's shameful. It makes you ashamed to say you are from there. It should never have happened, never," he said.

Speaking from home today Mr Brookshaw said the delay did not seem to have affected the New Zealand-bred horse.

Lord Gyllene's owner, Midlands property millionaire Mr Stan Clarke, 63, was visiting the stables today.

He watched in jubilation last night as his horse thundered past the finishing post.

For Lord Gyllene, it was back to normal today as stable routine resumed.

Lord Gyllene with trainer Steve Brookshaw

Labour victory at Shrewsbury

Shrewsbury Tory Derek Conway has been ousted from his seat as Labour's national red tide flooded into Shropshire, causing one of the biggest ever political shocks to hit the county. The Tories' night of gloom across

Shropshire deepened as Peter Bruinvels' hopes of winning the new Wrekin seat bit the dust.

The only glimmer of good news for the Tories came in North Shropshire where new boy Owen Paterson just scraped home with a 2,195 majority.

In Telford Labour's Bruce Grocott piled on the agony with a big win.

The dramatic night saw Labour take a firm grip on what has always been viewed as a typical Tory shire county.

Labour's Paul Marsden, pictured, claimed Shrewsbury and Atcham for the first time in his party's history.

Sole survivor

A Shropshire bodyguard is the sole survivor of the Paris crash which killed Princess Diana.

Trevor Rees-Jones, 29, escaped the tangled wreckage of Diana's Mercedes with serious head, face and chest injuries. The former paratrooper of Whittington, near Oswestry, was a front seat passenger.

Work to demolish a building dubbed the Shame of Newport – the former Tuckers ironmongers shop – is under way more than eight years after it collapsed. The building has been a boarded-up eyesore.

1998

RICHIE RULES WORLD

Telford's Richie Woodhall made an emotional visit to a Telford cemetery less than 24 hours after becoming a world boxing champion.

The 29-year-old fighter, who claimed the WBC super-middleweight title with an emphatic points victory over South African Thulane "Sugar Boy" Malinga at a packed-out Telford Ice Rink, kept a promise by laying his newly-won belt at the grave of former boxing pal Niki Grice.

"I promised his old man I would take the belt and lay it on his grave," said an emotional Woodhall shortly after being crowned champion.

Grice was just 25 when he died in a car crash in Wolverhampton in August 1991. He and Woodhall were big mates.

His father Harry Grice was among the 3,500-strong crowd at the ice rink to see Woodhall triumph over Malinga in brilliant fashion.

Woodhall, an Olympic bronze medallist and Commonwealth gold medallist as well as a former Commonwealth and European middleweight champion, was in control all through the fight and clearly deserved his unanimous points victory at the end of 12 hard-fought rounds.

"It was the greatest night of my life," he said afterwards. "The fans made it for me. I just hope I entertained them. I couldn't have done it without them."

Woodhall, who was beaten by American Keith Holmes the last time he fought for a world title 17 months ago, now plans to spend a few days resting with his family.

'BIG BANG' SHAKE-UP

Shropshire has been split into two in a "big bang" council shakeup which has seen the Telford & Wrekin district win its "independence" from the rest of the county.

Despite public opposition across Shropshire, Wrekin District Council won its battle to break away from under the Shropshire County Council umbrella, and become a unitary authority managing and running all its own services.

The newly-formed Telford & Wrekin Council has become, in effect, an independent county within a county controlling its own affairs.

Current and past members of the district authority packed into the council chamber for the final Wrekin Council meeting last night, hours before "a new day and a new dawn", as it officially became the Telford & Wrekin Council at midnight.

Council leader Phil Homer said he hoped the change to the unitary authority would not hit residents.

"This should be a seamless transfer. Customers should not notice the difference, although they can now ring this council rather than ringing the Shirehall in Shrewsbury."

Spillett success

Shropshire musician Adrian Spillett is celebrating the sound of success after gaining an early birthday present by winning the prestigious BBC Young Musician 1998 title.

Adrian swept to victory in Belfast, becoming the first percussionist to win the leading competition for teenage musical talent.

The 20-year-old, from The Mount, Shrewsbury, is a student at the Royal Northern College of Music in Manchester.

G8 summit

The world's most powerful men met at Weston Park in a G8 summit. They included Tony Blair, Bill Clinton, Boris Yeltsin, and Helmut Kohl, who hammered out an accord on international crime at the country manor on the Shropshire border. They then sat down to watch the FA Cup final on television.

1999

Biggest party for 1,000 years

They came from all over Shropshire and beyond, an unending torchlight procession to the summit of The Wrekin to celebrate a new year, a new century, a new millennium — and the return of the beacon.

By the time the final countdown began and the fireworks reached their crescendo, there must have been 3,000 on the summit.

It was, they agreed, the place to be. And free too.

The big moment was met with a big cheer among the masses gathered in the warm glow of a huge bonfire, although it was a mercifully mild night.

Some had brought beer, some had brought champagne. There were hugs and kisses and many sang Auld Lang Syne.

Almost unnoticed at first by many in the crowd, the revived Wrekin Beacon came on behind them, two red lights flashing in the mist which had enveloped the summit about half-an-hour before midnight.

After the cheers, the celebrations and the salutations, some began to drift away while others began to party.

So there was Land of Hope and Glory and a conga, Rule Britannia and the hokey cokey.

The celebrations on the summit had begun at 9pm when, before a crowd of around 200 people, chairman of Telford & Wrekin Council Councillor Dave Morgan, and forester Nick Edwards from Cressage, and saw mill manager Mike Harris, from Uppington — both from landowners Raby Estates — put the flaming torches to the huge bonfire.

Almost immediately there was the worst weather of the evening — strong wind and slanting rain — although happily it did not last long.

Over the next three hours the crowd was swelled by families with children, couples and young lovers, almost all dressed for bad weather, carrying torches and in millennium mood.

One absentee was John Wall, the Shrewsbury man who had begun the campaign to revive the Wrekin Beacon, an idea which was taken up by Telford & Wrekin Council and received overwhelming public support.

He had been invited as a special guest, but decided not to make the trek.

The big switch-on was performed by Councillor Dave Davies, the council's leader, pressing a button in the control room of the Wrekin telecommunications mast.

It is a modern successor to the Wrekin Beacon, much loved by generations of Salopians as a sign of home, which was turned off forever in 1965.

An RAF C130 Hercules transport aircraft on a training flight made a scheduled landing at Chetwynd airfield... and then sank into the soft ground. It took a major operation lasting several days to free it.

Rugby club ban

Oswestry rugby club has been barred from playing competitive games for an entire season in one of the most severe penalties handed down in the sport's history.

Four officers of the club have also been banned from any involvement in the sport for five years.

The judgment was handed down last night by the region's ruling body the North Midlands County as punishment for the club fielding a banned player under a false name.

Serck quits Newport

An engineering company is quitting Newport with the loss of 148 jobs.

Staff at Serck Audco Valves, a major employer in the town for years, were given the shock news in a statement from the management.

Serck Audco, which makes aluminium and bronze valves, blamed the continued uncertainty in the oil, gas and minerals markets for the closure.

A supervisor at the factory, who refused to be named, said workers had been told they had 90 days before the factory closed.

"This company has been at the centre of Newport for many years and this has come as a shock to everyone. It is a very sad day."

Monica mania failed to grip Shropshire when the former lover of President Clinton swept into the county virtually unnoticed.

America's most famous mistress Monica Lewinsky arrived in Shrewsbury on a whistlestop visit for a private reception at the Prince Rupert Hotel to round off the first leg of her whirlwind UK booksigning tour.

But despite media hype and previous high profile appearances, Miss Lewinsky's presence attracted barely a flicker of interest from locals.

2000

The worst floods in living memory ripped through Shropshire causing widespread misery.

Levels peaked in Shrewsbury on November 1 where the level recorded at the Welsh Bridge was 5.25 metres – 17ft 2ins – the highest level for 54 years.

Around 400 properties in Shrewsbury were affected. Elsewhere huge tracts of countryside were swamped, the Wharfage at Ironbridge was covered to the tops of the riverside railings, and Bridgnorth was also severely hit.

Onlookers in Shrewsbury watched as more than 100,000 gallons of water flashed through the county town every second.

A massive operation was co-ordinated by borough and county councils, police, fire and ambulance services at Shirehall.

The whole of the medieval town centre within the loop of the river became a no-go area for traffic as police and council officials set up barricades and turned traffic away.

Telford & Wrekin Council officials were out in force in Ironbridge, handing out sandbags to more than 20 properties.

And to compound the misery, the floods were preceded by severe gales, one of which badly damaged the historic Royal Oak at Boscobel. The tree is a direct descendant of the oak in which King Charles hid from the Roundheads in 1651.

In a flying visit to Shrewsbury on November 2, Prime Minister Tony Blair pledged urgent action to ensure there was never a repeat of the flooding hell.

He promised that work would quickly go ahead on a flood defence scheme. He praised the emergency services and council officials for their efforts in tackling the disaster.

But in a cruel twist, the county was to be hit by renewed floods in December, before shopkeepers and householders had finished clearing up after the first round of flooding.

This time Deputy Prime Minister John Prescott visited Shrewsbury on December 12, the day floods there peaked at 4.78m. In Ironbridge and Bridgnorth levels peaked the following day. The Bridgnorth flooding was as bad as that experienced in the early floods.

This dramatic picture shows the scene in the shadow of the English Bridge, Shrewsbury.

2001

COUNTRYSIDE CRIPPLED

The country way of life in Shropshire and Mid Wales was on the verge of collapse today with a massive restriction zone thrown around the region in a bid to halt the spread of foot and mouth.

The "infected area" zone stretches from Shrewsbury and Welshpool in the north and takes in Ludlow, Newtown and Llandrindod Wells before going on down to Chepstow in south Wales.

A whole raft of rural activities are banned. They include shooting, racing, hunting, point-to-point meetings, fishing where it involves going on farmland, rambling, exercising dogs and meetings in infected areas, climbing, birdwatching and orienteering.

No animals within the zone can be moved unless by special licence.

No visitors are allowed to infected farms without the express permission of MAFF vets. Other farms within the infected zone are allowed visitors but this is discouraged. Any visitors must disinfect their shoes and cars at the farm gate.

Rural rights of way and open countryside across the whole restriction zone are out of bounds to all members of the public, who face a £5,000 fine for breaching it.

The exclusion zone is adding to problems faced by the farming community with many rural businesses already laying off staff and a ban on scores of leisure activities.

The exclusion zone was set up as a new case was confirmed on the Powys/Shropshire border yesterday.

Today farmer Winston Jones was mourning the loss of his pedigree herd of 140 cattle.

Mr Jones of The Ditches, Churchstoke, was told yesterday that his prize Holstein milking herd, which has been built over three generations, had foot and mouth disease.

They were immediately destroyed and are expected to be incinerated today.

Mr Jones said he was devastated by the news. "It was sheer shock," he said.

"We have been so careful and yet this has still happened to us. We have hardly been off the farm, and the only vehicle coming on was the milk tanker."

MAFF vets believe the infection at The Ditches could be linked to Welshpool livestock market.

The Government has signalled the rural tourist industry and countryside businesses hit by the outbreak could receive millions of pounds in compensation.

Agriculture minister Nick Brown has said that only farmers who have livestock destroyed would be eligible for a payout but yesterday admitted others indirectly affected might be given financial aid.

(Within a week of the outbreak of foot and mouth disease in Essex in February, it was detected at a farm at Felindre, near Clun. The first confirmed Shropshire cases came on the weekend of March 17 and 18 in Chirbury and Brockton, near Shrewsbury. The Shropshire countryside became a vast no-go area, and agricultural shows, including the West Mid, were cancelled, although Minsterley Show went ahead in reduced form.

Almost all restrictions in Shropshire were lifted in mid-August and on November 6 the county was given the effective all-clear. By the end of the outbreak 59,716 animals in Shropshire had been destroyed, only a fraction of which actually had the disease).

The Long Mynd is among vast stretches of rural Shropshire closed by foot and mouth disease.

It's Sir Kevin

A Shropshire head has been knighted for his services to education.

Kevin Satchwell, of Thomas Telford School in Telford, is one of only a handful of teachers ever to receive a knighthood. The 50-year-old paid tribute to his family and staff and children at the school adding that they all shared in the honour.

Fossil discovery

Some of the oldest known ancestors of crabs and lobsters, dating back more than 500 million years, have been discovered in south Shropshire.

The fossilised creatures were found by experts in rocks near Comley, in the Shropshire Hills. Scientists say the fossils are the oldest known crustacean.

Terror victim

A Shrewsbury man was the only Briton to die on the planes used in the September 11 terror blitz on America.

Graham Berkeley, 37, an e-business director with a computer firm, was on United Airlines Flight 175, the second of the hijacked passenger jets to be crashed into the World Trade Centre in New York.

Noisy start to historic conference

Angry hunt supporters and countryside campaigners left Government ministers under no illusion about their feelings when they mobbed the Labour Party's rural conference in Shropshire.

More than 100 pro-huntsmen waved placards and blew horns at the opening of the historic event at the Harper Adams University College, Newport.

They let the Government know they face a bitter fight if they press ahead with plans to ban hunting.

On arrival at the campus the Secretary of State for Environment, Food and Rural Affairs, Margaret Beckett, was jeered as campaigners vented their anger at the Government's handling of the issue.

But Mrs Beckett brushed the chants aside to announce new cash to help boost rural economies. She said Labour was boosting rural bus services, schools and policing and was ensuring the survival of Post Offices.

The three-day event, Labour's first such rural conference, set out to tackle problems such as housing, transport and policing.

Pictured above are protesters at the opening of the event.

WHEN A BIG CAT ATTACKS..

Police are hunting a wild panther after the beast is thought to have savaged a family saloon car in Shropshire leaving huge dents, scratch marks and a giant paw mark as evidence.

It is feared the animal may now be injured and dangerous after a trail of blood was left at the scene. A pet cat belonging to the car owner, Gill Bonell, is also missing and may have been attacked.

Police confirmed they are investigating a suspected panther attack.

Mrs Bonell, of Knowlegate, near Ludlow, woke this morning to discover her Rover 400 had been "trashed" overnight.

Police suspect the panther could have caused the damage during a frantic attack on the family's pet, which could have taken refuge under the front of the Rover.

Thousands join countryside demo

Thousands of people from Shropshire and Mid Wales joined 400,000 marchers on the streets of London to send a clear message to Tony Blair: Hands off our countryside.

People from all walks of life – farmers, doctors, teachers, schoolchildren and pensioners – travelled to London to express their anger with the Government.

Honking horns, unfurling banners and chanting pro-hunt slogans, the Shropshire contingent made their presence felt at the Liberty and Livelihood March in the capital.

Among the campaigners was North Shropshire Conservative MP Owen Paterson and an 18-strong contingent from his extended family.

The MP, a champion of rights for hunters, said: "I think it is just astonishing. The numbers here are absolutely staggering. I just hope these bigoted MPs, who are driven by a totally wrong idea of the sort of people who go hunting, will start to listen."

The Shropshire and West Midlands ambulance services have sealed their merger and promised to further improve patient care.

They formally announced their link-up at a press conference at the Tweedale training centre at Madeley, Telford.

Responsibility for ambulance cover across Shropshire has passed to the West Midlands Ambulance Service NHS Trust, one of the biggest in Britain, although the county service will retain its own identity.

Final approval for the merger was given by Shropshire Health Authority after members agreed unanimously it represented the best option for the county.

TOWN CRASH FROM LEAGUE

Kevin Ratcliffe today quit as manager of Shrewsbury Town just hours after the club crashed out of the Football League.

His decision came after Town slumped to a 3-2 defeat against relegation rivals Carlisle, finally ending their hopes of league survival.

Shell-shocked Ratcliffe admitted: "The buck stops with me as I've brought in the players, I've picked the team but at the end of the day we haven't been good enough over the season.

"I do feel so sad that it has come to this as I've come here to do a job and haven't achieved that, and that is a great disappointment to me."

Heartbroken fans called for Ratcliffe's sacking in angry scenes after last night's match which ended 53 years of league history for Town in front of 7,000 fans.

More than 100 police officers were on duty at the Meadow last night.

Club chairman Roland Wycherley and directors Keith Sayfritz and Mal Whitrick today pledged to do everything possible to return the club to the Football League.

In a statement on behalf of the board, Mr Sayfritz said: "The most important people are our fans. We know that they have been let down extremely badly and all I can promise them is that we are aware of what has happened. I just want them to believe that Malcolm Whitrick, myself and the board are so, so sorry.

"Give us a day or so and then they can be certain of one thing – that we will do

Peter Wilding is consoled by Town physio Simon Shakeshaft after the defeat

everything we can to fulfil our duty to them and to get back into the Football League."

Ratcliffe said: "I did say at the beginning of the season that this will be a year of survival, but I didn't think it would come to us not surviving in the league, and I feel really sorry for that.

"I've had a great relationship with the board and we are going to leave on good

terms. During my time here the fans have been very supportive and I would like to thank them.

"I think we've played well enough at times, I don't think we've had the luck or decisions go our way, but at the end of the day you are judged over the season and not over a few games, the result against Carlisle hasn't got us relegated, it's the results over the season."

Speed camera debut

Shropshire's first fixed speed camera has finally gone live – a week behind schedule.

The county's inaugural speed camera at Bennetts Bank in Wellington should have been switched on to coincide with a West Mercia-wide launch but teething problems forced the delay.

The controversial cameras have been introduced in a bid to cut down road deaths.

Yet while anti-speed campaigners are warning motorists to slow down, a new report says speed cameras have been rigged to catch only the worst offenders.

Cameras in some key 30mph zones have been set so they only flash motorists who travel at 43mph or more because police cannot cope with the flood of fines.

National police guidelines say that cameras in 30mph zones should catch drivers who exceed 35mph because these are the areas where pedestrians are most likely to be killed.

Historic poll

History was made on May 1 in the Shropshire local council elections with revolutionary polling methods, including "smart" voting, used for the first time.

The votes in Telford & Wrekin and North Shropshire were entirely by post.

In the Shrewsbury & Atcham Borough Council area there was so-called "smart" voting – electors voted by touchtone phone, digital television, on the internet, and also by post.

Although the general feeling appeared to be that it was a success in increasing participation in the democratic process, financially it was less impressive, costing nearly £1 million – compared to a cost of around £70,000 for "normal" voting. In other words, it was 14 times more expensive.

2004

Workers erect flood barriers on The Wharfage, Ironbridge.

Flood defences triumph

Shropshire's new flood defences were hailed as a huge success after the barriers held firm against the rising River Severn.

But while homeowners and residents in Shrewsbury and parts of Ironbridge celebrated, others claimed the expensive defence system had caused unexpected problems further downstream.

The Environment Agency confirmed today the worst of the flooding was over and said river levels in Shropshire had already started to subside.

The river peaked in Ironbridge at 6.1m yesterday evening. In Bridgnorth, it peaked at 4.87m and the level at 8am today was 4.71m.

Workmen in Shrewsbury were today starting to dismantle the temporary defences outside the new council offices in Frankwell. Lyn Fraley, spokesman for the agency, declared the new pallet barrier

which protected the Wharfage in Ironbridge a huge success.

She said the defences in the Gorge and in Frankwell, Shrewsbury, had protected almost 100 homes.

"We are very pleased with the way they have performed. It is a good sign for future years," she said.

But there was discontent in other parts of the Ironbridge Gorge and in Bridgnorth, with several residents fearing the problem had simply been passed on to them.

Avon Horden, who lives on Severnside, across the river from the Wharfage in Ironbridge, said this was the first time that his home had been flooded in 40 years.

Mr Horden, 45, said: "We do not normally get floods here. We even got away with it during the really big floods in 2000.

"There really can be no other explanation than that this is being caused by the barrier along the Wharfage."

Parking charges came into force in Wellington and Newport today to a cry of outrage from traders, shoppers and motorists who claim they are being singled out for unfair treatment by the Borough of Telford & Wrekin.

At least one pay and display machine in Wellington was sabotaged by a vandal

stuffing paper into its cash slot.

In both towns, council car parks were unusually empty.

Telford & Wrekin Council deputy leader David Morgan said charges were part of a plan fostered by Government ministers to improve the environment by cutting congestion and pollution.

Disaster day for Telford United

Failed Telford United Football Club has been officially placed into liquidation with debts of almost £6.5 million.

A report by the club's directors showed the former Nationwide Conference outfit had assets of £78,000 but owed over £6 million – the bulk of the money being a loan for the construction of the New Bucks Head stadium.

The figures were revealed at a creditors' meeting which saw the axe formally fall on the doomed club.

After the meeting – attended by three of the club's directors and some creditors – liquidator Rod Butcher said there was now "little chance" of anyone getting the cash they were owed.

"From today Telford United Football Club Ltd is officially in liquidation and it is my task to realise whatever assets there are available,"said Mr Butcher, of Moore Stephens Corporate Recovery.

"But creditors have been warned today that they are not likely to see any of their money," he added.

The directors' report listed the Staffordshire-based Miras Group – owned by the football club's former chairman Andy Shaw who had bankrolled the building of the new ground for almost £5 million – as the main creditor.

Other directors Rob Cave, Paul Booth and Michael Ferriday were at the meeting at the Whitehouse Hotel, but Mr Shaw did not turn up.

The club was forced into liquidation after Mr Shaw's Miras Group went into receivership in March facing huge debts.

Last month supporters launched a new club – AFC Telford United.

Town are back!

Shrewsbury Town are basking in glory after clinching promotion to the Football League following a dramatic penalty showdown.

The club have bounced out of the Conference at the very first attempt.

Civic leaders are now considering a reception for Town's heroes who battled their way back into the third division defeating Aldershot 3-0 on penalties at Stoke's Britannia Stadium after yesterday's nailbiting clash ended at a 1-1 stalemate.

2005

LAST HUNTS SET OUT

Hunts across Shropshire rode out today for one last meet before the 300-year-old rural tradition is officially banned.

The Government's controversial Hunting Act, which outlaws fox hunting, deer hunting and hare coursing with dogs, will come into force at midnight. It follows the Countryside Alliance's failure to overturn the ban yesterday.

Hundreds of hunt members rode out into the countryside across the region today for their last legal hunt with dogs.

The North Shropshire Hunt, pictured, met in Lee Brockhurst, near Shrewsbury, where joint master Ann Carding said there were mixed feelings for the 400 people who attended.

"There is a lot of anger at the moment. We feel it's a very unjust law but we are going to enjoy our hunting and will carry on within the law until the act is repealed," she said.

More than 100 people turned out in Lapley to support the Albrighton Hunt.

Members said they had an emotional day thinking about the loss of an ancient rural pastime.

£36m IN THE RED

Shropshire's health service is heading for a huge £36 million debt and health bosses are looking at crisis measures – including hospital closures – to balance the books.

The largest single deficit of £29 million will be carried by the Shrewsbury and Telford Hospital Trust which runs the Royal Shrewsbury Hospital and the Princess Royal Hospital in Telford.

And one of the main conclusions of the review which was unveiled to health watchdogs today is that the trust is efficient but underfunded.

It has concluded that under the new Payments by Results system, the organisation should in future get another £15 million a year from its paymasters, the Shropshire County and Telford & Wrekin Primary Care Trusts.

Total NHS debt in the county by the end of the financial year is forecast to be £36 million.

Review programme director Clive Walsh stressed that at this stage no firm proposals or recommendations were on the table.

The various options will be put to NHS stakeholders over the next few weeks and then refined for three months in a public consultation exercise towards the end of January.

However, in the firing line are three community hospitals which could face the axe.

Management consultants claim that the "extreme option" of closing the hospitals at Bridgnorth, Whitchurch and Ludlow could save £2.4 million a year.

And major changes to the way both the Royal Shrewsbury and Telford's Princess Royal hospitals are run could save another £2.2 million.

Consultants say one site could become a "hot" centre dealing with emergency medical cases while the other becomes a "cold" site handling non-emergencies.

The consultants do not say which site would become either centre but the 'cold' site would inevitably be seen as the junior partner.

The controversial options, which are bound to stir up massive controversy, are contained in an independent report compiled by outside consultants into the cash crisis crippling the county's health service.

The Bridgnorth hospital site is currently undergoing major development to bring all the town's medical services under one roof.

Any move to close the site would provoke an outcry.

A fireball rises from a huge blaze which hit Snedshill trading estate in December.

2006

Bye bye bears

Shropshire's Merrythought teddy bear factory – one of the last soft toy manufacturers in Britain – today closed down with the loss of 48 jobs.

Bosses blamed the closure of the Ironbridge works on cheap competition from abroad.

The three-generation family business is run by 56-year-old Oliver Holmes. His grandfather founded the firm, which celebrated its 75th anniversary last year.

The shock news was broken to all 48 staff at a mass meeting.

A statement said: "The directors of Merrythought Toys regrettably announce the cessation of manufacture of their products in Ironbridge due to the ongoing effects of external economics.

". . . Despite the best endeavours of the management team and the absolute dedication of a loyal and talented workforce, it has proved impossible for Merrythought to remain competitive.

"The directors extend their most sincere thanks to all those who have supported the business."

The collapse of Merrythought is a tragic last twist in the tale of a 76-year-old Shropshire business that has been a household name among teddy bear collectors around the world.

It was in 1930 that Merrythought Toys opened a factory in Coalbrookdale in a former social room building rented from the Coalbrookdale Company.

In the years since Merrythought has been an integral part of the Ironbridge Gorge scene. It survived both floods of the River Severn and, on one occasion, a wartime raid in which bombs rained down not far away on the opposite side of the river.

All over the globe children – and adults – are proud owners of soft toys with the label "Merrythought,Ironbridge, Shropshire. Made In England".

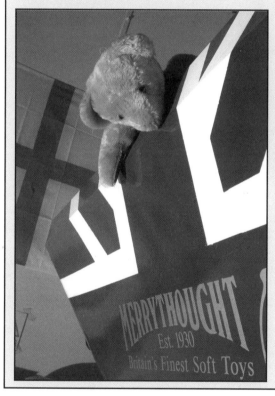

Sizzling summer breaks records

Record-breaking temperatures have left Shropshire basking in seemingly endless sun.

Weather experts have been flicking through the record books in a struggle to find anything like it.

July 19 was Britain's hottest July day ever, with 36.5C (97.7F) recorded at Wisley in Surrey, while Shropshire smashed the county's all time July record with 33.7C (93F) recorded at RAF Shawbury.

July was the hottest British month on record nationally, although in Shropshire it equalled that of 1983, according to Shropshire weatherman John Warner. The county's mean temperature during the month was 20C (78F). The hot spell finally broke on July 29.

But that was not all. Shropshire has enjoyed its warmest autumn since 1731, and July and September were the warmest since records began in 1659.

Amid all this sun and heat, it's easy to forget another statistic – that it was the wettest May since 1979.

Jenna Hodgson, 21 from Shrewsbury, pictured, was enjoying the sizzling July sunshine in the grounds of Shrewsbury Castle.

Well, there's always the beer..

Disappointed Shropshire rugby heroes Cleobury Mortimer were coming back down to earth today after their astonishing fairytale run of results came to an end at Twickenham.

The rugby minnows went down 46-3 to Dorking yesterday in the final of the Powergen Junior Vase.

Club supporters hailed their day out at Twickenham as one to remember, with the occasion being just as important as the result.

Team skipper Paul Harding praised his players and their supporters and said he was delighted at the way fans had cheered the team on.

POLICE HERO SHOT DEAD

A police officer has been shot dead after being called to reports of an argument in Shrewsbury. Constable Richard Gray, who had received five commendations for bravery, is the first Shropshire police officer to be murdered on duty.

The 43-year-old father of two from Bayston Hill, a member of the police armed response team, went to New Park Road in the Castlefields area on May 6.

He was shot by 33-year-old Peter Medlicott with a .222 calibre rifle he used for pest control. Medlicott then turned the gun on himself.

Tributes to Constable Gray, known as Ricky, came in from across the world and the flag at Shrewsbury's police headquarters in Monkmoor Road flew at half mast.

Scores of floral tributes from colleagues were laid on the ground underneath the police standard.

Detectives said the weapon used to gun down the police officer was "legally held". The results of post-mortem examinations carried out on the men revealed they both died from single gunshot wounds to the head.

West Mercia Chief Constable Paul West led the tributes.

He said: "In Ricky's four years with us his bravery, determination and professionalism as a police officer saw him recognised with a total of five commendations, two from his divisional commander, two from me, and a judge's commendation.

"In itself, that speaks volumes for the sort of man he was and his dedication and commitment to duty."

Constable Gray was born in Dundee, Scotland, and served with the 1st Battalion of the Black Watch in Northern Ireland as well as serving in Germany, Hong Kong, England and Scotland before joining first Cheshire Constabulary and then the West Mercia force.

Wettest June brings floods chaos

Some of the worst floods in living memory have caused widespread chaos across Shropshire with more than 70 people being rescued and 1,000 properties swamped by water.

Emergency services have been working around the clock to deal with thousands of call-outs caused by torrential rain.

In Ludlow, about 20 residents were evacuated from their homes when the Burway Bridge – on the main route into the town from the north – collapsed, causing a gas main to burst. Later a nearby house collapsed. Older residents said it had been 1926 since the town had experienced flooding anything like as bad.

Dan Needham, of New Road, Ludlow, said: "It was astonishing. The whole of lower Ludlow looked like a big lake."

Residents and businesses in Much Wenlock were faced with a "raging torrent"

of flood water cascading down the main High Street, forcing the emergency services to close routes into the town.

Among other hard hit areas was Coalbrookdale, where a massive volume of surface water left Dale Road submerged and "like a war zone."

The floods, which mainly hit the east and the south of the county, came during the wettest June in living memory. They followed hard on the heels of a thunderstorm which led to flash flooding which caused severe damage in the Alveley and Hampton Loade areas.

And one of Shropshire's premier tourist attractions, the Severn Valley Railway, has been thrown into crisis after the water swept away land underneath the track near Highley, leaving the rails suspended in the air. Damage to the line is expected to cost hundreds of thousands of pounds to repair.

Submerged vehicles at Coalbrookdale, which became "like a war zone"

Appendices

Campaigning in the 1908
Neilson v Stanier by-election

ELECTION

Beville Stanier was MP for Newport and,
later, Ludlow

A triumphant Bill Yates, arr
Wellington, after his 1955 g

A crowd gathers in Wellington awaiting the result, date unknown, but around the 1920s or
1930s

Edith Picton-Turbervill
was Shropshire's first
woman MP

Wrekin Labour Party agent Mellor Harrison, left, with successful Wrekin Labour candidate Ivor Thomas after the 1951 result

Gerry Fowler takes The Wrekin for Labour in October 1974

...ts a supporter in The Square, ...on victory

Paul Marsden became Shrewsbury's first Labour MP

John Biffen, right, chalks up another victory in the Oswestry seat

Matthew Green scored a historic victory for the Lib Dems in the Ludlow seat. He is seen in 2001 with Lib Dem leader Charles Kennedy

Elections

1900
General election October

Shrewsbury
Mr H.D. Greene, KC (C)   unopposed

Wellington
Alexander Brown (U)   3,480
Robert Varty (Liberal and Labour)   2,318

Unionist majority 1,162

Newport
Colonel W. Kenyon-Slaney (C)   unopposed

Oswestry
Stanley Leighton (C)   unopposed

Ludlow
Jasper More (U)   unopposed

1901
By-election May 24

Oswestry
The Hon. G. Ormsby-Gore (C)   4,518
Allan Bright (L)   3,430

Conservative majority 1,088. Con hold.

Caused by death of MP Stanley Leighton.

1903
By-election December 23

Ludlow
Mr Rowland Hunt (U)   4,393
Mr Fred Horne (L)   3,423

Unionist majority 970. Unionist hold.

Caused by death of MP Jasper More.

1904
By-election July 26

Oswestry
Allan Bright (L)   4,542
W. Clive Bridgeman (C)   4,157

Liberal majority 385. Lib gain.

Caused by elevation of MP the Hon. G. Ormsby-Gore to the peerage following death of Lord Harlech on June 26. Bright was first Oswestry Liberal MP for over 70 years. Campaign was marred by disorder.

Key

U – Unionist
C – Conservative
L – Liberal
Lab – Labour
Ind – Independent
Lib Dem – Liberal Democrat

Unusual parties spelt out
Winning candidate in bold

1906
General election. Polling various dates mid-January

Shrewsbury
Sir Clement Hill (U)   2,395
Edward George Hemmerde (L)   1,955

Unionist majority 440. No change.

Wellington
Mr Charles Henry (Lib. and Lab.)   4,806
Mr Hildebrand Harmsworth (U)   3,114

Lib majority 1,692. Liberal gain.

Newport
Colonel Kenyon-Slaney (C)   4,853
Frank Neilson (L)   4,677

Conservative majority 176. No change.

Oswestry
Clive Bridgeman (U)   5,011
Allan Bright (L)   4,508

Unionist majority 503. Unionist gain.

Ludlow
Rowland Hunt (U)   4,978
Fred C. Horne (L)   4,218

Unionist majority of 760. No change.

1908
By-election May 14

Newport
Sir Beville Stanier (U)   5,328
F. Neilson (L)   4,377

Unionist maj 951.

Caused by death on April 24 of MP W.S. Kenyon-Slaney.

1910
General election January (polling was on various dates)

Shrewsbury
Sir Clement Hill (C)   2,596
Mr J.H. Whitworth (L)   1,994

Unionist majority 602. Unionist hold.

Wellington
Mr C.S. Henry (L)   4,673
Captain C.P.B. Wood (U)   3,484

Liberal majority 1,189. Lib hold.

Newport
Mr Beville Stanier (C)   5,570
Mr W.E. Moulsdale (L)   4,324

Unionist/Conservative majority 1,246. Unionist hold.

Oswestry
Mr W.C. Bridgeman (C)   5,003
Mr E. Powell (L)   4,379

Conservative majority 624, Unionist/Conservative hold.

Ludlow
Mr Rowland Hunt (U)   5,769
Mr G.F. Forsdike (L)   3,365

Unionist majority 2,404. Unionist hold.

1910
Second general election December (various dates)

Shrewsbury
Sir Clement Hill (U)   2,423
Mr Thomas Pace (Lib and Lab)   1,855

Unionist majority 568. Unionist hold.

Wellington
Mr C.S. Henry (L)   4,404
Captain the Hon
George Forester (Con/Unionist)   3,286.

Liberal majority 1,118. Liberal hold.

Newport
Mr Beville Stanier (U)   unopposed

Oswestry
Mr W.C. Bridgeman (U)   4,867
Mr Edward Powell (L)   4,121

Unionist majority 746. Unionist hold.

Ludlow
Mr Rowland Hunt (U)   unopposed.

1913
By-election April 22

Shrewsbury
Mr G. Butler Lloyd (U)   2,412
Mr J.R. Morris (Ind)   1,727

Unionist majority 685. Unionist hold

Caused by death of Sir Clement Hill MP on April 9.

1918
General election December 14

Shrewsbury
Mr G. Butler Lloyd (U)   9,826
Ald A. Taylor (Lab)   5,542

Unionist majority 4,284, Unionist hold.

Wrekin
Sir C. S. Henry (Coalition Liberal)   unopposed.

Oswestry
Mr W. C. Bridgeman (U)   12,276
Mr T. Morris (Lab)   8,467

Unionist majority 3,809. Unionist hold.

Ludlow
Sir Beville Stanier (U)   unopposed.

In 1918 Wellington & District became part of the new Wrekin Division.
Sir Beville Stanier sat in the previous Parliament for Newport.

1920
By-election February 7

Wrekin
Charles Frederick Palmer (Ind)   9,267
Charles Duncan (Lab)   8,729
John Bayley (Coalition Liberal)   4,750

Ind majority 538. Ind gain.

Caused by death of MP Sir Charles Henry on December 27, 1919. A modern book gives John Bayley's voting figure as

4,759, but the contemporary WJ&SN gives it as 4,750.

1920
Second by-election November 20

Wrekin
Major General Sir Charles Townshend KCB DSO (Ind)	14,565
Charles Duncan (Lab)	10,600

Ind majority 3,965. Ind hold.

Caused by death of MP Charles Palmer, a Parliamentary journalist, on or about October 25.
Townshend was the general who had surrendered at the siege of Kut.

1922
By-election January 4

Ludlow
Viscount Windsor (C)	unopposed.

Caused by death of MP Sir Beville Stanier on December 15, 1921.

1922
General election November 15

Shrewsbury
Viscount Sandon (C)	10,999
M.J. Sunlight (L)	9,401

Con majority 1,598. Con hold.

Wrekin
Howard S. Button (C)	11,652
R.E. Jones (Lab)	10,603

Con majority 1,049. Con gain from Ind.

Oswestry
The Rt Hon W.C. Bridgeman (C)	12,837
Capt. R. Sidebottom (L)	6,660
Tom Morris (Lab)	6,105

Con majority 6,177. Con hold.

Ludlow
Viscount Windsor (C)	11,787
E.C. Pryce (L)	5,979

Con majority 5,808. Con hold.

1923
By-election April 19

Ludlow
Lt Col George Windsor-Clive (C)	9,956
Capt. Edward Calcott Pryce (L)	6,740
Mr Percy Frederick Pollard (Lab)	1,420

Con majority 3,216. Con hold.

Caused by succession of sitting MP Viscount Windsor to the Earldom of Plymouth, following death of his father the Earl of Plymouth on March 6.

1923
General election December 6

Shrewsbury
Joseph Sunlight (L)	11,097
Viscount Sandon (aka Dudley Ryder) (C)	10,548

Lib majority 549. Lib gain from Con.

Wrekin
Henry S. Nixon (Lab)	11,657
Arthur Nicholas Fielden (C)	10,274

Lab majority 1,383. Lab gain from Con.

Henry Nixon was Shropshire's first Labour MP

Oswestry
The Rt Hon William Clive Bridgeman (C)	11,528
Captain Russell Sidebottom (L)	9,713
Mr Sidney Ronald Campion (Lab)	3,477

Con majority 1,815. Con hold.

Ludlow
Lt Col George Windsor-Clive (C)	unopposed.

1924
General election October 29

Shrewsbury
Viscount Sandon (C)	13,220
Joseph Sunlight (L)	8,945
David B. Lawley (Lab)	1,614

Con majority 4,275. Con gain from Liberal.

Wrekin
Thomas Oakley (C)	14,003
Henry Nixon (Lab)	11,132

Con majority 2,871. Con gain from Lab.

Oswestry
Mr W.C. Bridgeman (C)	14,316
Captain Russell Sidebottom (L)	6,143
Mr T. Morris (Lab)	5,503

Con maj 8,173. Con hold.

Bridgeman became the First Lord of the Admiralty in the new administration.

Ludlow
Lt Colonel Windsor-Clive (C)	unopposed

1929
General election May 30

Shrewsbury
George Arthur Victor Duckworth (C)	14,586
Joseph Sunlight (L)	11,794
Albert Abraham Beach (Lab)	3,662

Con majority 2,792, Con hold.

Wrekin
Edith Picton-Turbervill (Lab)	14,569
Thomas Oakley (C)	11,707
William Edward Boyes (L)	6,575

Labour majority 2,862, Lab gain. County's first woman MP.

Oswestry
Major Bertie Edward Parker Leighton (C)	15,544
Prof John Share Jones (L)	10,565

Hugh Simon Evans (Lab) 6,944

Con maj 4,979, Con hold.

Ludlow
Lt Col George Windsor-Clive (C)	14,066
Thomas Hardwick (Lab)	5,323
Col Arthur Hanbury-Sparrow (L)	5,259

Con majority 8,743, Con hold.

1931
General election October 27

Shrewsbury
Mr G A V Duckworth (C)	18,505
Dr Betty Morgan (L)	9,358
Edward Porter (Lab)	2,567

Con maj 9,147. Con hold.

Wrekin
Colonel J. Baldwin-Webb (Nat Con)*	22,258
Miss E. Picton Turbervill (Lab)	14,162

Con maj 8,096. Con gain. *National Conservative.

Oswestry
Major Parker Leighton (C)	23,740
Mr W.E. Warder (Lab)	8,343

Con maj 15,397. Con hold.

Ludlow
Lt Col G Windsor-Clive (C)	19,700
Mr T Hardwick (Lab)	4,683

Con maj 15,017. Con hold.

1935
General election November 14

Shrewsbury
Mr G A V Duckworth (Nat Con)	18,401
Mr C C Poole (Lab)	9,606

Conservative majority 8,765. No change.

Wrekin
Colonel Baldwin-Webb (Nat Con)	20,665
Mr Geoffrey Theodore Barratt (Lab)	15,040

Conservative majority 5,625. No change.

Oswestry
Major B E Parker Leighton (Nat Con)	unopposed.

Ludlow
Lt Col G Windsor-Clive (Nat Con)	16,355
Mr Thomas Hardwick (Lab)	6,146

Con maj 10,209. No change.

1941
By-election September 26

Wrekin
Mr Arthur Colegate (Nat Con)	9,946
Mr Noel Pemberton-Billington (NI)*	7,121
Mr Arthur Patrick Kennedy (Ind)	1,638

Nat Con majority 2,825, Nat Con hold.

Caused by death on September 17, 1940, of MP Colonel Baldwin-Webb. *National Independent.

1945
General election July 5

Shrewsbury
Cmdr John L. Holt (C)	15,174
Flt Lt S. Chapman (Lab)	10,580
Mr A.S. Comyns-Carr (L)	8,412

Con majority 4,594. No change.

Wrekin
Ivor Owen Thomas (Lab)	22,453
Arthur Colegate (C)	17,422

Labour majority 5,031. Labour gain.

Oswestry
Colonel O.B.S. Poole (C)	19,082
Mr T.D.E. Boyd Carpenter (Lab)	10,777
Lt L. Corbet Burcher (L)	5,049

Con maj 8,305. No change.

Ludlow
Lt Col Uvedale Corbett*(C)	13,928
Squadron Leader A. Parry Jones (Lab)	6,358
Sgt C. G. Cameron (L)	4,307
Mr C.E. Edwards (Ind)	989

Con maj 7,570. No change. *Nicknamed "Streak".

1950
General election February 23

Shrewsbury
John Holt (C)	18,470
Mr R.B. Cant (Lab)	12,542
Lt Col N.W. Elliott (L)	6,126

Conservative majority 5,928. No change.

Wrekin
Mr I.O. Thomas (Lab)	19,730
Capt F.G. Bibbings (C)	17,039

Lab maj 2,691. No change.

Oswestry
The Hon W.D. Ormsby-Gore (C)	23,562
Mr A.G. Wait (Lab)	14,556

Conservative maj 9,006. No change.

Ludlow
Lt Col U. Corbett (C)	22,340
Mr J. Williams (Lab)	14,573

Con maj 7,767. No change.

1951
General election October 25

Shrewsbury
John Langford Holt (C)	21,503
Robert Bowen Cant (Lab)	14,735

Con majority 6,768. No change.

Wrekin
Ivor Thomas (Lab)	20,109
J.H. Cordle (C)	18,305

Lab majority 1,804. No change.

Oswestry
David Ormsby-Gore (C)	23,843
Arthur Wait (Lab)	14,471

Con majority 9,372. No change.

Ludlow
Christopher Holland-Martin (C)	22,073
Rex Barker (Lab)	14,596

Con majority 7,477. No change.

1955
General election May 26

Shrewsbury
John Holt (C)	21,319
Geoffrey Allen (Lab)	13,726

Con maj 7,593. Con hold.

Wrekin
Bill Yates (C)	19,019
Ivor O.Thomas (Lab)	18,541

Con maj 478. Con gain.

Oswestry
The Hon W.D. Ormsby-Gore (C)	22,859
Mark E. Boggin (Lab)	12,434

Con majority 10,425. Con hold.

Ludlow
C.J. Holland Martin (C)	20,816
Reginald (Rex) Barker (Lab)	12,937

Con majority 7,879. Con hold.

1959
General election October 8

Shrewsbury
J.A. (John) Langford-Holt (C)	19,970
(Kenneth) K.V. Russell (Lab)	11,338
Harold Shaw (L)	6,387

Conservative majority 8,632. No change.

Wrekin
W. (Bill) Yates (C)	22,030
(Donald) D.W.T. Bruce (Lab)	19,052

Con majority 2,978. No change. n.b. BBC TV cameras were at the count.

Oswestry
David Ormsby-Gore (C)	21,055
Glyn Thomas (Lab)	10,531
Dai Rees (L)	6,068

Con majority 10,524. No change.

Ludlow
Christopher J. Holland-Martin (C)	21,464
John Garwell (Lab)	14,138

Con majority 7,326. No change.

Shrewsbury Chronicle gives Holland-Martin's voting figure as 21,484 and his majority as 7,346.

1960
By-election November 16

Ludlow
Jasper More (C)	13,777
Dai Rees (L)	8,127
John Garwell (Lab)	7,812

Con majority 5,650. No change.

Caused by the death of MP Mr C.J. Holland-Martin.

1961
By-election November 8

Oswestry
John Biffen (C)	12,428
John Buchanan (L)	8,647
A.B. Walden (Lab)	8,519
J. Drayton (Patriotic Front)	839

Con majority 3,781. No change.

Caused by MP Sir David Ormsby-Gore (Lord Harlech) becoming Ambassador to the United States.

1964
General election October 15

Shrewsbury
Sir John Langford-Holt (C)	18,517
Jim O. Murphy (Lab)	12,658
Geoffrey K. Roberts (L)	7,180

Con majority 5,859. No change.

Wrekin
W. Yates (C)	21,765
D.W.T. Bruce (Lab)	19,078
John Davies (L)	3,839

Con majority 2,687. No change.

Oswestry
W.J. Biffen (C)	18,154
G.J. Costley (Lab)	11,407
T. Crowther (L)	8,745

Con majority 6,747. No change.

Ludlow
J. More (C)	17,290
Mike K. Prendergast (Lab)	10,763
John Griffiths (L)	8,768

Con majority 6,527, No change.

Shrewsbury Chronicle gives John Griffith's figure as 8,764.

1966
General election March 31

Shrewsbury
Sir John Langford-Holt (C)	17,569
Tom Pritchard (Lab)	14,603
Bill Marsh (L)	6,660

Conservative majority 2,966. No change.

Wrekin
Gerry Fowler (Lab)	23,692
Bill Yates (C)	22,846

Labour majority 846. Labour gain.

Oswestry
John Biffen (C)	17,727
G.J. Costley (Lab)	13,011
T. Crowther (L)	6,010

Conservative majority 4,716. No change.

Ludlow
Jasper More (C)	19,603
John Gilbert (Lab)	16,123

Conservative majority 3,480. No change.

1970

General election June 18

Shrewsbury

Sir John Holt (C)	22,619
Peter Kent (Lab)	13,413
Ian Brodie (L)	5,960

Con maj 9,206. Con hold.

Wrekin

Tony Trafford (C)	26,282
Gerry Fowler (Lab)	25,764

Con majority 518. Con gain.

Oswestry

John Biffen (C)	20,361
Neil Turner (Lab)	10,801
Dr E. P. Cadbury (L)	8,963

Con majority 9,560. Con hold.

Ludlow

Jasper More (C)	22,104
David Nagington (Lab)	12,800
Christopher Oddie (L)	5,444

Con maj 9,304. Con hold.

1974

General election February 28

Shrewsbury

Sir John Langford Holt (C)	21,095
Bill Marsh (L)	14,914
Derek Woodvine (Lab)	11,536

Con majority 6,181. No change.

Wrekin

Gerry Fowler (Lab)	30,642
Dr Tony Trafford (C)	24,121
Ian Powney (L)	11,487

Lab majority 6,521. Lab gain.

Oswestry

John Biffen (C)	20,438
David Evans (L)	13,428
John Bishton (Lab)	9,685

Con majority 7,010. No change.

Ludlow

Jasper More (C)	18,674
Eric Robinson (L)	10,687
Geoffrey Martin (Lab)	9,035

Con majority 7,987. No change.

1974

Second general election October 10

Shrewsbury

Sir John Holt (C)	19,064
Bill Marsh (Lib)	13,643
Derek Woodvine (Lab)	11,504

Con majority 5,421. No change.

Wrekin

Gerry Fowler (Lab)	30,385
Philip Banks (C)	23,547
Wally Dewsnip (L)	8,442

Lab majority 6,838. No change.

Oswestry

John Biffen (C)	19,165
John Bishton (Lab)	10,751
David Evans (L)	10,623

Con majority 8,414. No change.

Ludlow

Jasper More (C)	17,124
Eric Robinson (L)	10,888
Dr John Marek (Lab)	8,353

Con majority 6,236. No change.

1979

General election May 3

Shrewsbury

Sir John Holt (C)	23,548
Alan Laurie (L)	13,364
John Bishton (Lab)	11,558

Con maj 10,844. No change.

Wrekin

Warren Hawksley (C)	32,672
Gerry Fowler (Lab)	31,707
Ray Yarnell (L)	7,331

Con maj 965. Con gain.

Oswestry

John Biffen (C)	23,551
Peter Sandland-Nielsen (Lab)	10,150
David Evans (L)	9,405

Con majority 13,446. No change.

Ludlow

Eric Cockeram (C)	20,906
Eric Robinson (L)	12,524
Ivor Wymer (Lab)	5,717
Raymond Adshead (National Front)	358
Frank Turner (Ind)	106

Con majority 8,382. Con hold.

1983

General election June 9

Shrewsbury

Derek Conway (C)	24,397
Anthony Bowen (Alliance)	15,773
Alan Mosley (Lab)	9,080

Con majority 8,624. Con hold.

Wrekin

Warren Hawksley (C)	22,710
Bruce Grocott (Lab)	21,379
Mark Biltcliffe (Alliance)	14,208

Con majority 1,331. Con hold.

North Shropshire

John Biffen (C)	28,496
David Evans (Alliance)	16,829
Miss Helen Jones (Lab)	7,860
John Phillimore (Referenda)	135

Con majority 11,667. Con hold.

Ludlow

Eric Cockeram (C)	26,278
David Lane (Alliance)	14,975
Phil Davis (Lab)	5,949

Con majority 11,303. Con hold.

1987

General election June 11

Shrewsbury

Derek Conway (C)	26,027
Robert Hutchison (L)	16,963
Mrs Liz Owen (Lab)	10,797
Geoff Hardy (Green)	660

Con maj 9,064. No change.

Wrekin

Bruce Grocott (Lab)	27,681
Warren Hawksley (C)	26,225
George Cook (SDP)*	10,737

Lab maj 1,456. Labour gain. *Social Democratic Party.

North Shropshire

John Biffen (C)	30,385
Gordon Smith (L)	15,970
Rob Hawkins (Lab)	11,866

Con maj 14,415. No change.

Ludlow

Christopher Gill (C)	27,499
David Phillips (L)	15,800
Keith Harrison (Lab)	7,724

Con maj 11,699. No change.

1992

General election April 9

Shrewsbury

Derek Conway (C)	26,681
Ken Hemsley (Lib Dem)	15,716
Liz Owen (Lab)	15,157
Geoff Hardy (Green)	677

Con majority 10,965. No change.

Wrekin

Bruce Grocott (Lab)	33,865
Elizabeth Holt (C)	27,217
Tony West (Lib Dem)	8,032
Robert Saunders (Green)	1,008

Lab majority 6,648. No change.

North Shropshire

John Biffen (C)	32,443
John Stevens (Lib Dem)	16,232
Rob Hawkins (Lab)	15,550

Con majority 16,211. No change.

Ludlow

Christopher Gill (C)	28,719
David Phillips (Lib Dem)	14,567
Beryl Mason (Lab)	11,709
Nic Appleton-Fox (Green)	758

Con majority 14,152. No change.

1997

General election May 1

Shrewsbury

Paul Marsden (Lab)	20,484
Derek Conway (C)	18,814
Anne Woolland (Lib Dem)	13,838
Dylan Barker (Referendum Party)	1,346
David Rowlands (UKIP)*	477
Alan Dignan (FCSS)	257
Alan Williams (People's Party Party)	128

Labour majority 1,670. Labour gain.

It was Labour's first win of the Shrewsbury seat in history.

*United Kingdom Independence Party. Alan Dignan was standing for "Farming, Country and Shooting Sports". The strange-sounding "People's Party Party" is not a mistake – it was the correct title of Alan Williams' stated affiliation.

Wrekin

Peter Bradley (Lab)	**21,243**
Peter Bruinvels (C)	18,218
Ian Jenkins (Lib Dem)	5,807

Labour majority 3,025. Notional Labour gain.

Wrekin seat was a reshaped seat under boundary changes, which Tories had been expected to win.

Telford

Bruce Grocott (Lab)	**21,456**
Bernard Gentry (C)	10,166
Nat Green (Lib Dem)	4,371
Christopher Morris (Referendum Party)	1,119

Labour majority 11,290. Notional Labour hold.

Telford seat was new seat under boundary changes, caused by splitting the Wrekin constituency into two. It meant Shropshire returned five MPs, instead of four.

North Shropshire

Owen Paterson (C)	**20,730**
Ian Lucas (Lab)	18,535
John Stevens (Lib Dem)	10,489
Denis Allen (Referendum Party)	1,764

Con majority 2,195. Con hold.

Ludlow

Christopher Gill (C)	**19,633**
Ian Huffer (Lib Dem)	13,724
Nuala O'Kane (Lab)	11,745
Tim Andrews (Green Party)	798
Tom Freeman-Keel (UKIP)	385

Con majority 5,909. Con hold.

2001

General election June 7

Shrewsbury

Paul Marsden (Lab)	**22,253**
Anthea McIntyre (C)	18,674
Jonathan Rule (Lib Dem)	6,173
Henry Curteis (UKIP)	1,620
Emma Bullard (Green)	931
James Gollins (Ind)	258

Labour majority 3,579. No change.

Wrekin

Peter Bradley (Lab)	**19,532**
Jacob Rees-Mogg (C)	15,945
Ian Jenkins (Lib Dem)	4,738
Denis Brookes (UKIP)	1,275

Labour majority 3,587. Labour hold.

Telford

David Wright (Lab)	**16,854**
Andrew Henderson (C)	8,471
Sally Wiggin (Lib Dem)	3,983
Nicola Brookes (UKIP)	1,098
Mike Jeffries (Socialist Alliance)	469

Labour majority 8,383. Labour hold.

North Shropshire

Owen Paterson (C)	**22,631**
Mike Ion (Lab)	16,390
Ben Jephcott (Lib Dem)	5,945
David Trevanion (UKIP)	1,165
Russell Maxfield (Ind)	389

Con majority 6,241. Con hold

Ludlow

Matthew Green (Lib Dem)	**18,620**
Martin Taylor-Smith (C)	16,990
Nigel Knowles (Lab)	5,785
Jim Gaffney (Green)	871
Phil Gutteridge (UKIP)	858

Lib Dem majority 1,630. Lib Dem gain.

First time in modern history the Conservatives had lost the Ludlow seat.

2005

General election May 5

Shrewsbury

Daniel Kawczynski (C)	**18,960**
Mike Ion (Lab)	17,152
Richard Burt (Lib Dem)	11,487
Peter Lewis (UKIP)	1,349
Emma Bullard (Green)	1,138
James Gollins (Ind)	126
Nigel Harris (SAWOPD)	84

Conservative majority 1,808. Conservative gain.

Nigel Harris was standing for "Seeks A Worldwide Online Participatory Democracy".

Wrekin

Mark Pritchard (C)	**18,899**
Peter Bradley (Lab)	17,957
Bill Tomlinson (Lib Dem)	6,608
Bruce Lawson (UKIP)	1,590

Conservative majority 942. Conservative gain.

Telford

David Wright (Lab)	**16,506**
Stella Kyriazis (C)	11,100
Ian Jenkins (Lib Dem)	4,941
Tom McCartney (UKIP)	1,659

Labour majority 5,406. Labour hold.

North Shropshire

Owen Paterson (C)	**23,061**
Sandra Samuels (Lab)	12,041
Steve Bourne (Lib Dem)	9,175
Ian Smith (UKIP)	2,233

Conservative majority 11,020. Conservative hold.

Ludlow

Philip Dunne (C)	**20,979**
Matthew Green (Lib Dem)	18,952
Nigel Knowles (Lab)	4,974
Jim Gaffney (Green)	852
Michael Zuckerman (UKIP)	783

Conservative majority 2,027. Conservative gain.

Demolitions

1900 The old Crown Hotel, Shrewsbury, was "rebuilt" – an inscription on the facade of the new Tudor-style hotel said "Rebuilt AD 1900".

1905 May 9, demolition of the 140ft Lodge Stack at Donnington Wood, more or less the last part demolished of the Lodge Blast Furnaces owned by the Lilleshall Company.

1906 St Peter's Finger pub at Dawley (apparently); reported January 27 that the old iron bridge at Buildwas had probably been demolished by the time of writing.

1912 Demolition began on the wooden bridge at Cressage around September.

1916 Chimney stack at Day's Works, Horsehay, on July 22.

1925 The English Bridge, Shrewsbury, essentially demolished to construct a new, wider bridge.

1926 On February 13 the WJ&SN mentioned the demolition of London House in connection with the widening of Wyle Cop. It stood on the corner of Wyle Cop and Dogpole.

1928 WJ&SN reported August 4 that a dangerous corner which had been the scene of many accidents would be removed when the road improvement "at present in progress" of the Cock crossroads, Wellington, was completed. The old children's home was in the course of demolition (it appears to have been opposite the Swan on the Dawley side of the junction).

1930 August 8 the SC had a pic of the felling of a chimney stack at Hanwood.

1931 October 28, the 154ft high Tibberton paper mill chimney felled. Also The Castle on the top of Haughmond Hill partially collapsed on May 27. On October 6 the old chimney stack at Wombridge Forge, Oakengates, felled.

1933 In September one of the oldest licensed houses in Wellington, the New Inn, Albert Road, which was "in course of demolition" for the purpose of creating improvements at Hiatt Ladies College. It was delicensed in 1930.

1935 The old Ship Inn, Bridge Street, Shrewsbury, demolished, as was the Exchange Vaults/Exchange Hotel, Shrewsbury, both to provide for a new inner loop road scheme linking the English and Welsh Bridges (reported WJ&SN October 19). Pix of the demolition in progress in the Barker Street area appeared in the SC on September 27. Benthall waterwheel was scrapped according to information by somebody actually involved in scrapping it. The pole on top of the Long Mynd appears to have been felled – an interview with landowner Max Wenner in the SC of June 4 refers to it being "mysteriously removed a short time ago".

1936 WJ&SN of February 1 had a pic of the demolition a block of old houses at Ketley. The Buttery, a black and white building in Shifnal, dismantled in March and later re-erected in Castlecroft, Wolverhampton.

1937 WJ&SN had pic on November 27 of an World War One tank at Wellington recreation ground being scrapped. SC had a pic on April 23, of a garden chapel in the grounds of Luciefelde House, Shrewsbury, which it said would "soon have to disappear" because of the construction of new houses.

1938 February: Lloyds Mansions, in The Square, Shrewsbury, dismantled, but in the event never re-erected (reported with picture February 5). September 1, 140ft chimney stack at the Coalport China Works felled. The Clement Memorial in The Dingle, Shrewsbury, taken down to be rebuilt at Greyfriars. On April 22 the SC had a story which referred to the demolition of a portion of Messrs Della Porta's premises in Shrewsbury for the purpose of extending the County Buildings.

1939 SC had a picture in on February 24 of the old Dog and Duck Inn, Jackfield, which it said would "shortly disappear." On July 28 SC had a picture of "two old hotels (which) are included in this block of property at the Castle Gates end of Chester Street which is being demolished for

road widening. The housebreakers commenced work on Monday." The hotels were the Swan Hotel and the Greyhound Hotel. Buildings were demolished about now to create a "Much Wenlock bypass" with a widened road near the Gaskell Arms (before and after pix were in the SC on June 2).

1940 SC reported February 16 that demolition work was in progress on the chimney of the old Snedshill iron foundry. SC reported March 8 that the Union Buildings at the corner of High Street and Mill Street, Wem, "are to be pulled down by the county council for road improvement."

1941 SC had a picture on May 16 saying: "Demolition of the last remaining portion of the Friary of St Austin, Shrewsbury, is in progress. The old walls, which date from the 13th century, are being pulled down to make room for a business development."

1944 Gibbon's Mansion, a 16th century house off Wyle Cop, Shrewsbury (according to a story in the SS on July 12, 1986). The Wesleyan School, Whitchurch, either in 1944 or 1945 (according to Mr George Wild of Trefonen, whose grandfather Arthur Wild was head at the school).

1946 December, one of the best-known landmarks in mid Shropshire, "The Man on the George", was blown from its high perch on the George Hotel, St Georges "during a recent gale" where it had been its sign for 115 years. It was formerly the figurehead of a large sailing vessel named the Royal George and was brought from Birkenhead to St Georges by horse and waggon by Mr John Downes, of Snedshill.

1948 A block of shops on the river side of Tontine Hill, Ironbridge, are said to have been demolished in 1948, although a picture showing flooding – quite possibly the 1948 floods – shows them to be missing, with the site fenced off. Possibly they were demolished then in 1947.

1950 The 125ft high chimney stack in the centre of the ruins of the Old Stirchley Forge and Nail Factory was felled on April 18. The grandstand of Much Wenlock racecourse was demolished in 1950 or the 1950s (according to a 2006 story from Wenlock historian David Cole).

1952 Badger Hall (according to a contributor to a Radio Shropshire programme).

1954 July 18, Tong Castle deliberately blown up, having been declared dangerous. Buildwas Park Hall deliberately blown up by successive explosions on August 3 and 4. It had been unoccupied since being derequisitioned in 1946. It had been the seat of the Acton-Moseley family. Wallop Hall, between Westbury and Welshpool, demolished. Shifnal Toll House was hit by a lorry around March 1954 (an October 15, 1955, report says it happened "some 18 months ago") and the building was afterwards pulled down for safety reasons.

1955 Old warehouse in St Alkmund's Square, opening up view of St Alkmund's Church, Shrewsbury – the demolition is reported as being in progress in the Shropshire Magazine of July. Sundorne Castle, near Shrewsbury – WJ&SN carried picture of the demolition taking place on October 1. Apley Castle – a picture was carried in WJ&SN of October 29 showing it intact but saying "It is now being demolished... which is expected to take three months to complete."

1956 June 16, WJ&SN reported that Viscount Boyne planned to demolish two thirds of Burwarton House, near Bridgnorth, because it was too costly to maintain. On June 23 the WJ&SN made reference to the demolition of an old furniture repository in Shrewsbury's Butcher Row which had left an open space. According to an owner of Hinstock Hall, Hinstock Hall was partially demolished in 1956.

1957 Probably old Barclays Bank on corner of St Mary's Street and Castle Street, Shrewsbury, as SC said July 5 that work to rebuild the bank would start "soon".

1958 On May 2 the SC reported that the West Midland Trustee Savings Bank in Market Street, Shrewsbury, was to be demolished and rebuilt in the next 12 months.

1960 The 15th century Swan Hotel, Wellington, after death watch beetle hit the structure – a story with a picture of the start of demolition was carried in the WJ&SN on January 16, saying it had "started to disappear this week." A new Swan was opened on November 1. The Raven Hotel, Shrewsbury, in the summer. On October 23, a giant 135ft high chimney stack at the Lilleshall Company's Priorslee Works was felled. The Shropshire Magazine of May 1960 said that demolition workers were "hard at work tearing down the old Harbourmaster's House which stands near the bridge in Low Town, Bridgnorth." It noted that Cann Hall had "recently" been demolished. The "Red Church" at Jackfield was demolished in August 1960 (according to Derrick Pountney of Broseley). SC of May 6 said demolition of the old Shrewsbury Post Office would "start this month".

1961 First stage of the demolition of the Shrewsbury general market hall. Demolition men moved in on July 24. First job was to demolish the clock tower. Chetwynd Hall was demolished this year. On April 21 the SC had a story implying that the 14th century Church Farm Cafe, Shrewsbury, was in the process of demolition. It said the timbers were being dismantled and it would be re-erected (it never was), and referred to the fate of Gibbon's Mansion and Lloyds Mansion, neither of which was re-erected.

1962 August 18, demolition taking place at Ketley to make way for new church and block of flats. The Crown Hotel, Shrewsbury (a report in the SC of June 8 said "the complete demolition of the Crown Hotel... is not expected to take more than another 10 days.") Hiatt College in Wellington may have been demolished by June – there is a report in on June 9 of the opening of a new filling station in King Street, Wellington, which may have been on the site. Empty shops in Wellington High Street were demolished on September 17 as part of the town's redevelopment plan. Sutton Mill, Shrewsbury.

1963 Church Stretton Market Hall/town hall demolished as unsafe in July. Broseley Town Hall in December. Demolition of Shrewsbury's old general market hall was completed during the year. It started around late June. On August 9, the SC reported that the Column Lodge was to be demolished. The George Hotel, Shrewsbury, must have been demolished about 1963 (there is an Express &Star pic dated April 6, 1962, saying that permission is being sought to demolish it but there were objections). The original Little Wenlock village hall was probably knocked down in 1963. The metal roof of Shrewsbury railway station was removed (according to historian Roy Pilsbury). Ladywood Tileries, Jackfield, demolished in 1963 according to mention in Broseley Local History Society newsletter.

1964 August 14, demolition of houses, some of the first to go for the redevelopment of Wellington town centre. It was at Tan Bank near the junction with Foundry Road. Reported with pic November 20, demolition of old buildings in progress at the rear of Market Street, Oakengates. The almshouses in St Mary's Street, Shrewsbury, in May 1964 according to David Trumper.

1965 Old rectory at Norton-in-Hales. Reported in SJ August 6 that "with the start of demolition of the shops at nos 41 and 43, a well known name will disappear after over 80 years unbroken association with Market Street, Oakengates... Mr W.H. Mawdsley started business in Market Street in about 1885... The shops either side of Mawdsley's, i.e. Paynes and John Bull army stores, will also be pulled down." It was part of the Oakengates redevelopment scheme.

1966 March 8, The Vine Hotel, Newport. The old Fox and Hounds pub in Shawbury. Parts of Bradford Street and Broadway, Shifnal.

1967 Belmont Hall, Wellington (according to Allan Frost). SS of Jan 10 had picture of the Granville Buildings, St Georges, where demolition was in progress. On March 6, the SS had a picture of the old Methodist Church in Oswestry in the final stages of demolition. On April 11 the SS carried pictures of workmen demolishing the Coalport railway bridge spanning the main road at Hadley, and also the same day the demolition of the railway bridge between Bridgnorth station and the tunnel below the town – both presumably taken the previous day, April 10. On June 28

(Continued page 122)

Barclays Bank, Wellington, in 1964

Corfton Hall

Castlefields, Shrewsbury,

Benthall waterwheel, one of the wonders of the Ironbridge Gorge

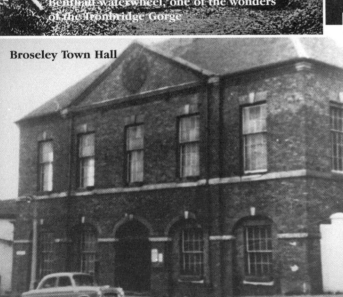

Broseley Town Hall

Sundorne Castle was knocked down in the mid 1950s

e Dog and Duck, Jackfield, in the floods of 1925

Manor House Hadley

A tragic victim of the 1960s

Larden Hall shortly before demolition

Despite attempts to preserve it, Ludlow's old Clifton cinema disappeared forever in the 1980s

CLIFTON

Essoldo Bingo

The old Shirehall, Shrewsbury, in 1968

the SS had a picture saying "work has started on removing the old canal bridge, Longdon-on-Tern. The road will be closed for two weeks while it is levelled and straightened." November 15, Broseley Methodist Church.

1968 Picture of the demolition of Constitution Hill School, Wellington, in SS September 26. Demolition started in Madeley to make way for a new shopping centre on January 31, starting with Madeley Rest Room. The 15th century Larden Hall, between Shipton and Easthope near Much Wenlock. Shrewsbury's old swimming baths were being demolished on December 31 (there was a SS picture this day saying "Demolition has started on Shrewsbury's old swimming baths which are being converted at a cost of £120,000"). Gasholders near Wellington cattle market – Shropshire Journal of October 25 said workers had moved in to raze the site.

1969 Merivale (also spelt Merival), Abbey Foregate, in September. In February, the Market and Corn Exchange in Whitchurch.

1970 The old Royal George pub, Shifnal. Dark Lane village (a booklet gives date as 1970/71 but a 1970 aerial pic shows work in progress). The Wrekin Beacon on August 26. Pole Cottage on the Long Mynd in April, with work starting on Good Friday. The Cuckoo Oak pub in Madeley. Work began on December 1 to demolish the old Shirehall. The Commercial Inn at Madeley.

1971 The old Shirehall in The Square, Shrewsbury, over several months at the start of the year. Seven shops in Ironbridge High Street in late September. April, the Norman chapel at Malinslee dismantled to make way for the new Telford town centre. The stones were stored opposite the Ever Ready works, Dawley. (according to a Telford Journal story and pic of 2007, it was rebuilt in 1984).

1972 Market Drayton town hall to make way for a new library and health centre. (was being demolished in February). Final act of demolition of five houses and two shops at Bayston Hill to make way for road widening scheme on the A49 (reported September 21).

1973 November, O.D. Murphy pop works on the A5, Wellington. The unique roof of the old Bridgnorth Cockpit Theatre was dismantled tile by tile for preservation at a new site (reported August 15), but no home had been found for the theatre. January 31, George Oakley's in Cheshire Street, Market Drayton.

1974 The old Plaza ballroom in Oswestry in December. April/May, the old Much Wenlock Primary School. The Castlefields redevelopment scheme in Shrewsbury, leading to much demolition of homes, was in full swing (report carried February 1). Demolition work was in progress at the old Wrekin Brewery in Market Street, Wellington (pic in Shropshire Star on November 21). The old carpet and wool factory off Cartway, Bridgnorth, a building dating from 1802 – this is according to a story carried the following year i.e. April 8, 1975.

1975 Demolition completed of The Plaza ballroom in Oswald Road, Oswestry. Demolition work completed at Oswestry's Great Western Railway station (picture on Feb 8). The 70-year-old 110ft tall chimney at the brickworks at Westbury on February 28. The 1925 wing of the Royal Salop Infirmary in October. The Grosvenor Cinema, Oakengates, on and around January 13.

1976 The Majestic Ballroom, Wellington – picture carried in SS of it in final stages of demolition on February 12. Probably also the old Regal Cinema, Craven Arms – SS story of February 17 said it was to be demolished to make way for a phone exchange. It had last been used as a cinema "about 10 years ago" and later for bingo and dancing, but had been derelict for nearly two years. On March 31 the footbridge linking High Town with Bridgnorth railway station was dismantled as the cost of repairs – £50,000 – was considered too much. The old Rainbow pub in North Street, Shrewsbury, in August. On April 1 there was a pic in SS where a new view from the Column at Shrewsbury had been created by the demolition of several large houses at the junction of London Road and Wenlock Road to make way for the new Meole-Column link road. Glass was removed from the front canopy of Shrewsbury

railway station. British Rail said it was to make the structure safe.

1977 Farcroft House, Market Drayton, (according to a book).

1978 St Andrew's School, Shifnal, in August.

1979 The Squirrel Hotel, Bridgnorth, in January and February.

1980 On February 19 a picture was carried saying "demolition work is nearly finished in Foundry Road, Wellington, in preparation for the planned sports centre." On June 10 a picture of Broome Hall in Oswestry was carried saying it was "being demolished to make way for housing". The 70ft chimney stack at the former laundry at the site of The Onny Press, Church Stretton, was demolished brick by brick (picture on August 19). Park Hall Camp, near Oswestry, was being returned to agriculture and recreational uses under a £670,000 reclamation scheme.

1981 Pitchcroft Bridge, over the A518 Wellington to Newport road, was "well under way" on February 10. Work began February 8 and expected to take two weeks. Oswestry's last air raid shelter, on the horse market, on May 8. Reported in SS September 10 that the Station stand at the Gay Meadow was being rebuilt in a £250,000 redevelopment. On November 29, the old Wellington swimming pool chimney was blown up.

1982 Morda House, Oswestry, after fire damage.

1983 Ironbridge A power station. First chimney stack was toppled in October, and demolition of rest was said to be taking place over succeeding two years.

1984 Reported with picture August 22, Charles Clark's car showroom in Chester Street, Shrewsbury, to make way for a new showroom and a major road widening scheme.

1985 Hengoed Church, on January 4. Demolished in a matter of hours.

1986 The larger of two gas holders in Wellington was due to be demolished in early March, with a second smaller tank being demolished later. A picture carried on April 8 showed it had been demolished by then. Ludlow Town Hall, during March. Shrewsbury's Beaconsfield club at Raven Meadows, in April, as part of the Hardanger shopping development at the Raven Meadows. An "old cinema and milk yard" in Waterloo Street, Ironbridge, March 28. Around August, buildings around the Upper Galdeford car park, Ludlow, including the old Portcullis pub.

1987 April, the old Clifton Cinema, Ludlow. AB Cranes, ie. the old Horsehay Works, there's a picture from on or about September 10.

1990 The Forest Glen was dismantled according to Allan Frost book The Wrekin Hill.

1993 The Free Bridge, Jackfield, work on demolition was (due to) begin the week beginning August 30.

1994 October (reported 18th) bulldozers moved in to demolish the main classroom and admin block of Hadley Manor School, but left 60 per cent for community use.

1995 The Beauchamp Hotel, Shrewsbury. The Ever Ready factory, Dawley, in June. The former Grand cinema in Wellington, around June.

1997 Work started to demolish the Tuckers building in Newport High Street, which had collapsed in 1989 and had been derelict since, being dubbed "the shame of Newport", on August 18. The old Salop Laundry in Laundry Lane, Shrewsbury, after an arson attack on May 31?

1998 August 4 – bulldozers move in to demolish the charity centre on the old Manor School, Hadley, site.

1999 The Green Man pub, Wellington, on January 30/31. It was reported in the SS on October 1 that the dilapidated wartime building at Higher Heath, used as a Roman Catholic chapel by Poles, in Manor Place, was to be demol-

ished. It would mark the end of an era for a Polish community living in the county since World War Two.

2000 April 3, the Empire Cinema, Shrewsbury (work had started, but was expected to last months). April 6, demolition was completed at Dawley Baptist Church, which was to be replaced by a new church and community centre. The old Bucks Head ground in Wellington was demolished – some had already taken place at the time of the last game on April 22.

2001 Grange Farm, Uffington, in January or February. The Shelton Hall Hotel, Shrewsbury, in April. Whitchurch's old cinema, the old Palladium, on July 10. Ludlow Town's ground at The Riddings (last game played c. July 31).

2002 Shifnal Cottage Hospital, about February 19. February 27, work begins on demolishing a Cold War nuclear bunker at RAF Shawbury. On March 13, the Atlas Foundry, Shrewsbury (it had been totally demolished by April 4). April, Top Ten Bingo Hall in New Street, Oswestry, closed and was soon demolished. July 29, Work started on demolishing St Austin's Street car park in Shrewsbury. August 29, The Century Cinema in Shrewsbury, formerly called the King's Hall Cinema (SS had a pic of early stages taken on August 7). Demolition (internally) of Telephone House, Shrewsbury, was under way on September 26, and work on proper demolition started October 16. Demolition completed on November 29. March 6, permission was given to demolish the old Somerfield supermarket in Market Drayton, despite English Heritage saying it should be preserved because of its hyperbolic roof.

2003 March, Wellington's last remaining traditional signal box. October, The Bush pub, Hadley. November, Wellington Methodist Church. Demolition of large parts of the Cross Houses Hospital began in September 2003 (according to book on its history by Mrs Freda Donnelly).

2004 The White House, Church Stretton, childhood home of Kenneth Horne, the radio star, must have been demolished about mid February. It was closed on September 2, 2003, when it was a residential and nursing home. On August 6, Highley Welfare Centre after over 70 years. Woodside flats were demolished c. August 11 – some doubt, as although work ceremonially started by Prince Philip in July, apparently it was months before demolition proper got under way. September 9, Demolition took place at the old New Yard premises of the Lilleshall Company in Gower Street, St Georges, to make way for new housing. February, planning permission was given to demolish Benbow House, Shrewsbury, as part of a scheme to redevelop the Furrows site.

2005 Shifnal squash club on July 25. Planning permission given c. May 24 to demolish one of Highley's oldest buildings, The Stone House, which was built in 1774. On September 7 and 8 a scout hut in the grounds of Criftins School in which General de Gaulle had once attended a church service during the war was taken down. October 18, demolition begins at the old nurses' home of the Robert Jones & Agnes Hunt Orthopaedic Hospital, Oswestry. On December 13 and 14, the landmark "Umbrella Tree" at the entrance to Arlescott Farm on the Broseley to Much Wenlock road was felled for safety reasons.

2006 April 7, Church Preen village hall. Dara Thai floating restaurant at Shrewsbury, starting c. June 7. July 12, The Harlescott Inn, Shrewsbury. Shrewsbury's old livestock market, by August 24. The old Cooper's boathouse at Longden Coleham in August following a fire at the site, now the Timberline timber yard. Work started c. August 29 on demolishing Woodside's local centre. Scheduled to take six weeks. Around September 21 demolition was taking place at the old MEB site at Ditherington. Demolition at Ellesmere's old Dairy Crest site at Ellesmere Wharf started about September 27. The Parkside Centre, Ketley, on October 6.

2007 Orleton Park School, Wellington, in January/February. Webster-Wilkinson/Coventry Gauge and Tool factory at Madeley, around March. Work started on demolishing the old Bridgnorth District Council Stanley Lane depot on April 25. July 7 and 8, first stage of dismantling Cosford signal box (for re-erection). *The Old School House, Shrewsbury, around February* (dismantled for re-erection).

Royal train carrying King George V and Queen Mary attracts crowds as it passes Welshampton in July 1911.

Prince Charles unveils a plaque at the 1979 Ironbridge bicentenary

A June 1982 visit to COD Donnington by the Queen

The Princess of Wales at NEC, Telford, 1988

Princess Margaret regularly used RAF Shawbury on her way to Keele University, where she was Chancellor

Prince Philip starts the demolition as part of the regeneration of Woodside, Telford, in 2003

Royal visits

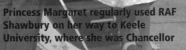

Royal visits

1900 July 24, the Duchess of York, Coalport China Works.

1907 November 23, King travelled through Newport in a car on his way from Stafford to Lilleshall Hall, where he had lunch. Big crowds in Newport. Planted a tree at Lilleshall Hall and afterwards caught the train at Newport in the afternoon to travel back to London.

1909 July 21, Princess Marie Louise of Schleswig-Holstein to Wellington, Shrewsbury and Welshpool. Stayed at Orleton Hall, Wellington. November 22 the Prince and Princess of Wales arrived at Powis Castle. On November 23 the princess visited Shrewsbury (St Mary's), Wenlock Abbey, Buildwas Abbey. November 24 she visited Ludlow, the first visit of any member of the royal family there since 1836. Her journey took in Bishop's Castle, Lydbury North, and return journey took in Shrewsbury. They left Powis Castle on November 26.

1911 Princess Alexander of Teck (n.b. Alexander is the correct spelling) on August 2 to open Shirlett Sanatorium, and also to Shrewsbury on August 4 when she visited St Mary's Church and popped in to some of the town's antique shops. On July 17 a royal train carrying King George V and Queen Mary passed through Ellesmere and Welshampton before changing engines at Whitchurch as part of a royal tour following the coronation. It was on its way from Machynlleth to Scotland.

1914 King George V to the Royal Show in Shrewsbury July 3, laid foundation stone of the new library at Shrewsbury School, and inspected the naval and military veterans. Also conferred the title of "Royal" on the Salop Infirmary.

1920 July 16, King and Queen passed through Shrewsbury Station on their way to south Wales. Stopped there while the engine was changed.

1921 The Queen, with Princess Mary, arrived at Shotton Hall to stay with her brother and sister in law, the Marquess and Marchioness of Cambridge. She went to Brogyntyn the following day, and on Saturday August 13 passed through Shrewsbury on way to Weston Park. On the way back the Queen stopped in Shrewsbury and went round some antique shops. She also went to St Mary's Church and the old council house. On the 15th she visited Pitchford Hall and went through Shrewsbury on the way to Adcote Hall.

1922 February 28, Princess Mary and Viscount Lascelles arrived at Shifnal railway station to be greeted by huge crowd after their wedding at Westminster Abbey and went to Weston Park for their honeymoon. They went back to London and on to Florence on March 8 but returned to visit Burwarton Hall on June 3 and Ludlow on June 6.

1923 Prince of Wales broke his return journey from Wales to London in Shrewsbury to present an award to the Ironbridge platoon of the 4th KSLI. (reported in WJ&SN on November 3, so probably happened November 2 or November 1).

1925 July 8, Princess Helena Victoria visited Shrewsbury and Wellington. August 5, the Queen of Romania visited Shrewsbury.

1926 November 3 the Duke of York opened National Institute of Poultry Husbandry at Edgmond. November 6, Princess Mary opened the extension of the Shirlett Sanatorium, the new wing of the Eye, Ear and Throat Hospital at Shrewsbury, and also visited Shropshire Technical Schools for Girls at Radbrook.

1927 August 11, Queen arrived in Shropshire on a visit to her brother the Marquess of Cambridge and the Marchioness of Cambridge at Shotton Hall. August 17 she visited Shrewsbury Floral Fete. She visited various places in the county and left on August 18.

1929 March 20, Princess Helena Victoria, granddaughter of Queen Victoria, to Shrewsbury and Wellington on behalf of the YMCA.

1932 January 22, Prince George for a series of cere-monies at the Orthopaedic Hospital, Gobowen. June 21 the Prince of Wales visited Shrewsbury to take part in the 50th anniversary of the removal of Shrewsbury School to its present site.

1933 The Princess Royal opened Shrewsbury bypass May 23.

1935 April 25, Duke of York presented new colours to the 2nd Battalion KSLI in the Quarry before a crowd of nearly 60,000.

1939 April 15, Princess Marie Louise to Shrewsbury. Went to Girl Guides gathering. On July 25, Queen Mary received a great welcome from Cosford RAF personnel and residents on her way to Patshull House to be the guest of the Earl of Dartmouth.

1940 April 1, Princess Royal inspected women war workers in Shrewsbury and Wellington, having spent the weekend in the district. April 19, King and Queen visited RAF Cosford.

1941 March 19, Princess Royal visited a Women's Land Army hostel at Shifnal. May 22 the Princess Royal, as president of the Girl Guides, paid visits of inspection at Church Stretton and Shrewsbury.

1942 March 10, Princess Royal inspected members of the ATS at Shrewsbury. July 16, King George VI and Queen Elizabeth to COD Donnington. They also visited RAF High Ercall on the same day when they were given a demonstration of Turbinlite equipment.

1943 September 20, Duchess of Kent inspected the Derwen Cripples Training College and the Orthopaedic Hospital, Oswestry. April 10 the Princess Royal attended a rally of the Women's Land Army in Shrewsbury and visited Copthorne barracks. December 7, Princess Royal visited various hospitals in Shropshire.

1944 March 31, Princess Royal toured Shropshire ATS depots.

1946 May 29, Princess Royal visited COD Donnington.

1949 July 6, Princess Elizabeth and Duke of Edinburgh to Royal Show, Shrewsbury.

1950 Duke of Gloucester started two day tour of Shropshire youth clubs on June 19.

1951 June 8, Princess Elizabeth to Newport and district to perform a double opening ceremony at the new hall of residence at Harper Adams Agricultural College and the National Recreation Centre, Lilleshall Hall.

1952 October 24, Queen and Duke of Edinburgh to Shrewsbury School in its 400th anniversary year. She cut the tape to open a new terrace to the main school building. First official visit to Shrewsbury by reigning monarch since 1914.

1953 May 20, Duke and Duchess of Gloucester to the Shropshire and West Mid Agricultural Society's 65th show at Shrewsbury.

1955 June 30, Duke and Duchess of Gloucester to the National Hunter Show at the West Mid Showground, Shrewsbury.

1956 Princess Margaret flew in to RAF High Ercall on May 26 to be taken by car to Wolverhampton on a royal visit, and left later by the same aerodrome.

1957 May 28, Duchess of Kent to Bridgnorth to take part in the celebrations marking the 800th anniversary of the granting of the Charter of Incorporation of the Borough, and afterwards went to Much Wenlock and Hadley Castle Works. On May 29 she went to Dames Agnes Hunt Memorial Village and Shropshire Orthopaedic Hospital, and also to Oswestry School. (n.b during her visit she made a special detour through Jackfield). August 21 Princess Alice, Countess of Athlone, visited Shrewsbury Flower Show. November 27, Princess Margaret arrived at RAF Shawbury in a Viking, leaving immediately for a two-day visit to Staffordshire.

1958 Duke and Duchess of Gloucester were at the West Mid Show, Shrewsbury, on May 21. June 11, the Princess Royal paid a surprise visit to a rally of the Shropshire Federation of Women's Institutes at Henley Hall, Ludlow. April 14 Princess Margaret touched down at RAF Shawbury en route for a royal engagement in Staffordshire.

1959 June 30, Princess Margaret arrived at RAF Shawbury, went to the Royal Normal College for the Blind at Rowton Castle, also went to a service at Ludlow, and to Bishop's Castle High School and Craven Arms, passing the Arbor Tree at Aston-on-Clun on the way. October 22, the Duchess of Gloucester visited RAF Shawbury.

1961 May 2, Queen Mother, Princess Margaret, and Anthony Armstrong-Jones arrived at RAF Shawbury on their way to Keele Hall. On May 4 the Princess Royal arrived at Davenport House, Worfield, home of her sister-in-law the Dowager Lady Boyce, staying several days. On May 6 (maybe also 5) Princess Alexandra inspected a regional rally of the junior Red Cross at Shrewsbury and also visited Little Wenlock.

1962 April sometime, the Duke of Gloucester, president of the National Association of Boys Clubs, visited clubs at Bridgnorth and Newport. July 5, Princess Margaret and Lord Snowdon paid a flying visit to the Grove School, Market Drayton, on their way to RAF Shawbury (after a trip to Staffordshire). October 25, Princess Marina, Duchess of Kent, to the Robert Jones and Agnes Hunt Orthopaedic Hospital.

1963 May 1, Queen Mother to the Harper Adams Agricultural College at Edgmond, and travelled on to Shrewsbury.

1964 Princess Royal on June 25 to open the new Monkmoor to Ditherington link road, and open the new TA headquarters at Sundorne and present new colours to the 4th Battalion KSLI. December 8, Princess Margaret and her husband Lord Snowdon flew out from RAF Shawbury after an engagement at Keele University, of which she was Chancellor.

1965 Princess Margaret arrived at RAF Shawbury on June 30 on her way to Keele University.

1966 June 29, Princess Margaret arrived at RAF Shawbury on her way to North Staffordshire, and on June 30 she visited Quinta School, near Oswestry, an approved school run by Dr Barnardo's Homes. July 23, Princess Marina had a three hour tour of RAF Shawbury.

1967 March 17, Queen officially opened the new £1.9 million Shirehall in Shrewsbury. Also visited Sutton Hill. Prince Philip to Park Hall Camp on May 26. Princess Margaret landed at RAF Shawbury on June 28 on her way to Keele University.

1968 Princess Margaret unveiled commemorative gates at Adams' Grammar School, Newport, on May 30. July 5, The Duchess of Gloucester opened the £750,000 maternity hospital at Copthorne.

1969 September 10, Princess Anne officially opened the High Ercall Multi Occupational Training and Education Centre. The Queen Mother came to Shropshire on November 4, arriving at RAF Shawbury and then a programme in Shrewsbury which included the Sir John Moore Barracks and the Katharine Elliot School for handicapped children.

1970 June 29 Princess Margaret visited Coalbrookdale, Priorslee Hall, the Eaton Yale and Towne factory at Halesfield, had tea at Oakengates Town Hall. October 13, Princess Margaret visited Condover Hall School for the Blind.

1972 April 27, Queen Mother and Princess Margaret arrived at RAF Shawbury on their way to the Potteries. July 14, Prince Philip visited Brookside, officially opened the £1 million Court Centre in Madeley, and also saw the Iron Bridge.

1974 Queen Mother visited the Sir John Moore Barracks at Shrewsbury on April 24.

1975 Queen opens Coton Hill House, Shrewsbury, on May 21. She also came to the 100th West Mid Show at Shrewsbury on that date. May 29, Prince Philip made a flying visit to Shrewsbury and Apley Park, near Bridgnorth, to see the work of youngsters involved in the Duke of Edinburgh Award Scheme. June 3, Princess Anne to Annscroft Stables and saw blind or partially blind riders from the Royal Normal College for the Blind. July 1, Princess Margaret officially opened the new pavilion and squash courts at The Grove ground in Market Drayton.

1976 Princess Anne officially opened Bridgnorth Sport and Leisure Centre on November 23. Also, the same day, opened the new Oswestry sports and leisure centre.

1977 Princess Margaret at RAF Shawbury c. March 18 on her way to Keele. New Copthorne General Hospital at Shrewsbury officially opened by Prince Charles on November 17 and renamed the Royal Shrewsbury Hospital, the Queen having given her consent for the name.

1979 Prince Charles to Ironbridge as part of bicentenary celebrations on July 5.

1980 Princess Margaret and UN Secretary General Dr Kurt Waldheim arrived at RAF Shawbury May 22 on their way to Keele University. Princess Margaret was also flown in to RAF Shawbury by Prince Charles on June 30 to open officially Shawbury's new scout and guide centre. October 24, Prince Charles rode at Ludlow racecourse, watched by future wife Lady Diana Spencer.

1981 Second phase of Telford town centre was opened by the Queen on Friday November 13. On July 17, Prince Charles was greeted by 20,000 people on the streets of Shrewsbury just 12 days before his marriage. He arrived at Shrewsbury by train at the start of a journey to Llansantffraid to open a £1 million animal feed mill. There was a civic reception for him.

1982 Queen paid a private visit to COD Donnington on June 4. She was Colonel in Chief of the Royal Army Ordnance Corps. She officially opened the new Central Processing Building. She arrived at RAF Shawbury and travelled by road, through High Ercall.

1983 On June 23 the Queen Mother had a private visit to RAF Shawbury.

1984 Princess Diana made her first official visit to Shropshire on December 11 when she came to Shrewsbury, where thousands turned out to see her. Some sang and waved, chanting her name. She visited Shrewsbury's Multi Skills Youth Training Centre in Castle Court, and later Condover School for the Blind. Princess Anne opened Telford Ice Rink on October 10. Prince Edward worked alongside other students during excavations at Wroxeter Roman City (reported August 16). Princess Margaret visited the refurbished Shrewsbury library on May 18 and also Whitchurch. She also came to Shawbury c. February 3 on her way to Keele University.

1985 Princess Margaret to Newport (Harper Adams and Adams Grammar) on May 16.

1986 January 7, Prince Edward spent four hours filming in the wind and snow-swept hills near Cardington as part of a series for the Duke of Edinburgh's award scheme. He was in a blizzard on top of the Lawley before returning to the Royal Oak pub in Cardington where he chose a speciality on the menu, Shropshire Fidget Pie. March 19, Princess Anne took part in horse trials at Downton Castle, Ludlow. July 11, Queen was driven through Shrewsbury on her way to RAF Shawbury after a royal visit to Mid Wales. The Queen Mother carried out a farewell royal tour of the Sir John Moore Barracks in Copthorne Road, Shrewsbury, on

June 28 for the final passing out parade at the Light Infantry Depot, where training was ending after 105 years.

1987 Prince Philip to GKN Sankey, Hadley, May 20. March 6, Prince Charles went to Blists Hill, but had to cut out Coalbrookdale from his programme because bad weather had disrupted his helicopter trip, to the disappointment of children waiting there. He inaugurated the wrought ironworks at Blists Hill (in his role as patron of the Ironbridge Gorge Museum). Princess Anne took part in a charity race event at Ludlow racecourse on April 16. Duchess of Kent visited Robert Jones and Agnes Hunt Hospital on November 4. On November 25 Princess Margaret was at RAF Shawbury on her way to Stoke on Trent.

1988 November 2, Princess Di opened NEC in Telford. April 26, the Princess Royal, Princess Anne, visited Lilleshall National Sports Centre, and opened the Old Ben Homes at Lilleshall. On June 7, the Princess Royal officially opened the Festival Town Centre, Market Drayton.

1989 Prince Charles opened the Museum of the River in Ironbridge on May 8. Princess Anne visited Shrewsbury on June 14 to watch disabled riders at the West Mid showground and Prince Philip opened Shrewsbury's £10 million link road and new £2 million district council headquarters in Wem on July 21. On September 25, the Princess Royal opened Shropshire Rural Housing Trust's sheltered development at Shawbury and also visited MOTEC at High Ercall, where she went on the skidpan.

1990 Princess Anne, The Princess Royal, opened officially Telford hospital on February 12. It became known afterwards at the Princess Royal Hospital. Princess Margaret toured RAF Shawbury for the first time on May 23 (she had only previously passed through).

1991 April 16, the Duchess of York opens the new social education centre at Telford College of Arts and Technology; visits Innage Grange at Bridgnorth; and refurbished barracks at Shrewsbury. May 17, the Princess Royal to RAF Cosford, the West Mid Show at Shrewsbury, and the Save the Children Fund shop at Wyle Cop, Shrewsbury.

1993 July 14, Prince Charles visited Waste Refineries International at Eaton, between Bishop's Castle and Craven Arms.

1994 Princess Margaret was given a bright and breezy welcome on October 13 as she arrived to open a new court complex in Shrewsbury. She was greeted by over 150 brownies and guides before going on a tour of the new magistrates courts in Preston Street.

1995 Princess Royal arrived at RAF Shawbury on July 7 to present awards and certificates to graduates from the ATC course and Advanced Flying Training course.

1996 A visit of the Duchess of Kent to Oswestry and Market Drayton on March 12 was abandoned when driving snow and poor visibility grounded the royal helicopter. July 9, Duke of Edinburgh paid a flying visit to RAF Cosford to see how the base was operating in a new training role and the facilities on offer.

1998 Princess Anne to the Princess Royal Hospital and BOD Donnington on January 23, and visited Shropshire again – and the Shropshire Star at Ketley – on May 15.

2000 March 15, Princess Anne to the Orthopaedic Hospital at Gobowen to see the Midland Centre for Spinal Injuries.

2001 February 21, Prince Charles came to Boscobel House, following in the footsteps of Charles II in the 350th anniversary year of the King hiding in the royal oak. He plants a sapling to ensure the future of the royal oak tradition. May 15, Princess Anne officially opens the Secret Hills Discovery Centre at Craven Arms and also unveils a £2 million new air ambulance at RAF Cosford. August 25, Zara Phillips, daughter of the Princess Royal, spotted clubbing at the Park Lane nightclub in Shrewsbury. October 15, The

Duchess of York opened a £55 million extension to the Muller factory, Market Drayton.

2002 December 12, the Prince of Wales's opening of the new £650,000 Jubilee stand at Ludlow racecourse was scuppered at the last minute because a snowstorm stopped his helicopter from getting there.

2003 Earl and Countess of Wessex to Cleobury Mortimer, Much Wenlock and Shrewsbury on March 31. July 10, Queen and Duke of Edinburgh in their first joint official visit to the county since 1952. Duke signalled the demolition of derelict flats at Woodside, which heralded the beginning of a major regeneration scheme on the estate. Later they opened the Ludlow Library and Museum Resource Centre. Prince Charles visited Ludlow racecourse on November 24 after a previous visit was postponed because of the weather.

2004 April 2, Princess Anne opened an extension at the Wakeman School, Shrewsbury, and unveiled a plaque at the Shrewsbury flood defences and then went to Ditton Priors and on to open a new clubhouse at Chelmarsh Sailing Club. June 25 Princess Anne made a whistlestop visit to RAF Cosford and Harper Adams University College.

2005 October 31, Princess Anne opens a sports block at Telford College of Arts and Technology.

2006 c. May 8, Princess Anne visited the Harper Adams University College. October 19, Princess Anne opened the new Old Hall School on the Wrekin College Campus.

2007 Princess Anne opened the new National Cold War Exhibition at the RAF Museum, Cosford, on February 7. Prince Charles visited RAF Shawbury on May 3. October 3, Princess Anne due to make several visits in the county, including officially opening the Harris Centre at Walford and North Shropshire College, Baschurch.

> *This is not a complete list of royal visits as some, particularly involving minor royals, have been left out.*

SHROPSHIRE
& MID WALES
£1¼m
CANCER FUND

Miss
Shropshires

Miss Shropshires

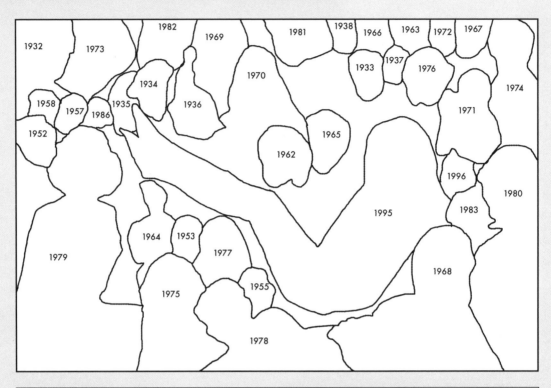

Miss Shropshires

1932 Mrs J C Beckett, of Bayston Hill.
1933 Miss Kathleen Worsley, of Much Wenlock.
1934 Miss Irene Meloy, of Market Drayton.
1935 Miss Dorothy Lewis Price, of Dawley.
1936 Miss Joyce Hartshorne, of Montford Bridge.
1937 Miss Muriel Evans, aged 20, of Mountfields, Shrewsbury.
1938 Miss Hilda Bunce, 18, of Worthen.
1952 Miss Rosemary Sharp, of Shop Lane, Rodington (first Miss Shropshire since 1938).
1953 Miss Kathleen Bright, 26, of Dorrington.
1954 ?
1955 Miss Beryl Lewis, 16, of Moston Road, Shrewsbury.
1956 Mrs Gwen Owens, 21, of Hunter Street, Mountfields, Shrewsbury. She was formerly Miss Gwen New of Cross Houses – she had married less than a month before taking the title.
1957 Mrs Gwen Owens, for the second successive year. Her name also sometimes appears as Gwenda in contemporary newspapers.
1958 Mrs Edith Easom, 22, of Albert Road, Shrewsbury.
1959 Miss Carol Lewis, 17, of Wem.
1960 Miss Carol Lewis, of Wem, for the second year.
1961 Mrs Gwenda Owens, 26, of Preston Street, Shrewsbury, for the third time.
1962 Pat Fisher, 17, of Whitchurch.
1963 Mrs Irene Claffey, 24, of Calcott Lane, Bicton Heath.
1964 Mrs Joan Taylor, 24, of Jubilee, Astley.
1965 Mrs Shirley Wallis, 22, of Harlescott Grange.

1966 Miss Angela Holden, 19, of Monkmoor Road Avenue, Shrewsbury.
1967 Mrs Margaret Weston, of Manor Gardens, Dawley.
1968 Mrs Carol Wainwright, 26, of High Street, Wem, for the third time – she had won the competition as Miss Carol Lewis in 1959 and 1960.
1969 Miss Belinda Banks, 18, of Darwin Gardens, Shrewsbury.
1970 Pat Mason, of Gravel Hill, Ludlow.
1971 Miss Valerie Titley, 17, of Summer Crescent, Wrockwardine Wood. During her year's reign she married, becoming Mrs Valerie Karcz.
1972 Patricia Wilkes, 26, of Mendip Close, Little Dawley.
1973 Miss Glenda Allan, 16, of Greenacres Way, Newport.
1974 Lynda Hambleton, of Donnington.
1975 Janet Whittaker, 22, who lived near Farndon.
1976 Miss Christine Parker, 20, of Tilley Green, Wem.
1977 Debbie Pragnell, 18, of Newport.
1978 Heather Couch, 27, from Rossett, Wrexham.
1979 Miss Catrin Bevan, 18, of Pontesbury.
1980 Angela Tanner, 19, of Pontdolgoch, near Caersws.
1981 Lyn Corbett, 21, of Much Wenlock.
1982 Sharon Lloyd, aged 20, of Stirchley Village.
1983 Kendra Taylor, 19, of Dawley.
1984 ?
1985 ?
1986 Deborah Mitchell, 20, of Telford.
1995 Bianca Mustone, aged 18, from Bridgnorth.
1996 Lynsey Perks, 18, of Little Dawley (some reports give Stirchley).

CHRONOLOGY

1900

January 21: Major C.B. Childe of Kinlet Hall killed in action in the Boer War during the advance of General Buller's force to the relief of Ladysmith.

January 24: The Hon Neville Windsor Hill-Trevor of Chirk, Lt Lawley and Lt Hugh McCorquodale, of Cound, were killed in action at Spion Kop.

July 31: Fourteen men of the Shropshire Regiment killed and 45 injured in the Transvaal through a supply train leaving the rails.

October 8: First patients enter Florence House, Baschurch, founded by Agnes Hunt, a convalescent home for sick and crippled children.

November 13: Cinematograph entertainment plays to large and enthusiastic audience at Dawley Town Hall.

November 18: The parish church of Stokesay – restored as a memorial to the Rev J.D. La Touche – reopened by the Bishop of Hereford.

1901

January 1: A new pumping station in connection with sewerage works opened in Coleham, Shrewsbury.

February 4: First students admitted at the new Technical School for Girls at Radbrook, Shrewsbury.

February 27: 50 out of 51 members of Salop County Council elected without opposition.

March: Major work at Shrewsbury railway station sees new ground floor excavated.

April 8: Miss Muriel Darby of Little Ness laid the foundation stone of Trinity Hall, Coalbrookdale.

May 9: Welcome home at Shrewsbury to the Shropshire Service Co of Volunteers on their return from South Africa.

September 26: Opening of Harper Adams Agricultural College, Edgmond.

October 17: William Evans of Ironbridge won the Quoiting Championship of England.

November 1: General Baden-Powell enthusiastically received during a short stay at Shrewsbury Railway Station.

c.November 11 (reported in WJ&SN November 16 as happening "this week"): Huge derelict boat Sabrina breaks free from its moorings near the Welsh Bridge, Shrewbury, and crashes and is pinned against the bridge.

1902

February 24: British convoy including the 13th (Shropshire) Imperial Yeomanry captured by Boers.

March 5: Opening of a new Free Library and museum in Whitchurch.

March 18: Richard Wigley hanged at Shrewsbury for murder of Miss Eliza Bowen at the Lion Inn, Westbury.

April 16: Destructive fire at Hinstock National Schools.

June 30: Coronation bonfires lit on hills over Shropshire.

August 24: A portion of the Iron Bridge fell into the River Severn.

August 26: Opening of Dawley Coronation Grounds.

October 24 New church dedicated at All Stretton.

October 25: Lady Meyrick opens new reservoir at Church Stretton.

December 14: Ten men hurt in collapse of portion of an old bridge at Shrewsbury station.

DEATHS: August 14, Mr A. Salwey, first chairman of Salop County Council.

1903

January 20: Inquiry into corrupt practices during the municipal election in Castlefields Ward, Shrewsbury, exposes widespread bribery and corruption in Shrewsbury council elections going back at least 30 years. (Conservative victor F.G. Morris was unseated and nine people were jailed in July 1903 for 21 days. Some 300 electors were disenfranchised for five years.)

May 23: Formation at Shrewsbury of the Shropshire Association for Protection Against Reckless Motor Driving.

May 30: Buffalo Bill's Wild West show came to Shrewsbury in a field next to the barracks in Copthorne.

July 19: 500th anniversary of the Battle of Shrewsbury commemorated.

September: New County police offices open at Swan Hill. Shrewsbury.

October 10: Ironbridge Quoit Club won the English championship for the third year running.

Late October: Worst floods for years. Frankwell flooded c. October 27.

December 16: Roof of Wellington RC Church collapsed.

December 31: By this date Salop County Council had registered 65 cars, and 28 motorcycles, and had issued 105 licences.

1904

January 1: New Motor Car Act came into force. Shropshire's designated licence plates letters were "AW". AW 1 went to Captain Foster, of Woodcote Hall, Newport.

March 7: Lady Forester Hospital, Much Wenlock, opened.

April 26: Three men killed at Granville pit, St Georges.

April 29: Buffalo Bill's Wild West show visited Wellington, watched by around 10,000 people.

May 16: Alfred Ditcher, aged four, killed by a motor car at Pant. Believed to be Shropshire's first motor car fatality.

July 3: Slight earthquake shock in several towns and villages in Shropshire.

July 22: Boer War memorial to Shropshire soldiers unveiled in Shrewsbury.

July 25: Winston Churchill spoke at Ellesmere and Powis Hall, Oswestry, in support of the Liberal candidate in the Oswestry by-election.

August 18: An airship took off from Shrewsbury Flower Show, the first airship flight in the West of England. The woman passenger Miss G. Bacon was the first woman to fly in a British airship. It landed safely at Admaston.

September 25: Disorder at the Primitive Methodist Chapel, Wrockwardine Wood, when two rival preachers attempt to conduct the service.

November 12: Mr Hildebrand Harmsworth opened the new grandstand on the football ground at Wellington, seating 400.

November 14: Electric lighting works opened at Church Stretton by the Hon Mrs Mostyn.

DEATHS: June 4, Joseph Della Porta, Shrewsbury businessman; November 23, the Rev Holland Sandford, rector of Eaton-under-Heywood, after whom Sandford Avenue in Church Stretton is named.

1905

January 17: Wellington free library opened to the public – the reading room had opened on May 18, 1904.

January 18: Five schoolchildren die falling through ice at Kynaston's Pool, Bettisfield.

January 19: Wem Town Hall, also known as Wem new market hall, formally opened.

April 15: Ex-Wellington Town player Harry Hampton scores the two winning goals as Aston Villa win the English Cup.

May 30: Four die in a fire in Cheshire Street, Market Drayton, at the shop of Frank Parker, saddler and harness maker. They were Parker, his two children and their nurse. His wife survived.

July 27: The Rev W.G. Haslehurst, Rector of West Felton, killed while mountaineering in the Swiss Alps.

August 14: Opening of the Morgan Free Library, Wem.

September 17: Sunday School classes and Bible classes went to Wrockwardine Wood Methodist Chapel to find they were locked out. They processed to the nearby Cinder Hill and held open air services, attended by hundreds. It was the climax of a rumbling internal dispute which led to a schism in the church lasting decades.

First week or so of October: Six die at Broad Oak, Albrighton, Shrewsbury, in outbreak of diphtheria.

October 23: General Booth, founder of the Salvation Army, visits Madeley.

November 10: Trefonen "non-provided" school destroyed by fire.

November 20: The Perseverance Ironworks, Shrewsbury, destroyed by fire.

December 5: Shrewsbury School severely damaged by fire.

DEATHS: January 5, John Plimmer, born at Upton Magna, one of the founders of New Zealand. December 5, Henry Eckford, the "Sweet Pea King" of Wem. Reported May 13, Quartermaster Sergeant William Charles Parker, of Woodhouse Lane, Batchcott, Richard's Castle, who fought at Rorke's Drift in the Zulu War. November 22, Sergeant Major J.I. Nunnerley, originally from North Shropshire and one of the survivors of the Charge of the Light Brigade.

1906

January 1: Balderton Hall, a largely Elizabethan mansion near Harmer Hill, severely damaged by fire.

January 10: Prime Minister Sir Henry Campbell-Bannerman addressed a meeting of Liberals in Shrewsbury, at the general market hall, but was continually interrupted by some of the 6,000 crowd and gave up his speech after half an hour.

January 20: Joseph Chamberlain addressed a meeting of about 6,000 at the Castle Car Works, Hadley.

February 25: Opening of Wrockwardine Wood Central Hall.

March 17: Huge mill fire at Eaton upon Tern at the mill run by John Heatley.

May 1: Rail-motor trains began running on the Great Western line between Wellington and Craven Arms.

June 27: An earthquake affected parts of Shropshire and Wales.

August 19: Opening of new Roman Catholic church in Wellington.

December 4: Electric light inaugurated at Ludlow.

December 25: It was a white Christmas, with snow falling on Christmas evening.

DEATHS: March 6, General Sir W.F. Gatacre in the Upper Sudan.

1907

January 10: Opening of Newport Parish Church Room in New Street, Newport.

January 10: Opening of Oakengates Parish Hall.

Reported January 26: "The Severn at Shrewsbury is frozen over, and skating in various parts of the district is being indulged in by large numbers."

February: An Order by Shropshire County Council compelling dog owners to put their dogs on a lead or chain when out between the hours of sunset and sunrise caused widespread protest. It was somewhat relaxed in April.

February 19: Mr Rowland Hunt, in a speech in the House of Commons which resulted in his being temporarily banned by the Unionist Whips, vigorously condemned Mr Balfour's "wobbling" policy on the fiscal question.

May 20: Serious fire at Messrs Morris & Co in High Street, Bridgnorth.

June 22: Restored Colours of the Shropshire Regiment replaced in St Chad's Church, Shrewsbury.

September 8: The Rev Dr S. Parkes Cadman preached at Wellington Wesleyan Church during a visit to his old Shropshire haunts.

October 15: 18 die in rail accident in Shrewsbury.

November 1: Mr Lloyd-George, President of the Board of Trade, addresses a meeting of Liberals in the Anstice Hall, Madeley.

DEATHS: February 21, in the sinking of the Berlin off the Hook of Holland, Arthur Frederick Herbert, aged 40, a King's Foreign Messenger, of Orleton Hall, Wellington.

1908

January 20: General Baden-Powell explained his "Boy Scouts" scheme to an audience at Shrewsbury.

January 26: Opening of a RC church at Ludlow.

April 16: Annie Lloyd, aged 75, a blacksmith's widow, strangled at her home at Ffynnondeg, Sychtyn, near Oswestry. An accused man was later acquitted.

June 25: Mr Milnes Gaskell of Wenlock Abbey made a Privy Councillor in the King's Birthday Honours list.

July 9: The Rev F.E.B. Wale, vicar of Holy Trinity, Shrewsbury, killed by a fall in the Alps, Switzerland.

July 20: Opening of new workhouse infirmary at Newport.

Reported July 25: Shrewsbury's Hercules statue painted by pranksters.

September 30: Farmers from 22 counties in England and Wales attend a meeting in Wellington over a meat warranty dispute with butchers. Moves are set afoot to form a united farmers' body – it is the start of the formation of the National Farmers Union.

December 24: Arthur Phillips of Market Drayton patents his 'air navigation machine'. He is probably Shropshire's pioneer aviator.

DEATHS: April 24, W.S. Kenyon-Slaney, of Hatton Grange, near Shifnal, the MP for Newport; October 25, the Rev Preb George Edward Yate, vicar of Madeley, in his 84th year.

1909

January 22: New pump station opened at the Conduit Head, Radbrook, to increase the water supply of Shrewsbury.

February 4: Around 4,000 at the Shrewsbury market hall to hear Austen Chamberlain speak.

April 2: Serious fire at Messrs J & B. Blower house furnishers at Pride Hill, Shrewsbury.

April 21: Serious fire at Marrington Hall, near Chirbury.

May 10: Opening of Shrewsbury Isolation Hospital.

May 28: Decided at a public meeting in Shrewsbury to reconstruct the Old Potteries Railway Line and work it as a light railway.

May 30: £5,000 damage caused in a fire at the furniture works of Messrs Stone & Sons, Wellington.

June 26: Opening of new Free Bridge at Jackfield.

July 31: New tower of Kemberton Church dedicated.

September 9: A Shropshire Aviation Club formed at Shrewsbury.

September 16: Service of thanksgiving at Shrewsbury Abbey on completion of the work of repairing the tower, putting in the new clock, and rehanging the bells.

October 23: Public drinking fountain unveiled at Dawley in memory of Captain Webb, first man to swim the English Channel.

November 20: George Bernard Shaw was principal speaker at a meeting in the Music Hall, Shrewsbury. His subject was "The Ratepayers, the Budget, and the Break up of the Poor-Law".

November 24: New dual secondary school formally opened at Bridgnorth i.e. it was the new home of the Bridgnorth Grammar School and Bridgnorth Girls High School.

DEATHS: May 19, Herbert Meyrick, fourth son of Colonel Sir Thomas Meyrick and Lady Meyrick, of Apley Castle. Herbert tried to swim a horse across Apley Castle Pool, came off, and drowned. He was 34. His parents had already lost another son in the Boer War.

1910

January 8: "One of the most destructive fires in Wellington for years" hit Messrs Aston's furnishing department at the corner of Walker Street and Tan Bank.

January 14: Testing of the new Minsterley Bridge with two traction engines weighing together 28 tons.

February 16: Deanery Hall, Pontesbury, was gutted by fire in the early hours. The hall had just been completed and had not even been formally opened.

February 17: Gale destroys the grandstand of Shrewsbury Town FC at Copthorne.

March 31: New elementary school opens at Coleham, Shrewsbury.

June 23: Cae Glas Park, Oswestry, opened.

July 29: Skating rink at Tan Bank inaugurated.

August 20: First practice match at Shrewsbury Town's new ground, the Gay Meadow.

August 26: Opening of new swimming baths at Wellington.

September 10: Shrewsbury Town's first game at the Gay Meadow, v Wolverhampton Wanderers Reserves.

October 6: Opening of new High School for Girls, Ludlow.

November 7: Formal opening of new Castle Bridge over the River Severn in Shrewsbury.

November 19: Baden-Powell inspects scouts at Ludlow.

November 24: Formal opening of new County school for infants at Hartshill Road, Oakengates.

November 25: Final negotiations to effect the purchase of the Castle Car Works, Hadley, were completed on November 25. The property came into the possession of Messrs Joseph Sankey & Sons Ltd, Bilston.

November 28: Aquatate Hall, near Newport, burned down.

December 4: Seven miners killed through the breaking of a rope in a pit shaft at Kemberton Colliery.

DEATHS: November 16, John Randall of Madeley (who had celebrated his 100th birthday on Sept 1).

1911

March 24: Star Hotel, Market Place, Shifnal, gutted by fire.

April 13: After lying derelict for over a quarter of a century, the Shrewsbury and Llanymynech and the Kinnerley and Melverley sections of the "Potteries, Shrewsbury, and North Wales Railway" were formally reopened for traffic as the Shropshire and Montgomeryshire Light Railway.

May 5: Duke of Teck visited Shrewsbury School to officially open the new concert hall.

May 24: Unveiling of restoration of the North Gate, Bridgnorth

July 31: An aircraft piloted by James Valentine landed at Brockton, near Madeley, causing a sensation and attracting huge crowds.

August 2: Shirlett Sanatorium opened by Princess Alexander of Teck.

August 23-24: Lloyd George, the Chancellor of the Exchequer, stayed overnight at the Raven Hotel, Shrewsbury.

September 5: Opening of Besford House, Belle Vue, Shrewsbury, as a home for pauper children.

October 2: The Rev T.J. Rider, vicar of Baschurch, killed after having seizure and falling from his horse while out cub hunting with the North Shropshire Hounds near Tilley.

November 15: Formal opening of the Priory School, Shrewsbury, one of nine secondary schools which Salop County Council had provided.

November 23: Miss Morrison, "a well known young suffragette", gained an "excellent hearing" from large numbers of people in the Square, Wellington.

November 29: Coalbrookdale High School formally opened.

December 15: Wem Grammar School formally reopened after being "practically rebuilt and considerably enlarged."

DEATHS: October 8, Wellington-born Hesba Stretton, novelist, real name Sarah Smith, died at Ham, aged 79.

1912

January 15: Sidbury Church, near Bridgnorth, destroyed by fire.

February 20: Edward German, composer, conducted his opera Merrie England in his native town of Whitchurch.

March 1: General coal strike called. Miners of Shropshire joined those of the country generally in striking for a minimum wage. The strike ended on April 6.

May 23: A girls secondary school opened in Whitchurch.

June 10: Lord Barnard started the new engine and pumps at Shrewsbury Waterworks.

June 16: Ten men injured in a motor charabanc accident at Preston Gubbals.

July 18: At Hinstock Horticultural Show airman Gustav Hamel gave an exhibition of flying in a Bleriot monoplane.

July 20: First use of news photos in the Wellington Journal & Shrewsbury News.

July 23: The sale of a portion of the Duke of Sutherland's Lilleshall estate commenced at Wellington Town Hall, four days' transactions realising the sum of £278,052.

July 26: A new secondary school for girls opened at Oswestry.

August 24: New village hall opened in Chirbury.

September 10: Two army airmen, 2nd Lt Hotchkiss of Craven Arms and Lt Bettington killed near Oxford when their monoplane crashed.

September 24: A new county school at King Street, Wellington opened (official opening followed December 6).

October 12: The Wesleyan Day Schools, Clee Hill, destroyed by fire.

DEATHS: Lord Wenlock died in London on January 15. George Maw, formerly of Benthall Hall, died at Kenley, Surrey, on February 7. On May 25, Mary Caroline, Duchess of Sutherland, died. Lady Billson died at Llanrhaeadr Hall on August 6. On December 3, Lady Boughey of Aqualate.

1913

January 7: A memorial to Samuel Taylor Coleridge, the poet, unveiled at High Street Church, Shrewsbury.

February 8: A new X-ray department opened at the Salop Infirmary.

May 23: Lovers Henry Wilkinson, aged 17, and Ethel Mary Owen, 26, who was pregnant, drowned themselves in Colemere.

May 24: The Earl of Powis opened The John Crump Bowring Memorial Cottage Hospital and Memorial Ground at Wellington.

June 18 and 19: Mr B.C. Hucks, the well-known aviator, gave exhibitions of flying at Market Drayton and Ludlow.

July 11: Women's suffrage pilgrims marched from Shrewsbury to Wellington and then on to Wolverhampton.

August 26: The inhabitants of Church Stretton adopted the Commoners Act of 1908.

September 22: The Rev Joseph Miller, aged 74, vicar of

Bolas Magna, married schoolteacher Miss Dilys Wynne Roberts, aged 20.

October 20: Richard Henry Lea, station master, killed on the railway line at Market Drayton.

November 10: Disastrous fire at the yard of Mr Nicholas, builder and contractor, Coleham, Shrewsbury.

December 11: A new parish hall opened at Church Stretton.

December 12: Foundation stones laid of the Lyon Memorial Hall, Hodnet.

December 19: A servant girl and a waggoner employed at Bog Hall committed suicide.

DEATHS: April 9, Sir Clement Hill, MP for Shrewsbury. On April 27, "tragic death" of the Rev R.E. St. A. Arkwright, vicar of St Chad's, Shrewsbury. June 27: Death of the Duke of Sutherland. On October 4, Orlando J.C. Bridgeman died at Shrewsbury in his 91st year. November 2: J.W. Sankey, of Penn, chairman of Sankey's of Bilston and Hadley. On June 19, Mrs Wynne-Corrie of Park Hall died when she got in a lift at the hall and it dropped violently into the basement. She was wife of a former High Sheriff.

1914

March 5: Mr J.A. Pease, president of the Board of Education, opened a new secondary school for boys in Oswestry.

March 11: New parish hall opened at Stapleton.

March 12: Opening of King's Hall, Shrewsbury.

March 22: Richard Reynolds died from the effects of being knocked down by two dogs at Much Wenlock.

March 26: The Rev David Wigley Abbott, vicar of Cardington, found dead in a pond near Cardington vicarage. He had shot himself in the head. Verdict: suicide.

April 13: Old Parr's Cottage, Middletown, reopened after restoration.

April 14: Acton Burnell Hall destroyed by fire.

May 24: A new railway station opened at Church Stretton.

June 30 – July 4: The Royal Show came to Shrewsbury. During his visit King George V conferred the title of "Royal" on the Salop Infirmary.

July 17: Mrs Lyon opened the new parish hall at Hodnet.

August 4: In consequence of outbreak of war, orders of mobilisation arrived at Shrewsbury, the HQ of the No 4 military district.

October 3: Clun was lit by electricity.

November 7: Fire at a cinematograph show at Trimpley Hall, Ellesmere.

December 13: A ferryboat which had plied across the River Severn for 70 years sank at Coalport.

DEATHS: Annabelle Lady Boughey, of Sundorne Castle, in London on February 18. On December 25 W.L. Dodgson of Ludlow, a brother of author Lewis Carroll, died. April 6: Major H.C. Williams-Wynn died from injuries received by being thrown from his horse while riding at the Wynnstay point-to-point races. May 2: Death of the Rev Silvester Horne (Ipswich MP), of Church Stretton, in Canada. Funeral was in Stretton on May 15.

1915

January 31: The Six Bells Hotel and two adjoining houses destroyed by fire in Clun.

February 12: At Salop Assizes Mary Jones and Lilian Jones, mother and daughter, sentenced to death for the murder of the new-born child of the latter near Oswestry (Upper Hengoed) – they were later reprieved.

April 8: The "Wingfield Gardens" suburb opened in Shrewsbury.

April 12: A fire at Hanwood Barytes Mill caused £1,000 damage.

May 24: A recreation ground and tennis courts opened in Church Stretton, the ornamental iron gates at the entrance being the work of a Belgian refugee.

June 21: Grindley Brook flour mill destroyed by fire.

June 26: Decided at a meeting in Shrewsbury to form a county regiment of Volunteers consisting of men too old or otherwise debarred from joining the regular army or navy.

July 15: Serious accident at Shrawardine Bridge on the Shropshire and Montgomeryshire Railway, the engine and carriages being derailed and the lives of the passengers temporarily imperilled.

September 12: Fire at Bettisfield Camp, near Whitchurch, two huts being destroyed and another partially burned.

September 14: Mrs Hayes and her servant Alice France fined at Shrewsbury Police Court for being in communication with German POWs.

October 11: Fire at Whixall Hall.

Misc: The first kerbside petrol pump in Britain installed at the premises of Legge and Chamier in Shrewsbury. Ludlow Castle scheduled as an ancient monument.

DEATHS: John Maddock, ironmaster, of Maddock's of Oakengates, died (reported October 23). August 7, Captain Derriman, Chief Constable of Shropshire, died in France of wounds received in action. On December 5 electrical pioneer Thomas Parker, of Severn House, Ironbridge, who was born in 1843, died.

1916

January 14: Earthquake shocks in various parts of Shropshire and the Midlands.

January 15: William Burd, ferryman, drowned at Buildwas.

February 24: A church hall and parsonage opened at Lea Cross.

March 13: Three killed when a Daimler beer lorry plunged into the brook at Cound Arbour.

May 19: Mytton Roller Flour Mill, near Shrewsbury, destroyed by fire.

June 21: Mrs Harley of Condover – sister of Field Marshal Viscount French – on her return from France and Serbia, received a cordial welcome from members of the Shrewsbury branch of the NUWSS.

September 29: Field Marshal Lord French visited Shrewsbury and inspected the members of the Shropshire Volunteer Force.

November 15: Pte Ernest Collison killed by a crater mine explosion at the Old Oswestry Coppice.

November 16: L/Cpl James Bayley fatally injured by a bomb explosion at Park Hall Camp, Oswestry.

December 13: New drill hall opened at Ironbridge.

December 20: Huge fire at Messrs Cock and Sons tannery in Barker Street, Shrewsbury, causing £50,000 damage.

DEATHS: Viscount Clive in London on October 13, of wounds received in action. On May 1, William "Fatty" Foulke, Dawley born footballer who played in goal for Sheffield United and Chelsea.

1917

February: River Severn frozen over for about a mile in the Ironbridge Gorge – the last known time the Severn froze over completely in the Ironbridge Gorge.

February 2: Lt Barnett and Cpl Bradley fatally injured through the explosion of a bomb at Prees Heath Camp.

May 12: Spire of Rowley Church, near Westbury, struck by lightning and demolished.

May 16: A lieutenant and a private fatally injured by a bomb explosion at Park Hall Camp.

May 21: Moreton Say Church hit by lightning and damaged.

June 26: 2nd Lt John Charles Merrick killed at Prees Heath Camp through the premature explosion of a faulty bomb.

July 9: Private Denis Jetson Blakemore, of Shrewsbury, executed for desertion.

July 23: Lilleshall House, with gardens, pleasure grounds, park, historic remains of abbey etc. bought by a syndicate for £45,000.

July 27: Sale of Duke of Sutherland's Lilleshall estate realised over £300,000.

August 15: Harley Church tower struck by lightning.

September 28: Viscount French inspected a contingent of Shropshire Volunteers at Shrewsbury.

October 25: Fire at Bettisfield Camp.

November 21: Fire at L & NWR Co's goods yard at Castle Foregate, Shrewsbury.

December 19: Thomas Cox executed for murdering his wife at Ludlow.

DEATHS: March 7, Mrs Harley of Condover, sister of Field Marshal Viscount French, killed in the bombardment of Monastir, Serbia. She was aged 61. She was, at some stage, awarded the Croix de Guerre. March 21, William Anstice died in London. July 6, Alderman Thomas Corbett, Shrewsbury businessman and alderman.

1918

January 18: Collision between goods train on the railway between Oswestry and Whittington resulted in the death of a fireman, another fireman and two drivers being injured.

March 6: Boscobel House purchased by the Earl of Bradford.

May 23: Sgt Whitfield VC welcomed home at Oswestry on his return from France.

June: The 4th King's Shropshire Light Infantry awarded the Croix de Guerre for its heroism in the Battle of Bligny.

June 19: Young woman killed by an aeroplane at Hungerford, near Craven Arms, i.e. Harrit (Harriet??) Bounds, at Lowe's Field, Holdgate.

July: Victoria Cross awarded to Lt Richard Douglas Sandford RN, 'a scion of one of Shropshire's oldest county families, the Sandfords of Sandford, near Whitchurch'. He was in the Zeebrugge raid when he was in command of the submarine C3.

July 9: Leopold Coney, a schoolboy, killed by lightning at Cleobury Mortimer.

July 26: Edward Keeling killed by lightning near Shrewsbury.

September 3: Opening of the Silvester Horne Institute, Church Stretton.

October 15: Recreation room and library opened at Market Drayton.

December 26: Park Hall, a Queen Anne mansion near Oswestry, burnt down.

DEATHS: April 27, the Hon G.H.W. Windsor-Clive, formerly Ludlow MP. July 25, death of Lord Wenlock. Wilfred Owen, the Shrewsbury poet, November 4.

1919

March 9: Serious fire at Tern Hill aerodrome.

May 19: The Hughley estate of the Earl of Bradford sold by auction for £24,163.

May 24: Reception at Shrewsbury of the cadre of 4th KSLI.

June 5: Welcome at Shrewsbury to the cadre of the 6th KSLI "Pals".

June 10: The Bank House, Broseley, opened by Lord Forester as a social club.

June 21: Cadre of the 10th KSLI welcomed at Shrewsbury.

June 24: Admiral von Reuter and his comrades who scuttled German warships at Scapa Flow taken as prisoners of war to a camp near Oswestry.

July 12: German prisoner of war named Oster shot by a sentry at Park Hall camp.

August 5: Welcome home at Shrewsbury to Shropshire soldiers and sailors who served overseas in the Great War.

Misc: The Marquess and Marchioness of Cambridge came to live in Shropshire (according to a 1929 report).

DEATHS: January 9, the Rt Hon C.G. Milnes Gaskell of Yorkshire and Wenlock Abbey. April 5, Major A. Wynne Corrie of Park Hall, Oswestry, died at Bournemouth. January 19, Sir Bryan Leighton of Loton Park, in London. Reported March 8, death of Geo. Skidmore, of Cleveland Street, Shrewsbury, who had been marooned on an island for seven months after shipwreck. On December 27, Sir Charles Henry, the Wrekin MP. His Shropshire residence was at Brooklands, Wellington.

1920

March 8: A World War One tank was presented to Wellington in recognition of its fundraising for the war effort.

April 16: St Georges Hall, Garrick Street, Wolverhampton, collapsed and killed two men, including Harry Plimmer, of Bank Road, Dawley.

Reported April 24: Mitchell's Fold at Stapeley Hill was handed over to the Office of Works to be preserved as an ancient monument.

Reported May 22: It was decided to re-erect Shrewsbury's old armoury at a site near the Welsh Bridge.

May 27: After a lapse of seven years, Shropshire and West Midland Agricultural Society revived its annual show at Gravel Hill, Shrewsbury.

Reported July 17: Shrewsbury Town Council had settled at its new Guildhall, formerly called Newport House on Dogpole. Its council meetings were still being held at the Shirehall.

August 18: Shropshire Horticultural Society's floral and musical fete, suspended since 1913, held in The Quarry, Shrewsbury.

August 29: An 11hp Riley of Coventry car driven by Captain Riley, a former RAF airman, ascended to the summit of The Wrekin. It was claimed (wrongly) to be the first motor car ascent of the Wrekin.

September 19: Worthen war memorial unveiled.

September 30: Criftins Parish Hall opened.

October 10: The unique Ruyton-XI-Towns cave war memorial unveiled.

Misc: *The Hampton Loade ferry was swept away in a storm* (according to report of a new ferry opening in 1958). Shrewsbury bus garage built at Ditherington with "full blossoming" i.e. opening? on November 11.

DEATHS: October 17, Mr J.A. Kilvert of High Ercall, who took part in the Charge of the Light Brigade, died at Wednesbury. October 25, Mr C.F. Palmer, MP for the Wrekin. November 11, the Rev Preb Thomas Auden at Church Stretton, a historian and author.

1921

January 1: Wellington College renamed Wrekin College.

January 3: Lady Harlech becomes Shropshire's first woman magistrate.

February 13: Hanwood war memorial unveiled.

April 3: Thomas Hall of 2 Station Cottages, Ditton Priors, murdered his three children and then killed himself.

April 3: Little Wenlock war memorial unveiled.

May 1: Pontesbury war memorial unveiled.

Reported May 21: Peplow Hall estate, belonging to Sir Beville Stanier, sold.

May 22: Coalbrookdale War Memorial unveiled and dedicated.

August 5: Formal opening of the new Shropshire Orthopaedic Hospital – the former Park Hall Military Hospital near Oswestry.

Also August 5: During a bazaar at Lymore Hall (near Montgomery), the floor of a room collapsed and precipitated nearly 20 persons, including Lord Powis, into the cellar.

August 28: Alveley war memorial unveiled. Also August 28, war memorial cross unveiled at Maesbury by local war heroes J.V. Campbell VC and Sgt Harold Whitfield VC.

September 13: Billingsley Colliery closed with loss of 200 jobs.

October 18: Peace Memorial Hall opened at Meole Brace.

Armistice Day: Market Drayton war memorial unveiled.

November 11: Sir Frederick Sykes, director of Civil Aviation, opened the Pugh Memorial boat house on the riverside on the grounds of Shrewsbury School.

December 4: Rushbury war memorial unveiled.

December 12: Public war memorial hall at Much Wenlock declared open by Lord Forester.

December 27: Dedication and opening of the Oswestry War Memorial gates at the entrance to Cae Glas Park.

DEATHS: December 15, Sir Beville Stanier, Ludlow MP since 1918, at the Citadel, Hawkstone. He was a Unionist. July 29, death of Sir Thomas Charlton Meyrick, Bart, at Apley Castle, son of the late St J. C. Charlton of Apley Castle and Jane, only daughter of the late Mr Thomas Meyrick, of Bush, whose surname he subsequently adopted.

1922

January 21: A meeting of ex-servicemen at Shrewsbury decided to form a county committee of the British Legion in Shropshire.

Reported March 25: Charles Darwin's birthplace, Mount House, Shrewsbury, was bought by HM Office of Works to house a large body of postal engineering staff.

May 6: Wellington War Memorial unveiled by Maj-Gen Sir Charles Townshend.

May 9: Sir John Leigh of Lilleshall Hall returned unopposed as Conservative MP for Clapham.

May 31: Earl Haig welcomed to the county by people of Oswestry, and on June 2 addressed members of the British Legion in Shrewsbury.

June 3: General Berthelot of the French Army visited Shrewsbury and pinned the Croix de Guerre to the regimental colour of the 4th KSLI.

July 29: Shropshire War Memorial in Shrewsbury unveiled by the Lord Lieutenant, the Earl of Powis.

September 2: Lady Forester opened the war memorial footbridge connecting Coalport and Jackfield.

October 25: New secondary school at Bishop's Castle opened.

October 28: Formal opening of a new grandstand at the Gay Meadow.

October 29: Fire at the railway engine sheds at Oswestry causes thousands of pounds worth of damage.

November 25: Lord Berwick opens the Empire Cinema,

Shrewsbury.
DEATHS: Colonel Sir Robert Henry Anstice, son of the late John Anstice of Madeley Wood Hall, at Brighton on April 9.

1923

January 18: Port Hill suspension bridge opened at Shrewsbury.

February 18: Miss Harriet Manning died at Bodbury Hill, Church Stretton, from exposure.

April 7: Railwaymen's war memorial unveiled and dedicated at Shrewsbury railway station.

May 7: Three day sale in London of the Brownlow Collection of pictures, furniture, etc, raised £115,869.

June 20: First lady barrister appears at Shropshire Assize Court.

July 24: William Griffiths executed at Shrewsbury for the murder of his wife at Eccleshall.

July 31: John Walker Williamson, 19, killed by lightning at Alveley.

August 2: Marjorie Adams, a child, killed by a falling lime tree in the Quarry, Shrewsbury.

August 10: Three cottages destroyed by fire at Norton, near Shifnal.

September 14 (reported): Outbreak of foot and mouth disease at Stanwardine Park Farm, Baschurch. By December 21, 90 Shropshire farms were infected.

November 22: New isolation hospital opened at Monkmoor, Shrewsbury.

Misc: Shrewsbury Town FC won the Birmingham League championship shield in the 1922-23 season.

1924

Reported January 12 (in WJ&SN): Shrewsbury Castle bought for the town of Shrewsbury.

March 2: Ironbridge War Memorial unveiled.

April 23: Edward German conducted Merrie England at the Town Hall, Whitchurch, at the jubilee concert of the choral society.

June 16: At Ascot Races the Gold Vase won by "Audlem" trained at Tern Hill.

July 10: The National Assembly of the Church of England adopted a measure for creating a bishopric of Shrewsbury out of the Shropshire parishes, with the Abbey Church of Shrewsbury as a cathedral.

July 16: A fire at Messrs Groom's timber yard in Wellington caused damage estimated at £3,000.

September 22: Serious fire at Mawley Hall, Cleobury Mortimer.

November 25: Disastrous fire at the works of the Castle Mills Engineering Company, Dinham, Ludlow.

December 28: Four die in road accident at Stokesay. Car crashed through iron railings at Stokesay Bridge and crashed into River Onny. Two of the six in the car rescued.

DEATHS: March 9, W.H. Foster at Apley Park, Bridgnorth. November 24, Thomas Dutton "The Shropshire Giant," died at Market Drayton. May 17, General Townshend, the former Wrekin MP, died. Although he was an Independent he later joined the Conservative Party. August 31, death of John Percy Wood, of Craven Arms, aged 42, who had a poultry and grocery business. June 16, Lord Acton of Aldenham Park died.

1925

January 3/4: Gales and floods hit Shropshire.

January 16: Reported in the SC today that the Bog Mines closed down 'last week' throwing a large number of men out of work.

April 20: Cressage village hall opened.

July 14: Brimfield Court destroyed by fire.

October 12: New bridge opened at Longnor.

October 22: The third arch of the old English Bridge collapsed during demolition work. Nobody was injured.

November 28: Miss Edith Picton-Turbervill selected as prospective Labour candidate for the Wrekin Division.

December 3: A village hall opened at Oreton.

December 8: Messrs H. Addison & Co's furniture works destroyed by fire in Wellington.

DEATHS: Miss Mary Cholmondeley, distinguished novelist, daughter of the Rev Richard Hugh Cholmondeley of Condover Hall, on July 15.

1926

January 12: A new automatic telephone system was inaugurated at Shrewsbury.

January 21: Shrewsbury Castle, a gift to the town from Shropshire Horticultural Society, opened by Lord Barnard for the use of the public, town council meetings, and the like.

February 12: Reported in the SC that Buildwas Abbey had been taken over by the HM Government Office of Works.

March 4: The House of Lords rejected by 61 votes to 60 a motion directing that the Shrewsbury Bishopric Measure should be presented for the Royal Assent.

March 4: Newport Girls High School opened.

April 2: SC reported that the Coalport China works would be probably transferring to Stoke towards the end of that month.

April 13: The first bypass road in Shropshire opened at Gobowen.

May 5: New public hall opened as Pontesbury.

June 29: The Memorial Hall at Upton Magna destroyed by fire.

August 15: Earthquake in Shropshire and the Midlands.

August 20: Report in the SC today of a landslip at the Lloyds, Jackfield.

November 17: Edgton Recreation Room opened.

December 15: New village hall opened at Pitchford.

December 18: Allatt's School, Shrewsbury, closed after 126 years.

December 30: Original foundation stone of the English Bridge relaid.

1927

January 21: Village halls opened at Eaton Constantine and Acton Scott.

January 27: Berrington Hospital opened by Lady Berwick.

February 7: Between 200 and 300 tons of rock fell from the Castle Walk into New Road, Bridgnorth.

February 23: John Thomas Giles sentenced to death at Salop Assizes for the murder of his wife at Ellesmere, but afterwards reprieved.

April 23: Alexander George McCorquodale, of Cound Hall, marries Barbara Cartland (later Dame Barbara Cartland) at Westminster.

July 30: Hartshill Park, Oakengates, opened.

Reported in WJ&SN August 6: Lilleshall Hall, recently residence of Sir John Leigh, sold to Mr H. Ford who would open the grounds to the public.

August 13: Queen Mary crosses over the new English Bridge, the first car to do so. When the official royal opening of the bridge by the Prince of Wales on October 26 was called off, the Queen's crossing was adopted retrospectively as the royal opening.

September 6: A 40ft pole was erected on the summit of the Long Mynd, made out of a growing tree and given by Mrs Gibbon. It was to replace one "taken down six years ago" (the SC of September 9 reported).

September 16: English Bridge opened to all traffic.

October: First performance at The Hippodrome Cinema (later the Regal) at Market Drayton.

October 21: Viscount Chelmsford opened Walker Technical College, Hartshill.

October 29: At a meeting at Shrewsbury it was decided to form a Shropshire branch of the English Folk Dancing Society.

November 15: Manufacture of beet sugar started at a new factory at Allscott.

December 19: Village hall at Weston-under-Redcastle opened.

December 21: A new Upton Magna Memorial Hall opened, replacing one destroyed by fire.

DEATHS: February 12, Col F.A. Wolryche-Whitmore at Larden, Much Wenlock. On March 16, Captain James Foster of Woodcote Hall, Newport. July 30, Lt Col James Patchett at Haybridge Hall, Hadley, who was managing director of Shropshire Iron Works. On October 24, the Marquess of Cambridge, brother of the Queen, at Shropshire Nursing Institution, Shrewsbury.

On March 6 Sir Francis Boughey of Aqualate Hall hanged himself on a windlass on one of the hall's outbuildings (verdict, suicide while temporarily insane). October 8, authoress Mary Webb.

SCHOOL CLOSURE: The SC reported on April 29 that Eaton-under-Heywood Parochial School had closed, following the blowing down of the bell turret in a gale on January 28, 1927, and the general condition of the school.

1928

January 1: John Bayley and Edward German were knighted in the New Year Honours.

January 2: Alveley Parish Hall opened.

March 23: The Salopian Society in London decided to admit women as members.

April 26: Annscroft Church Hall opened.

June 14: Easthope Church destroyed by fire.

June 21: New church of All Saints, Gobowen, consecrated.

July 5: Launch of cruiser HMS Shropshire, the naming ceremony being performed by the Countess of Powis, wife of the Lord Lieutenant of Shropshire.

September 26: Clun Town Hall handed over to parish council.

October 6: Sultan of Muscat and Amon (sic) visited Wroxeter.

October 18: Dedication of mission church, Eaton-on-Tern.

November 1: For the first time in history a woman candidate, Liberal Mrs Amelia Florence Hanna, took part in the Shrewsbury council elections. She was beaten in the Kingsland and Coleham ward on November 1 by 210 votes.

November 11: Oakengates War Memorial – wrought iron gates to recreation ground – unveiled.

November 21: Majaraja Paliata visited Ludlow.

November 25: A severe flood, the worst since 1880, caused severe damage to the centre arch centring – i.e. preliminary timber supports – of the new road bridge being built at Atcham, delaying work.

Misc: Ludlow Agricultural Society was wound up. Alderman Deakin formally set in motion the new diesel engine at Shrewsbury electricity works.

DEATHS: December 13, Mr T.J. Watkins of Shrewsbury, former Shropshire billiards champion. On April 10, Shropshire novelist Stanley John Weyman.

1929

Reported SC January 18, with pic: Subsidence at Jackfield.

Reported SC January 25: Effective sacking of the Rev L Baker Short of Shrewsbury High Street Unitarian Church for political sermons and bad language.

February 2: Increase in motor traffic of 62 per cent since 1925 is reported to Salop County Council.

February 10: War memorial tablet at Dawley unveiled by Col J.T. Campbell VC.

March 26: New church at Easthope dedicated to replace one burnt down.

March 30: WJ&SN reported that St Georges sports were abandoned because of lack of support.

May 7: Mrs Marion Wallace Cock, nee Scott, Shrewsbury's first woman magistrate, sworn in.

May 19: New Roman Catholic church opened at Church Stretton.

June 13: Sultan of Zanzibar visited Shrewsbury.

June 20: Former Madeley doctor called Twells on trial for murder in Canada.

July 19: St Saviour's School for Girls at Shrewsbury opened.

July 26: Parish hall erected to the memory of the late Miss L. Betton-Foster opened by Mrs Betton-Foster at Richards Castle.

September 9: Shrewsbury Town Council adopted first part of a scheme for the development of the Racecourse Estate.

September 30: "Talkies" came to the Empire cinema, Shrewsbury.

October 4: Sir Chas Hyde opened the museum of Roman relics at Shrewsbury.

October 14: Shrewsbury Philharmonic Society disbanded.

October 24: Mr Herbert Morrison, Minister of Transport, opens new Atcham Bridge.

October 25: Lymore Hall, a 17th century black and white mansion near Montgomery, sold for demolition.

November 10: Kinnerton Primitive Methodist Chapel destroyed by fire.

November 30: New tower of St George's Parish Church dedicated.

December 9-ish: Flooding in Shrewsbury affects about 250 houses.

December 24: George William Stewart, aged 18, of Waterloo Street, Ironbridge, killed in a fall of debris from the old Bedlam Furnaces, Ironbridge, "an old pile of buildings in the process of demolition".

DEATHS: Marchioness of Cambridge on March 26. Colonel Sir John Anstice, former mayor of Wenlock on August 1; Mr J.L. Della Porta on July 7. Mr J. Leonard, known in the Shrewsbury district as "Jack the Ragman" and "Whistling Jack", found dead in a ditch at Churncote, April 10. Sir Offley Wakeman, February 9. Countess of Powis, of shock after car crash at Towcester, on April 29. On September 21, nine-year-old Helen Crosby of Bridgnorth died from injuries received in an accident while swinging on the North Gate.

1930
March 31: Wellington Guardians held a farewell dinner.
April 29: Criftins CofE School destroyed by fire.
May 16: Viscount Bridgeman opened Newport Cottage Hospital.
June 12: 5,483 acres of the High Ercall estate sold at auction, including Ercall Hall, the Cleveland Arms and so on.
July/August: Much Wenlock church spire removed for safety reasons.
August 28: A new senior council school opened at Monkmoor.
September 11: Prince and Princess Takamatsu of Japan paid official visit to Shrewsbury.
October 4/5: Squadron Leader Michael Rope of Shrewsbury killed in the R101 airship disaster.
October 21: St Catherine's Hall, Coton Hill, Shrewsbury, officially opened by Canon A.C. Thompson.
December 6: Reported that that week the Chief Constable of Shropshire Major Becke had started a system of patrolling the roads of the county with a police car to prevent motoring offences and lessen the number of accidents.
Misc: The Plaza cinema, Bishop's Castle, opened.
DEATHS: November 1, Colonel H Heywood-Lonsdale DSO, aged 66, chairman of Salop County Council since 1920.
SCHOOL CLOSURES: On December 26, the SC reported that the Shrewsbury Lancasterian School closed for the Christmas holidays 'on Friday' (i.e. December 19) and would open in January as an ordinary council school.

1931
January 12: Shrewsbury Town Council decided to install automatic light signals in the town. Four locations chosen – the General Post Office Corner, the junction of Cross Street and Castle Foregate, New Street corner (Frankwell), and Coleham Head.
February 2: Retail Newsagents' Convalescent Home opened at Lilleshall Old Hall by Viscount Burnham.
February 2: Result of a referendum into a proposal to build a Church Stretton bypass – 446 in favour, 164 against, and 12 spoiled papers, a majority of 282.
February 18: Henry Cadman, stationmaster at Admaston for 20 years, knocked down and killed by an express as he crossed the line.
February 20: Ludlow bypass opened by Sir Henry Maybury.
May 27: "The Castle", a round structure which had stood on the summit of Haughmond Hill for generations, partially collapsed.
July 16 and 17: Two men died after separate falls at Buildwas power station.
July 23: New county council senior school opened at Harlescott.
July 24: Wem Senior Top School opened by Mrs Cholmondeley.
September 12: First Baldwin-Webb trip, to London, with 3,000 going from the Wrekin Constituency.
October 29: First electricity showroom in Shropshire opened in Wellington.
December 19: Opening of St Mary's Hall, Jackfield.
December 22: St Georges bypass opened on Holyhead Road at Priorslee.
SCHOOL CLOSURES: August 28 saw the last of the Wem Undenominational School, known as the British Schools, which had been superseded by the new Council Schools. The school closed at the beginning of the month.
DEATHS: December 23, Mr Lionel Powell of Sutton Court, Diddlebury 'the well known impresario,' aged 55. February 11, R.A. Clarke, (i.e. Richard Augustus Clarke), well known solicitor, sportsman and public name in Wellington.

1932
March 18: "Forbra", owned by William Parsonage of Ludlow, won the Grand National.
March 31: RAF mechanical transport depot at Harlescott officially closed.
May 1: Richards Castle church tower struck by lightning.
May 9: New church at Wattlesborough dedicated by the bishop of Hereford.
June 1: New recreation ground opened at Prees.
June 4: 3,200 Salopians visited London on a "Baldwin-Webb" outing organised by Wrekin MP Colonel Baldwin-Webb to celebrate the second anniversary of him being adopted as Parliamentary candidate.
July 9: New golf course opened at Oswestry.
July 15: Mr J.C.L. Mellish, a Shrewsbury schoolboy, killed through falling from a window at the school.
August 13: Methodist church opened at New Hadley.
August 31: Sir Alan Cobham came to Harlescott where he held a "National Aviation Day".
Reported September 3: Investigations/boreholes made in previous week in an attempt to discover a supposed passage between Lilleshall Abbey and the back of Longford Church, and also another alleged passage from Wombridge to the Abbey.
September 6: Mrs J.C. Beckett, of Bayston Hill, selected at Shrewsbury Music Hall as "Miss Shropshire" for Shrewsbury Carnival – she is the first Miss Shropshire.
October 5: New urban council offices opened at Wem.
October 13: Buildwas Power Station opened by Mr P.J. Pybus (Minister of Transport).
December 25: Kinlet church damaged by fire.
Misc: The final synod of the Shrewsbury district of the Primitive Methodist Church opened at Oakengates, Wellington bus garage built.
DEATHS: Mr C.F. Leake, editor of the Wellington Journal, at a London nursing home on February 17. On June 14, Lord Wenlock at Freeburg, Germany, the title becoming extinct. Lord Forester of Willey Park, October 10.

1933
April 29: Resolved officially to change the name of the Shropshire Orthopaedic Hospital to The Robert Jones and Agnes Hunt Orthopaedic Hospital.
May 23: Princess Royal opens Shrewsbury bypass.
May 25: New open air swimming baths opens at Market Drayton.
May 27: 4,000 Salopians on Baldwin-Webb trip to Southampton-Bournemouth.
May 29: New village hall opens at Morville.
June 24: A new Welfare Hall for miners opened at Highley.
June 30: New senior school opened at Wrockwardine Wood.
July 13: Work begins on removing the Charlton Mound, Oakengates, a 30ft pit mound near the centre of the town. It was cleared mainly by foreign students of the International Voluntary Service organisation.
November 8: Riding at Liverpool, Gordon Richards, the Shropshire-born jockey, rode his 247th winner of the season, a new record, beating the 246 winners in a season by Fred Archer in 1885.
Misc: Wem electricity supply was switched on. Hadley choir won the Welsh National Eisteddfod for the third time.
DEATHS: Sir Robert Jones, who helped found the Shropshire Orthopaedic Hospital, died January 14. On December 7, in China, Miss Stella Benson, (married name Mrs O'Gorman Anderson) a well known novelist and native of Shropshire. February 7, Major Arthur Ainslie Johnson, clerk to Salop County Council, found dead in the Shirehall, with a self-inflicted gash to his throat.

1934
February 8: A portion of Wem National School destroyed by fire.
February 21: Madeley pensioners' new Rest Room opened.
March 7: Mr Alan Charles Heber-Percy, third son of Mr and Mrs Heber-Percy of Hodnet Hall, killed while steeplechasing at Cheltenham.
April 1: The Borough of Shrewsbury was greatly extended, with a new boundary virtually doubling its area.
April 27: Reported that the Long Mynd had been sold to Mr Max Wenner. About 5,200 acres were sold.
June 2: Opening ceremony at St Georges recreation ground

on completion of an improvement scheme.
June 12: Sir Oswald Mosley addresses a "large gathering" at the Music Hall, Shrewsbury, including "a large number of members of the movement, clad in their black shirts."
June 13 and 14: Visit of Amir Abdullah, Amir of Trans-Jordan, to Shrewsbury.
June 16: 5,000 Salopians went on fourth Baldwin-Webb outing to Isle of Wight and Aldershot Tattoo.
July 2: Start of a week of performances at Ludlow Castle for the tercentenary performance of Milton's "Masque of Comus". About 3,000 were involved in the Shropshire Historical Pageant.
July 14: WJ&SN had pic of a policeman on traffic duty in "experimental" white uniform during a heatwave in Shrewsbury.
July 28: The Iron Bridge scheduled as an ancient monument and closed to traffic.
August 2: Opening luncheon for the Boat House Restaurant, Ellesmere.
August 4 (reported): Permission given to extend Ironbridge Power Station by installing a second 50,000 kw turbine.
September 6: The FA Commission, sitting at Birmingham, ordered the closing of Wellington Town's ground for 14 days after "scenes" in the English Cup tie against Oakengates the previous Saturday.
September 27: Oswestry Town Council conferred the Freedom of the borough on Sir Walford Davies.
October: Midland Gliding Club formed on the Long Mynd.
November 9: Marion Cock elected to become Shrewsbury's first woman mayor.
November 14: Granada Theatre, Shrewsbury, opened.
November 22: New elementary school opened at Alveley.
Misc: Sir H.W. Walford Davies, of Oswestry, was appointed "Master of the King's Musick".
DEATHS: Lady Wenlock, of Monkhopton House, September 12.

1935
January 6: Stirchley Church Room destroyed by fire.
January 26: "Forbra", winner of the 1932 Grand National, owned by Mr C.M. Parsonage, of Ludlow, broke a fetlock while steeplechasing at Newbury and was destroyed.
February 12: Bridgnorth Town Council decided to buy College House for £1,225 to use as municipal offices.
March 12: Max Wenner, of Batchcott Hall, Leebotwood, granted an injunction to stop gliding on the Long Mynd because it interfered with his grouse shooting.
April 1: Fire destroyed ancient black and white buildings in Shropshire Street, Market Drayton – some of the few parts of Drayton to have escaped the town fire of August 1651.
April 19: For the annual Good Friday football match between Wellington and Shrewsbury at the Buck's Head there was an attendance of 11,836, the largest gate in the history of the Birmingham League.
April 20: It was reported that the war on the musk rat in Shropshire was nearly won.
May 4: Wellington Town won the Birmingham League championship.
May 8: Sir Oswald Mosley, leader of the British Union of Fascists, delivered a "rousing speech" to a large audience in Market Drayton High Street.
May 11: 7,000 Salopians visited London on fifth annual Baldwin Webb outing.
May 24: Shropshire Yeomanry rode through Shrewsbury for the first time in over 40 years.
June 2: A man and woman, members of a charabanc outing from Birkenhead, drowned when a boat capsized on the Mere, Ellesmere.
June 3: Shrewsbury Town's application for admission to Third Division (Northern Section) was not successful. It was its first application to join the league.
June 11: Gift of the Linden Field sports ground to Much Wenlock by members of the family of Lady Catherine Milnes Gaskell.
July 4: Shelton water works, erected at a cost of £102,253, inaugurated.
July 9: New factory for canning condensed milk and cream opened at Minsterley.
July 30: Fire destroyed The Court House, a half timbered Elizabethan building at Shrawardine.
August 22: Two men killed in a 100ft fall at Ironbridge power station.

August 27: One of the biggest fires in Oswestry for years guts a furniture warehouse in Bailey Street.

August 31: Opening of new grandstand at Wellington Town's Buck's Head stadium.

October 12: Ackleton Malthouse almost entirely destroyed by fire.

October 21: Opening of new parish hall, Wombridge.

DEATHS: Lady Catherine Milnes Gaskell, of Wenlock Abbey, noted authoress and public worker, aged 78, on August 21. On November 15, three-times mayor of Shrewsbury Alderman William Maynard How, aged 79. On August 14, Viscount Bridgeman of Leigh, at his residence, Leigh Manor, near Minsterley. He was former Home Secretary and First Lord of the Admiralty.

1936

February 3: Most of the committee members of Shrewsbury Town resigned following an extraordinary general meeting when it was decided to apply for admission to the Northern Section of the Third Division and that the club should be converted into a limited liability company.

February 29: In one of the races of the Wheatland Hunt point to point at Haughton, near Bridgnorth, Bernard Towers, 34, of Bridgnorth was thrown at the water jump and died.

March 2: Bellstone Hall, Shrewsbury, renamed Morris Hall in memory of Mr J.K. Morris.

March 23: During a terrific thunderstorm a schoolboy Dennis Crane, aged 11, was killed by lightning at Constitution Hill Boys School in Wellington, a pilot died when his plane crashed trying to land at Childs Ercall, and a bungalow at Cold Hatton was destroyed by fire.

March 30: Newport Rural District Council met for the last time before being amalgamated with Wellington Rural Council.

April 13: New church hall opened at Whixall. Also April 13, Winifred Mary Oliver, aged 10, of Hadnall, fell 30ft to her death off a cliff at Grinshill.

May 2: Wellington Town won Birmingham League for second successive season.

May 8: Severe damage in fire at the Crown Furniture Works, Orleton Lane, Wellington.

June 13: 5,000 Wrekin residents visited Southampton, the Aldershot Tattoo and the Queen Mary, on a Baldwin-Webb trip.

June 27: Ernest Robert Hill, aged 18, sentenced to death at Salop Assizes charged with murdering his former sweetheart, 18-year-old Dorothy Clewes, of Market Drayton, at Moreton Say. Reprieved by Home Secretary.

July 2: The Bishop of Shrewsbury consecrated new Roman Catholic Church of St Peter's in Ludlow.

July 25: Ashes of A E Housman interred at Ludlow Parish Church.

September 4: SC reported new excavations at Uriconium "began this week".

October 7: A fire at Tern Hill Aerodrome destroyed a large portion of the officers quarters.

October 9: Shropshire's first nursery school opened at Hodnet.

November 22: Serious fire at Newport Grammar School, also this day three shops gutted by fire at Clee Hill on the junction of the Tenbury road and the main Ludlow road. They were a butchers, a bakers and a grocers.

December 16: Flooding in Frankwell, Ironbridge etc.

Misc: The Montgomeryshire Canal was closed through a breach near Welsh Frankton, and never repaired.

DEATHS: January 22, founder of the County Home for Ailing Babies at Wellington, Mrs Flora Dugdale of Newport. Well known in Shrewsbury as "Napoleon", William Twycross, of The Trumpet, Hills Lane, on January 25. World famous preacher, Dr S. Parkes Cadman, a native of Ketley, in America on July 12, aged 71. On March 10 the 'father' of Shrewsbury Town Council and twice borough mayor Ald. William Gowen Cross of Mardol, aged 87. On April 4, Thomas Oakley, Unionist MP for the Wrekin from 1924 to 1929. May 1, Shrewsbury's first woman councillor, Mrs G.M. Murrell. May 1, A.E. Housman, author of A Shropshire Lad. Ald. Richard Devereux Bromley, twice mayor of Shrewsbury, on Aug 30. Sir Edward German of Whitchurch, November 11.

1937

January 4: Max Wenner, owner of the shooting rights on the Long Mynd, falls to his death from an airliner.

January 11, Madeley Senior School (now Abraham Darby School), opened.

January 18: Official opening of Wellington's new cinema, The Clifton, by the Mayor E.R.H. Herbert of Orleton Hall.

February 21: The last railway engine on the Bishop's Castle Railway was the Bishop's Castle Company's old engine Carlisle which worked the trip into Craven Arms goods yard, where she was to be broken up.

March 1: The Welsh flag flown from Shrewsbury Castle for the first time in honour of St David's Day.

March 18: Official opening of Shrewsbury's 1,000th council house.

May 29: Wilderhope Manor formally opened as a youth hostel.

June: Highley colliery bridge over the River Severn completed.

June 25: SC had a pic of firemen working on a thatched cottage at The Newnes, Ellesmere, which was reputed to be the birthplace of Dick Whittington and which they 'saved from destruction'.

June 30: Three members of 90 Squadron, Bicester, killed when their Blenheim bomber crashed at Stanton Long.

July 3: New cricket pavilion at Wrekin College opened by Dr Grace, nephew of W.G.

August 3: Constable Harry Speake (Henry Geo. Andrew Speake) aged 21 died when he went into the River Severn at Emstrey, Shrewsbury to chase absconders who were getting away. He died of heart failure.

October 2: Official opening of Ketley playing fields.

November 22: Fire destroyed Woofferton Saw Mills.

November 22: Opening of the Majestic Cinema, Bridgnorth.

December 1: Mr J. Floyer Benthall of Benthall Hall fell 80ft down a disused well near the hall. Discovered later, and rescued, he was not badly hurt.

Misc: New youth hostel opened at Malthouse Farm, Wheathill, near Burwarton. The Comrades Club, Wellington, renamed the Sir John Bayley Social and Ex-Servicemen's Club. The drinking fountain in Burway Road, Church Stretton, suffered considerable damage when hit by a lorry 'belonging to the railway company' reported the Shrewsbury Chronicle of August 13. According to projectionist Ken Williams, The Royal cinema in Dawley opened this year, 1937 (although a story on its closure in 1962 gave the date as 1938).

DEATHS: Col. Harold William Alexander Francis Crichton-Browne, explorer, soldier and author, of Buildwas Park, died at London nursing home aged 71, on October 1. March 24, Samuel Meeson Morris, four times mayor of Shrewsbury, aged 80. April 10, Alderman William John Legge, of Upper House, Madeley, aged 86, oldest member of Wenlock Borough Council and a leading figure in industry.

1938

January 1: Donnington village stores burned down.

January 18: Emperor of Abyssinia arrived for a short stay at Walcot Hall, Lydbury North.

March 22: A workman unearthed hundreds of valuable old silver coins dating from between 1554 and 1633 while excavating at Donnington.

March 30: Official opening of the new grammar school at Whitchurch.

April 7: Rowley's House, Shrewsbury, opened as a museum for housing Viroconium finds.

May 7: WJ&SN reported that Shrewsbury Town had had their most successful season, winning the Midland League at their first attempt, the Shropshire Senior Cup for the 17th time, and being finalists for the Welsh Senior Cup.

May 18: Wellington Town dropped out of Birmingham League and joined Cheshire League.

May 21: The 7th annual Wrekin Baldwin-Webb outing to Empire Exhibition, Glasgow.

May 30: An application by Shrewsbury Town to secure admission to the Third Division (Northern Section) failed for the fourth time.

June 30: Shrewsbury's new fire station opened at Cross Hill.

July: Last known journey on the Newport-Shrewsbury

branch of the Shropshire Union Canal, when a barge took 20 tons of coal from Norbury junction to Longdon-on-Tern.

August 1: One-way traffic scheme came into operation in Shrewsbury.

August 13: Chad Valley in Wellington was first toy firm in the world to receive a Royal Warrant as manufacturers of dolls, toys, and kindergarten amusements to the Queen.

August 18: Sub Lt A.N. Young, an officer in the Fleet Air Arm, broke the British amateur gliding record for a single seater, staying aloft 15hr 45 mins above the Long Mynd.

August 21 Major James Geoffrey Stewart-Smith, of Kinver, killed at the Long Mynd on his first flight in a glider. It was the first fatal gliding accident there.

August 24: Inspector Faulconbridge, aged 50, killed in a fall during fire drill at Shrewsbury fire station.

October 27: An area of 400 square miles in and around Shrewsbury was blacked out in a big exercise to test air raid precautions.

October 30: "Disastrous" fire at Wem totally destroyed a block of business premises including Messrs Moss motor engineers in Market Street.

November 15: Shrewsbury's new technical college buildings opened by Kenneth Lindsay, parliamentary secretary to the Board of Education.

DEATHS: On January 24, in London, Captain Adrian Jones, born in Ludlow on February 9, 1845, and believed to be the world's oldest sculptor. May 8, at Brogyntyn Hall, George Ralph Chas. Ormsby-Gore (Lord Harlech) died.

1939

January 5: 29 degrees of frost registered at Shrewsbury, the lowest temperature ever recorded.

February: Report in SC implied Benthall Pottery had just closed. Certainly had closed by then.

February 3: It was officially announced that a £1 million "war" depot was proposed at Donnington.

Reported February 10 in SC that work on Church Stretton bypass had now commenced.

February 23: 1,420 acres of Lord Harlech's Brogyntyn estate was sold.

May 20: Ugly scenes in Wellington when a meeting of Blackshirts was broken up by a crowd pelting them with eggs and fruit.

June 8: Successful revival of Shrewsbury horse races.

June 9: Sir Kingsley Wood, Air Minister, toured Shropshire RAF stations.

July 24: Shifnal RDC's new council chamber and offices opened.

July 27: Shifnal's new cottage hospital opened by the Countess of Bradford.

Reported August 5: Excavation of the ancient Ancient Briton city on top of the Wrekin.

September 1: Evacuation of children from big towns and cities into Shropshire began.

September 5: John Hulton-Harrop of Betton Strange becomes first Fighter Command casualty when his Hurricane is shot down by mistake by a Spitfire.

December 9: Acting Corporal Thomas William Priday (of Gloucestershire) of the KSLI steps on a mine during a patrol and becomes Army's first battle casualty.

December 19: Landslide at Wesley Road, Ironbridge, causes family living at 5 Lloyds Road to abandon their home.

DEATHS: Former world famous athlete, T.C. Cope, i.e. Crim Cope, of St Georges, on February 19, aged 81. On March 6, T.P. Deakin, honorary Freeman of the Borough of Shrewsbury, and twice mayor.

1940

January 29: Biggest snowfalls in living memory followed a period of severe frost.

February 3: Alterations and extensions to the Shropshire County Council buildings at Shrewsbury opened by the Lord Lt, the Earl of Powis.

February 7: Five separate landslides in a cutting near Bridgnorth which held up rail traffic on the Worcester to Shrewsbury line.

April 1: Opening of new Wellington Senior School at Orleton Lane, Wellington (later Orleton Park School).

April 24: Opening of Wellington Rural District Council's offices and first "home" at Tan Bank.

May: COD Donnington officially opened.

May 30: Four men electrocuted at Farley Quarry near

Much Wenlock. They were tipping rocks when their tipping lorry touched a 11,000 volt overhead cable.

June 28: It was announced by the Admiralty that HMS Whirlwind, a destroyer which had been "adopted" by St Leonard's Mothers' Union, Bridgnorth, had been sunk.

July 20: Salop County Council decided to sack all staff who were conscientious objectors or supporters of subversive organisations.

August 17: George Robey, the world famous comedian, entertained troops at the YMCA canteen, Shrewsbury.

August 29: In the early hours a string of bombs fell across Bridgnorth. Two killed.

August 31: Shortly before midnight a bomb fell on a cottage on Ellesmere Road, Shrewsbury, killing a woman and her two grandchildren.

September 17: Wrekin MP Colonel James Baldwin-Webb killed when a children's evacuee ship City of Benares in which he was a passenger was torpedoed in Mid Atlantic.

November 16: German bomber crashed at Monkhopton.

December 7: A DSO was awarded to Shropshire air ace, Pilot Officer Eric Lock, who had previously won the DFC and bar.

Misc: General de Gaulle's family stayed at Gadlas Hall, Ellesmere, after the Fall of France, and the General was a regular visitor.

DEATHS: January 14, Alderman William George Dyas, aged 67, four times Mayor of Wenlock. February 29, death of Col Sir Charles Edward Yate, of Madeley Hall, a distinguished soldier and figure in political life.

SCHOOL CLOSURES: March 20: Constitution Hill School buildings, Wellington, closed as an elementary school after nearly 100 years.

1941

January 28: Widespread foot and mouth disease broke out in Shropshire, Cheshire and Herefordshire.

February 10: Shrewsbury experienced its worst floods for 60 years.

March 23: Landslide wrecked Rock Cottage at Lincoln Hill, Ironbridge. The family escaped.

June 4: Comedian George Robey entertained at a concert party in the YMCA canteen, Ditherington.

June 30: The Yew Tree Cafe, Prees Heath, burnt down.

July: Squadron Leader the Rev Herbert Cecil Pugh, padre of RAF Bridgnorth since 1940, died heroically while tending injured airmen aboard the troopship Anselm which was sunk by enemy action off the coast of West Africa. He was awarded a posthumous George Cross.

July 11: Dr Benes, president of the Czechoslovakian Republic, paid a visit to the Czech State School at Hinton Hall, Whitchurch, the only Czech secondary school not under German domination.

August 3: Shropshire air ace Eric Lock was presumed killed after going missing during an operation over France.

December 20: Whitchurch Town Hall, aka the Regent Cinema, destroyed by fire.

Misc: Mrs M.J. Rotton, of Stokesay Court, was elected the first woman alderman of Salop County Council.

DEATHS: January 8, Mr H.O. Derwas, of Victoria Road, Oswestry, last of an old Shropshire family dating back to the 14th century. On February 11 Mr W. Morris, aged 64, of Ratlinghope, last seen making his way home in a blizzard, was found dead on the Long Mynd. On March 11 Sir Walford Davies, Master of the King's Musick and a native of Oswestry. January 10: At Cound Hall, death of former High Sheriff (i.e. of 1912) of Shropshire, Alexander Cowan McCorquodale.

1942

May 10: The Scouts' VC, the Bronze Cross, awarded posthumously to Patrol Second L.H.E. Humphries, aged 13, of the 3rd Broseley Troop, was handed to his mother. He had died in an unsuccessful bid to save a fellow scout from drowning in the River Severn the previous July.

May 24: Mr Frank Cyril Hopwood, a Lieutenant in the Home Guard and licensee of the Buffalo Hotel, Clun, fatally shot during a machine gun demonstration.

October 24: Bus crashed into a telegraph pole at the river bridge at Tern Hill. Eight passengers were taken to the RSI.

December 6: High Ercall Institute was destroyed by fire.

DEATHS: January 28: "One of the most travelled women in England, having made lone trips into unknown lands in all parts of the globe, Miss R. Humphreys, died at her home at Swan Hill Court, Shrewsbury, aged 75." On December 22, J.V.T. Lander (i.e. John Vernon Thomas Lander), coroner for Wellington and district for half a century, died. On January 18, Viscount Boyne, of Burwarton House, aged 78. November 6, Herbert Edward Forrest, of Bayston Hill, aged 84, author, historian and researcher. December 26, William Owen Wilding, of Lyth Hill, aged 66, managing director of Wilding and Son printers.

1943

January 9: Major fire in the gun store at COD Donnington.

February 21: A fire at the Castle Maltings, Castle Foregate, Shrewsbury, caused considerable damage, gutting the third and fourth floors of the four-storey building.

March 2: Four people found dead in a house at Sunnyside, Stafford Road, Newport. Edward Ernest Leek, 47, manager of a Newport boot shop and a lieutenant in Newport Home Guard, had shot and killed his wife, their six-year-old son, and his mother in law, before shooting himself.

March 30: Shropshire's first cooking depot opened at Horsehay.

April 22: Big fire in Corve Street, Ludlow, involving the premises of Messrs Flemon's drying kiln, Ludlow Laundry, an adjoining house and the Labour Exchange.

May (first week of): The Raven Hotel, Shrewsbury, opened as an American Red Cross Service Club.

May 5: In its first fatal accident in its 51 years, Harold Howes, 36, was killed on the Castle Hill Railway, Bridgnorth, while doing work on one of the cars.

May 14: Wellington British Restaurant was opened by Miss Phyllis Neilson-Terry "the famous actress".

July 15: At a ceremony in the Shirehall, Shrewsbury, a plaque was presented on behalf of the Admiralty in recognition of the county's Warship Weeks efforts to raise funds to buy HMS Shropshire, and in return a county plaque was presented to be placed on the cruiser's quarterdeck. Later in the year the ship was transferred to the Royal Australian Navy.

September 9: Body of ATS girl Louisa Edith Jenny Price, aged 18, of Higher Tranmere, was found partly stripped and mutilated in woods on the Wrekin. She had attended a dance given at the Forest Glen by American soldiers the night before. Sgt Michael Pihosh, 22, a Military Policeman, was acquitted of her murder (verdict on November 23).

September 24: Lady Mountbatten, Superintendent in Chief of the St John Ambulance, made a tour of inspection of ambulance brigades and nursing divisions in Shropshire.

November 27: Bishop Percy's House in Cartway, Bridgnorth, formally handed over to Bridgnorth Boys Club as their new headquarters.

DEATHS: Reported March 27, Squadron Leader Viscount Clive, descendant of Clive of India and heir to the Earl of Powis, killed on active service in Britain, aged 38. He was a Mosquito pilot. February 18, O.D. Murphy, of Haybridge Hall, Hadley, died. He was MD of the Wrekin Brewery Company and a former Mayor of Wenlock. On March 20, Major G.E. Capel-Cure died at Badger Hall. July 31: Lady Startin, wife of Admiral Sir James Startin, died at Linley Hall, Bishop's Castle. October 1, the Earl of Plymouth, a former Conservative MP for Ludlow, died aged 54. On November 30, Major Rowland Hunt, MP for Ludlow from 1903 to 1918, died at Linley Green, Broseley.

1944

March 31: Flight Lieutenant Cyril Douglas "Sid" Swain of Wem was among 50 prisoners executed for taking part in "The Great Escape".

June 6: The 2nd Battalion of the KSLI landed on D-Day and made the deepest penetration inland of any of the invading troops on the day.

October 16: Sergeant George Harold Eardley of the KSLI won the VC at Overloon, Holland.

December: There were Home Guard stand-down parades at various Shropshire towns.

December 24: On Christmas Eve a V1 bomb containing what purported to be letters from POWs landed about a mile east of Newport, the blast smashing windows in the town.

December 26: England players Stanley Matthews and Tom Lawton played for "Shropshire Sportsmen" against the RAF in a charity match at the Gay Meadow before a crowd of 6,000. Shropshire Sportsmen won 14-3. Lawton scored six.

DEATHS: Brigadier General V. Campbell, the Tally Ho VC of World War One, and formerly of Broomhall, Oswestry, died on May 22.

1945

January 2: A 79-year-old gamekeeper, Mr William Chaplin, of Patsmarsh, Worfield, shot dead by an alleged poacher in a wood.

March 19: In a sensational case of the day, Reginald Gough, 31, of Bank Farm, Hope Valley, was found guilty at Stafford Assize Court of the manslaughter of 13-year-old Dennis O'Neill, who died at the farm on January 9. He was from Newport. Gough's wife Esther, aged 29, was cleared of manslaughter but guilty of wilful neglect. Gough got six years penal servitude, the judge saying his behaviour had 'shocked the world and shocked England'. His wife was jailed for six months.

April 16: Work on felling rotten limes in The Quarry, Shrewsbury, began.

April 18: Private Fred Grice, of Slaney Street, Oakengates, arrived home after escaping from a POW camp in Germany. The street was decorated with flags and bunting to welcome him.

April 23: Shifnal Rural Council held its first meeting at the new council chamber at The Grove.

May 1: Two German prisoners of war were shot dead while reportedly trying to escape from a military site near Wem.

May 19: The WJ&SN reported that the Maltings at Shrewsbury was closing as an infantry training depot for the KSLI and North Staffordshire Regiment. It had been used since early in the war.

June 24: The old County Theatre in Shrewsbury extensively damaged by fire.

August 11: Some 1,500 members of the Shropshire Civil Defence Services attended the final stand down parade in the grounds of Shrewsbury School.

August 30: At a ceremony in Shrewsbury Castle Mr S.M. Bruce, High Commissioner for Australia, received a plaque commemorating the adoption of HMAS Shropshire by the county.

September 2: Ernie Clements of Wrekin Cycling Club became the first double cycling champion by winning the British League of Racing Cyclists time trial championship having previously secured the national road race title.

September 22: Shrewsbury bypass reopened. Since September 1943 it had been used as a vehicle storage depot of the 60 Vehicle Reserve Depot, receiving new vehicles from factories and later despatching them to embarkation ports. Normal turnover was 1,000 a week and the largest number there at one time was 1,500.

October 16: Church Stretton bypass officially opened.

October 26: Reported in SC that Shrewsbury was to adopt blitzed town Zutphen in Holland.

October 30: Bridgnorth had its biggest fire for many years at the premises known as the Bargain Bazaar, 57 High Street.

October 31: Shropshire-born champion jockey Gordon Richards rode his 3,000th winner at Newmarket.

November 10: By scoring all seven goals for Shrewsbury Town in a Midland League match against Notts County Reserves, centre forward W.G. Richardson beat the Shrewsbury individual scoring record in one match.

December 17: An Oxford training plane crashed in a field at the foot of The Wrekin, the two airmen were killed.

December 22: WJ&SN reported that St Dunstan's training centre for blind servicemen and women was transferring from Church Stretton to Ovingdean, Brighton, in the new year.

DEATHS: December 12, Freddie Fox, 57, a well known jockey and native of Ryton, Dorrington, died in a road accident in Oxfordshire. He was champion jockey in 1930. January 4, Fred Lawton, of Brockton Court, Shifnal, one of the best known band leaders in Shropshire was found dead in bed. He committed suicide. December 10, Thomas Vickery, of Astley Abbotts, designer, maker, and exhibitor of grandfather clocks, aged 63.

1946

January 1: Percy Thrower took up his duties as Shrewsbury parks superintendent.

February 9: The worst flood in living memory left a trail of damage in Shropshire and the border counties. On February 9 it was 18ft 9ins above summer level at Montford Bridge.

February 22: It was reported that the first bananas for over six years had arrived in Shropshire.

April 12: SC reported that Attingham Hall was to become an adult college.

May 14: Oswestry Youth Club building was opened by Sir Offley Wakeman.

June 15: Four German "special category" prisoners escaped from prison camps at Wem and Hawkstone, but were soon recaptured.

June 20: The Captain and representatives of other officers and crew of HMAS Shropshire entertained at Shrewsbury and Powis Castle.

Reported June 29: Wellington Town FC buys the Buck's Head ground from Messrs Butler's.

July 6: Former Foreign Secretary Anthony Eden guest of honour at the first Wrekin fete since the war, held in Orleton Park, Wellington.

July 25: Nearly 30,000 people – an all time record (until then) – attended the first post war Shropshire and West Midland show at Shrewsbury, held on one day instead of the usual two.

December 31: The first 999 scheme in Shropshire for emergency telephone calls came into operation at Shrewsbury.

DEATHS: Mr Thomas Wainwright Bromley, first chairman of Shropshire NFU, on October 4, aged 86.

1947

January 1: Big fire in scrap aircraft site at High Ercall airfield.

January 5: Ceremonies at the collieries in Shropshire to mark the nationalisation of the mines.

February 5: Roads blocked and villages isolated by worst snowstorms for many years.

February 25: At the height of a night snowstorm, fire gutted one of the moulding shops at the tile works of Messrs. J. Doughty & Son Ltd, Jackfield.

March 5: Worst blizzard of winter hit Shropshire.

March 20: Disastrous floods followed the great thaw, and the Severn at Montford Bridge reached the previous year's level, itself a 150-year record.

April 1: Shrewsbury Borough Police Force merged with Shropshire Constabulary.

April 9: Coal lorry careered down Tontine Hill, Ironbridge, hitting and overturning another lorry, before plunging through a wall and into the River Severn, taking a parked Co-op van with it into the water. Nobody was hurt.

May 8: Long Lane signal box on the outskirts of Craven Arms demolished when one of about 15 railway wagons derailed at the crossing and crashed through it. The signalman had a miracle escape.

May 10: A war memorial recreation ground opened at Alveley.

May 21 and 22: Record crowds attend the first two-day West Mid since the war.

May 31: Shropshire honoured its county regiments at a ceremony in the Quarry, Shrewsbury, when addresses of honour and silver trumpets and bugles were presented.

June 17: Reported in SC that Shrewsbury Town Council had decided at their meeting 'on Monday' to gradually abandon the conduit water system which had brought water to the town from Conduit Head since 1552.

August 21: Celebrating its diamond jubilee, Shrewsbury Flower Show broke all records for attendance figures, with receipts more than double their previous best.

September 3: Film technicians were at Bomere Pool to shoot lake scenes for the making of the film "Precious Bane" starring Ann Todd. The movie appears never to have been made.

September 6: Dick Meyrick, Shropshire bowler, won the British Crown Green Coronation Cup at Meole Brace, the first occasion for a Shropshire man to win this cup.

September 8: In a railway accident at Jackfield, crossing keeper Mrs E. Baynham, aged 68, was killed.

November 15: Harold Shipton of Shrewsbury married Miss Janet Attlee, daughter of Prime Minister Clement Attlee.

SCHOOL CLOSURES: Hope Bowdler School.

DEATHS: Lord Berwick of Attingham Park, aged 70, on June 12.

1948

January 12: For rescuing a 13-year-old girl from drowning in the River Severn, Mr P. Wenlock, of Water Street, Castlefields, Shrewsbury, was presented with the Royal Humane Society's testimonial. It was his seventh river rescue.

January 14: For the third successive year, heavy rain caused severe flooding in Shropshire and adjoining counties.

January 25: The church bells and tower of All Saints Church, Gobowen, were dedicated.

January 27: Shropshire Orthopaedic Hospital, near Oswestry, gutted by fire. Patients were moved to safety by the nurses and military and civilian helpers. Nobody hurt.

February 13: The bodies of two women who were victims of a great blizzard in 1947 found on Wilderley Hill, near Picklescott, after 12 months.

February 28: Dawley old folk's rest room officially opened.

March 20: The Chief Scout, Lord Rowallan, attended a great county rally at the Quarry, Shrewsbury.

March 30: The Dower House at Quatt was badly damaged by fire.

April: Millichope School, near Craven Arms, opened.

April 29: In a fire which trapped a family of seven at their home in Copthorne Road, Shrewsbury, Mrs Edith Harper and three of her children died.

May 1: Dawley War Memorial Gates dedicated.

May 20: Record attendance of over 45,000 at the two-day Shropshire and West Midland Show, Shrewsbury.

June 12: Big parade at Copthorne Barracks, Shrewsbury, to mark the merger of the 2nd Battalion King's Shropshire Light Infantry with the 1st Battalion.

July 25: A new memorial wall to Old Salopians killed in WW2 unveiled at Shrewsbury School.

July 31: New village hall at Willey opened by Princess Alice, Countess of Athlone.

August 2: Mr R.G. Meyrick of Nalgo (Shrewsbury) bowling club, won the British Crown Green Amateur Bowling Association's individual merit at Derby.

August 17: Sporting friends in his native Ironbridge made a presentation to Billy Wright, the England and Wolves footballer, in recognition of his football achievements.

August 28: A service held around the Captain Webb Memorial in Dawley to pay homage to the Channel swimmer born 100 years before a few yards from the memorial.

September: At Shropshire Orthopaedic Hospital there was an outbreak of typhoid which killed seven people and infected over 100 more. It began in September and ended on October 23.

December 1: Thousands of pounds damage caused by night fire at the beer and mineral water bottling stores of Messrs Drew & Co, King Street, Oswestry.

December 2: Opening of new parish hall at Cleobury Mortimer.

December 10: Official opening of new parish church hall at Moreton, Newport.

Misc: RNIB school opened at Condover. Attingham Hall was (due to) open as an adult college in the autumn of 1948. Shropshire Fire Brigade was formed, taking over from the National Fire Service.

DEATHS: Lt Col Dickin of Loppington House on May 30. Dame Agnes Hunt died on July 24. Admiral Sir James Startin, of Linley Hall, Bishop's Castle, called 'the bravest of the brave' by the Times for his numerous acts of personal bravery and lifesaving, on September 25, aged 93.

1949

February 18: SC reported that Walford Manor, Baschurch, had been bought by Salop County Council to be used as a farm institute. (A later story talked of courses beginning in October).

April 8: Picture of the external illuminations on the Empire Cinema, Shrewsbury, on after 10 years, the first night of the lifting of the ban on street illumination.

April 30: Wolverhampton Wanderers won the FA Cup with three Shropshire-born players in their team – Billy Wright, Johnny Hancocks and Roy Pritchard.

May 7 (i.e. pic in WJ&SN this day): Major work being done at the Bucks Head, Wellington, to level the famous slope at

the Wellington Town ground.

May 13: There was a £50,000 fire in the paint shop of the Chatwood Safe and Engineering Co, Shrewsbury.

July 6: Princess Elizabeth and the Duke of Edinburgh visited the Royal Show at Shrewsbury – the fourth to be held in the county town since 1845.

July 20: Official opening of new children's recreation ground at Orleton Lane, Wellington, by the donor, Mrs O.D. Murphy.

July: Filming of Hollywood film Gone To Earth starring Jennifer Jones started in Much Wenlock at the end of this month.

September 20: The Cumberland opened at Broseley.

October 14: SC had a picture of a new 'self service' shop at Harlescott in which customers brought purchases to the pay desk in a wire basket, where they were checked by a counter clerk.

December 7: Gordon Richards and Billy Wright were the chief guests at a dinner at the Forest Glen to honour Shropshire sporting celebrities.

December 10 (reported): Shropshire Association of Parish and Town Councils inaugurated.

December 17: Television came to Shropshire with the opening of the Sutton Coldfield transmitter.

DEATHS: On June 3, the death aged 79 of the Rt Rev A.J. Moriarty, RC Bishop of Shrewsbury since 1934.

1950

February 27: A new Shrewsbury bus station opened adjoining old St Chad's School. It had moved from the Square and Upper Barker Street.

March 25: Overley Hall, near Wellington, opened as a Sunshine Home Nursery School for blind children.

April 9: Fire gutted a 17th century block of three thatched cottages at Norton crossroads, near Shrewsbury.

April 12: In a week of pageantry RAF Bridgnorth conferred the honour of the Freedom of Bridgnorth.

May 12: Two killed in explosion at the Ironbridge Metal Co., Madeley Wood. Victims were managing director Mr F. Frankel and employee Mrs K. Healey.

June 3: Shrewsbury Town were admitted to the Third Division (Northern Section).

June 17: In the King's Cup race a plane crashed at Newport and the pilot was killed.

August 21: Shrewsbury Town's first home match in the Third Division against Wrexham attracted a crowd of 16,070 to the Gay Meadow. Town won 2-1. A further 1,000 people were shut out of the ground.

September: Outbreak of dysentery centred on Whitchurch. The first case was in September and from October 20, 1950, to March 29, 1951, there were 74 cases in Whitchurch.

October 12: The Iron Bridge declared free of toll after the official handing over of the bridge by the Ironbridge Trust to Salop County Council.

October 15: Provincial premiere of Gone To Earth in Shrewsbury's Granada Cinema.

Misc: Shropshire's worst year for polio deaths – 11. There were also 62 notifications of the disease.

DEATHS: August 14, one of the best Shropshire athletes of his day, Mr E.C. Climer, of Wem, died aged 76. On September 25, on a holiday at his birthplace of Ellerdine, John Beard, CBE, of London, former president of the TUC, aged 78. "Nipper", aka Arthur Edward Cook, a local character, buried in Stottesdon churchyard on March 3.

1951

January 4: Frank Griffin, 40, became the first person executed at Shrewsbury since 1923, for the murder of the 74-year-old licensee of the Queens Head Inn, Ketley.

On or about April 10, Tom, Jimmy and Kit, the last remaining horses of Wellington goods yard's cartage fleet, replaced by two motor vehicles.

May 3: Shrewsbury's Festival of Britain celebrations opened with folk dancing in the castle grounds.

July 14: A memorial to Richard Baxter, the famous 17th century divine, unveiled on the village green at Rowton, his birthplace.

September 6: The 300th anniversary of the escape of Charles II after the Battle of Worcester celebrated with a thanksgiving service at Boscobel and by the planting by the Earl of Bradford of a sapling grown from an acorn of the oak tree not many yards away up which Charles hid.

September 24: Last Bridgnorth Borough Petty Sessions held.

September 29: Chief Guide, Lady Baden-Powell, visited Shropshire.

November 6: Official opening of Picklescott village hall.

November 20: New Castle Walk footbridge opened in Shrewsbury by the Mayor, Cllr A.H. Jones.

December 31: Passenger train services ended on the Much Wenlock to Craven Arms railway line.

Misc: One way system introduced in Pontesbury, mainly because of safety fears for village schoolchildren.

1,000 tons of rock were blasted off High Rock, Bridgnorth, to remove an overhang and sweep it back. The famous Tailor's Hole was lost as a result.

DEATHS: August 31, Giles Reid Walker, in a road collision in South Africa, a "well known aviator and sporting motorist" whose parents lived at Ruckley Grange, near Shifnal. Famous for the lupins bearing his name, Mr G. Russell, of Albrighton, aged 94, on October 15.

1952

January 14: A new bus station opened in the Upper Car Park, Barker Street, Shrewsbury, moving the station from Bridge Street.

February 23: The last of the avenues of limes at Shrewsbury Quarry felled.

April: Jackfield hit by a serious landslip.

April 10: Bridgnorth Rural District Council's new offices and council chamber at Westgate officially opened.

May 21 and 22: The Shropshire and West Midland Show was held at Shrewsbury without the cattle, pig and sheep sections owing to widespread foot and mouth outbreaks (discovered on April 26 at Willoughbridge, nr Market Drayton).

May 31: "The Dodger" train made its last journey from Wellington to Coalport on the closing of the line.

June 19: As part of the fourth centenary celebrations of Shrewsbury School, a high cross at the top of Pride Hill presented to the town.

September 8: A lorry bound for Ironbridge power station ran away down Madeley Hill and into Ironbridge. Three people seriously injured.

September 12: An Anson plane from RAF Shawbury crashed into the Wrekin in mist, killing the pilot.

November 6: 1st Battalion KSLI welcomed by cheering crowds on their return to Shrewsbury after being away fighting in Korea for 16 months. There was a civic reception at Shrewsbury.

November 6: Wind of 94mph recorded at Shawbury.

DEATHS: Major B.E. Parker Leighton, Conservative MP for Oswestry 1929-45, at home at Sweeney Hall, Oswestry, aged 76, on February 15. On April 28, Sir John Bayley, founder of Wrekin College, in Ramsgate aged 99. On July 5 the chairman of Allied Iron Company's Shropshire group, Mr W.H. Watkins, died aboard his yacht at Poole harbour, aged 63. On September 2, Mr B. Jackson, aged 24, of Gobowen, when practising for the Isle of Man TT races at the Isle of Man. November 9, the Earl of Powis, of Powis Castle, who had been Lord Lieutenant of Shropshire for 55 years, aged 90. April 26, death of Robert Fleming Prideaux, aged 72, Shrewsbury town clerk of 31 years.

1953

Around January 10: Shrewsbury Town beat Finchley 2-0 to go into the Fourth Round of the FA Cup for the first time ever.

January 31: They lost in the Fourth Round on about January 31 4-0 to Southampton before a record gate of 17,249 at the Gay Meadow in the club's first-ever all-ticket match.

March 5: A dormitory and the music room at the Royal Normal College for the Blind in the grounds at Rowton Castle destroyed by fire, but boys evacuated safely.

April 29: Oswestry Town FC received the Birmingham League Championship shield.

May 15: News appears for the first time on the front page of the Shrewsbury Chronicle.

June 1: Gordon Richards, the Shropshire jockey, knighted in the Coronation Birthday Honours.

June 6: Sir Gordon Richards wins the Derby for the first time at his 28th attempt.

June 29: Milton's famous Masque "Comus" performed at Ludlow Castle.

July 5: Colonel John Hunt, leader of the successful

Everest expedition, given a great welcome on his return home to Weir Cottage, Llanfair Waterdine.

September 10: An extension to Midland Red's Wellington garage opened.

October 12: Many thousands of pounds damage was caused by fire in the paint shop at Sankey's Hadley Castle Works.

October 13: Ironbridge power station floodlit to celebrate its 21st birthday.

November 5: John Allen, aged 33, of Stretford, Manchester, escaped over the wall of Shrewsbury Jail, believed to be the first escape of its kind for 40 years. Recaptured four days later. He was serving 10 years for housebreaking and larceny.

November 15: British middleweight boxing champion Randolph Turpin married Miss Gwyneth Price, daughter of a North Wales hill farmer, at Wellington Register Office in Walker Street.

November 23: Celebration dinner at Donnington in honour of Sir Gordon Richards' knighthood and first Derby win. It was part of a three-day programme in which the champion jockey was feted in his native district.

Misc: William Brookes School at Much Wenlock opened (as Much Wenlock County Secondary School). The Mere and Cremorne Gardens were given as a gift to Ellesmere by Lord Brownlow in commemoration of the coronation on June 2.

DEATHS: The High Sheriff of Shropshire, Lt Col W.W. Hayes, of Harcourt, Stanton, killed when his car crashed into a tree at Tushingham on March 11. On March 14, Robert Nathaniel Moore, founder of Madeley Rest Room, aged 72. March 18, Mr Rowland Francis Meyrick, of Apley Castle, descended from the famous Charlton family, aged 85. Arthur Phillips, Market Drayton aviation pioneer (SC had a p1 report on his death 'last week' aged 80 on May 15, 1953.)

1954

January 26: Desmond Donald Hooper, a 28-year-old gardener, of Atcham Camp, executed at Shrewsbury for murdering a 12-year-old girl.

February 3: During a prolonged spell of frost and snow, the River Severn froze almost completely over at Shrewsbury.

February 18: Fire gutted the 17th century Mary Knoll House, near Ludlow.

March 4: A Spitfire crashed in a farm yard just 50 yards from Church Pulverbatch School where 45 children were having lessons. Pilot killed.

April 30: In what was described as Shrewsbury's most dangerous ever fire, damage estimated at over £20,000 was done to the oil refinery of Messrs Morris and Co in Castle Foregate.

May 26: Alderman Mrs M. Hoy elected first woman mayor of the Borough of Wenlock since the office was instituted in 1468.

July 18: Tong Castle deliberately blown up.

July 28: Opening of nurses' home at Oswestry Orthopaedic Hospital.

July 28: Two Shrewsbury climbers, Peter Kaighen (29), lodging in Sundorne Crescent, and Anthony Lawson, 25, of St Michael's Vicarage, went missing while climbing the Matterhorn. Believed to have fallen to their deaths.

July: Reported on July 31 that rabbit killer disease myxomatosis had spread to Shropshire, having been found at Marshbrook, near Church Stretton.

August: Shropshire's central ambulance station at Abbey Foregate, Shrewsbury, came into operation, with 14 ambulances and six service cars (report September 4, said it came into operation "last week").

August 3: Buildwas Park Hall deliberately blown up.

September 22: Oswestry's new municipal covered attested cattle market built at a cost of £20,000 opened.

October 8: Wellington gave an enthusiastic welcome to Dr Roger Bannister, guest of honour at a Shropshire Youth Clubs ball.

October 15: New Colours presented to the 1st Battalion KSLI in Germany.

December 11: New recreation ground at Hadley, made possible by a gift of £10,000 by Messrs Joseph Sankey and Sons in celebration of their centenary, officially opened.

DEATHS: Sister of Captain Matthew Webb, Mrs Margaret Elizabeth Barnett, aged 88, at Grove House Nursing Home, Church Stretton (reported WJ&SN January 9). On February 9, Mr G.N. Dickin, of Loppington Hall, a member of one of Shropshire's oldest families, aged 79. On August 27, the

former managing director of Sankey's, Col H.B. Sankey, of Whiston hall, Albrighton, in his office at Bilston, aged 59.

1955

January 24: Trench Boys' Secondary Modern School opened.

February: A newspaper article suggested that Dawley could be used as an "overspill" area for Birmingham.

February 24: A spell of severe weather which had lasted over a week culminated in a blizzard with snow up to 10ins deep in Shropshire.

March 26: Over two inches of rain in 24 hours caused severe flooding in Shropshire and adjoining counties.

March 31: Harlescott secondary modern school opened.

April 24: Two soldiers drowned when a boat overturned on The Mere, Ellesmere.

April 28: In honour of the bicentenary of the KSLI, the honorary Freedom of the Borough of Shrewsbury was conferred on the regiment. Later there were ceremonies in Bridgnorth and Hereford.

May 18: The West Mid Show at Shrewsbury on May 18 and 19 first to be televised. Also particularly wet, with 12 hours of rain, hail and occasional snow on the eve of the show.

May 28: Children's playground nicknamed "Tricia's playground" opened by Lord Newport at Cremorne Gardens, Ellesmere.

June 14: Manual telephone exchange operated in Lydbury North by village postmistress Mrs Esta Griffiths Jones for 48 years, switched over to automatic operation.

August 2: Severe fire virtually destroyed the well known Chelmick tea rooms near Church Stretton.

August 4: Minesweeper HMS Rodington, named after Shropshire village, commissioned.

August 21: A family of three had a 'miraculous escape' when a motorcycle and open side car combination plunged 400ft off the Burway, Church Stretton.

September 4: Wellington police moved from building in Church Street to new headquarters in Glebe Street (official opening was October 10).

October 4: Wrockwardine FC played a practice match under floodlights installed by their own voluntary efforts and became the first club in Shropshire, either amateur or professional, to do so.

Reported October 15: Apley Castle, Wellington, sold the preceding week for demolition.

Misc: 1955 was Shropshire's worst year to then for road deaths to date – 63 were killed.

DEATHS: May 16, Dr C.A. Alington, a former head of Shrewsbury School, aged 82.

1956

January 11: Three airmen killed when two Provost aircraft collided in mid air at Stoke-on-Tern. One airman successfully baled out.

February 7: Severe damage done by fire to the interior of the Ritz Cinema, in Market Drayton Town Hall, where the large assembly hall was let out as a cinema.

May 5: The ship's bell from HMAS Shropshire presented to the county to hang in the council chamber at the Shirehall.

July 17: A new attested cattle market opened at Harlescott, Shrewsbury.

August (end of): Rolls-Royce took over the Sentinel Works at Shrewsbury

September 6: One person was hurt when a passenger train and a parcels express train collided about 200 yards north of Ludlow railway station.

September 17: First day of school of Dawley Secondary Modern School (later called Phoenix).

September 17: Production started at the new Ever Ready factory, Dawley. (n.b. one report said it started in August).

October 4: Wellington's first traffic lights came into operation, at the Bucks Head junction.

October 11: Speech by Wrekin MP Bill Yates at the Tory Party conference in Llandudno ended in uproar. He attacked Britain's policy over Egypt and Cyprus.

December 13: Boxer Tommy Nicholls of Wellington returned home after winning silver in the Melbourne Olympics. He was a southpaw featherweight.

December 18: Shropshire extended a warm welcome to 35 Hungarian refugees who arrived in the county and who were taking up residence at Ash Grange, near Whitchurch, which had been handed over by Salop County Council to the Red Cross.

December 25: It was a white Christmas. Snow started shortly after lunchtime on Christmas Day and led to snowdrifts of up to 4ft from a fall which averaged 4ins.
Misc: Electricity was continuing to be extended to thousands of rural properties in the county.
DISEASE: Fourteen people died of respiratory TB in Shropshire in 1956, the lowest figure ever recorded and less than a quarter of the figure for 1946. The number of polio cases notified in the county during 1956 was ten, a decrease of nine compared with the previous year, with none proving fatal.
DEATHS: Ossie Pointon of the Forest Glen, who popularised the "All Friends Round the Wrekin" toast started by his father, on June 19. On December 11, Frank Davies, former chief constable of the old Shrewsbury Borough police force, aged 78. September 10, Sir Arthur Colgate, aged 72, at Ryde, Isle of Wight, Wrekin MP 1941-45. December 19, George Whitfield, Oswestry VC, when he was apparently knocked down by an Army lorry while cycling.

1957

January 14: Christ Church School, Cressage, opened.
February 12: Springfield Hotel in Wenlock Road, Shrewsbury opens.
March 14: Sooty and Harry Corbett visited Wellington's Chad Valley Works.
March 16: New attested cattle market at Bridgnorth Smithfield opened.
March 23: Labour leader Hugh Gaitskell addressed a county rally at Wellington Drill Hall. The local Labour candidate was Donald Bruce.
June 17: Diesel train service (was due) to start operating between Shrewsbury, Wellington and Birmingham. It was not to be a full service (SC said on June 7), but would be supplemented by steam.
July 6: The Majestic Theatre in Whitburn Street, Bridgnorth, was struck by lightning while 500 cinema-goers were watching a gunfight in a Western. Nobody hurt.
August 26: Hampton Loade ferry was swept away down the swollen River Severn. Ferryman William J. Parkes, aged 66, managed to leap aboard the Arley ferry to safety as his ferry swept past.
September 4: Wyle Cop Youth Club, Belmont, Shrewsbury, destroyed by fire.
September 10: A new secondary modern school opened at Pontesbury.
September 13: 50 firemen fought a blaze which caused damage put at over £23,000 to the warehouse premises and plant belonging to Messrs S.E. and A. Ridley Ltd in Mill Street, Bridgnorth.
September 26: Portway House, Wellington, a former YWCA hostel, officially opened as nine bedsits for elderly ladies.
Reported December 14: County health officials unveiled a campaign to warn children about the risk of lung cancer in later life arising from smoking.
December 31: The Captain Webb Memorial taken down from its original position and moved to a new site in front of Dawley library.
Misc: Baschurch secondary modern school (later the Corbet School) opened.
DEATHS: Richard Mansell, twice mayor of Shrewsbury, on May 23, aged 91. On March 21, the Earl of Bradford, at Weston Park, aged 83. Sir Richard Leighton, Bt, of Loton Park, on September 25 aged 64. On April 13, Stephen Ward, MBE, of Ercall Lane, Wellington, aged 84, a well known agriculturalist and pioneer in the formation of the NFU – it was his motion in 1908 which led to the NFU being set up.

1958

January: Secondary modern school for boys opened at Oldbury Wells, Bridgnorth.
January 4 or 5: A 19-year-old from Wellington died of polio at Shrewsbury, Shropshire's first polio death since 1954 when there were two deaths.
January 15: The Canadian anti-polio Salk vaccine was used for the first time in Shropshire, with an initial supply of 900 doses.
Reported February 7 in SC: More than 200 square miles of Shropshire hill country was soon to be classed as one of Britain's areas of outstanding natural beauty.
According to a newspaper report dated March 6, the "New Plaza" cinema at Bishop's Castle had closed "until further

notice" according to a notice on the building.
March 22: Sir Gordon Richards opened a dispensary for sick animals at Stafford Street, Oakengates.
Reported May 24: Workmen were ripping up the Cock island in Wellington and putting in traffic lights. Hoped to have the traffic controlled by traffic lights before the end of August.
June 5: Arthur Rowley became Shrewsbury Town's first player manager since the club entered league football.
June 9: Dorrington station closed to passengers, along with Condover, Leebotwood, Marshbrook, Onibury, Bromfield, and Berrington and Eye. All Stretton and Little Stretton halts also closed.
July 6: One of Shropshire's biggest ever military parades. Thousands of people paid homage to the TA in Shropshire for a drumhead parade, incorporating a Bligny day service, in the Quarry, Shrewsbury.
September 20: The last run over the section of the Lilleshall Company's railway lines between the Priorslee Furnaces and the New Yard, about two miles away. The company was closing the line.
Reported September 27: Since February over 40,000 children, expectant mothers and others, vaccinated against polio in Shropshire.
October 1 and Oct 2: Prime Minister Harold Macmillan and his wife visited Wellington and Shrewsbury on a meet-the-people tour. Following day he went to Cruckton ploughing match.
Reported November 1: "The National Trust announced the gift of Benthall Hall by Mrs J. Floyer Benthall and Sir Edward Benthall, of Lindridge, Devon."
Reported November 1: 500 men boycott the cookhouse at Donnington Army base in protest over food.
November 20: Shrewsbury crematorium officially opened at Emstrey.
SCHOOL CLOSURES: Eyton School, Eyton-on-the-Weald-Moors, shut on July 25.
DEATHS: On January 8, Wynne Corrie, i.e. Mrs Mary Wynne Fletcher, a well known Shrewsbury Amateur Operatic Society soprano, together with her two children and their 19-year-old nursemaid, in a road crash near Rugby.

1959

February 5: Landslide at the Royal Salop Infirmary caused part of the hospital to be evacuated.
March 20: SC reported today that the Minister of Housing and Local Government had confirmed an order designating 300 square miles of the Shropshire hills as an Area of Outstanding Natural Beauty.
Good Friday (i.e. March 27): Shropshire's last remaining blast furnaces, at Priorslee, closed after 107 years.
April 7: Official opening of the new £500,000 Shrewsbury Smithfield at Harlescott.
May 8: SC reported that Shrewsbury Town had made it back to the Third Division after only a single season in the Fourth, after beating Watford 4-1.
June 30: Milton's Masque of Comus performed at Ludlow Castle. Princess Margaret saw the floodlit performance, in the culminating event of her royal visit.
July 7: Two women and a baby stabbed to death at Harmer Hill.
July 13: New premises of Barclays Bank, on the corner of Castle Street and St Mary's Street, Shrewsbury, opened.
August 29: Official opening of Sankey FC's new ground at the Hadley Castle works.
September: The Norah Wellings toy factory at Victoria Toy Works, King Street, Wellington, closed.
September 8: Secondary modern school for girls opened at Oldbury Wells, Bridgnorth.
September 23: Harold Macmillan visits Shifnal in whistlestop tour to support Tory candidate Bill Yates.
September 26: Aneurin Bevan at the Majestic Ballroom, Wellington, in support of Labour candidate Donald Bruce. Over 700 present.
September 29: Stirling Moss and his wife Katie injured in a head-on collision at Chetwynd.
October 3: Shrewsbury Telephone Exchange became operational.
October 15: Set of commemorative gates leading to the site of Abraham Darby's historic furnace officially opened to mark the 250th anniversary of the founding of the Coalbrookdale Company.
October 31: The Crown Hotel, Shrewsbury, closed.
November 21: Shrewsbury Town's first game under floodlights – albeit for only part of the game, as it was a 3.15pm

kickoff – played at the Gay Meadow v QPR.
November 25: Official inaugural floodlit game (7.15pm evening kickoff) at the Gay Meadow, v Stoke. Shrewsbury won 5-0.
December: Hiatt College (for ladies), Wellington, which dated from May 1847, closed in December at the end of term.
Misc: *Old Man Parr's cottage at Winnington burned down in mid summer 1959.*
DEATHS: On October 3, John Vernon Lander, 75, retired Wellington and district coroner, aged 75. He had overcome polio as a young man.
SCHOOL CLOSURES: March 7, reference made in WJ&SN to the closing of Little Wenlock School i.e. that school must have been closed quite recently.

1960

February 15-20: Sale of contents of the Raven Hotel, Shrewsbury.
April 13: Stirling Moss found guilty of dangerous driving at Chetwynd. Banned from driving for 12 months.
May 4: Wrekin MP Bill Yates stormed out of the House of Commons after being denied an emergency debate on Cyprus. He wanted to impeach the Foreign Secretary, Selwyn Lloyd.
May 6: The 1st Battalion of the KSLI marched through towns and villages in the county and Herefordshire to "show the flag" and the fortnight of marching ended today.
May 28: Adam Faith came to Oakengates as the grand finale to Oakengates shopping week. He was appearing at the Granada, Shrewsbury.
Reported June 11: Said to the last of its type, the old guillotine-style canal lock at Eyton-on-the-Weald Moors was soon to be dismantled and preserved as a relic at the British Transport Commission Museum in London.
June 26: Shropshire's first ever Catholic rally took place at Woodcote Hall, Newport.
July 2: Severn Valley Motor Club held its first hill climb at Loton Park, Alberbury.
July 22 and 23: The All England Schools Inter County Athletics Championships held at the cinder track at Shrewsbury Technical College.
August 11: 35 soldiers, the last National Service intake to be trained at the regimental depot of the KSLI in Shrewsbury, passed out.
September 1: New Clifford Williams factory opened at Dawley Bank.
September 3: The Wellington Journal and Shrewsbury News started putting news on the front page for the first time since it was founded on January 2, 1854.
September 19: Shrewsbury Technical College opened in London Road (the official opening followed on May 5, 1961).
September 7: Ellis Boyce, 30, of Lea Cross, Shrewsbury, won the Isle of Man Junior Manx Grand Prix, setting a new record speed.
September: Robbie Brightwell of Donnington left for the Rome Olympic Games, where he twice smashed the UK and national record for the 400 metres, but did not qualify for the final.
October 15: Ludlow CofE secondary school opened at Burway.
October 31: The Plaza cinema at Bishop's Castle, opened in 1930, closed (but also see 1958 when it was carrying a 'closed until further notice' sign).
November 24: Outbreak of foot and mouth – the worst in Shropshire since 1952 – at The Beeches, Ollerton. Hundreds of cattle, sheep and pigs were slaughtered.
December: About the 3rd Shropshire suffered its worst floods since 1946. The Severn at Shrewsbury rose 18ft. 500 homes were affected in Shrewsbury.
December 5: Withdrawal of the freight service between Dawley and Stirchley and Coalport East. Stations at Madeley Market and Coalport East closed.
December 5: George Riley, a 21-year-old butchers assistant of 38 Westlands Road, Copthorne, sentenced to death at Staffordshire Assizes for murder of widow and near neighbour Mrs Adeline Mary Smith.
DEATHS: On January 8, the former Suffragan Bishop of Shrewsbury, the Rt Rev Robert Leighton Hodson, aged 74, at Llandudno. February 23, Colonel John George Burton Borough, of Chetwynd Park, aged 69. Reported September 10, Miss Edith Picton-Turbervill, one of the first women to enter the House of Commons when she was elected as

Labour MP for the Wrekin in 1929. October 29, Mr E.P. Everest i.e. Edward Percy Everest, "Mr Flower Show", at his home in Shrewsbury aged 78. On December 4, Vincent Greenhous, aged 74, at his home at Shoot Hill.
SCHOOL CLOSURES: July, Tong School.

1961

January 2: Bishop's Castle's first ever factory opened – E.R. Hammersley and Co. Ltd of Cradley Heath, which opened a clothing factory in the Plaza cinema, which had closed some months before.
February 9: George Riley executed at Shrewsbury jail. Shropshire's last execution.
February 13: Three railway workers killed in collision between passenger train and freight train a few yards from Baschurch station.
March: Shirlett Sanatorium closed.
March 8: Five die when ambulance bursts into flames at Atcham.
April 26: All time record attendance for Shrewsbury Town of 18,917 in Third Division tie against Walsall.
April 29: Arthur Rowley, Shrewsbury Town's player manager, became a soccer immortal by beating the aggregate scoring record of 379 set up by Dixie Dean. He scored with a header at Bradford.
May 14: New swimming baths opened at Dinham, Ludlow.
May 17: Two riders of the Royal Artillery motor cycle display team hurt when their machines collided during a display at the West Mid Show.
May 22: First celebration of communion at the ruined Lilleshall Abbey for over 400 years.
October 20: Two prisoners escaped from Shrewsbury Jail, using a rope and a home-made hook to get over the prison wall. Recaptured after six days.
October 31: Dawley's Civic Trust scheme, first completed in Shropshire, officially opened. It involved a facelift for Dawley.
November 4: Belmont Hall, Wellington, opened.
Reported December 30: Long stretches of the River Severn at Shrewsbury froze over for the first time since 1947. On Christmas morning there was a hard frost of 16.5F, but it was not a white Christmas.
SCHOOL CLOSURES: July: Constitution Hill infants school, Wellington, closed at the end of this month.
DEATHS: On February 27, Brigadier A.G.W. Heber-Percy at Hodnet Hall. On February 5, George "Woppy" Phillips, well known Shrewsbury scrap man. Born in 1886.

1962

January 1: Shrewsbury MP John Holt knighted in the New Year honours for political services.
Reported January 30: Bob Norry, 22, of Coalbrookdale, a member of 22 SAS, killed during a 36,000ft parachute drop on Salisbury Plain.
Reported February 9: Constable Bob Roberts, a Shropshire policeman, awarded the George Medal for his attempts to arrest a gunman after a manhunt in the Mid Wales hills in August 1961.
February 10: Reported that a phantom clock raider was scaling public clocks in Shrewsbury and stopping them.
May 29: Government announces decision to go ahead with Dawley New Town.
June 9: Singer Frankie Vaughan mobbed by fans when he attended Wellington Carnival at the Bucks Head.
July 21: Last passenger train left Much Wenlock for Wellington.
September: Telephone House, Shrewsbury, completed.
September: New Walker Technical College opens at Bennetts Bank, Wellington.
September 3: "The Twist" singer Chubby Checker besieged by autograph hunters during sightseeing trip in Bridgnorth.
September 7: Reported that the George Hotel, Shrewsbury, had been sold and would close on January 30, 1963.
September 12: Philip Larkin opened Wellington library extension.
September 26: Shrewsbury Town's Arthur Rowley set up an all time British league scoring record when he got the 411th goal of his career, beating the record set by Jimmy McGrory of Glasgow Celtic. He scored with a shot at the Gay Meadow against Millwall.
October 19: John Profumo, secretary of state for war, lays the foundation stone at the new Territorial Army centre at Sundorne Road, Shrewsbury.

November 16: Two men killed at Highley colliery.
November 17: Reported that Graham C. Murphy had given his family home, Haybridge Hall, Hadley, to Wellington Rural Council, fulfilling his wish to provide a suitable memorial to his parents, the late Mr and Mrs O.D. Murphy. The hall was to be converted into flats for old people.
December 14: The Beatles play Shrewsbury Music Hall the first time.
December 21: 40 street lamps turned on on the A5 through Ketley, illuminating "darkest Ketley".
December 25: It was minus 10C, lowest Christmas temperature recorded in Shropshire to then, followed by blizzards on Boxing Day.
Misc: Wem Smithfield closed. Sprinter Robbie Brightwell won the European championships over 400m, and got a silver in the Empire Games. Bowler Dick Meyrick won the British Crown Green Bowling Association merit title, the first time the trophy had been won twice in succession in its 52 year history. The Royal Cinema, Dawley, must have closed about now (a story datestamped August 10 says it closed "recently").
SCHOOL CLOSURES: Easter: Closure of Wrockwardine Wood Junior School, Gower Street, St Georges, known as the Board school. July 1962: i.e. at the end of the summer term the temporary county modern school at High Ercall was due to close. (this reported in SC Feb 9). It opened in 1947 in former WAAF accommodation and had 200 boys.
September: The Millichope School, secondary school for boys, moved to Apley Park over the summer break, the term starting at the new location in September.
DEATHS: Major Sir Jack Becke, chief constable of Shropshire from 1918 to 1935, on March 29 at Northwich infirmary, aged 83. On June 11, John Evan Woollam, of Dawley Road, Wellington, aged 90, a longstanding local councillor. July 11, Robert Gwynne, who founded Gwynne & Sons in Wellington, in his 87th year.

1963

January and February. A big freeze gripped the county with temperatures around freezing day and night. There was skating on the frozen Severn at Shrewsbury. There was a thaw on February 8.
January: Much Wenlock's War Memorial Cinema closed.
January 16: Dawley New Town officially designated. The target population of the new town, which was essentially based on Dawley and Madeley, was about 90,000, which represented a growth of about 50,000 on the existing population.
February 8: RAF Bridgnorth closed. The last passing out of recruits at RAF Bridgnorth was on February 8 and the base closed soon after.
February 28: Beatles played at the Granada in Shrewsbury.
April 26: Beatles played at the Music Hall, Shrewsbury.
April 28: Shrewsbury railway station's high roof dismantled to make way for modern steel canopies. The roof had been erected in 1904.
About June 10: First half of the new Shrewsbury market opened to the public.
June 8: Official opening of Apley Park Secondary Modern Boarding School by Viscountess Boyne.
June 27: Wellington Girls Modern School officially opened at Dothill.
June 28: A workman was killed when the market hall cellar collapsed during demolition work at Shrewsbury.
July 6: Harold Wilson spoke at Wrekin Labour Party's annual gala in Oakengates.
September 7: Last passenger train ran on the Severn Valley Railway from Bridgnorth to Shrewsbury.
September 9: Official closure date of the Wellington to Crewe line for passenger traffic. Both above due to Beeching axe.
September 11: Reconstructed Powis Hall, Oswestry, opened.
Mid September: Church Stretton's Regal cinema closed.
October 4: The Wellington Journal & Shrewsbury News published for the first time on a Friday. Previously it had been a Saturday paper.
November 5: New subscriber trunk dialling automatic telephone system put into operation at Wellington.
Misc: Wellington Journal and Shrewsbury News bought by Midland News Association.
DEATHS: On August 18, Paul Miller, Shrewsbury Town's goalkeeper, in an open air pool at Trentham Gardens. April 24, Gerald (Gerry) Cuff, who delighted hundreds of thou-

sands of children in the ATV "Pop Eye" series. He was licensee of Shrewsbury's Yorkshire House Hotel. He was 58.

1964

January: RAF High Ercall closed.
Reported January 17: Shropshire constabulary's first woman sergeant was this week promoted to inspector, to become the first woman in the county to hold the rank. She was Mrs Hilda Mary Hazelhurst, a war widow.
January 17: SC reported that Robbie Brightwell of Shropshire was named captain of the England athletics team in the Tokyo Olympics.
January 31: Wrekin Beacon due to be switched off today but given last minute stay of execution after local protests.
February 6: A 15-year-old schoolboy, John Howard Brazier, fell to his death from a window at Apley Park School.
May 8: Ken Dodd got a tumultuous reception at "the back of the sheds" in Shrewsbury.
May 9: Weston Park opened to the public for the first time.
May 10/11: Statue of Hercules in Shrewsbury Quarry was decked out in "football kit" by youths who used bright red paint to dress him in a football shirt and shorts.
May 29: Shropshire's first Twist champions chosen at a dance at Sankey's ballroom.
June: Shrewsbury's new post office was opened.
June 13: Three men, all members of a coach party from Stockport, killed on the Mere, Ellesmere, when their hired dinghy capsized.
June 26: Official opening of Shropshire's first Catholic secondary school, the BRJ at Wellington.
July 17: Opening of rebuilt and revamped Marks and Spencer store in Shrewsbury.
August 26: Littlewoods store opened at Castle Street, Shrewsbury.
October 5: Shropshire Star launched.
October 24: Official opening of the new TA Centre, Trench.
November 18: The pannier market, the last stage of the new market hall, Shrewsbury, opened.
December 10: TV personality Mr Pastry at Shrewsbury for the official opening of the new nursery special school at Woodcote Way.
December 13: The Hampton Loade ferry swept away, killing the 22-year-old ferry operator.
December 14: Flooding hits Shropshire, but not as bad as 1960 floods.
December 29: The stocks at Norton, near Sutton Maddock, partially demolished when they were struck by a skidding van.
Misc: Last passenger train from Wellington to Stafford on September 6. Four Salopians competed in the Tokyo Olympics - Robbie Brightwell, who was skipper of the British Olympic athletics team; Worfield hurdler Mike Parker; horseman Ben Jones of Newport; and boxer Johnny Kingston Elliott of Hadley. Brightwell was 4th in the 400m but ran the final leg of the 4x400m to edge the British team into 2nd place.
SCHOOL CLOSURES: *Coalbrookdale High School.* July 24: Stanton C.E. Controlled School at Stanton, nr Moreton Corbet, closed after 233 years. SC reported on October 23, 1964, that Shropshire education authority had confirmed the decision to close Ash CofE Controlled School, Whitchurch.
DEATHS: November 9, Thomas Edward Barnwell, the first Shropshire police officer to solve a crime by fingerprint detection methods, when he was a Sergeant at Hadnall. He was acting chief constable for the county from about November 1943 for two years. He was 81 and lived in Shrewsbury.

1965

January 1: At the stroke of the New Year the Wrekin Beacon switched off, but was revived, albeit temporarily, at Easter i.e. ceremonially turned on again April 20 after money raising by a group of businessmen – sand and gravel contractors, but it seems it was switched off again forever not long after when the money ran out.
January 11: Fatal rail crash at Shrewsbury in which Coton Hill signal box was demolished, killing the signalman.
January 12: Kynaston's ironmongers in Noble Street, Wem, burnt down.
January 30: Shrewsbury Town reached 5th round of FA Cup for the first time, beating Millwall 2-1 at the Den.

February 8: Alf Ramsey calls together England squad at Lilleshall and experiments with 4-3-3 formation – the birth of the wingless wonders.

February 19: First Shropshire Journal was printed, replacing the Wellington Journal and Shrewsbury News, which appeared for the last time on February 12.

February 20: Shrewsbury Town beaten 2-0 by Leeds in the 5th round of the FA Cup at Elland Road.

March 18: Wellington Town play their first match under floodlights at the Bucks Head (against Leeds).

April 20: Wrekin Beacon ceremonially turned back on.

May 14: New ferry at Hampton Loade launched exactly five months after the old one capsized killing owner's son Robert James.

May 23: Detachments of the Ist Bttn KSLI and 4th Bttn KSLI marched through Much Wenlock to exercise the privilege of "Freedom of Entry."

May 29: Haybridge Hall officially opened as an old folks home.

July 11: 4,500 acres of the Long Mynd became the property of the National Trust.

Reported July 23: Lord Harlech, Tory MP for Oswestry 1950-61, appointed president of the British Board of Film Censors.

Reported August 27: A new Silhouette factory completed at Whitchurch to make bras. The first 100 girls had moved in at the end of March.

September 16: Shrewsbury's new general market hall officially opened.

September 29: The Rolling Stones played at the Granada, Shrewsbury.

October 15: Reported in SJ that the run down of the Army Technical Stores Sub Depot at Aston Park, Wem, was continuing with a view to it closing in March 1966.

November 15: Work on Dawley New Town officially began, on Tweedale industrial estate.

December 10: New village hall at High Ercall opened, replacing a 1945 village hall.

December 20: River Severn flooded, rising to a peak in Shrewsbury of 17ft 6ins.

Misc: The Welshpool to Whitchurch line closed to passenger rail traffic. Oakley Manor in Shrewsbury was converted into council offices. Great train robber Robert Welch was held at Shrewsbury jail and a car park, picnic area and three large trees slide into Ellesmere Mere in a landslide. Chelmarsh reservoir built. In July the Severn Valley Railway Society was formed.

SCHOOL CLOSURES: Alberbury School after 103 years. On June 25, the SJ reported the old Mill Bank School, Wellington, was now deserted following the transfer of pupils to a new school in North Road.

DEATHS: On March 28, Richard Beesly, 57, joint managing director of McConnel, Ludlow, and a former county councillor, gored to death by a bull at his home, Ashford Hall, Ludlow.

1966

January 1: Wrekin Beacon went out forever now or about now.

Reported January 28: Flu bug hits the county. In Highley at one time only 99 of the 244 children attending the local county and primary school were present in the previous week.

February 9: A Dawley man who scaled the perimeter wall and broke in to Shrewsbury jail appeared in court.

March 8: Work started on building houses for Dawley New Town, at Sutton Hill.

Reported April 1: Preston School near Wellington was suffering its worst ever epidemic. Chicken pox meant this week that 26 of the 51 pupils were absent.

April 18: New Shirehall and law courts, Shrewsbury, opened for public business.

May 22: A landslide near the Greyhound crossroads, Oakengates, caused the A5 to close.

June: A squad of 27 England players trained at Lilleshall National Sports Centre from June 6 to 17 in the final runup to the World Cup.

June 5: Last civic parade of the doomed Bishop's Castle Borough Council.

June 11: New Salvation Army HQ opened in Oakengates.

June 23: Three died when two RAF Shawbury Chipmunks collided near Tibberton Grange, Newport.

June 23: A 300ft wing of Ellesmere College was gutted by a £100,000 fire.

July 3: Ironbridge War Memorial rededicated, having been

moved from the Market Place to the gardens at the end of the Iron Bridge. It was moved so its original site could be used as a bus bay.

August 7: One of Shrewsbury's biggest ever fires caused over £1 million damage in Barker Street when it gutted the wool warehouse of John Smith and Sons (Shrewsbury) Ltd and the showrooms and store of ironmongers A.D. Foulkes.

September: Last performance (i.e. Born Free) at The Regal Cinema, Market Drayton.

November: Closure of Oswestry station to passenger and goods traffic. Last journey between Oswestry and Gobowen was on November 5.

November: Snedshill brickworks, owned by Lilleshall Co, closed at the end of the month, after 164 years.

November 30: Official opening of Reynolds House, Ketley, Shropshire's tallest flats.

December: Randlay Brickworks closed.

December 31: The Crown Hotel, Bridgnorth, closed on or about December 31.

Misc: Sycamore helicopters at RAF Tern Hill were grounded after three accidents. It was announced that the top security jail at Stoke Heath was being turned into a Borstal. A private plane hit a hillock near Welshampton, killing all three on board. A High Court judge sat for the last time at courts at Shrewsbury's old Shirehall in The Square.

SCHOOL CLOSURES: Wenlock Edge School at Lutwyche Hall closed, as did Wroxeter School. Mill Mead School, Shrewsbury, according to letter from former matron in SS May 1, 2007.

DEATHS: January 6, Trench bus firm proprietor Alfred Thomas Brown, aged 79. September 18, Patrick Whalley, 29-year-old chairman of Furrows, killed when his Ferret armoured scout car overturned during an Army exercise. He was in the Shropshire Yeomanry.

1967

January 11: First American soldier arrives at the former RNAD at Ditton Priors which was being handed to the Americans for storage of ammunition and equipment. He had been sent to liaise with local contractors.

January 12: First Shropshire Assizes in the new court at Shrewsbury's new Shirehall.

January 15: Five young people die in head on crash between two cars in Lawley.

February 13: Wrekin MP Bill Yates hurt in a two car crash at Church Aston in which a 19-year-old girl died.

March 5: Ex-LMS loco 45116 made Shrewsbury station's last steam-hauled passenger journey.

April 1: Major council shake-up saw the end of borough councils at Ludlow, Oswestry and Bishop's Castle. Ludlow Town Council amalgamated with Ludlow Rural District Council; Oswestry Borough Council was absorbed by Oswestry Rural District Council. Bishop's Castle ceased to exist as a borough.

April 1: Grosvenor Cinema at Oakengates closed.

May 9: Runaway lorry ploughed into a stone cottage at the New Road junction with Shineton Street in Much Wenlock.

June 2: Jackie Kennedy, widow of President John Kennedy, in Oswestry to attend private funeral of Lady Harlech. Senator Robert Kennedy also attended. It was at the Roman Catholic Church in Upper Brook Street.

July 27: Madeley Wood Colliery closed.

July 31: Dawley Development Corporation announced that it had accepted a report from a working party and had agreed to set up a company to be called the Ironbridge Gorge Museum Trust Ltd to preserve industrial relics in the Ironbridge area.

August 2: Mick Jagger had been househunting and had looked at Longnor Hall, near Shrewsbury.

August 10: Shrewsbury's new borough courtroom was used for the first time after a £20,000 renovation of the building – the old market hall (official opening had been on August 9).

August 24: Bill Yates formally relieved of his position of Tory prospective parliamentary candidate for The Wrekin. It followed his controversial comments over the Arab-Israeli conflict.

October 1: Shropshire Constabulary, created in 1840, merged with Worcester City, Worcester County and Hereford County, to form West Mercia Police.

October 1: Ellesmere Comrades and Social Club gutted by fire.

October 10: Wrekin's former MP Bill Yates said he was emigrating.

October 18: Doric columns erected in the middle of a field at Hodnet as a memorial to Brigadier A.G.W. Heber Percy.

October 25: Foot and mouth disease broke out near Oswestry with disastrous effects for farmers.

December 14: Two pedestrians killed by train at Baschurch level crossing.

Misc: Ironbridge Gorge Museum Trust was registered as a limited company.

Half a mile of the Attingham Park boundary wall was demolished and replaced by a wooden fence.

DEATHS: Lady Harlech, on May 29 or 30, in a car crash near Harlech. On July 28, Mr G. Emery Tudor, chairman of Shrewsbury Town, aged 62.

SCHOOL CLOSURES: Legge's Hill infants school. Broseley. On July 21 Bourton CofE School closed near Much Wenlock after 148 years.

1968

January 1: Panda cars go on patrol in Shrewsbury.

January 23: Men of the 1st Battalion KSLI were sent to Mauritius to put down race riots.

February 26: Fire at Shelton Hospital kills 24 patients.

March 5: Wellington police receive panda cars.

March 28: RAF Shawbury given the Freedom of the Borough of Shrewsbury.

April 1: Ironbridge Gorge Museum Trust trustees met for the first time.

April 2: Five killed – three brothers, a maid, and a waitress – in a fire at The Hotel, Church Stretton.

April 22: After a three-week standoff, George Moore finally evicted from his grocery and bakery shop at the bottom of Madeley High Street. It was being demolished to make a new roundabout.

May 25: Sir Gordon Richards opened Oakengates Town Hall.

June: US Army completed its withdrawal from the Ditton Priors ammunition depot.

June 20: The 17th Training Regiment Royal Artillery left Park Hall Camp (to go to Woolwich).

June 25: Foot and mouth restrictions lifted i.e. at midnight June 25/26.

July 2: Hailstones the size of golf balls fell in one of Shropshire's worst storms in memory.

July 10: KSLI loses its identity by becoming part of the Light Infantry.

September 9: A serious fire gutted nearly half of a three storey building of the Coalbrookdale works of Allied Ironfounders in what was said to be Shropshire's worst industrial fire for years.

September 18: A siege started at The Warden House, The Slade, Weston-under-Redcastle, when gunman John James held his wife and four young children hostage and held police at bay, firing several shots. It ended on October 4 when a woman hostage grabbed the gun while James slept and threw it out of the window. The 17-day siege was the longest peacetime siege in recent British history. James was sent to Broadmoor for an indefinite period on December 11.

October 21: Ben Jones, whose parents Arthur and Gladys had a fish and chip shop in Audley Road, Newport, won a gold medal as part of the British showjumping team at the Mexico Olympics.

October 23: Dawley New Town expanded to take in Wellington and Oakengates to create an enlarged new town to be called Telford.

November 23: Ifton Colliery closed.

December 2: New Shrewsbury swimming baths opened.

SCHOOL CLOSURES: The Bog School.

1969

January 15: Oswestry's new Smithfield opened on the edge of town, and the old town centre site closed.

January 17: It was reported in the SS that the "first courses have begun" at the former bomber airfield at High Ercall which had been turned into a £500,000 road transport training centre.

January 24: Two crewmen died when a Jet Provost plane crashed into Abdon Burf on Brown Clee Hill.

January 31: Highley Colliery closed.

February 13: It was reported that "work has started on Shrewsbury Civic Society's plans to restore the Bear Steps".

March 27: A £1m appeal launched to create a "world famous open air museum" at Blists Hill.

April 29: A fire in a giant stores building at COD Donnington was said to be one of Shropshire's biggest since 1948.

May 1: First girls were admitted to Oswestry School since its foundation in 1407.

May 3: Wellington Town played their last game in the Southern League – they were being renamed Telford United in the new season.

May 18: It's a Knockout recorded at the Quarry before a crowd on nearly 10,000. Shrewsbury beat Chester in the first round.

June: The new Ironbridge Power Station began generating. (?)

June 27: A Rembrandt painting owned by Lt Col A. Heywood-Lonsdale, of Shavington Grange, near Market Drayton, sold at auction in London for £483,000, believed to be a record price for a self portrait of the painter.

June 29: The last communion administered at Craeiglwyn Chapel, near Oswestry, which closed after 101 years.

August 15: Reported that many British troops were moving on to the streets of Belfast, including Shropshire soldiers of the 3rd Battalion Light Infantry.

September 3: Shrewsbury were joint winners of the 1969 It's a Knockout competition, sharing the victory with the German team of Wolfsburg in the finals at Blackpool.

September 19: Wrekin Brewery in Wellington closed about September 19.

October 6: Natural gas arrived in Oswestry.

November 2: Last service at Coalbrookdale Methodist Chapel, which then closes due to falling congregation.

December 10 (today or reported today): Myford House, Horsehay, a home for unmarried mothers opened in 1943, closed, partly because it was now more socially acceptable.

December 31: Maw & Co tileworks at Jackfield closed today or about today.

SCHOOL CLOSURES: Shelve School on July 18.

1970

January: Members of the Welsh Nationalist Society staged sit-in at Shrewsbury police station because it was the HQ of the "secret police".

April 16: Colours of the KSLI laid up in the sanctuary of Bridgnorth's St Leonard's Church, in the town where the KSLI was born 214 years previously. They were the colours of the 1st Battalion KSLI.

May 2: Telford United and Macclesfield made history as first finalists of the FA Challenge Trophy at Wembley. Telford lost 2-0.

May 23: Severn Valley Railway steam enthusiasts began running trains from Bridgnorth as the old SVR line reopened for steam hauled passenger trains.

May 25: Pilot killed when his aircraft spun in to the ground during an air display at Sleap airfield.

June: Ludlow's Picture House, claimed to be the oldest cinema in England, closed.

June 12: An ammunition train carrying 50 tons of 120mm tank shells in collision with a parcel train at Shrewsbury station. The freight train driver leapt clear just before impact.

August 10: Over 5,000 workers at GKN Sankey in Telford went on unofficial strike for six weeks, costing the firm £6 million in lost production and making over 25,000 workers idle throughout the motor industry. The strike ended on September 18.

August 19 and 20: Two inches of rain hit Shrewsbury Flower Show – worst weather to hit it for 50 years.

September 22: The National Canine Defence League Kennels opened at Roden.

November 16: Official opening of Whitchurch Civic Centre.

Misc: Hodnet Hall gardens reopened after the hall had been modernised and reduced in size by two thirds (due to reopen on Good Friday). The floating restaurant at Shrewsbury, near the Welsh Bridge, opened.

SCHOOL CLOSURES: Princes Street School, Wellington, opened in 1858, closed c.July. The decision was taken to close Ironbridge CofE School (reported January 13).

1971

January 4: Double gas explosion at Willows Road, Oakengates, destroyed one house and damaged two others, but caused no fatalities.

May 1: Telford United won the FA Challenge Trophy at Wembley, beating Hillingdon 3-2 after being 2-0 down.

June 19: Ketley recreation centre officially opened.

August: Madeley Court Centre opens (but official opening was July 14, 1972).

August 21: Maesbury Mill destroyed by fire.

Reported October 2: Dutch elm disease spread into Shropshire.

October 4: The Eastern Primary road (Sutton Hill part) opened around October 4.

October 5: Last two-week sitting of Shropshire Assizes began. Was being replaced by a Crown court in January 1972 taking on the functions of Shropshire Quarter Sessions and Shropshire Assizes.

November 17: The remainder of the former naval depot at Ditton Priors was auctioned off piecemeal.

Misc: On July 10 the Offa's Dyke long distance path was opened at Knighton. *The RAF quit Buntingsdale Hall, Market Drayton.* Shrewsbury (Castlefields) bowler Tony Poole becomes British Crown Green Champion (reported August 9).

Shropshire's conversion to North Sea Gas was continuing.

1972

February: Shropshire's homes and businesses hit by phased power cuts due to a miners' strike. On February 18 the Wilberforce inquiry recommended pay rises and the NUM recommended acceptance. Miners voted to return to work on February 28. They had been on strike for six weeks.

March 18 (reported): Edge & Sons, at Lamledge Lane, Shifnal, closes with 139 redundancies. It had been founded in Coalport in 1800.

April 20: The Bell pub at Alveley reopened after 36 years.

April 24: The Paradise Lost strip club in Castle Street, Hadley, shut down by magistrates.

May 22: Tweedale fire and ambulance stations became operational.

June 8: Cruckton's new village hall, formerly Cruckmeole School, officially opened.

June 30: No 27 Maintenance Unit at RAF Shawbury closed.

July 28: Reported in Bridgnorth edition of the SJ that a new police station had opened in Bridgnorth "this week".

August 25: Reported in SJ that archaeologists at the site of the Roman city of Viroconium had discovered the foundations of a baths basilica which could be unique in Britain.

August 25: Reported in North edition of the SJ that Wem swimming pool had opened "this week". There was no official opening.

August 28: Prince William of Gloucester killed in a plane crash shortly after taking off from Halfpenny Green airfield.

September 6: Flying pickets went on the rampage on building sites in Telford.

Reported October 13: The Express & Star Ltd bought Powysland Newspapers – the Shrewsbury Chronicle, Bridgnorth Journal, Newport and Market Drayton Advertiser, and Telford Observer.

November 15: Lorry crashed into the crowded Greyhound Inn, Ketley Bank, just before closing time. Five were hurt. The pub was virtually demolished.

Reported November 17 in Shrewsbury edition of the Shropshire Journal that work began on the main part of a new £10 million district general hospital at Copthorne.

Reported December 1: Work on rebuilding Shrewsbury's 62-year-old weir was completed. It was due by the end of September but summer floods delayed the work. However, it was finished before heavy rain arrived in mid November.

DEATHS: On August 28 Corporal Ian Roderick Morrill, aged 29, of Oakley Avenue, Shrewsbury, shot dead by a sniper in Belfast only 11 days after arriving. He was in the 1st Battalion Light Infantry. On November 1, Lady (Teresa) Berwick of Attingham Hall in a car crash at the entrance to Attingham Park. She was a passenger. On April 16 former Clun schoolboy, Second Lt Nicholas Hull, killed in Belfast. On September 7 Ted Ireland, the founder editor of the Shropshire Star.

1973

January 5: First edition of the Telford Journal (combining old Shropshire Journal and Telford Observer) printed.

On January 20: Two men jailed in the celebrated Paradise Lost Club case. One got two years for keeping a disorderly house, the other 12 months for aiding and abetting. They denied it.

Reported March: Lord Barnard sold the site of Viroconium to the nation (reported March 6).

April 16: The Granada cinema in Shrewsbury reopened as a bingo club.

April 19: Major gas explosion in Temeside, Ludlow. Two people were seriously injured.

May 16: Home Secretary Robert Carr officially opened Shrewsbury's new £482,869 police station at Monkmoor. It had actually become operational on April 1.

July 20: Trench Secondary Modern School officially renamed the John Hunt School.

August 23: Shropshire won the Minor Counties cricket championship for the first time in its history.

September 25: Shropshire produced its first British light middleweight boxing champion in Larry Paul.

October 2: The first shops, Carrefour and Sainsbury's, opened at Telford town centre.

October 3: A celebrated trial began at Shrewsbury of building workers accused of being flying pickets who conspired to intimidate workers at Shrewsbury and Telford in the September 1972 building workers strike. The accused included Ricky Tomlinson, who later became an actor. They were convicted, and sentenced on December 19.

November 2: Two crewmen died when a Hawker Hunter crashed in a field near Besford Wood.

November 26: The fuel crisis continues to bite with it being reported that police patrol cars in Shropshire were being restricted to 50mph by the West Mercia chief constable as a fuel-saving measure, and then on December 8 a universal 50mph speed limit was brought in for all roads for the public.

Misc: Shropshire's new fire service headquarters at St Michael's Street, Shrewsbury, came into full operation. The Department of the Environment bought Viroconium.

SCHOOL CLOSURES: Closure (due) in July of the Our Lady of Zion School, Acton Burnell.

DEATHS: Reported on December 11 of Offley Lander, of Sunnycroft, Wellington, an industrialist.

1974

January 1: Industry put on a three day week to save power due to industrial action by the miners. The three day week was to remain, the Government announced on January 26, as was the 10.30pm curfew on television programmes, as the power crisis continued.

March 21: The first streaker to appear in a Shropshire court was fined £5 after being spotted by police running nude across the White Lion Meadow car park in Whitchurch for a bet.

April 1: Under a major local government shake-up, Wrekin Council was formed from the amalgamation of various rural and urban councils. Among other changes, out went Bridgnorth Rural District Council, in came Bridgnorth District Council, and Bridgnorth Rural Borough Council became Bridgnorth Town Council; also in came Shrewsbury & Atcham Borough Council, and North Shropshire District Council.

May 2: Market Drayton bypass opened.

August 18: Announced that the Royal Normal College for the Blind at Rowton Castle and at Albrighton Hall was to move to Birmingham.

September 9: Troops opened fire on duck shooters near Park Hall Camp, Oswestry, mistaking them for terrorists, seriously injuring one man.

October 10: 70 council representatives, engineers and technical experts came to Ironbridge where the Iron Bridge was on show in an open day arranged to mark the completion of major restoration work to save the bridge from collapse. The two-year programme involved putting a concrete slab on the river bed.

December 2: Announced that the Milk Marketing Board's Wem creamery, where about 80 people were employed, was to close in two phases in 1975.

Misc: Shrewsbury parks superintendent Percy Thrower, who had become a television star, retired. A bungalow was wrecked in a gas blast at Temeside in Ludlow – the second in 18 months (i.e. November).

SCHOOL CLOSURES: Hadley County Junior School?

DEATHS: January 15, Lord Powis, Colonel Edward Robert Henry Herbert. Inherited Orleton Hall in 1924, and later lived at Powis Castle, Welshpool.

1975

January 14: Highley girl Lesley Whittle, 17, kidnapped. Her body was found on March 7 in a drain at Bathpool Park, Kidsgrove.

February 1: Millions of gallons of water flooded 15 acres of land near Ellesmere when the embankment of the Shropshire Union Canal collapsed for a stretch of 20 yards at Hampton Bank, Welshampton. Burrowing water rats and erosion were blamed.

April 5: Aerospace Museum at RAF Cosford opened to the public for the first time.

April 9: Harrier jet crashed at Powkesmoor Coppice, Ditton Priors, but the piloted ejected successfully.

May 2: Announced that Park Hall camp, Oswestry, was to be shut by the end of the year and 190 civilian jobs were to be axed. The MoD had decided not to continue training junior soldiers at the camp. It would mean the end of Oswestry's long links with the Army. It had been a garrison town for 36 years.

May 3: Blaze at Shrewsbury's Copthorne Hospital. Nurses and staff pushed and carried 26 women patients to safety.

May 15: The Grand cinema, Wellington, successfully applied for a seven-day bingo licence.

June 5: Britons voted "Yes" in the Common Market referendum. In Shropshire there was a 63 per cent turnout, with 113,044 voting yes (72.3 per cent) and 43,329 voting no (27.7 per cent). Total nationwide yes was 67.2 per cent against 32.8 per cent no.

June 14: The Granada cinema at Oswestry closed, although traders were making an effort to reopen it.

July 6: Three Harlescott children from the same family, Nicola Watt (13) and her brothers Andrew (10) and Timothy (9), swept to their deaths while paddling in the River Severn at Pimley, Shrewsbury.

August: (reported August 14) Climbers Michel Piolle of Shrewsbury and David Edwards of Wellington killed in the French Alps.

August 15: Reported that the Government reduced Telford's population target from 220,000 by 1991 to 145,000 by 1986, 150,000 by 1986.

September 16: Gatacre playing fields and pavilion officially opened in Oswestry.

September 30: Six workmates collapsed within minutes as they were handling zinc waste at a small steel fabricating factory – Wheeler and Pearsall – on the Rose Hill industrial estate, Tern Hill. They were taken to hospital in what was described as the Royal Salop Infirmary's biggest ever medical emergency. One of the men died on October 16.

October 10: The Wrekin Toy Factory making Chad Valley toys at Wellington was closed with immediate effect. (n.b. it was revived, reopening in June 1976).

October 23: Zamira Menuhin, daughter of violinist Yehudi Menuhin, married Jonathan Benthall, son of Sir Paul and Lady Benthall, of Benthall Hall, in a civil ceremony at Kensington Register Office. It was formally blessed at Benthall Parish Church two days later on October 25.

November 4: Announced that fork lift truck firm Eaton Ltd, at Halesfield – which was the first multinational organisation to be attracted to the new town in 1970 – was pulling out of Telford with the loss of 100 jobs.

November 24: Announced that one of Oswestry's biggest employers, engineering firm Davies and Metcalfe, which provided 80 jobs (once up to 250) at its factory on the Gobowen Road, was to close down.

December 1: Owen Owen took over the Maddox department store in Shrewsbury.

December 5: New Wrekin television mast started transmitting.

December 11: M54 Wellington bypass opened.

December 11: Donald Neilson – the notorious Black Panther – caught in a struggle with two police constables near Mansfield and charged with murder of Shropshire heiress Lesley Whittle.

December 31: Final closure of the Park Hall Army Camp was due at the end of this month.

Misc: Dorrington creamery closed. Oakengates ring road built.

SCHOOL CLOSURES: Attingham Park Adult College at the end of November. Hook-a-Gate primary school, opened in 1894.

DEATHS: On September 17, Sir Offley Wakeman, aged 87, a member of Salop County Council for 42 years.

1976

January 14: Explosive device, a booby trap bomb, found in an AA phone box on the A49 near Church Stretton.

February 18: A 16-year-old boy appearing at Shrewsbury magistrates court at the old market hall dived head first through a window after being remanded in custody and plunged 25ft onto a 74 year old woman in the street below. Both were taken to hospital.

April 15: It was announced that the Warner-Swasey factory at Shrewsbury was to close with 200 job losses. It was said there would probably be some work until October.

April 22: New Granada Bingo and Social Club on the site of the old Grand Cinema in Tan Bank, Wellington, opened.

April 24: Two men killed when a light plane crashes at Chirk.

June 7: Dawley Police Station closed with move of the HQ of the South Telford police sub division to Malinslee House, Telford.

June 21: Chad Valley toy factory in Wellington High Street reopened (it had been closed the previous October).

July 1: Donald Neilson found guilty of murder of Lesley Whittle.

July 3: Hosepipe ban introduced in Shropshire as continuing hot weather causes water crisis.

July 14: Fire swept through Loppington House, near Wem, a nursing home for severely mentally and physically handicapped children. In all 81 children were saved. All were accounted for.

July 21: Black Panther Donald Neilson given five life sentences at Oxford Crown Court.

July 23: Official opening of Coalport China Works museum.

July 26: Oswestry's new sports and leisure centre officially opened.

August 7: First Telford Super Saturday event, attracting 20,000 people.

August 9: Dawley bypass opened.

August 16-18: Huge fire on tinder-dry Haughmond Hill destroys 150,000 trees over 120 acres. Soldiers joined in the battle against the flames.

August 24: Shropshire given authority to use Green Goddess fire engines to help with a fire crisis after, on August 23, the fire service in the county had its busiest day ever with at one point every fire appliance committed.

August 26: Wem creamery was closing with the loss of about 63 jobs (according to SS report on April 27).

August 28: Parts of Shropshire had their first rain since August 6, but not in any measurable amount. However, heavier rain fell on August 29.

September: Geoff Hurst, England's 1966 World Cup hat-trick hero, became player-manager of Telford United.

September 29: Final service held at St Leonard's Church, Bridgnorth.

September 29: The RAF said a final farewell to Tern Hill when helicopters flew to their new home at RAF Shawbury, signalling the closure of RAF Tern Hill.

October 3: Top hang glider pilot Anthony Jones, of Churchstoke, killed when he plunged to the ground near Wentnor.

October 8: Two-man crew of RAF Folland Gnat jet trainer killed as it crashes near farms and cottages at Besford, about half a mile from the northern perimeter of the runway at RAF Shawbury.

October 11: Telford United's centenary match with the 1966 England World Cup side drew a gate of 8,032 to the Bucks Head, the biggest gate for many years. All the 1966 side, except Ray Wilson, turned up for the game. Telford United's manager was hat-trick hero Geoff Hurst.

December 19: Elsich Manor, Seifton, a historic building, severely damaged by fire. It had been empty for some time.

Misc: Ironbridge A Power Station stopped generating electricity. St Julian's Church, Shrewsbury, closed. The footbridge over Hollybush Road, Bridgnorth, was demolished. The first office block at Telford town centre, Malinslee House, opened. Tern Hill airfield closes in December. Bridgnorth sports centre was due to open in the summer. Controversy as Victorian glass canopy is removed at Shrewsbury station.

DEATHS: On March 14, Colonel Arthur Heywood-Lonsdale, aged 75, a former Lord Lieutenant of Shropshire, of Shavington Grange. Was also a former High Sheriff and chairman of Salop County Council etc. Was CBE. On May 18, in Bardi, Italy, Mr T Sidoli, aged 91, who had founded the Sidoli catering business in Shrewsbury. Lt Col Harold Arthur Golden, Chief Constable of Shropshire from 1935 to 1946, in Norwich, aged 80 (reported April 20). Former vicar of Oakengates, the Rev Gordon Cartlidge, aged 94 (death

reported in SS December 1).

SCHOOL CLOSURES: *Great Wollaston, Cleeton St Mary and Woodcote.* Hodnet old 1863 school buildings in May.

1977

January 11: Reynolds Woodware furniture factory in Lower Broad Street, Ludlow, gutted in fire.

January 12: Shropshire was in the grip of snow during what was said to be the worst winter weather for 14 years. There was further heavy snow on the evening of January 13 causing drifts up to 8ft deep.

January 20: Miss World Cindy Breakspeare, Miss Jamaica, visited Shrewsbury for the annual dance of Shrewsbury Rolls-Royce Diesel Division, at Tiffany's.

January 21: Glynwed's Aga foundry at Ketley closed, with about 100 job losses.

February 22: The new £7 million Shrewsbury Hospital, Copthorne (North) had just started taking its first patients at clinics in the outpatients department, the SS reported on Feb 22

March: Anthrax outbreak hits some Shropshire farms (reported March 25) and a number of cattle die.

March 4: Eric Clapton and Ronnie Lane played a jam-session style gig at the Drum and Monkey pub at Bromlow, near Minsterley.

April: Dudmaston Hall, Bridgnorth, was (due to be) given to the National Trust by Lady Labouchere. It was due to be completed by April.

April 1: Prime Minister James Callaghan opens the Silkin Way path in Telford. He was also confronted by Telford Hospital Action Group demonstrators on a walkabout in the new town shopping centre.

June: Events were held across the county to celebrate the Queen's silver jubilee.

June 18: Wem Corn and Seeds, a former maltings, burned down.

June 22: Ironbridge Gorge Museum won the Museum of the Year Award.

July 8: J.C. Hulse, engineering firm at Hinkshay Road, Dawley, closes.

July 31: Pool Hill Junior School, Dawley, burnt down on the evening of July 31-August 1.

October 2: Methodist Church in Madeley High Street closes.

November 20: The Royal Salop Infirmary closed when its last 52 patients were transferred to the new Copthorne General Hospital in the biggest such move in the county's medical history (the Copthorne hospital opened at the same time, but the official opening was not for another year).

December 22: In his latest stunt, poacher and prankster Poddy Podmore dressed as Santa and climbed on the walls of Shrewsbury Jail laden with gifts for the prisoners.

December 23: Punk sensations the Sex Pistols played at the Village night club in Newport.

December 31: RAF Cosford hospital closed on the last day of this year.

Misc: Edstaston Village Hall opened. First Telford Development Corporation houses were handed over at Leegomery.

DEATHS: Lord Forester of Willey on January 4. Dawley Marine Neil Bewley shot dead in Belfast on August 12. Weekend of January 1 and 2, Sir Edward Hanmer, aged 83, of Bettisfield Park, Whitchurch, one of Shropshire's best known racing personalities. Explorer and mountaineer Eric Shipton, from Sidbury, near Bridgnorth, the original choice to lead the 1953 Everest expedition, death reported April 1 in SS.

1978

February 24: Proposed new M54 motorway downgraded from three lanes to two.

March (reported 16th etc): A 33ft yacht, the Eyton Rose with five Shropshire men on board – Michael Sandford, Stephen Warrow, Keith Mitchell, Ben Steele, and Bill Pilliner – disappeared in the Bay of Biscay. It had left Weymouth on February 27 for the Mediterranean.

May: Film superstar Richard Burton filming "Absolution" at Ellesmere College.

September 23: The Little Theatre, Donnington, severely damaged by fire.

October (reported on November 1): Wartime aircraft recovery enthusiasts discover remains of Leading Aircraftman

John Toplis Carr in a crash site at Helshaw Grange, near Tern Hill airfield, who was killed on April 10, 1941 in a mid-air collision.

October: The last stage of Wellington's ring road started at end of October/early November. It principally involved road widening and junction improvements along Bridge Road between Wrekin Road and Springhill.

November 2: A man died when his Ford Capri plunged into the Mere at Ellesmere.

November: Big bread queues outside bakeries and shops in Shropshire in a national bakery workers strike.

November 17: The new Copthorne General Hospital at Shrewsbury officially opened by Prince Charles and renamed the Royal Shrewsbury Hospital, the Queen having given her consent for the name.

December 6: The four cooling towers of Ironbridge Power Station were floodlit, the first in Britain to be floodlit, as part of the forthcoming 200th anniversary celebrations of the Iron Bridge.

Misc: The Dawley-Donnington distributor road opened. Midland Motor Museum opened at Bridgnorth. The United Malting Company, Wem, closed. Telford's 100,000th resident moved in.

SCHOOL CLOSURES: Eaton Constantine School on July 21 after 128 years.

DEATHS: Some time in March, Percy Edward Pointon, owner of the Forest Glen. The business passed to his niece, Mrs Joyce Pitchford. Reported April 28: Flt Lt John Arthur Rigby, only son of former Mayor of Much Wenlock Arthur Rigby, killed when RAF Jaguar aircraft he was piloting crashed in Scotland.

1979

January: There was a "winter of discontent". Most Shropshire schools were closed for two days (reported January 9) because of a fuel crisis. On January 22 Shropshire public services were hit by a one-day strike by members of the National Union of Public Employees, hitting ambulance cover, schools and other major facilities. There were rail strikes in January too. Hospitals were hit by an ancillary workers dispute, with corridors becoming dirty and rubbish piling up outside the RSH.

January 22: Fire ripped through Bridgnorth Town Council's headquarters at College House.

January 28: Mrs Joan Lillian Hicks, of Pant, fell 150ft to her death from the snow-topped cliffs at Llanymynech while walking with her husband Ivor Hicks, who took an overdose and killed himself on June 19.

March 5: A 14-year-old boy injured by flying debris when the 85ft chimney at the old Ifton Brickworks, St Martins, was felled by explosives.

March 10: Shrewsbury Town reached the Sixth Round of the FA Cup, in which they drew 1-1 with First Division Wolves at Molineux, but lost the replay at the Gay Meadow 1-3 on March 13.

April 21: Floodlights were switched on to illuminate the Iron Bridge as part of the bicentenary celebrations of the bridge.

May: Granville Colliery, Shropshire's last pit, stopped production.

May: Mayor of Shrewsbury and Atcham, Bernard Lingen, launched a £1.25 million Cobalt Unit appeal to build a cancer treatment centre at the Royal Shrewsbury Hospital.

May 17: Shrewsbury Town promoted to Second Division for first time, beating Exeter City 4-1 at the Gay Meadow to clinch the Third Division title.

June: A new footbridge opened over the River Severn from Frankwell to Shrewsbury town centre.

July 5: The Prince of Wales visited Ironbridge as part of the bicentenary celebrations of the Iron Bridge. He unveiled a plaque. Three days earlier there had been a parade through the town with crowds lining the streets.

July 7: Government lifted the ban on Telford Development Corporation building houses for direct sale to the public.

August 7: Sidney Noble, the man known as "Doctor Death", interrupted his 10 year sentence in Shrewsbury Prison to marry at Shrewsbury Register Office to Lorna Sellars, of Kettering. Noble had administered stupefying drugs to older women before robbing them.

September 9: Shropshire golfer Sandy Lyle, aged 21, of Hawkstone Park, won the European Open at Turnberry.

September 15: Clun New Memorial Hall officially opened.

Reported September 26: Colonel John Kenyon launches campaign to save the "Shropshire" name which he says is in

danger of being replaced by "Salop".

November 19: Salop County Council decided to break with tradition, switching its quarterly meetings from Saturdays to Fridays, despite a warning that it would lead to a council dominated by housewives, the retired and people of independent means.

Reported November 27: Closure announced of Market Drayton's Silhouette factory with loss of 235 jobs (due to take effect early 1980).

December 27: All Saints Church, Gobowen, almost completely destroyed by fire.

Misc: Ludlow's Clifton Cinema sold to a bingo firm. An international song festival in Shrewsbury in February was a disastrous financial flop, losing £26,000. The National Trust acquired Carding Mill Valley. The 10,000th Telford Development Corporation rented house was completed. Darby House in Telford town centre completed. Wellington ring road completed.

1980

February 4: Ludlow bypass opened.

February 25: Paul Coffey, formerly of Shrewsbury where he was a deputy charge nurse at Shelton Hospital, became Britain's youngest heart transplant patient, aged 23.

March 1: The county council voted 48-5 in favour of the change from the title Salop County Council to Shropshire County Council – a two-thirds majority had been needed. (see April 1) It followed a campaign led by Colonel John Kenyon of Pradoe, West Felton.

March 7: Announced that Salop County Council was to close down its £1m refuse incinerator at Stafford Park, Telford, at the end of the month.

March 7: Bulldozer operator unearthed 2,906 Roman coins buried in about 280AD at Hatton Farm, near Childs Ercall.

April 1: Salop County Council officially renamed Shropshire County Council.

April 1: Shropshire Star did not publish for the first and only time in its history because of industrial action by print union NGA.

April 19: Prince Bernhard of the Netherlands arrived in Bridgnorth for a remembrance service for the 53 Dutch airmen who trained at RAF Stanmore at the end of the war and who died in the Royal Netherlands Air Force.

May 10: Final film ever at Ludlow's Clifton cinema. It was "10" with Dudley Moore. The cinema closed and switched entirely to bingo as an Essoldo bingo hall.

May 9: Chad Valley toy factory in Wellington closed on or about May 9.

May 12: Film star Richard Todd was in Ludlow when his son Peter married 28-year-old actress Janet Wantling, whose parents lived in Corve Street, Ludlow. The wedding was at St Laurence's Church.

July: *Overley Hall school for the blind closed.*

July 1: Clive Barracks at Tern Hill officially opened.

August 15: Education Secretary Mark Carlisle threw out, on the grounds of the £985,000 cost, Shropshire County Council's proposals to introduce comprehensive education in Newport, meaning that when Shrewsbury went fully comprehensive in 1981 that Newport would be the only stronghold of grammar schools left in the county.

September 12: Comedian Ken Dodd opened Dawley's new traffic-free centre and market. The work included moving the Captain Webb Memorial from the Paddock Mount back to close to its original position outside the Lord Hill.

September 20: 67-bed youth hostel opened at Coalbrookdale.

October 5: Seventeen arrested after clashes between rival groups of skinheads from Telford and Wolverhampton which forced the cancellation of a concert by top chart band Bad Manners at Oakengates Town Hall. Six people were hurt.

October 23: Part-time fire stations at Shifnal, Ironbridge and Oakengates closed.

October 24: Prince Charles rode at Ludlow racecourse. Among those watching were Lady Diana Spencer and Camilla Parker-Bowles.

October 31: Telford Central fire station at Stafford Park officially opened.

December 15: Woman killed when her car plunged 300ft off the Burway in Church Stretton.

December 31: In the New Year Honours, Shropshire farmer and chairman of the Milk Marketing Board Stephen Roberts, was knighted.

Misc: Shrewsbury's first pedestrianisation scheme came into force with traffic being banned from part of the Square.

A new population target for Telford of 150,000 was set. The old Ironbridge A power station closed (according to SS story on October 21, 1981, which also said it had last generated in 1976).

ROAD DEATHS: By December 27 there had been 64 road deaths on Shropshire roads, equal to the worst figures for a decade.

1981

January 5: A man arrested under suspicion of being the Yorkshire Ripper was named as Peter Sutcliffe, a lorry driver who had made a number of deliveries – 'more than a handful' according to his boss – to the old Eaton Yale Ltd on Halesfield and would have stayed overnight in Telford area.

January 26: First turf cut of the new Shropshire and Mid Wales Cobalt Unit at the Royal Shrewsbury Hospital by appeal head Bernard Lingen.

February 5: GKN Sankey at Hadley Castle announces 986 redundancies.

February 6: Around 500 demonstrators outside Charlton Arms Hotel, Wellington, as employment secretary James Prior arrives for a speaking engagement with local Tories.

March 18: Gordon Banks, the England World Cup goalie, relieved of his duties as Telford United team manager.

April 20: Parachutist killed when parachute fails to open on a free fall jump at Prees Heath airfield.

May 1: Production ended at BKL Alloys Ltd aluminium refinery at Stafford Park, Telford, with closure to follow by end of month with loss of 118 jobs.

May 1: Various Shropshire weekly newspapers, such as the Telford Journal, Bridgnorth Journal, and Shrewsbury Chronicle, adopted the tabloid format.

May 4: Over 17,000 people (SS of May 5 said "well over 12,000") joined hands round The Wrekin to get into the Guinness Book of Records as the longest ever human chain in a charity event.

May 13: Frank Bough, television presenter, officially opened a new athletics stadium at Park Hall, Oswestry.

May 23: Mrs Edith Bumford killed in gas explosion at her terraced home in Kendal Road, Harlescott.

June 3: Announced that Decca at Bridgnorth was to close with the loss of 528 jobs (however Taiwan firm Tatung took over).

June 22: The 15th century former water mill near Oswestry, Llanforda Mill in the Candy Valley, gutted by fire.

June 27: A 100-year-old 39ins water main burst at 2am in Oswestry, sending millions of gallons of water down streets in the town ripping up roads, washing away gardens, and flooding shops and houses.

July 13: Mytton Mill, Forton Heath, severely damaged in Shropshire's biggest blaze for nearly two years.

July 17: The Shropshire and Mid Wales Cobalt Unit Fund reached its target of £1.25 million. The appeal was launched in the middle of 1979. Work on the 16-bed unit had already begun at the Royal Shrewsbury Hospital.

August 23: The Unicorn Hotel, Wyle Cop, Shrewsbury, closed (according to SS, August 19).

September: Shrewsbury's grammar schools finally faded into history as a new comprehensive system took over as the autumn term began.

September 22: Telford jobless figure is 20.9 per cent.

September 28: One-way system around Telford town centre introduced.

September 29: Dawley Christian Centre in Dawley High Street officially opened.

October 3: Gobowen Parish Church rededicated after big restoration campaign by parishioners following a severe fire on December 27, 1979.

October 14: A terrace house at 65 West Street, St Georges, destroyed in a gas blast. Occupant died later.

November 4: Official opening of the 2.5 kilometre section of the North East Primary Road from the Greyhound island on the old A5 to Wombridge interchange.

November 6: Hadley district centre officially opened.

November 27: Wellington's £1.3 million new swimming pool opened by Olympic swimmer Duncan Goodhew.

Overnight December 10/11: Heaviest December snowfall in Shropshire for many years. Four inches fell in Telford.

December 10: Prime Minister Margaret Thatcher spoke at the centenary dinner of Shrewsbury Conservative Club, the Beaconsfield, at the Radbrook Hall Hotel, Shrewsbury.

December 11: Mrs Thatcher visited Walford College of Agriculture at Baschurch.

December 12: Coldest December spell on record so far.

Between 6am and 9am temperatures recorded by Shawbury Met Office fell to minus 22.3C (minus 8.6F), the lowest since records began. Then Lilleshall weatherman John Warner recorded minus 25C (minus 13F) during the night of December 12/13, and around lunchtime on Sunday, December 13, a blizzard started in Shropshire in which between 8ins and 12ins of snow fell.

December: Coldest December since 1890, and combination of cold and snow not exceeded since 1878.

SCHOOL CLOSURES: Jackfield School. Various other school closures in July – Weston and Wixhill Primary School; Lee Brockhurst School; Hales Primary School; Loppington School; High Hatton School. (It had been reported also (on April 17, 1980) that Quinta School at Weston Rhyn was to close next year, i.e. this year 1981.)

DEATHS: Night of January 27/28, the Rt Rev Dr Arthur Stretton Reeve, former Bishop of Lichfield, aged 73 from Ashford Carbonell. February 25, former Shrewsbury boxer Pat Cowhey aged 69. March 15, Mrs Noel Lindsay Fielden, MBE and OBE, of Longden Manor, in car crash at Battlefield. Reported July 27, Mellor Harrison, former chairman of Wrekin Council. October 14, Councillor Bernard Lingen, the man whose name was synonymous with Shropshire's £1.25 million cobalt unit, was found dead after a suspected heart attack. November 7, Shropshire former champion jump jockey Tim Brookshaw, of Tern Hill, aged 52, five days after a riding accident. Inquest, reported on December 8, gave cause of death as a sudden attack of pneumonia.

ROAD ACCIDENTS: Unofficial figures indicated that 67 people died in road accidents in Shropshire during 1981, the worst year on record.

1982

January 10: England's lowest ever temperature – minus 26.1C (minus 15F) – recorded at Harper Adams Agricultural College, Edgmond. The winter was compared to that of 1947 or even of 1684.

January 12: Main social hall at the Derwen Training College for the Disabled, Gobowen, destroyed by fire.

February 27: Morda House, Oswestry, gutted by fire.

March 13: It was reported in the SS that a receiver had been called in to printers and stationers Wildings of Shrewsbury to try to save the jobs of the workforce by selling the business as a going concern.

March 17: Former Bridgnorth man Mark Anthony Paul Bartholomew jailed for life on March 17 for the murder of the rector of Quatt, the Rev Denis Manning, aged 65.

April 1: The new Shropshire Health Authority took full responsibility, in a shake up, taking over from Salop Area Health Authority from which it differed little.

April: Workmen on the M54 site at Priorslee found a hoard of silver coins. They were probably buried during the Civil War (inquest reported on November 14).

May: Shrewsbury's once world-famous Silhouette factory was said (on May 2) to be closing down in the next few weeks.

May 19: Sergeant Philip Currass, of Market Drayton, killed in helicopter accident along with other special forces soldiers during the Falklands War.

June 21: Pride Hill was made pedestrian-only on or about June 21.

July 6: Runaway lorry in Ironbridge killed four people.

July 20: Squadron Quartermaster Corporal (Corporal-Major) Roy Bright, aged 36, of Guest Road, Broseley, killed by IRA bombing of horse troop in Hyde Park. He was carrying the regimental standard of the Blues and Royals. (He died of his injuries on July 23).

August 8: Shifnal War Memorial Club destroyed by fire.

August 13: Shropshire plans for a complete change to comprehensive education rejected. Education Secretary Keith Joseph decreed that Newport, which still had grammar and secondary modern schools, should stay that way.

October 8: Rowley's House Museum in Shrewsbury opened.

November 12: Announced the Haybridge Works (part of Flather Bright Steels), Wellington, was to close (date not fixed) and operations would move to Tipton.

December: McClures women's dress shop in Wellington closed around December 1.

Misc: McDonald's opened a fast food restaurant at Telford town centre.

1983

February 22: Fire at the Do It All superstore in Telford town centre caused over £1 million damage.

Reported March 28: Weekday pub closing time in Wrekin area extended to 11pm, from 10.30pm.

April 27: The Clifton Cinema, Wellington, closed (but reopened in 1987).

May 14: Telford United won the FA Challenge Trophy at Wembley, beating Northwich Victoria 2-1.

June 23: The Court Works at Madeley closed after almost 200 years – the announcement was on June 23, and it was said that the closure would be completed within three months. The firm, founded in 1795, employed 250.

June 24: A £165 million fire at COD Donnington covered a large area of Shropshire with asbestos fallout.

June 27: Wellington new bus station (due to) open, on ring road – services transferred from Charlton Street and Queen Street.

Reported July 4: Closure of Whitchurch engineering firm W.H. Smiths, once one of the area's biggest employers, was complete.

July 21: Telford's £27m new hospital was given the go-ahead, but only on the casting vote of the chairman of Shropshire Health Authority Frank Jones after a 9-9 voting tie on the package of cuts and economies to pay for it.

July 26: Farmer fined the maximum £200 for breaching advertising control regulations by burning an advert advertising his fruit farm business into the side of The Lawley, near Church Stretton. Letters burned in paraquat were 60ft high and it was over 1,000ft wide.

August 29: Reported today that Beddoes & Son ironmongers in Ironbridge was closing. A new roundabout on the doorstep made it impossible for vehicles to stop.

October 28: Hinstock bypass opened to traffic, although the official opening was not until December 8.

November 25: The M54 opened.

Misc: Telford's West Midlands Tennis and Racquet Centre was opened in the summer – by January 1984 it was insolvent and collapsed, but was rescued.

1984

January 13: Telford Enterprise Zone came into force.

March 4: Filming began in Shrewsbury of A Christmas Carol starring George C. Scott.

March 24: Body discovered of Shropshire rose grower Hilda Murrell who was abducted, stabbed, and left for dead in the shadow of Haughmond Hill. She died of hypothermia and her unsolved killing prompted various conspiracy theories.

May 12: Shrewsbury Town reached best ever league position, eighth in the old Second Division.

June: Lilleshall Company moves its head office from Gower Street, St Georges to Gloucester – was expected to take place at the end of June.

June 8: The (Japanese) Maxell video tape factory in Telford officially opened. It was in the vanguard of a wave of foreign investment into Telford.

June 27: St Mary's RC School, Madeley, burned down.

July 19: Earth tremor rocked Shropshire.

July 28: Hosepipe ban came into force for Shropshire.

Reported August 6: David Ottley, of Leegomery, Telford, won the silver medal in the javelin at the Los Angeles Olympics, the first Briton to win an Olympic medal in a throwing event in 60 years.

August 10: An entire family – the parents and two children – killed when their car was in collision with a lorry at Rowton Castle.

September 4: Opening of the Football Association-GM Soccer School at the National Recreation Centre, Lilleshall. Twenty-five of the country's top 15-year-old players would be given two years intensive training, supervision and education.

September 8: The last Telford Super Saturday event organised by Telford Development Corporation held.

October 2: Gang of seven armed robbers got away with £454,000 after a hold up on an armoured security vehicle near Weston-under-Redcastle, one of Britain's biggest ever cash robberies raids to stop.

October 5: Announced that Bridgnorth's biggest employer, Taiwanese electronics giant Tatung, was pulling out of the town to move to Telford.

October 19: Newport's A41 £6 million bypass opened.

November 3: Opening of new £3 million police station in Telford (official opening April 16, 1985).

December 7: Premiere in Shrewsbury of A Christmas Carol. It was at the Empire Cinema.

SCHOOL CLOSURES: Marton School on July 20.

1985

February 12: In the early hours Talbot Chambers in Market Street, Shrewsbury, burned down. It was the old Talbot Hotel, a Georgian building at which the then Princess Victoria stayed in 1832.

February 16: Telford United made it to the Fifth Round of the FA Cup, being beaten 3-0 by cup holders and table-toppers Everton at Goodison Park. Around 10,000 Telford fans travelled for the game.

February 22: Cascades, the first nightclub in Telford town centre, opened.

March 29: A.B. Cranes, Horsehay – the old Horsehay Company – officially closed with the loss of 307 jobs.

March 29: Bridgnorth bypass opened.

April 23: Radio Shropshire began broadcasting.

May: The Lord Chief Justice, Lord Lane, sat for a week at Shrewsbury Crown Court to get back to the "grass roots" of justice.

May 4: Opening of Shropshire Regimental Museum at Shrewsbury Castle.

May 17: Shropshire County Council declared the county a nuclear-free zone, the effect of the declaration was to send a message that it did not want nuclear weapons or nuclear waste in the county.

July 5: A car left the treacherous Burway road on the side of the Long Mynd and plunged 300ft down the hillside. Shrewsbury-based Army chaplain Colonel Brian Wright, 54, rescued from the car jammed in a gully half way down the slope. He suffered only minor injuries.

July 21: Shropshire golfer Sandy Lyle, of Hawkstone Park, won the Open.

August 13: A double decker bus carrying 65 people, mostly schoolchildren, smashed into the low railway bridge in Coalbrookdale, at the foot of Jiggers Bank. A 10 year old girl was slightly injured.

August 19: In only the third successful prosecution of its type since 1911, eight men appeared before Bridgnorth magistrates where they admitted their involvement in a cock fight held at Eardington, near Bridgnorth, and received fines.

September: Corporal punishment in Shropshire schools ended at the start of the autumn term.

September 9 (reported): Huge pollution alert along River Severn after 50,000 gallons of toxic pig slurry spilt into the River Perry at Ruyton-XI-Towns and killed thousands of fish in one of the county's worst incidents of river pollution for years. Shrewsbury was put on an emergency water supply.

October 11: Closure of Telford Bottling Company, aka Telbo, at Halesfield, with loss of 46 jobs.

November 28/29: Temperatures at Shawbury had plunged to minus 12C (10F) overnight, making it the coldest place in Britain and the coldest November night since records began some 40 years previously.

December 6: Bombshell report suggests closure of eight Shropshire secondary schools and major reorganisation of almost all the rest.

December 8: Stunt rider Kirk Owen tried to create a new European record by leaping across the River Teme at Ludlow, but crashed on landing and spent nearly a month in hospital.

Misc: At the "end of the year" 35-year-old Alan Molyneux became Shropshire's first Aids fatality. He was a haemophiliac from St Martins who was given contaminated blood. His death was reported on January 20, 1986. Telford's Tatung factory opened.

DEATHS: January 26, former Shropshire MP Lord Harlech after a car crash on the A5 just outside Montford Bridge. As president of the British Board of Film Censors, his signature was a famous sight on cinema screens. On December 2, Philip Larkin, the poet, who had once been Wellington librarian. December 21, John Edward Charles Lewis, a former editor in chief of Shropshire Weekly Newspapers, aged 75. Was former editor of the WJ&SN. December 30, John Rocke, former High Sheriff of Shropshire in 1971.

1986

January: Work began this month on repaving of the pedestrian area of Wellington town centre for 300 metres from the top of New Street to the end of the Square. The work took five months.

January 22: In what was said to be the biggest public meeting ever held in Bridgnorth, nearly 800 concerned parents, teachers, and school governors attended a debate on proposals for a revamp of secondary education in the town. It was in the town's sports and leisure centre.

January 23: 850 people packed into the Corbet School, Baschurch, in a public meeting about the school's planned closure, which they vehemently opposed. It was one of a number of such meetings and campaigns in Shropshire around this time caused by the threat to schools through the "Towards 2000" report.

March 6: South Shropshire district councillors decided to demolish the top of Ludlow Town Hall immediately after an emergency report from structural engineers warned that the facework was liable to collapse at any time.

March 10: Work started on demolition of top half of Ludlow Town Hall.

March 20: South Shropshire district councillors gave go ahead for complete demolition of Ludlow Town Hall.

April 29: Final court hearing at Madeley Magistrates Court, Upper House.

May 3: Woodside Primary School, Oswestry, destroyed by fire treated as arson.

May 8: Historic Pell Wall Hall, near Market Drayton, gutted in suspected arson.

May 12: Telford Central railway station opened by Lord Murray.

May: New courts building complex at Malinsgate, Telford, opened (official opening was October 13, 1986).

June 10: Announced that the William Lee foundry, Oakengates – formerly the John Maddock's foundry – would shut in five weeks' time.

June 28: Final passing out parade at the Sir John Moore Barracks, the Light Infantry Depot, Shrewsbury, where recruit training was ending after 105 years. The Queen Mother was in attendance.

July 5: Woman teacher, 29-year-old Lesley Hawkins, died on her first parachute jump, at Forton airfield, Montford Bridge.

September 5: In a revamped package of proposed closures and mergers of Shropshire secondary schools Baschurch, Church Stretton and Ercall Wood were taken off the closure hitlist but the Wakeman School was added to it.

September 27: Mrs Eve Roberts spots mammoth bones while walking her dog at Condover quarry. It leads to the recovery of the famous 12,700 year old Condover mammoth.

November (reported in SS November 27): Ironbridge Gorge designated a World Heritage Site by Unesco. To come into force on January 1, 1987.

November: Medieval silver bowl was found during excavations at Shrewsbury Abbey.

November 14: Shropshire County Council's Labour administration's falling rolls secondary education package was reduced to tatters with defeats on key points. Wellington's Ercall Wood School was reprieved, but the Manor School at Hadley was effectively put in its place for closure. Among other major decisions, the Lakelands School at Ellesmere was reprieved. At Shrewsbury, all the schools were to stay. Nor was Church Stretton school to close, and no change at Market Drayton, Wem, and Whitchurch.

December 19: Telford Development Corporation given a new five-year lease of life by the Government. Announced in the Commons that it would not be wound up until the end of September 1991. It was the first time a firm target date had been set for winding-up.

December 22: Oswestry bypass opened six months ahead of schedule.

DEATHS: Shropshire-born racing legend Sir Gordon Richards, on November 10.

1987

January: Ellesmere Creamery closed this month (according to SS story of October 31, 1986).

January 6: Official opening of British Telecom's new national nerve centre, Whittington House, Park Hall, Oswestry.

January 14: Over 100 Shropshire schools closed as Siberian weather paralysed most of Shropshire. Many side roads blocked by snow.

February 15: What were thought to be Shropshire's first "test tube" twins were born at Royal Shrewsbury Hospital's maternity unit to Ros and Malcolm Adams of Shrewsbury.

March 2: Nearly 50 people ferried to hospital after two passenger trains collide on Shrewsbury to Aberystwyth line at

Westbury.

March 22: Around 1,000 protesters, including families, children in pushchairs, doctors and nursing staff turned out for a demonstration in Broseley in support of Broseley Hospital, which was threatened with closure.

March 26: Nearly 1,000 placard waving health workers packed the Square in Shrewsbury to protest against controversial health cuts proposed for Shropshire.

March 26: Shropshire Health Authority voted 12-6 against a controversial package of cuts, defying a direct instruction from regional bosses to get their budget back on course.

March 31: Links between the Little Theatre at Donnington and the Army, going back 34 years, formally ended and civilians took over.

April 20: Three people injured when a runaway horse galloped into the crowd during the Eyton-on-Severn point to point race.

April 23: Five black coffins signalling the "death of the NHS in Shropshire" led a protest around Shrewsbury as health workers took part in a last ditch stand against health cuts.

May 4: The third, and last, Ironbridge duck race held.

May 12: The Clifton cinema, Wellington, officially reopened in its 50th anniversary year (using the old circle). Over 200 people watched Crocodile Dundee.

June 30 (reported): Discovery of bones of third baby mammoth at Condover quarry site.

July 3: A balloon carrying adventurers Richard Branson and Oswestry's Per Lindstrand ditched in the Irish Sea. They were trying to become the first people to cross the Atlantic by hot air balloon. Instead they were granted the world distance record for a hot air balloon flight.

July 23: Last three patients moved out of Cross Houses Hospital, near Shrewsbury, which closed.

August 15: Concorde flew over the Iron Bridge and Shrewsbury flower show for the centenary flower show.

October 22: Telford Marks & Spencer opened.

November: Shropshire band T'Pau were at No. 1 with China In Your Hand. It topped the chart for five weeks.

November 18: Excavations at the site of Shrewsbury Abbey had revealed a complete water mill dating back to the 1800s.

December: According to historian Peter Hutchinson, C & W Walker engineering works, Donnington, closed down December 1987.

DEATHS: Tiger Joe Minor, Hadley boxer? On January 16, former chief constable of Shropshire Robert Fenwick, CBE, QPM, collapsed in Shrewsbury baths and was dead on arrival at hospital. February 28, county councillor Tom Marston in a car crash near Church Stretton. March 20, at the age of 52 of Chief Superintendent Colin Glover, head of Telford police. Reported May 11, Brigadier David Parker, commander of Donnington Garrison, aged 54. Reported June 10, Major George Leake, aged 73, of Walcot. He was on a fishing trip on the west mainland of Orkney and the boat capsized. He reached shore but had an apparent heart attack. He was a former director of Shropshire Weekly Newspapers.

SCHOOL CLOSURES: Acton Burnell Primary School must have closed (a story in on December 21, 1995, refers to it closing "eight years ago"). Apley Park School closed July.

1988

March 16: Shropshire chartbusters T'Pau played at Telford ice rink.

March 18: The Pride Hill Shopping Centre opened in Shrewsbury.

April: Inaugural meetings held of a range of new parish councils set up in Telford area. They include parish councils for Wellington, Oakengates, Dawley Hamlets, Great Dawley, Madeley, St Georges & Priorslee, Wrockwardine Wood, Stirchley & Brookside, Hollinswood & Randlay.

April 4: Seven people were hurt, one seriously when, for the second year running, a horse bolted during the Eyton-on-Severn point-to-point. The horse galloped into a beer tent.

April 10: Shrewsbury-born golfer Sandy Lyle became the new US Masters champion.

April 25: Huge fire at COD Donnington – the second major blaze in five years.

June 3: Telford magistrates issued a summons for MP Ron Brown, who had thrown down the ceremonial mace in the House of Commons during a debate, causing damage. The private case was brought by Telford solicitor John McMillan. However the DPP later stepped in to stop the prosecution.

c. September: Telford boxer Richie Woodhall won a bronze in the Seoul Olympic Games.

November 3: 10-screen cinema opened in Telford.

c. November 4: Sarah Ryan of Wrekin College was BBC choirgirl of the year..

November 8. Anna Humphries, a 15-year-old schoolgirl, disappeared on her way home from school at Penley, on the north Shropshire border. There was a huge international manhunt for Shropshire man David Evans, a convicted rapist who went missing at the same time. Evans was eventually arrested in France after which Anna's body was recovered from the River Severn at Hampton Loade on November 27. Evans was subsequently jailed on July 5, 1989, for at least 30 years for murder.

December 14: Shropshire chartbusters T'Pau played at Telford ice rink for a second time.

December 24: Clifton Cinema in Wellington closed.

Misc: Television programme "Take Me Home" was filmed in Telford, which was the fictional town of Woodleigh Abbots.

DEATHS: Shropshire's most famous gardener, Percy Thrower, on March 18.

1989

January 30: Last day of trading at Wellington Smithfield.

January 31: First patients moved in to the new Telford Hospital.

February 3: An Asian jungle cat was knocked over and killed near Ludlow and was subsequently stuffed and put on display at Ludlow Museum.

February 20: The IRA set off bombs at Tern Hill barracks while the Parachute Regiment was stationed there. Guards spotted the bombers and opened fire on them, but they escaped. The police were not notified for 40 minutes. The barracks were evacuated in time.

c. March: Broseley Cottage Hospital closed.

March 23: Ironbridge bypass opened.

April 7: Shropshire farmer's daughter Suzanne Younger took the Miss UK title. Later she went on to reach the final 10 in the Miss World competition.

June: The canteen-cum-ballroom at GKN Sankey, Hadley, burnt down by arsonists.

July 11: The first patient was welcomed at the new Shropshire and Mid Wales Hospice at Bicton Heath, Shrewsbury.

August 3: Tuckers ironmongers shop collapsed at Newport, trapping two elderly passersby.

c. September: Wellington Cottage Hospital closed.

September 22: Darwin shopping centre in Shrewsbury officially opened.

November: Parents of Adams' Grammar School pupils, Newport, voted overwhelmingly to opt out of local authority control (story on Nov 9 in SS).

November 28: £500,000 raid on a Brinks Mat security van making the trip to Lloyds Bank in Dawley.

December: Newport Cottage Hospital closed.

Misc: Oswestry and District Hospital closed in the second half of 1989. Monkmoor Hospital closed in the "summer" of 1989.

SCHOOL CLOSURES: July 22, Lyneal School.

1990

February 12: The Princess Royal officially opened Telford's £27 million hospital.

March: Council chambers in Telford (March 7) and Oswestry (March 13) came under siege from angry anti-poll tax demonstrators.

March 10: Three brothers, aged six, five and three, died after being trapped in a disused freezer outside their Clee Hill home.

March 19: The last livestock market was held in Bridgnorth town centre after 154 years.

March 26: The new Bridgnorth livestock market started operating at Tasley.

March 27: It was announced that Owen Owen, Shrewsbury, the former Maddox department store, was to cease trading at the end of July.

March 30: Poultry processors J.P. Wood of Craven Arms declared processing was to stop with the loss of 500 jobs and the business closed by the end of June.

April 2: An earthquake with its epicentre near Clun reached 5.2 on the Richter scale, the worst quake in Shropshire for a century.

May 19: Telford shopping centre was sold by Telford Development Corporation to the Universities Superannuation Scheme. It had a price tag of more than £100 million.

June 3: Eleven British holidaymakers, six of whom were from Telford, died in a coach crash in France.

September 1: Telford won Entente Florale – the "European Cup" of towns of flowers.

November 22: Market Drayton Cottage hospital closed.

December 12: Ellesmere Cottage Hospital closed.

December 13: Shropshire County Council plans for a new £1.09m bridge over the River Severn at Ladywood, Jackfield, turned down by Government following a public inquiry because of the impact it would have on the Iron Bridge 400 metres away.

1991

April 1: King Charles Barn in Madeley, where King Charles hid in 1651, severely damaged by fire.

April 11: Official opening of Shropshire and Mid Wales Hospice (at Shrewsbury) by Duchess of Kent.

April 12: Official opening of Bridgnorth's new Smithfield livestock market and auction centre at Tasley (although the first auction had been held in March 1990).

April 14: Shropshire golfer Ian Woosnam won the US Masters title at Augusta.

May 25: Parking charges introduced on Ironbridge car parks – the first parking charges in the Wrekin district.

June (c. June 11) Marshall Osborne at Jackfield goes into receivership.

July 29: English Bridge gyratory system, Shrewsbury, comes into operation.

August 12: Police shot dead a young man, Ian Gordon, who was brandishing an air pistol near Wellington Railway Station. It provoked tensions with the black community and there were disturbances in Wellington and Hadley.

September: Telford City Technology College (later Thomas Telford School) took its first pupils.

September 30: Telford Development Corporation wound up after 23 years.

December 18: Fire caused hundreds of thousands of pounds damage at Ludlow racecourse.

SCHOOL CLOSURES: July 24, Stockton Norton School, near Bridgnorth.

1992

January 2: Two children and their mother killed in house fire at Sandcroft, Sutton Hill.

January 9: Shropshire chart topping band T'Pau split up.

January 16: A temporary Bailey bridge put up at Buildwas to replace the corroded Buildwas bridge that was being replaced (reported on January 16).

January 21: Angel Hotel, Ludlow, was badly damaged by fire.

February 1: Cable television came to Telford (first homes expected to be able to buy it from February 1).

February 16: Kevin O'Donnell, a former Shropshire student and an IRA member, shot dead by SAS in Northern Ireland.

March 4: Whitchurch bypass officially opened.

May 10: Last direct train from Shropshire to London.

c. July 21 (reported 23rd): Bishop's Castle Railway Museum, claimed to be the first in Shropshire devoted purely to the railways, opens officially in Bishop's Castle.

July 25 (or thereabouts): 8,000 New Age hippies held an illegal festival at a hilltop site at Anchor, between Newtown and Clun.

August 11: The new £65 million M54 extension and Shrewsbury bypass opened.

August 25: IRA bomb blitz in Shrewsbury in which Shropshire Regimental Museum severely damaged.

September 28: Dominic Sasse, 37, of Ludlow, a poet hailed by literary critics as the new Tennyson, killed in an Airbus airliner crash at Kathmandu.

November 12: It was announced by Express Foods that its Ruyton-XI-Towns creamery would be axed next year. Dairy Crest revealed the same day it would be shutting its Four Crosses plant.

SCHOOL CLOSURES: July 21, Ellerdine School.

1993

February 3: Reported that the old Methodist chapel at Hadnall, a 130-year-old listed building, had partially collapsed because of passing lorries.

February 7: Stirchley county primary school severely damaged in an arson attack, causing £2 million damage.

February 22: Huge fire at Cox's Chemicals at Overley and major petrol spillage when a tanker overturned in Copthorne, Shrewsbury, caused hundreds of residents to be evacuated, and gave Shropshire's emergency services one of their busiest ever nights.

March 25: Ellesmere Smithfield held its last sale.

March 31: In the early hours a UFO was in a direct overflight of RAF Cosford and RAF Shawbury (according to MOD investigator Nick Pope).

May 27: Masked raiders snatched nearly £500,000 worth of gold and watches from Robinsons Jewellers in Shrewsbury in what was possibly the county's biggest ever jewellery robbery.

August 7: The Free Bridge at Jackfield closed with a horse-drawn carriage from Blists Hill Museum making a final journey across it.

September 21: Armed raiders got away with £400,000 in raid on a Brinks Mat security van outside Lloyds Bank in Broseley.

c. August 25: The Forest Glen was being rebuilt at Blists Hill Museum. Work began in early April and was (due to be) completed in mid September. (picture used August 25).

Reported September 28: The Telford campus of Wolverhampton University opened its doors to residential students.

October 12: The Lord Hill statue in Shrewsbury was hoisted off the top of its column for repairs after being cut into five pieces before being lowered to the ground. (his restored head was returned to the Column on October 6, 1995).

October 22: Announced that Venture Pressings Ltd, a joint GKN Sankey-Jaguar Cars venture, was pulling out of Telford, with 220 workers being made redundant.

December 8: The Lamentation of Christ, an old master dating from the 16th century which was discovered hanging in Little Ness Church, sold at Sotheby's to an American dealer for £210,000. Its new home would be an American museum.

1994

January 8: Two killed when a light aircraft struck The Wrekin in dense fog.

January 12: Severn Valley Railway steam engine ploughed into a car on a level crossing at Hampton Loade, pushing the vehicle 80 yards and killing the driver.

February 25: Shropshire's controversial "homes with hangars" Skypark scheme at Shawbirch thrown out by Environment Secretary John Gummer.

February 25: Ever Ready battery plant in Hinkshay Road, Dawley, closed.

April 8: Announced that M54 Wellington bypass stretch was to be ripped up and completely relaid at a cost of £12 million.

April 15: Shropshire at the centre of one of Britain's largest water pollution scares after a huge chemical spill was traced to an industrial estate in Wem. Drinking supplies to nearly a quarter of a million people hit, although Shropshire homes were not affected. The spill was of solvent.

April 30: Shrewsbury Town won the new Division Three title trophy with a 4-1 win at Scunthorpe.

May 24: Newly restored Forest Glen Pavilion officially opened to the public at Blists Hill Museum.

June: The Three Fishes pub in Shrewsbury became a pioneering non-smoking pub; also, controversial voucher parking scheme launched in Shrewsbury in June.

July: Film star Hugh Grant came to Shropshire and Llanrhaeadr to film The Englishman Who Went Up A Hill But Came Down A Mountain. He filmed on the SVR at Hampton Loade.

July: Reported on July 29 that forgotten treasures worth up to £2.5 million were discovered packed into the attics and cellars of Stokesay Court, near Ludlow, where they had lain undisturbed since 1941. They included art, furniture, ceramics and glass. They were discovered by relatives after the death of the owner of the mansion, Lady Magnus-Allcroft.

August: Two standing stones at "Shropshire's stonehenge"

– the Mitchell's Fold stone circle at Stapeley Hill – had been deliberately pulled over by some sort of machine and repairing the vandalism could cost as much as £23,000 (reported August 10, date of the vandalism not mentioned). They were later repaired.

August 11: Wells Soft Drinks announced it was to pull out of Burford and move to Warwickshire, with the loss of up to 350 jobs in the south Shropshire community. The plant was closing at the end of 1996, it was said.

August 27: Traffic started flowing on the new Jackfield Bridge.

September 7: Announced that the MEB's divisional office at Spring Gardens, Ditherington, Shrewsbury, was to close with the loss of 270 jobs there.

September 28: Start of four-day "sale of the century" auction at Stokesay Court of a hoard of "forgotten treasures" found there. Realised £4,217,644.

October 3: First day of business of new Shrewsbury Magistrates Court complex. Court at The Old Market Hall, Shrewsbury, closed down at the same time leaving the building virtually redundant. (official royal opening was October 13).

October 18: New Jackfield Bridge officially opened.

November 7: Operation Bumblebee, West Mercia police's biggest crackdown on burglars, swung into action across Shropshire with dozens of dawn raids.

Misc: New footbridge was opened linking High Town, Bridgnorth, with the SVR over Hollybush Road.

SCHOOL CLOSURES: Hadley Manor School, in September.

DEATHS: Wolves and England football legend Billy Wright, September 3. He had been born in Ironbridge. He was 70. Wolves and England footballer Johnny Hancocks of Oakengates, February 19. KSLI veteran and historian Ned Thornburn in December. c.November 18, Fred Davies, the coracle ball boy who for decades had collected the ball from the River Severn. He was 83.

1995

February 24: Thousands of protesters (i.e. 2,500) poured into Shrewsbury for what was said to be biggest mass demonstration in Shropshire. They were supporting the county council as it rubberstamped a budget £6 million over the Government's spending limit on February 24, becoming only the second county to challenge its budget.

April 24: The 17th century old barn in Church Street, Madeley, where King Charles II slept during his flight after the Battle of Worcester in 1651, severely damaged in what police believed was an arson attack.

May: Old Clifton Cinema in Wellington, which was an entertainment centre for laser gun game company Quasar, severely damaged by fire. It had opened about 18 months previously.

May 2: Shropshire Regimental Museum in Shrewsbury Castle reopened by Princess Alexandra following restoration after the 1992 bomb attack by the IRA (first day open to public was May 16).

June: Market Drayton residents went to the polls in a referendum about traffic.

June 14: Fire gutted old Grand Cinema – being used by Factory Furniture Direct – in Wellington.

June 21: It was reported on June 21 that Ironbridge coracle maker Eustace Rogers, aged 80, had vowed to give up his craft, four months after thieves raided his workshop and stole a treasured photograph of his grandfather.

July 24: Shropshire Records and Research Centre in Shrewsbury opened.

August 19: There was a long, hot summer, which led to a hosepipe ban in Shropshire introduced on August 19.

September 2: The centuries-old Arbor Tree in Aston-on-Clun, traditionally dressed with flags, collapsed.

Reported October 10: A villager in Ellerdine Heath feared a curse had descended on the village after an ancient boulder was moved. Mrs Mary Davies said at least five neighbours had fallen ill after the Ice Age glacial debris was moved from a field yards from her home by a farmer who was unaware of its significance.

October 15: Lady Forester Hospital in Broseley reopened as the Lady Forester Day Care Centre.

October 23: Hope House Hospice opened at Morda, Oswestry.

Reported October 27: A tulip tree symbolising Shrewsbury's blossoming friendship with its twin town of Zutphen in Holland died – the sixth year running a friendship tree had died. A malicious poisoner was suspected.

November 19: Wem Town Hall burned down.

December: Ancient stocks at Norton, between Bridgnorth and Telford, seriously damaged by a car smashing into them after skidding on ice. Exact date in December not certain. (the stocks were removed, repaired, and returned in August 1996 following repairs costing £9,000 paid for by the motorist's car insurance).

December 9: Seventeen people were hurt when a coach plunged off an isolated road in Shropshire at midnight (i.e. 8/9), rolling over twice as it crashed 30ft down a hillside near Snailbeach in frosty conditions.

December 16: A new Arbor Tree, a rooted cutting from the old tree, was planted at Aston-on-Clun.

December 27: Armed police cordoned off part of Bishop's Castle after man with a shotgun was holed up in the tourist information centre in the High Street. He later gave himself up to police.

December 29: Main hall, canteen, and gymnasium at Phoenix School, Dawley, burnt down by arsonists.

DEATHS: Writer Edith Pargeter, best known as Ellis Peters, at her home in Madeley on October 14, aged 82. December 14, Viscount Boyne, the Lord Lieutenant of Shropshire, aged 64.

SCHOOL CLOSURES: Acton Reynald girls school closed in the summer.

1996

January 12: Big fire at Crudgington Creamery.

January 13: National Rivers Authority abandoned its planned £6 million flood defence scheme for Shrewsbury after failing to win the backing of Shrewsbury and Atcham borough councillors, who feared the defences would harm the appearance of the town.

January 18: Prime Minister John Major visited Shrewsbury in the first visit by a premier to the county town for 15 years. Stayed at the Lord Hill Hotel and on January 19 visited Telford.

February 26: Greenacres Primary School, Shrewsbury, destroyed by £1.2 million arson attack, started by two boys aged just eight and nine.

March 6: Wem gripped by ghost fever after picture by amateur photographer Tony O'Rahilly shows spirit of a young girl haunting the fire-ravaged Wem Town Hall.

March 7: Shropshire rocked by a powerful earth tremor with epicentre at Harmer Hill.

March 14: Government gave official go ahead for Wrekin Council to become a go-it-alone unitary authority.

March 23: Beef banned from menus in all 250 Shropshire LEA schools following fears about mad cow disease.

c.April 13: New Coalport Village Hall opened.

May 31: G and R Cadwallader haulage firm of Oswestry closed after 42 years today with the loss of 138 jobs, a victim of the BSE crisis.

July 5: Hundreds of people climbed Oswestry hill fort carrying pieces of a special mozaic and linked up to spell out the words A Fair Deal For Shropshire, calling for improved funding for Shropshire County Council.

July 31: Bedstone College severely damaged by fire.

August 8: Three people killed in a crash between an ambulance and lorry on the A49 at Hadnall. Two of the dead were in the ambulance.

September 14: Broseley Pipe Works Museum opened.

October 1: Announced that Britain's sole military helicopter flying school was to be based at RAF Shawbury.

October 4: Tony Blair visited New College in Wellington, dropping in after the Labour Party conference.

December 7: The first fare paying passengers for 30 years travelled the Cambrian Railway line in Oswestry. The historic 350-yard trip was the culmination of years of work by a dedicated band of steam enthusiasts.

SCHOOL CLOSURES: Hilltop School, Ludlow, on September 30. It looked after children who had suffered mental, physical or emotional abuse. Probably Ford, Wattlesborough and Yockleton (piece in August 30, 1996, about the new Trinity CE Primary School in Ford which was opening and replaced them).

DEATHS: Geoffrey Parfitt, who established Shrewsbury's regimental museum and masterminded its restoration after it was bombed by the IRA, aged 69 on July 19. On August 7, Lt Col George Ellis, 89, of Preston Gubbals, who was credited with helping make the West Mid Show one of the country's top agricultural shows. September 26, Mrs Elsie Day, aged 110, Shropshire's oldest woman.

1997

January: Oswestry balloonist Per Lindstrand and tycoon Richard Branson made unsuccessful attempts to become the first to circumnavigate the world by balloon (first started in Morocco on January 7, ended with an emergency landing in Algerian desert next day).

February 22: Announced that a controversial futuristic sculpture derided as looking like a scrap heap on the Forge traffic island in Telford was being removed for "safety reasons".

March 12: No Smoking ban was introduced in Telford shopping centre on this, national No Smoking Day.

April 7: Shropshire horse Lord Gyllene won the Grand National.

March 31: Two young Scout leaders, Stuart Perkins and David Weaver, crushed to death under tons of sandstone boulders after a camp fire triggered a rockfall at 1am during a scouts' annual trip to Pinkham House Farm, Cleobury Mortimer.

April 14: Wellington post office (due to) open at new site in Market Street, after switching from Walker Street.

May 1: In the general election, Labour won Shrewsbury seat for the first time in history. It was the first modern election with five Shropshire seats – The Wrekin had been split in two, into The Wrekin, and the new Telford seat.

May 31: Old Salop Laundry, in Laundry Lane, Sutton Farm, Shrewsbury, which was derelict was seriously damaged in an arson attack.

July 19: Seven people hurt when a horse ran amok at Newport show.

July 26: Man dies in a glider crash on the Long Mynd.

August 17: William A Lewis car dealership on Burway Trading Estate, Ludlow, severely damaged in £1 million fire.

August 18: Work began to demolish Tuckers, the partially collapsed shop in Newport which had become dubbed "The Shame of Newport".

August 31: Bodyguard Trevor Rees-Jones, of Whittington, near Oswestry, is sole survivor of the car crash in Paris which killed Princess Diana.

September 8: Jackfield war memorial footbridge closed for safety reasons – it later reopened after repairs.

October 6: Oakley Grange, an 18th century house in Oak Street, Shrewsbury, destroyed in an arson attack.

DEATHS: On February 24, Harold Gale, of Lilleshall, the sacked chief executive of Mensa, who died 24 hours after a road crash in Muxton.

1998

January 6 and 7: Floods hit Shropshire, the Severn flooding in the Ironbridge Gorge and Shrewsbury.

January 11: 2,000 farmers attended a rally at Oswestry livestock market in support of a campaign for a fair deal for British beef.

January 15: Kids International, Telford's biggest event, scrapped after nine years.

January 17: Shrewsbury brought to a standstill by a rally against proposed education cuts involving 4,000 protesters.

January 22: The Empire Cinema, Shrewsbury, closed after 75 years, with the showing of its last film – the James Bond movie Tomorrow Never Dies.

January 22: Drugs worth over £1 million were seized on the A53 near Market Drayton, possibly Shropshire's biggest haul.

January 23: Campaigners carried a symbolic coffin to Downing Street marking the "death" of Shropshire education.

January 23: Last routine operation was performed at the Eye, Ear and Throat Hospital at Shrewsbury.

January 30: The Eye, Ear and Throat hospital at Shrewsbury closed after 117 years (although the audiology clinic did not close until March 6).

February 16: An unidentified married couple from Highley won over £2 million on the lottery.

March 5: The National Trust unveiled Sunnycroft, its first property in Telford, a late Victorian gentleman's villa in Wellington.

March 27: Telford's Richie Woodhall became World WBC Supermiddleweight champion at Telford ice rink.
March 29: Adrian Spillett, 20, of Shrewsbury became BBC Young Musician of the Year, first percussionist to do so.
April 1: County is split into two for administrative pur-

poses between Shropshire County Council and Telford & Wrekin Council. Last meeting of old Wrekin Council was March 31, change came into effect at midnight that night.

May 16: G8 summit of world leaders held at Weston Park.

May 25: Direct rail link from Shropshire to London restored by Virgin Trains.

July 4: A woman, Mrs Margaret Ostle of Newport, was struck and killed by a glider on the Long Mynd.

July 5: The Elim Pentecostal Church, Hadley, burned down by arsonists.

July 17: Telford firm Truprint announced it was to quit the county with 240 job losses.

July 17: Tory leader William Hague launched a nationwide "listening to the people" exercise, starting in Shrewsbury.

July 29: A 28-year-old man, Nick Pugh, of Ludlow, was shot and seriously injured by police at Snitton, near Ludlow.

August 3: Two Royal Mail investigators shot in Ellesmere, one of them, Andrew Gardner, died. A postman was arrested.

August 10: Tesco in Telford started 24 hour shopping.

August 23: Six Shropshire young farmers hurt when a runaway double bed hurtled down a hill and into a ditch during a charity bed push.

September 28: Lloyds Bank in Much Wenlock closes after over 70 years in the town.

October 10: Major fire in the turbine hall at Ironbridge Power Station.

October 28: Worst floods in Shropshire for 30 years.

October 31: St Austin Friars/Barker Street multi storey car park closed at the end of this month as it was beyond economic repair.

November 20: Centrex at High Ercall closed with the loss of 30 jobs.

November 29: Two young women killed by fumes at the Crown Inn, Wentnor.

December 2: New eight screen multiplex officially opened in Shrewsbury with launch party for VIPs and guests. (opened to public on December 4)

December: About now Laura Ashley's in Oswestry closed (had been announced c. November 26 and closure was expected "before Christmas").

DEATHS: Dick Meyrick, legendary Shropshire bowls player, on December 3.

1999

January 24: Two decorative belt or strap ends from the 9th century discovered by metal detector enthusiasts at Frodesley.

January 26: The 70-year-old Mid Shropshire Bowls League votes to let women play in all their competitions.

February 3: Wheathill Youth Hostel, near Burwarton, closes after 60 years.

February 16: Fire at Brookside County Primary School, Telford, causes £1 million damage.

February 22: Sowland Ltd, Baschurch, a ground working firm, went out of business with the loss of 50 jobs.

March 3: A winding up order is made for Telford Tigers in the High Court over an unpaid tax bill.

March 9: Shrewsbury Golf Club votes to give women equal status to men.

March 9: The transfer is finalised of 13,000 Telford & Wrekin Council homes to a housing trust.

March 10: A smoking ban is introduced in public areas at the Charles Darwin Centre, Shrewsbury.

March 17: Whittington Castle is handed to Whittington Castle Preservation Trust on an 18 month licence. It is a community-led charitable trust.

March 20: President's moll Monica Lewinsky comes to Shrewsbury during a tour to promote her book.

April 12: Oswestry Rugby Club banned from competitive games for a season and four club officers banned from the sport for five years for fielding a banned player under a false name. The club had already been docked 90 league points.

April 14: The badge or crest of the wartime cruiser HMS Shropshire was returned "home" to the county by veteran Australian sailor Roy Purdon who had kept it for 57 years having removed the crest from the cruiser when it was handed over to the Australian navy during the war.

April 18: Seven people evacuated after a chemical tanker crashes on the A49 at Dorrington, coming to rest in a beer garden.

May 3: Telford's own radio station, Telford FM, launched.

June 22: Telford United change their nickname from the

Lilywhites to The Bucks.

July 23: Rock legend Robert Plant performs a secret pub concert at the Three Tuns, Bishop's Castle.

c. July 31: At the end of the month the Serck Audco factory at Newport closed with the loss of 148 jobs.

August 9: A new railway museum opened at Bishop's Castle featuring items from the golden age of steam.

August 26: A massive Hercules transport plane got bogged down on the grass airstrip at Chetwynd airfield and was eventually freed and took off on August 30.

October 4: It was revealed that former Prime Minister John Major had a "secret" half sister living in Shropshire. She was Kathleen Lemon, aged 75, of Whitchurch.

October 5: £2 million damage at C.J. Wildbird Foods Ltd at Upton Magna in a fire in the birdseed warehouse.

October 7: Rebekah Gilbertson, an ex student of Moreton Hall School near Oswestry, chosen as Country Life's girl of the millennium.

October 23: Telford boxer Richie Woodhall lost his world championship title at Telford Ice Rink to Marcus Beyer.

November 9: Shropshire pilot Martin Rutty sets a world record by flying from London to Sydney. He and business colleague Tim Gilbert become the first people to fly between the two countries in a single-engined helicopter.

November 25: The Thomas Telford School in Telford named as the most successful comprehensive in England, with 99 per cent of its pupils gaining five or more good GCSEs.

December 2: Wall paintings hidden for hundreds of years discovered by decorators stripping plaster at All Saints Church, Worthen. (reported in SS today)

December 22: Revealed that the Shrewsbury Quest tourist attraction had closed amid financial troubles. It was an evocation of medieval life leaning heavily on the Brother Cadfael connection. (reported in SS today)

December 31: The new Wrekin Beacon was turned on at midnight on New Year's Eve for the new millennium.

DEATHS: c. January 14, Shropshire's Mr Ice Cream, Camillo Sidoli. Stan Hall, veteran journalist who covered Shrewsbury Town for 30 years, January 9, aged 82. Colonel Guy Thornycroft, Shropshire soldier and former High Sheriff and ex-deputy lieutenant, c. January 13. Shropshire horseracing legend Captain Tim Forster, April 21. June 14, Sir George Labouchere of Dudmaston Hall. June 28, David Hutchison, chief executive of Telford & Wrekin Council. About November 17 George Nightingale from Church Stretton, one of the world's top cyclists in the 1930s and 1940s, aged 84.

2000

January 1: New millennium celebrated at midnight 31/1. Shropshire sky ablaze with fireworks. Thousands gathered round a bonfire on the summit of The Wrekin and saw revived Wrekin Beacon switched on at stroke of midnight.

January 1: Early on New Year's Day body of a young Telford man, Jason McGowan, found hanging at Ketley in circumstances which grabbed national attention. Relatives claimed he had been victim of racist lynch mob.

January 6: Shrewsbury Quest tourist attraction went into voluntary liquidation.

January 10: Work started on redevelopment of Telford United's Bucks Head stadium.

January 12: Span of Jackfield and Coalport War Memorial Bridge removed for restoration.

January 18: Announced that the remains of a near-2,000 year old harbour had been discovered at Wroxeter Roman City.

January 24: Telford's first crematorium opened.

January 26. Market Drayton got first 20mph zones in Britain. It had been picked for a nationwide trial.

February 21: Rebuilt Wem Town Hall reopened.

March 8: Ludlow Castle illuminated at night to make town look more attractive.

April 8: Shrewsbury Quest reopened with new management.

April 22: Telford United play last game at old Bucks Head before its demolition. (Some demolition had already taken place).

April 25: Shropshire's wettest April since records began in 1903.

April 28: The Jackfield and Coalport Memorial Bridge lifted back into place after £500,000 renovation.

May 6: Shrewsbury Town staged "great escape", beating Exeter City 2-1 to survive in the Football League.

May 20: Prime Minister's wife Cherie Blair had a baby boy, named Leo after his Shropshire grandfather.

June 12: Spectator stand at Oakengates Leisure Centre athletics stadium severely damaged in arson attack.

June 12: One of Ludlow's biggest factories, DMS Plastics, severely damaged by fire.

June 23: Superstar Joan Collins visited Telford to open £3m office complex.

July 9: Mother and two children killed in fire at Southgate, Sutton Hill in Telford.

July 15: Jackfield and Coalport War Memorial Bridge officially reopened.

July 21: Sunlight Laundry, formerly Laundrycraft, in Whitchurch, closed, with 86 job losses.

August 5: Mother and two daughters die in house fire in Halifax Drive, Leegomery.

August 11: Coach firm Williamsons Motorways and Williamsons Holidays of Knockin went out of business after nearly 80 years. (reported today)

August 14: Eddie the Eagle Edwards officially opened a controversial new Tesco store in Ludlow.

September 11: After protests at fuel depots massive queues built up at filling stations in Shropshire and Mid Wales, as elsewhere.

September 15: Newport builder Craig Phillips won reality TV show Big Brother.

September 18: Last baby born at Wrekin Hospital, and first delivered at new maternity unit at Telford's Princess Royal Hospital.

September 19: Jim Elliot of Acton Scott Working Farm Museum became first person to become world ploughing champion three times.

September 20: H.H. Wardles (Metals) of Fenns Bank, near Whitchurch, announced it was closing, with up to 125 jobs lost. Some jobs were saved in a partial buyout later.

September 28: Gang of four youths banned from every shop in Bayston Hill for five years in first court order of its kind in the county. It was the first gang order ever issued.

October 5: The bodies of a former Shropshire family – a mother and four children – found in Cornwall. They were Lesley Ford, Sarah-Jane Tranter, 17, Anne-Marie Tranter, 16, Steven Tranter, 14, and Craig Tranter, 13. A man appeared in court accused of murder.

October 16: St Julian's Craft Centre in Shrewsbury would shut in February, it was announced.

October 17: Hatfield rail crash leads to dropping of Shropshire's revived direct rail link to London (exact date unknown, probably around 2001).

October 21: First match at the still incomplete new Bucks Head ground. Telford United lost 1-0.

October 26: Mountaineer Julian Freeman-Attwood, from Rednal, conquered the 6,550 metre high Mount Targo in Central Tibet.

October 30: Famous Royal Oak tree at Boscobel severely damaged in gale.

October 31: Start of flooding in Shropshire.

November 1: Shropshire floods reach climax, peaking at the Welsh Bridge in Shrewsbury at 5.25 metres – 17ft 2ins – on November 1, highest level for 54 years. In Shrewsbury 400 properties were affected. Elsewhere huge tracts of countryside were swamped, the Wharfage at Ironbridge was covered to the tops of the riverside railings, and Bridgnorth was also severely hit.

November 2: Prime Minister Tony Blair visited emergency control room at Shrewsbury.

November 3: Hampton Loade ferry sank.

November 11: Shrewsbury Quest closed for good.

November 16: Bishop's Castle Railway Museum severely damaged by fire.

November 25: Shropshire's wettest autumn since local records began, with 14ins of rain in three months.

December 1: Athena nightclub opened in Telford at former Cascades site.

December 4: Midland Centre for Spinal Injuries opened at the Robert Jones and Agnes Hunt Orthopaedic and District Hospital at Gobowen.

December 8: New storms and severe flooding – almost as severe as the late October/early November floods.

December 12: Deputy PM John Prescott visits flooded Shrewsbury. The River Severn peaked at Shrewbury at 4.78m.

December 13: River Severn peaks at Ironbridge p.m. at 6.5m, and at Bridgnorth at 5m, as high as in October.

December 16: A canal embankment at Adderley, near Market Drayton, gave way, draining canal and flooding a farmhouse nearby.

DEATHS: March 18, George Phillips, possibly the last exponent of the Dawley twang in full measure, aged 85. Shropshire actor Peter Jones, April 10. c July 7, Jack Insall, author of the All Friends Round The Wrekin series of books. Former Tory MP Sir Julian Critchley, who lived in Ludlow, on September 9.

2001

January 13: New Dawley Baptist Church officially opened.

January 17: Bridgnorth brought to standstill as 200 pro-hunters congregated in the High Street in a show of defiance as MPs voted on future of foxhunting.

January 31: i.e. at the end of the month, Pritchard's Tailors and outfitters in Cross Street, Oswestry, opened in 1878, closed.

February: IK Precision shut Whitchurch plant.

February 9: £2.6 million Secret Hills Discovery Centre opened at Craven Arms.

February 12: New Newport library opens at former Tuckers site (official opening February 22).

February 15: Telford Sea Cadets hut at Donnington, Telford, suffered about £200,000 damage in a suspected arson attack.

February 21: After public protests, Telford & Wrekin Labour group drops plans for parking charges in Newport and Wellington.

February 22: Shropshire countryside plunged into crisis after outbreak of foot and mouth disease in Essex. By the end of the outbreak 59,716 animals in Shropshire had been destroyed.

March 6: Traffic in Scotland Street, Ellesmere, reverted to a two-way system after a controversial one-way experiment.

March 9: Cherie Blair officially opened Telford's Princess Royal Hospital's £1.8 million maternity unit.

March 18: Shropshire's first confirmed outbreaks of foot and mouth disease, at farms at Chirbury (confirmed "at the weekend" according to SS report on Monday 19th) and confirmed at Beech Field Farm, Brockton, near Shrewsbury, on the 18th.

March 21: The West Mid Show postponed due to FMD.

March 26: Newport Show called off due to FMD.

March 31: By end of month there are three confirmed FMD cases in Shropshire.

April 3: Vast burial pits for slaughtered animals created at Tern Hill airfield.

April 18: Hundreds of sheep on the Long Mynd shot as "dangerous contact" animals in latest anti-FMD measure.

April 19: Burwarton Show and Bishop's Castle Show cancelled.

April 20: Last service at Our Lady of the Rosary Church, Donnington.

April 23: Adams School, Wem, renamed Thomas Adams School.

April 25: Deputy Prime Minister John Prescott launched pioneering scheme in Waters Upton which would see a return of various village services, all under one roof.

May 30: Prime Minister Tony Blair visited Newport, giving election speech in Cosy Hall.

May 31: By the end of the month total of confirmed outbreaks of foot and mouth disease in Shropshire stood at 11.

June 2: Telford MP Bruce Grocott made life peer.

June 5: Crowds turn out in Shrewsbury to see Tory leader William Hague and wife Ffion.

June 16: Kevin Satchwell, head of the Thomas Telford School, knighted in Queen's Birthday Honours List.

June 23: Two die in a microlight crash at Nash, near Ludlow, and a charity parachutist, Iain Johnstone of Clun, dies on his first jump at Prees.

July 6: Jury return a suicide verdict on Errol McGowan, a Telford man who, some claimed, had been victim of a racist lynch mob.

July 7: Large parts of the Long Mynd reopened to the public almost five months after being sealed off through foot and mouth disease.

July 7: Wem Library at Talbot House officially opened.

c. July 10: Pennerley Methodist Church closed after 132 years of worship.

July 20: Scientists announced they had found the world's oldest crustaceans in rocks at Comley, near Church Stretton. They are 511 million years old.

July 30: Ludlow Town played their last game at their ground at The Riddings, before bulldozers moved in.

August 18: Almost all foot and mouth disease restrictions lifted in Shropshire.

August 22: Charlton Bowling Club at Hadley destroyed by

fire.

August 25: Zara Phillips, daughter of the Princess Royal, spotted clubbing at Park Lane nightclub in Shrewsbury.

September 1: "Traditional" AW element of Shropshire vehicle number plates, used since 1903, disappears with introduction of a new number plate system.

September 10: Chemical incident at D. Leonardt & Co, Highley, led to 27 people being taken to hospital by coach.

September 11: Only Briton to die on the planes in the September 11 terror blitz on America was Graham Berkeley, of Shrewsbury.

September 26: A new police station opened in Ludlow at a cost of £330,000. Eyebrows were raised because it had no cells.

October 1: Shrewsbury & Atcham Borough Council handed over 5,744 houses to Severnside Housing and its funding partner the Nationwide Building Society in a deal worth £50 million to the council.

October 14: Shropshire golfer Ian Woosnam won World Matchplay Championship at Wentworth.

October 16: On Whitchurch Town Council six councillors resigned as part of a long-running saga over the suspension of the council clerk and her assistants.

October 18: Telford taxi driver Azhar Ali Mehmood sentenced to life for murdering his teenage girlfriend, her mother and sister in an arson attack in Leegomery – possibly worst multiple murder in Shropshire history.

October 25: Telford United put all its players up for sale as it faced a deepening cash crisis.

October 29: Midland Centre for Spinal Injuries at Shropshire Orthopaedic Hospital officially opened.

November 6: Shropshire given the foot and mouth allclear when it was removed from the at-risk register.

November 9: Mount Gilbert School officially opened on the site of Hinkshay School.

November 15: Cotsbrook School, near Shifnal, seriously damaged by fire only three weeks after reopening.

November 17: Two boys died when a car in which they were passengers plunged into the River Severn at Shrewsbury.

December: Whitchurch magistrates court closed.

December 3: A syndicate of 12 workers at D. Leonardt & Co, Highley, won £1.1 million on the lottery.

December 10: Shrewsbury Labour MP Paul Marsden defected to the Liberal Democrats.

DEATHS: July 14, Vesey Holt, a deputy lieutenant of Shropshire. November 23, television clean-up campaigner Mary Whitehouse, who was a former Madeley teacher.

2002

January 4: Madeley Co-op closed, ending 93 years of the Co-op in Madeley.

January 7: Work on Shrewsbury's floods defence scheme got under way at Frankwell.

January 17: Telford world champion boxer Richie Woodhall retired.

January 27: Hiscocks shop, Coalbrookdale, closed after 42 years.

January 31: Bridgnorth Magistrates Court closed.

February 12: Shrewsbury livestock market opened for the first time in nearly a year following the foot and mouth crisis.

February 12: Flooding hit Shrewsbury and Ironbridge.

March 11: First sod was cut at Atlas Foundry site in Frankwell, Shrewsbury, for a £10.7 million headquarters for Shrewsbury and Atcham Borough Council.

March 22: Fire in Fish Street, Shrewsbury, threatened Bear Steps heritage complex. However, firefighters saved it.

March 25: Sir Bobby Charlton kicked off work at Ludlow Town FC's new £1.4m stadium.

April 3: Shropshire Ambulance Service merged with West Midlands Ambulance Service.

May 2: Conservatives won control of Shrewsbury and Atcham Borough Council for first time in 23 years.

May 13: Sir Michael Beetham Conservation Centre opened at the RAF Museum, Cosford.

May 15: Whittington Castle Preservation Trust signed a 99-year lease for Whittington Castle, effectively buying it on behalf of local villagers.

May 26: Dozens of people who had appeared as extras in the 1949 film Gone To Earth attended a special screening in Much Wenlock.

May 29: Telford & Wrekin Council became "Borough of Telford & Wrekin". Richie Woodhall and Iris Butler were made first Freemen of the new Borough.

June 6: Teagues Bridge Community Centre, Trench, destroyed in arson attack.

June 11: Go-ahead was given for over 70 homes on old battlefield site off Upper Brook Street, Oswestry.

July 6: £1.3 million Salvation Army headquarters at Oakengates officially opened.

July 12: Telford personal injury claims firm Claims Direct goes into receivership.

July 19: Labour held its first-ever rural conference. The venue was the Harper Adams University College at Edgmond. It lasted three days.

July 24: Buildwas post office closes after almost 50 years.

July 31: A 4 metre high Jubilee Column in Telford town park daubed with graffiti only days after it was unveiled.

August 6: £7 million Enginuity attraction opens at Ironbridge Gorge Museum.

September 17: Bronze Age cremation cemetery was found during work on Hodnet bypass.

September 22: Over 400,000 people, including many from Shropshire, joined Countryside March in London.

September 23: Earth tremor rocked Shropshire in the early hours. It measured 4.8 on the Richter Scale and the epicentre was at Dudley. Little damage, but it was thought to have caused a leak at a gas main near Ludlow.

September 30: Enterprise Jewellers in Bridgnorth went bust, with the loss of 219 jobs.

October 11: Ludlow woman Helen Perry became first woman in Britain to give birth using her own frozen eggs.

October 17: A car was damaged in a suspected panther attack at Knowlegate, near Ludlow.

October 27: Severe gales claimed life of an 11-year-old girl at Tern Hill.

November 22: J.C. Pickering toy and bicycle shop in Mardol, Shrewsbury, closed after 120 years.

December: A new police station was officially opened at Donnington.

December 4: Double-decker bus had its roof sliced off at Oakengates railway bridge, luckily without injuries.

DEATHS: May: last Shropshire soldier to see action in World War One, Jim Andrews, of London Road, Shrewsbury, aged 102. Shrewsbury Town goalscoring machine Arthur Rowley, on December 18. Reggie Lloyd, in October, former south Shropshire councillor and longest serving member of Shropshire County Council.

2003

January: Hampton Loade ferry sank.

January 4: Shrewbury Town beat Everton 2-1 at the Gay Meadow in the Third Round of the FA Cup, but at the end of the month were beaten by Chelsea 4-0 in the Fourth Round.

March 10: Nesscliffe bypass partially opened (official opening March 21).

March 17: M54 service station opened on outskirts of Telford.

April 8: Controversial car parking charges brought in at Telford town centre for first time.

April 15: Shropshire's first fixed speed camera came on line at Bennetts Bank, Wellington.

April 29: Shrewsbury Town beaten 3-2 at home by Carlisle in a must-win match and consequently dumped from the Football League after 53 years.

May: Nightingale House care home, Baschurch – the "Florence House" where Dame Agnes Hunt had launched a pioneering "cripples hospital" – closed.

May 1: Historic polling day in Shropshire local council elections, with revolutionary polling methods, including "smart" voting for the first time. Votes in Telford & Wrekin and North Shropshire were entirely by post, while Shrewsbury & Atcham Borough Council had "smart" voting by internet, digital television, touch-tone phone, and also post.

May 3: Shrewsbury Town played their last game in the Football League, losing 2-1 to Scunthorpe at the Gay Meadow.

June: The name Oswestry Town disappeared as a result of a merger with TNS (Total Network Solutions) of Llansantffraid. From the summer, the team was known as TNS.

July: Various activities to mark 600th anniversary of the Battle of Shrewsbury.

August 16: Rumours nightclub in Wellington closed because it had been unable to get insurance following arson attacks.

August 25: Hunt by armed police after 6ft long cat spotted

at Bayston Hill. Nothing found.

September 2: Shropshire appeared at Lords in the Minor Counties Association Knockout Trophy final, but were beaten by Cambridgeshire.

September 10: Hodnet bypass opened.

October 1: Official merger of the Princess Royal Hospital, Telford, and the Royal Shrewsbury Hospital.

October 13: Flood barrier tested on The Wharfage, Ironbridge.

October 15: The King's Social Club, Donnington, burnt down.

October 25: Dawley's Holy Trinity Church hit by fire.

December 9: Shrewsbury Town played Telford United at the Gay Meadow in the first league game between the two sides since 1937. The 2003 game had a bumper crowd of over 6,700 and was a goalless draw.

2004

January 9: Shrewsbury's £1.7 million new cinema and digital media centre opened at the Old Market Hall.

February 5 and 6: Flooding hit Shrewsbury and Ironbridge giving new flood defences their first test. They passed with flying colours.

February 11: Over 20 swallows spotted at Diddlebury – more than a month early.

March 16: The last ever Shrewsbury and Atcham Borough Council meeting – a committee meeting – held at Oakley Manor council chamber, Shrewsbury.

March 23: New Shrewsbury council headquarters officially opened for business and greeted its first customer.

March 27: Farewell dinner for Shawbury & District Round Table, which was becoming defunct after 29 years.

April 1: Oswestry maternity unit officially declared open again after a six month closure.

April 1: Speed cameras at Spring Gardens, Longden Road, and Mytton Oak Road, Shrewsbury, became operational.

April 3: W T Smith butcher at Wem High Street closed after over 65 years.

April 9: RAF Cosford became the Defence College of Aeronautical Engineering, Cosford, about now.

April 26: Hampton Loade ferry, a new boat built by the Blists Hill Museum, officially relaunched.

April 30: The Government used its capping powers on Telford and Wrekin Borough Council, meaning the council had to find £30,000.

May 16: Shrewsbury Town return to the Football League at their first attempt after a 3-0 win on penalties against Aldershot in the Conference playoffs at the Britannia Stadium, Stoke.

May 26: Village square of Baron-sur-Odon, south west of Caen in France, named after the 4th Battalion King's Shropshire Light Infantry, in the presence of a handful of surviving veterans who had liberated the village and seen their first major combat there in June and July 1944. In a separate ceremony, the previous day, veterans of the 2nd Battalion of the KSLI attended a ceremony at Lebisey, on the northern outskirts of Caen, to commemorate their achievement in pushing the farthest inland of any of the ground troops on D-Day in June 1944.

June 15: Telford United officially goes bust with debts of £6.5 million, but a new club formed, playing three leagues lower.

June 17: Shrewsbury and Atcham Borough Council's new headquarters at The Guildhall – as the building was named – officially opened.

June 26 and 27: West Mid Show was held on Saturday and Sunday for the first time.

July 4: Little Dawley Methodist Church held its final service after 167 years.

July 8: Coldest July day since records began at RAF Shawbury – 11.4C.

July 8: The threat of capping lifted from Telford and Wrekin Borough Council.

July 16: The Royal National Institute for the Blind school at Condover closed.

July 16: Shropshire and Mid Wales Hospice renamed the Severn Hospice.

July 27: It was revealed that 87 people had died in Shropshire since March 2003 after being infected with the ESBL superbug. The extent of the problem became clear when Telford and Wrekin coroner, Michael Gwynne, went public about his concerns.

August 18: Shropshire's Alison Williamson was the toast of the county after winning bronze in the women's archery event in the Athens Olympics.

August 20: Parts of Oswestry town centre pedestrianised – Cross Street, Bailey Head, Bailey Street, and Albion Hill.

September 18: By special arrangement, the Red Arrows staged a flypast of The Wrekin as part of the Shropshire Star's 40th birthday celebrations.

October: The Shropshire Star celebrated its 40th birthday with the launch of a £5 million appeal to build a hospice in Telford.

October 18: Wellington and Newport parking charges brought in for the first time by Telford & Wrekin Council.

October 23: A woman swept to her death in her Land Rover Freelander at a flooded ford at Neen Savage.

October 26: Chief executive of the Shrewsbury & Telford Hospital Trust, Neil Taylor, quit.

October 31: Last ever service at Ketley Bank's Hilltop Methodist Church, which was closing due to falling congregations.

November 18: Telford and Wrekin Borough Council leader Phil Davis ousted in no confidence vote by council's Labour group.

November 24: Over 100 people gathered in Shrewsbury to witness the unveiling of the Darwin Gate sculpture in Mardol Head. Said to be the first public sculpture of its kind in Shrewsbury since 1897.

December 6: Parking charges introduced at Telford's Princess Royal Hospital.

December 7: About 130ft of embankment of the Llangollen Canal between Hampton Bank and Bettisfield collapsed, draining the canal for a mile.

December 25: A white Christmas – snow fell in Shropshire.

December 27: Pregnant 14-year-old, Amy Williams, of Sutton Hill, found naked and strangled in Madeley churchyard.

DEATHS: February 4, Lord Forester of Willey. c. March 12, Lady Kathryn Dugdale, lady in waiting to the Queen for nearly 50 years, aged 80. She lived at Tickwood Hall, Much Wenlock. August 29, Vera Davies, of Linley Hall, near Broseley, possibly Shropshire's oldest driver at the age of 98, after a car crash. Veteran Shropshire photographer Dan Arden, on December 2. May 20, Len Murray, Hadley-born former TUC general secretary.

2005

January 2: Athena nightclub in Telford closed.

February 10: Wem Town Council voted to take over running of the town's swimming pool from North Shropshire District Council to stop it being mothballed.

February 17: Last legal hunts across Shropshire.

February 18: Shrewsbury's floating restaurant officially ceased trading.

February: Sub post offices at Ketley Bank, Ketley, Arleston, St Georges, Belle Vue, Porthill, and Oswestry closed.

March 8: Hampton Bank on the Llangollen Canal, closed after a major breach, reopened.

March 9: Dawley Bank post office closed.

March 13: Man killed in a paraglider crash on Long Mynd.

March 14: Coalport Bridge reopened after repairs lasting nearly a year.

March 17: Moston Road post office, Shrewsbury, closed.

March 24: Announced that Ironbridge power station would close by 2015.

March 31: Wem Town Hall closed.

March 31: The last public session held at Wem Swimming Pool, after which it was boarded up.

March 31: English Heritage bought Ditherington Flax Mill.

April 5: Shrewsbury MP Paul Marsden defected from the Lib Dems to Labour.

April 22: Iron Age roundhouse discovered during dig by archaeologists at the site of the New Meadow in Oteley Road, Shrewsbury.

April 24: Fire caused £500,000 damage to a row of shops at Priorslee.

April 29: Shifnal squash club closed.

May 3: Prime Minister Tony Blair and Chancellor Gordon Brown visit Wellington on an election visit.

May 5: Lion Hotel, Llanymynech closed. Princess Victoria stayed there in 1830.

May 6: After a four-week trial, Andrew George, 37, of Shrewsbury, sentenced to life imprisonment after being found guilty of murder of Hilda Murrell, the Shrewsbury rose grower whose killing in 1984 had sparked a host of conspiracy theories.

May 6: Phillip Raymond Powell, of Sutton Hill, told he must serve at least 30 years after admitting the murder and rape of 14-year-old Amy Williams, whose body was found in Madeley churchyard.

May 7: AFC Telford United promoted in their first season in the UniBond League.

May 18: Constable Mark Milton, a police officer who sped at up to 159 mph on the M54 "to familiarise himself with his new patrol car" cleared of speeding and dangerous driving.

May 19: Eglantyne Jebb chosen as the most influential Salopian of the 20th century by Shropshire Society in London.

May 26: Otis Ferry, joint master of the South Shropshire Hunt, found guilty of disorderly behaviour following an invasion of the House of Commons in a pro-hunt demo. He was given a conditional discharge.

June 16: Bridgnorth couple Keith and Louise Gough won £9 million (£9,001,406) on lottery.

July 1: Revamped Oakengates Theatre relaunched as "The Place".

July 5: The Bishop of Hereford decided to withdraw the licence for St Anne's Church, Lea Cross, in the latest move in a long running ownership battle between parishioners and the diocese.

July 13: Parking charges in Wellington and Newport scrapped by Telford & Wrekin Borough Council after nine months, on a 47-2 vote.

July 18: Three naked ramblers arrested at Quina Brook near Wem during a John O'Groats to Land's End walk. Breach of the peace action against them dropped before coming to court.

July 20: The first train ran at Llynclys Station in 40 years, where almost a mile of track laid as a tourist attraction.

July 22: Row of shops at Leegomery destroyed by fire.

July 23: Historic cricket pavilion at Shrewsbury School severely damaged by fire.

July 29: Lloyds of Ludlow folded.

August 8: Wem Swimming Pool, closed since the end of March, reopened, run by Shrewsbury-based Swim With Style.

August 29: Lloyds TSB bank on Pride Hill, Shrewsbury, made history by opening on Bank Holiday Monday, one of only three in the country opening their doors.

September 3: Oswestry Co-op in Smithfield Road closed.

September 5: Ellesmere Town Hall officially bought by Ellesmere Town Council from North Shropshire District Council, securing its future.

September 6: Self-styled MI5 spy Robert Hendy-Freegard, a former Newport barman, jailed for life at Blackfriars Crown Court.

November 3: The Mawley Oak, dating back to the Middle Ages, blown down in the early hours near Cleobury Mortimer.

November 8: An announcement that the big Army repair organisation, ABRO, at Donnington was to close by March 2007 with the loss of 628 jobs caused a huge outcry.

November 9: The average price for a home in some parts of Shropshire broke through £500,000 mark for first time.

November 22: Shropshire health services revealed to be £36 million in debt.

November 24: Fire destroyed new hotel called The Sleep Inn nearing completion at Emstrey, Shrewsbury.

December 9: HSBC's Shifnal branch closed.

December 15: Well-known Wellington nightspot of the 1970s and 1980s, The Town House, reopened as "Fusion".

December 21: Peter Roscoe and Geoffrey Hardy of Castlefields, Shrewsbury, became first same sex couple in Shropshire to "marry" under new civil partnership legislation.

December 23: Fire devastates Snedshill industrial estate.

December 31: Oswestry's Vic nightclub closed.

DEATHS: June 18, Tony O'Rahilly, who took the 1995 picture of the "Wem Ghost". December 16, Frank Davies of Shrewsbury, joint founder of the Lingen-Davies cancer appeal which raised cash to build a cobalt unit at the Royal Shrewsbury Hospital. February 21, Major Ervin Miller, aged 90, American wartime base commander of Atcham airfield.

2006

January 7: Thousands joined protest marches in Ludlow, Whitchurch and Bridgnorth to fight against possible closure of community hospitals in those towns.

January 7: Littlewoods store in Cross Street, Oswestry, closed after over 50 years.

January 20: Cave war memorial in Ruyton-XI-Towns given Grade II listed status.

February: Condover Hall school for the blind reopened as a base for Condover Horizon, a school for pupils with autism.

February 27: Oswestry's historic Cross was reinstated in its original position in the centre of the town about now.

March 2: Residents in Church Stretton went to polls in a local referendum to vote over proposals for a new leisure centre.

March 16: Dawley Bingo Club – the New Royal – opened for last time.

March 17: Government gave a stay of execution for ABRO at Donnington, which was to stay open for at least three years longer than feared. It had been on target for closure in 2007.

March 17: Empty Harlescott Inn, Shrewsbury, gutted in second arson attack.

March 18: Powneys Bookshop, Shrewsbury, closed.

March 23: Shrewsbury Town chairman Roland Wycherley officially cuts first sod of the New Meadow stadium.

March 24: Community hospitals at Ludlow, Whitchurch and Bridgnorth officially reprieved by health bosses.

March 26: Last ever service at St John's Hill Methodist Church, Shrewsbury, held on Mothering Sunday.

April 4: The new Battlefield livestock market in Shrewsbury was officially opened, although in fact it had been operating since the end of March.

April 9: Hundreds of people from Cleobury Mortimer travelled to Twickenham to watch Cleobury's rugby players take on Dorking in the final of the Powergen Junior Vase. Cleobury Mortimer lost 46-3.

April 20: Shrewsbury Sports Village at Sundorne officially opened.

May 16: Mrs Sharon Moore of Much Wenlock began a sit-in at the Shropshire Primary Care Trust headquarters as part of a fight to win NHS treatment with the breast cancer drug Herceptin. She and supporter Julia Black ended their sit-in after four days i.e. May 19 – and shortly afterwards i.e. May 22 Mrs Moore heard she had won her fight to receive Herceptin on the NHS.

May 26: Shrewsbury Town goalkeeper Joe Hart signed for Manchester City in a transfer deal worth £1.5 million.

May: Wettest May since 1979. Gobowen post office was due to close by the end of May.

June 3: Dance sensation Hollie Robertson of Middleton, near Ludlow, won BBC TV's Strictly Dance Fever dancing talent show, with dance partner Darrien Wright.

June 12: Work started on Clun Bridge to improve approaches.

June 13: Cambrian Visitor Centre at Oswestry's old railway station opened.

June 15: Filming under way at Stokesay Court, near Craven Arms, for blockbuster movie "Atonement" starring Keira Knightley.

July 3: Fundraisers and campaigners took along spades to make the cutting of the first sod of the new Telford Hospice a community event.

July 4: Flash floods hit Albrighton and Cosford after a storm.

July 7: Telford building firm C.J. Pearce collapsed – it went into administration.

July 12: Controversial plans to merge West Mercia Police with other forces to create a regional superforce scrapped.

July 19: Shropshire smashed the county's all time temperature record for July with 33.7 (93F) recorded at RAF Shawbury.

July: July equalled hottest Shropshire July on record (1983). Mean temperature in county was 20C (78F).

August 8: Small fire hit Charlton Arms Hotel at Wellington, after which the hotel closed, never (to date) to reopen.

September 5: The first phase opened of the £70 million Hadley Learning Community (official opening September 8).

September 7: Three patients were treated for Legionnaire's disease at the Royal Shrewsbury Hospital. One of them later died.

September 11: Work started on a £20 million project to stop part of the Ironbridge Gorge sliding into the river.

September 18: New radio station, The Severn, launched.

September 18: New Highley-Alveley footbridge became operational (officially opened December 15).

September 20: Shrewsbury Post Office at the corner of Pride Hill and St Mary's Street closed. Moved to new site at W H Smith.

September: Shropshire weatherman John Warner said July

and September warmest since records began in 1659.

October 1: Riot lasting several hours and involving over 30 inmates at Stoke Heath young offenders institution.

October 19: Princess Anne opened new Old Hall School on the Wrekin College campus.

October 31: Coroner Michael Gwynne recorded verdicts of accidental death on 11 people, including six from Telford, killed in a coach crash in France in 1990. Inquest held in Telford.

November 3: A multi million pound new hospital extension at Bridgnorth Hospital officially opened.

November 6: Revealed that the bulk of Celestica workers in Priorslee, Telford, would be axed in December and the factory would close by March.

November 21: Syndicate of 33 workers at Palethorpes pie factory in Market Drayton won nearly £7 million on Euro Lottery.

November 27: Merrythought toy factory at Ironbridge closed after 76 years.

December 4: Lloyds TSB at Pontesbury closed.

December 9: Floods peak at Shrewsbury.

December 10: Floods peak at Ironbridge at 5.76 metres.

December 23: Cheswardine post office closed.

Misc: Lloyds TSB training centre at Forgegate, Telford town centre, was closed some time in 2006.

DEATHS: January 8, Ian Ridgway, assistant clerk to the Lord Lieutenant, in road crash. April 20, Sir Douglas Osmond, Shropshire Chief Constable from 1946 to 1962, aged 91. Former Oswestry borough mayor David Lloyd c. September 26, aged 64. c. October 11, Colonel John Kenyon, the man who led the campaign to restore the name "Shropshire" in place of Salop. December 4, Sir Peter Gadsden, former Lord Mayor of London and well known in Shropshire public life. February 3, Shropshire cycling star Ernie Clements.

SCHOOL CLOSURES: St Peter & Paul RC Primary School, Salters Lane, Newport – the Victorian school closed in July, and school moved to a new site at Coppice Drive. July 14, Orleton Park School, Wellington, closed. July 15, Old Hall School, Wellington, closed at its original site (moved to new site on Wrekin College campus). Ketley Infant School (renamed Meadows Primary School after merger with Ketley Town Junior School in 2005) closed its doors for the last time on July 19 after 109 years. Grafton School closed July 21.

2007

January 8: Temperature in Shropshire reaches 15C (59F).

January 10: One man dies and three are injured as two Squirrel helicopters collide at RAF Tern Hill.

January 17: The future of RAF Cosford is thrown into doubt by the announcement that it had lost out to RAF St Athan in South Wales for a contract worth £14 billion to become a national super centre for training.

January 18: Birmingham Airport's managing director, Richard Heard, is killed during a gale which brings down a branch through his car windscreen near Bridgnorth. The gale causes extensive damage and power cuts affecting thousands of Shropshire homes.

January 31: Oswestry maternity unit closed despite a big campaign in the town to save it.

February 1: Prime Minister Tony Blair visits Telford on the day it was revealed he had been questioned a second time in the 'cash for honours' affair. He addressed a conference on sport in schools at Telford International Centre.

February 2: Allscott sugar beet factory closes.

February 7: The National Cold War Exhibition opened at the RAF Museum, Cosford.

February 20: An online petition by Telford man Peter Roberts against road pricing closed with almost 1.8 million signatures, forcing Tony Blair to respond by email to all who signed.

March 16: Official opening of the Hadley Learning Community.

March 21: Kevin Whitrick, 42, of Orleton Lane, Wellington, committed suicide while using a webcam in an internet chatroom, believed to be Britain's first internet suicide.

March 23: Leading Seaman Faye Turney, aged 26 (nee Boswell), of Oxon, Shrewsbury, among 15 Royal Navy sailors and Marines seized by Iranians off the Iraqi coast, provoking an international crisis. They are later released.

May 3: In local elections, Tories take overall control of Oswestry Borough Council for the first time in its 34-year history, and also become the largest party for the first time on Telford & Wrekin Council. They also took control of North Shropshire District Council and South Shropshire

District Council for the first time.

May 5: Last league match at the Gay Meadow.

May 6: Constable Richard Gray shot dead when attending a "domestic incident" at Castlefields, Shrewsbury. He is the first officer in history to be murdered on duty in Shropshire.

May 6: Skydiver killed after landing badly at the British Falconry and Raptor Show at Chetwynd Park.

May 14: Final Shrewsbury Town game at the Gay Meadow, a 0-0 draw in the first leg of the League Two playoff semi final against MK Dons. As if in a nod to old times, the ball went into the River Severn during the match.

May 18: Funeral in Shrewsbury of murdered Constable Ricky Gray.

May 26: The largest crowd ever to watch Shrewsbury Town – 61,589 – are at the new Wembley stadium. Shrewsbury lose 3-1 to Bristol Rovers in the League Two playoff final.

May 30: Final competitive match played at the Gay Meadow – Shrewsbury Town Women v Wrockwardine Wood Jacs.

June 6: Reported that Telford shopping centre had been sold for £442 million to the Hark Group and Apollo Real Estate Advisers.

June 10: Red Arrows display at Cosford Air Show cut short after an unidentified airborne intruder entered the restricted display airspace.

June 19: Thunderstorms followed by flash floods wash away roads and cause severe damage in the Hampton Loade and Alveley areas. Ground under the Severn Valley Railway line near Highley is washed away, leaving tracks in the air.

June 22: Announced that Shropshire's ambulance control centre at Abbey Foregate is to close.

June 23: Gunman opens fire on the dancefloor at the Buttermarket nightclub, Shrewsbury, hitting a 24-year-old Telford man in the arm.

June 25: Continual heavy rain causes severe flooding in East Shropshire. Cars are submerged, houses swamped and roads blocked. Coalbrookdale particularly badly hit. Worst flooding in living memory in parts of the county.

June 26: Flooding at Ludlow washes away the Burway Bridge on the main route into town from the north. Across Shropshire, 70 people are rescued and 1,000 properties are swamped. It is the wettest June since 1860, with the county receiving two months' rain in under a week.

June 27: A house collapses at Ludlow due to the flooding.

July 14: First match at the New Meadow, Shrewsbury – Shrewsbury Town v A-Line All Stars. Shrewsbury win 4-0.

July 16: Councillor Tony Pound of Ludlow Town Council received hospital treatment after a fracas at a council committee meeting. He said he had been punched.

July 20: Renewed heavy rain leads to widespread flooding across Shropshire in the wettest summer in living memory. Much Wenlock, Ludlow, Craven Arms, Aston-on-Clun, Ditton Priors and Ketley are among areas hit. Total cost of flooding in Ludlow alone put at £5 million.

July 25: Government gives the go ahead for Shropshire's five remaining district and borough councils to be scrapped and replaced by an all-purpose single council from April 2009. Move will split the county into two unitary authorities – Telford & Wrekin (which is already a unitary authority), and a new Shropshire County.

July 28: Bishop's Castle Agricultural Show not held due to the wet summer – decision not to go ahead taken on July 18.

August 2: Burwarton Show called off for the first time in its history due to the wet weather. Decision was taken on July 22.

August 18: First ever league game at the New Meadow, Shrewsbury – Shrewsbury Town v Bradford.

August 31: Benthall Church becomes redundant.

SCHOOL CLOSURES: Albrighton Junior School in July (amalgamated with Albrighton Infant School). *The Bridge School, Stirchley, in January.*

DEATHS: Lord Biffen – John Biffen, North Shropshire MP from 1961 to 1997, on August 14, aged 76. Former Telford United manager and Shrewsbury Town coach Derek Mann aged 63 on January 27 or 28. Doreen Bourne, editor of Shropshire Magazine for nearly 20 years, c. February 12. On April 9, in Utah, Professor Harold Shipton, nicknamed "Shippy", a scientific genius from Shrewsbury who married Janet Attlee, daughter of serving Prime Minister Clement

Attlee. Telford United legend Jack Bentley, on May 26. Former Shrewsbury Town footballer Frank Griffin, on June 4.

SOURCES

(Unless otherwise stated, all up to October 5, 1964, are sourced from the Wellington Journal & Shrewsbury News, and all after that date are from the Shropshire Star. Dates given are dates of publication)

1900 – Disaster for Regiment, August 4; Paardeberg, March 31; cinematograph, November 17; letter, November 10. Picture: Shropshire Regimental Museum.
1901 – Queen, January 26; Westbury murder, December 7; furious driving, August 17; telephone, January 26. Main picture: Shropshire Archives.
1902 – Musical snowmen, September 27; execution, March 22; Hinstock, April 19; Ludlow, October 25; Ironbridge, August 30. Picture: Shropshire Regimental Museum.
1903 – Reckless driving, May 30; Buffalo Bill, June 6; bribery, January 31. Picture: David Trumper.
1904 – War memorial, July 23; colliery, April 30; Wem hall, February 6; road accident, May 21. Picture: Ray Farlow.
1905 – Kangaroo, July 22; school fire, December 9; marriage, August 5; ice accident, January 21; ironworks fire, November 25. Picture: Shropshire Archives.
1906 – Prime Minister, January 13; fancy dress, January 5, 1907. Picture: main, Ray Farlow. Fancy dress, Shropshire Archives.
1907 – Rail crash, October 19. Picture: source unknown.
1908 – Suffragette, May 9; Baden-Powell, January 25; murder, April 25; vicar, July 11; Hercules, July 18. Picture: Shropshire Archives.
1909 – Bridge, July 3; Webb memorial, October 30; Lloyd George, May 15; Lord Hill, July 24. Pictures: Ironbridge Gorge Museum (main), and Ray Farlow.
1910 – Disaster, December 10; football ground, SC, September 16; park, June 23; fire, February 19. Picture: Ray Farlow.
1911 – Aeroplane, August 5; Potts line, April 15; hotel fire, March 25; sanatorium, August 5. Picture: Ray Farlow.
1912 – Coal strike, March 9; Titanic, May 18; German, SC, February 23. Picture: Shropshire Archives.
1913 – Bolas romance, September 27; lovers drown, May 31; Bowring ground, May 31. Picture: source unknown.
1914 – War, August 8; Royal show, July 4. Picture: Shropshire Regimental Museum (main) and Ray Farlow.
1915 – Prees, SC, January 22 and also August 20; POWs, SC, June 18; chief constable, SC, August 13; Doyle, SC, March 26; court case, September 18. Picture: Ray Farlow.
1916 – Tally Ho VC, October 28; discovery, September 16; fire, December 23. Picture: Shropshire Regimental Museum.
1917 – Mrs Harley, March 17; Cox execution, December 22; no leave, SC, August 3; shot at dawn, synthesised. Picture: George Morris.
1918 – Armistice, November 16; Bligny, synthesised; VCs, May 11 and July 27; Park Hall, synthesised. Picture: Whitfield, from his family; Park Hall, Shropshire Archives.
1919 – Tribute, August 9; Lilleshall Hall, June 7; von Reuter, June 28. Picture: David Trumper.
1920 – Women jurors, SC, October 8; Dawley victim, April 24; Mosley wedding, SC, May 14; Wrekin, September 4. Picture: source unknown.
1921 – Royal shopping, SC, August 19; new hospital, SC, August 12; Lady Harlech, SC, January 7; gossip; Billingsley, September 17. Picture: Ray Farlow (main), Shropshire Archives (hospital).
1922 – French honour, June 10; war memorial, August 5; Princess Mary, February 25; cinema, December 2. Picture: Ray Farlow, and (school) Olive Farr/David Trumper.
1923 – Incident, November 3; Shrewsbury Town, SC, May 18; tree, August 11; tobacco, September 29. Picture: Ray Farlow.
1924 – Discovery, September 27; Dutton, November 29; Everest, SC, June 27; earthquake, February 23. Picture: Ray Farlow.
1925 – Drowning, January 10; English Bridge, August 8 and October 24; mine, SC, January 16; Queen, SC, August 7. Picture: mine, source unknown; bridge, sourced from souvenir programme.
1926 – Lords, March 6; strike, SC, various special editions in May; Coalport, SC, April 2; Gobowen, April 17; phone, January 16. Picture: David Trumper.
1927 – Cartland, SC, April 29; Marquess, October 29; landslide, BJ, February 12; Allscott, November 19. Picture: Ray Farlow.
1928 – Statue, SC, August 10; Easthope, June 16; Webb, April 28; HMS Shropshire, SC, July 6. Picture: Derrick Pountney (main – n.b. shows the ship probably in the 1930s), and David Trumper.
1929 – Caning, January 12; talkies, SC, October 4; long skirts, SC, December 6. Picture: Roy Pilsbury.
1930 – Church spire, August 9; R101, October 11; Criftins School, May 3; electrical standards, May 24. Pictures: Stephen Sanders.
1931 – Chimney, SC, October 30; castle, May 30; throne claim, SC, April 10; Baldwin-Webb trip, September 19; electricity showroom, October 31. Picture: David Trumper.
1932 – Abbey tunnel, August 27; power station, October 15; Forbra, SC, March 25; Miss Shropshire, SC, September 9. Picture: Shropshire Archives.
1933 – Bypass, May 27; Gordon Richards, December 9; hospital, May 6; Furrows, SC, September 15. Picture: Age Concern (bypass), and Jean Beard.
1934 – Blackshirts, SC, June 15; football, September 8; pageant; Ironbridge, August 4; mayor, SC, November 9. Picture: SC (Mosley), Shropshire Archives.
1935 – Crowds, April 27; KSLI, April 27 (first two pars SC of April 26). Picture: main, source unknown; KSLI, Shropshire Newspapers.
1936 – Pargeter, SC, October 9; storm, March 28; coins, February 29; nursery, October 10. Picture: Shropshire Newspapers.
1937 – Tribute, March 6; outrage, September 18; railway, February 27; airline death, January 9; police death, August 7. Picture: Sid Rowlands (funeral), Shropshire Newspapers.
1938 – Emperor, January 22; air raid exercise, October 29; Wem fire, November 5. Picture: Ray Farlow.
1939 – Blackshirts, May 27; war start, September 9; fighter pilot, synthesised. Picture: Gwen Edwards/Shropshire Newspapers (main), and Shropshire Newspapers.
1940 – Blitz, synthesised; Wrekin MP, September 28; air ace, September 28; conscientious objectors, July 27. Pictures: Baldwin-Webb, WJ&SN; bomb damage, Shropshire Archives.
1941 – Lock, August 9; town hall, December 27; flooding, February 22; Dr Benes, July 19. Picture: source unknown.
1942 – Invasion, June 6; baseball, SC, October 16; scouts' VC, May 16; bear, August 8. Picture: COD Donnington.
1943 – Bridgnorth railway, BJ, May 8; Sleap, synthesised; Forest Glen, SC, November 26. Picture: Bill Wren.
1944 – KSLI, August 5; Great Escape, May 27; marriage, February 5 and SC of April 7; V1, N&MDA, December 29, also part synthesised. Pictures: KSLI, John Eaves; Sid Swain, via Roy Dolton; V1, unknown.
1945 – VE Day, May 12; election, SC, July 27; cinema fire, SC, June 29; POWs, May 12; twin town, SC, October 26. Picture: Mr Griffiths of Oswestry.
1946 – Great flood, February 16; 999, January 4, 1947; Percy Thrower; bananas, SC, February 22; Harry Rogers, October 5. Picture: source unknown.
1947 – Floods, March 22; police farewell, April 5; wedding, synthesised; runaway lorry, April 12. Picture: WJ&SN.
1948 – Hospital fire, SC, January 30; typhoid, synthesised; Billy Wright, October 2; Dame Agnes, SC, July 30. Pictures: hospital, unknown; squatters, Arthur and Marjorie Mann.
1949 – Television, SC, December 23; Gone To Earth, July 30; royal week, July 9. Pictures: David Mitchell (televisions); WJ&SN/Gordon Riley (Montgomery).
1950 – Factory blast, May 20; Shrewsbury Town, June 10; polio, synthesised; film premiere, October 21. Picture: SC.
1951 – Crime, March 29, 1952; hanging, January 6; KSLI, BJ, November 30; princess, June 9. Picture: source unknown.
1952 – Jackfield, April 12; royal visit, October 25. Pictures: W. Lea (Jackfield); royal visit, SN; Disley, source unknown.
1953 – Sir Gordon, November 28; Marton, SC, May 15; John Hunt, SC, July 10. Pictures: SC (school); source unknown for Sir Gordon Richards.
1954 – Tong Castle, N&MDA, July 23; myxomatosis, July 31; oil fire, May 8; Hooper, January 30. Pictures: Express & Star (main), and SC (Hooper).
1955 – New town, December 17; KSLI, July 23; All Black, January 15; floodlighting, October 8; Trench school, February 5. Picture: Liverpool Daily Post.
1956 – Cattle market, July 21; Tommy Nicholls, December 15; refugees, December 22; rock and roll, October 13. Pictures: SN (main), and source unknown for Tommy Nicholls photo.
1957 – Lightning, July 13; memorial, January 4; smoking, December 14; runaway ferry, August 31. Picture: Shropshire Magazine.
1958 – vaccine, January 18; Rowley, June 7; overspill, November 15; Cock island, May 24; food boycott, November 1. Picture: WJ&SN.
1959 – RSI, SC, February 6; pagan rites, SC, August 28; furnaces, March 7; Stirling Moss, October 3. Pictures: SN (hospital), and WJ&SN.
1960 – Moss, SC, April 15; National Service, August 13; flooding, December 10; KSLI, May 7. Pictures: David Trumper (Raven Hotel), and SC.
1961 – Riley, February 11; Rowley, May 6; ambulance, March 11; Baschurch, February 18; escape, October 28. Pictures: SN (Riley), source unknown (Rowley).
1962 – New town, June 2; clock raider, February 10; coldest Christmas, December 29; George Medal, February 10. Pictures: John Rea/SN (main), SC (Beatles advert).
1963 – Big freeze, January 26; go ahead, January 19; RAF Bridgnorth, BJ, February 15; Beatles, May 4. Picture: David Wallace/WJ&SN.
1964 – Beacon, January 24; newspaper, synthesised; Brightwell, last par January 17, rest SC, October 30. Pictures: SN (beacon), and SS.
1965 – Long Mynd, July 12; new town, November 15; beacon, April 21; Rolling Stones, SJ, October 1. Pictures: SN.
1966 – Lilleshall, June 10; trains, November 7; fire, June 24. Pictures: SS (World Cup), and unknown.
1967 – Foot and mouth, October 26; Queen, March 17. Pictures: SS.
1968 – Shelton fire, February 26; Telford, October 23; gunman, September 19 (with some synthesised). Pictures: SS.
1969 – Highley, January 31; knockout, September 4; troops, August 15; television, September 3. Picture: SS.
1970 – Floral disaster, August 21; cinema, SJ, May 22; Sankeys, September 18. Pictures: SS.
1971 – Willows Road, SJ, January 8; Telford win, May 3. Pictures: SS.
1972 – Power crisis, February 17; Paradise, April 24; pickets, SJ (Telford edition), September 8; discovery, SJ (Wellington & Oakengates edition), August 25; air crash, August 28. Pictures: Express & Star (air crash) and SS.
1973 – Telford shops open, October 2; cricket, August 24; petrol, November 29; Ludlow gas, April 20; protest, October 3. Picture: SS.
1974 – Three day week, January 3; shooting, September 10; Poddy, November 14. Pictures: SS.
1975 – Kidnap, January 15; M54, December 11; hospital rescue, May 5; poison drama, October 1; TV mast, December 6. Pictures: SS.
1976 – Water crisis, July 3; Neilson, July 1; final service, BJ, October 1. Pictures: SS.
1977 – RSI, November 21; jubilee, June 8; Sex Pistols, N&MDA, December 30; Telford, April 5. Pictures: SS.
1978 – Theatre, September 23; Tessa, August 11; towers, December 7; royal honour, November 17. Pictures: SS, and Frank Leath (Prince Charles).
1979 – Shrewsbury Town, May 18; health fears, February 9; birthday bridge, July 2; Granville, May 25. Pictures: SS.
1980 – Salop, March 1; Diana, October 25. Pictures: SS.
1981 – Demo, February 7; torrent, June 27; Friends, TJ, May 8; Cobalt, July 17. Pictures: SS.
1982 – Lorry disaster, July 7; winter (synthesised); education, August 13. Picture: SS.
1983 – Donnington blaze, June 24; M54, November 25; hospital, July 22. Picture: SS.
1984 – Princess Di, December 11; Hilda, March 26; movies; soccer school, September 5; robbery, October 2. Pictures: SS.
1985 – Sandy, July 22; radio station, April 23; Stan Storton, February 18. Pictures: SS.
1986 – Heritage site, November 27; mammoth, synthesised; town hall, March 18; education, November 15. Pictures: SS.
1987 – Balloon pair, July 4; health cuts, April 23; train, March 3; dog, April 13. Picture: SS.
1988 – Warrant, June 3; T'Pau, March 17; manhunt, Express & Star, November 12. Pictures: SS.
1989 – IRA blitz, Express & Star, February 20; building collapse, August 3; first patients, January 31. Picture: SS.
1990 – Coach tragedy, June 4; poll tax, March 8 and March 14; Clun, April 6. Picture: SS.
1991 – Shooting, April 12 and 13; TDC, September 30; hospice, April 12. Picture: source unknown.
1992 – Terror, Express & Star, August 25; train, May 11. Pictures: SS.
1993 – Disaster night, February 23; jewellery raid, May 28; Brinks Mat, September 23. Picture: source unknown.
1994 – Treasure, July 29; pollution, April 16; air crash, January 10; vandals, August 10. Pictures: SS.
1995 – Arbor tree, September 2; Wem hall, November 20; boulder, October 10; scrapyard, December 7. Pictures: SS.
1996 – BSE, blend of March 23 and March 29; demo, July 6; flood defence, January 13; ghost, March 6. Pictures: Tony O'Rahilly (ghost) and SS.
1997 – Grand National, April 8; Labour win, May 2; survivor, September 1; demolition, August 18. Picture: SS.
1998 – Richie, March 28; big bang, April 1; Spillett, March 30; G8, May 16. Picture: SS.
1999 – Serck, April 1; rugby ban, April 13; Monica, March 20; millennium party, January 1, 2000. Picture: SS.
2000 – Floods, synthesised. Picture: SS.
2001 – Foot and mouth, March 12; Sir Kevin, June 16; fossil, July 20; September 11, synthesised. Picture: SS.
2002 – Rural conference, July 20; big cat, October 17; countryside demo, September 23; ambulance, April 3. Picture: SS.
2003 – Town crash, April 30; speed camera, April 15; poll, synthesised. Pictures: SS.
2004 – Flood defences, February 7; parking, October 18; Telford disaster, June 15; Town promoted, May 17. Picture: SS.
2005 – Hospital debt, November 22; last hunt, February 17. Pictures: SS.
2006 – Merrythought, November 27; rugby final, April 10; sizzling summer, synthesised. Pictures: SS.
2007 – Police murder, synthesised; floods, June 26. Pictures: SS.